Conservation
of
ISLAND BIRDS

Case studies for the management of threatened island species

Edited by

P. J. MOORS

Proceedings of a symposium held at the
XVIII ICBP World Conference
in Cambridge, England, in August 1982
under the Chairmanship of Sir Peter Scott

ICBP Technical Publication No. 3

Copyright © 1985, International Council for Bird Preservation, 219c Huntingdon Road, Cambridge CB3 0DL, England.

British Library Cataloguing in Publication Data

Conservation of island birds: case studies for
    the management of threatened island birds.
    — (International Council for Bird Preservation
    technical publications, ISSN 0277-1330; 3)
    1. Birds, Protection of   2. Rare birds
    I. Moors, P. J.   II. Series
    639.9'78   QL676.5

ISBN 0-946888-04-3

Photoset by Paston Press, Norwich, England.
Printed and bound by Page Bros (Norwich) Ltd, England.

INTERNATIONAL COUNCIL FOR BIRD PRESERVATION

ICBP is the longest-established worldwide conservation organization. It is devoted entirely to the protection of wild birds and their habitats. Founded in 1922, it is a federation of 270 member organizations in 86 countries; these organizations represent a total of some three million members all over the world.

Central to the successful execution of ICBP's mission is its global network of scientists and conservationists specializing in bird protection. Its ability to gather and disseminate information, identify and enact priority projects, and promote and implement conservation measures is unparalleled. Today, ICBP's Conservation Programme comprises over 70 projects throughout the world.

Birds are important indicators of a country's environmental health. ICBP provides expert advice to governments on bird conservation matters, management of nature reserves, and such issues as the control of trade in endangered species. Through interventions to governments on behalf of conservation issues ICBP can mobilize and bring to bear the force of international scientific opinion at the highest levels. Conferences and symposia by its specialist groups also attract worldwide attention to the plight of endangered birds.

Publications include the international *Bird Red Data Book*; ICBP maintains a comprehensive databank concerning the status of all the world's threatened birds and their habitats from which the *Red Data Book* is prepared. The most recent edition, *Threatened Birds of Africa*, was published in autumn 1984. A series of Technical Publications (of which the present volume is the third) gives up-to-date and in-depth treatment to major bird conservation issues.

ICBP, 219c Huntingdon Road, Cambridge CB3 0DL, UK.

UK Charity No. 286211

CONTENTS

ICBP   iii

FOREWORD by Christoph Imboden,
Director, ICBP, Cambridge   viii

EDITOR'S PREFACE
by P. J. Moors   ix

PART I: PROCESSES AFFECTING POPULATIONS OF ISLAND BIRDS

1   Island Birds: Will the Future Repeat the Past?
    Warren B. King   3

2   Population Processes in Island Birds: Immigration, Extinction
    and Fluctuations
    Jared M. Diamond   17

3   Island Biogeographic Theory in Bird Conservation:
    An Alternative Approach
    T. M. Reed   23

4   The Spread of Commensal Species of *Rattus* to Oceanic Islands and
    their Effects on Island Avifaunas
    I. A. E. Atkinson   35

PART II: REGIONAL SURVEYS OF THE STATUS OF ISLAND BIRDS

5   The Conservation of Landbirds on Islands in the Tropical Indian
    Ocean
    A. W. Diamond   85

6   Threats to Birds on Subantarctic Islands
    G. W. Johnstone   101

PART III: ISLAND CONSERVATION IN ACTION

7 Methods of Eradicating Feral Cats from Offshore Islands in
   New Zealand
   C. R. Veitch   125

8 Eradication Campaigns against *Rattus norvegicus* on the Noises
   Islands, New Zealand, Using Brodifacoum and 1080
   P. J. Moors   143

9 The Impact and Eradication of Feral Goats on the Galapagos Islands
   Luis Calvopina   157

10 Breeding Success and Mortality of Dark-rumped Petrels in the
   Galapagos, and Control of their Predators
   R. J. Tomkins   159

11 A Programme to Save the Dark-rumped Petrel, *Pterodroma
   phaeopygia*, on Floreana Island, Galapagos, Ecuador
   Malcolm C. Coulter, Felipe Cruz & Justine Cruz   177

12 The Diet of the Osprey on Tiran Island: Management Implications
   for Populations on the Northern Red Sea Islands
   Uriel N. Safriel, Yehuda Ben-Hur & Adam Ben-Tuvia   181

13 Status, Habits and Conservation of *Cyanoramphus* Parakeets in the
   New Zealand Region
   Rowland H. Taylor   195

14 The Puerto Rican Parrot and Competition for its Nest Sites
   James W. Wiley   213

15 The Restoration of Nonsuch Island as a Living Museum of
   Bermuda's Pre-colonial Terrestrial Biome
   David B. Wingate   225

16 Multiple Use of Cousin Island Nature Reserve, Seychelles
   A. W. Diamond   239

PART IV: A PROGRAMME FOR THE PROTECTION OF ISLAND ECOSYSTEMS

17 Conservation of Island Ecosystems
    Cameron B. Kepler & J. Michael Scott   255

FOREWORD

By Christoph Imboden, Director,
International Council for Bird Preservation

Islands, according to myth, were places of enchantment. From earliest times, explorers have brought back tales of remote tropical paradises inhabited by strange animals and plants. Desert islands have been a part of our literary heritage since Daniel Defoe and Benardin de Saint-Pierre. However, the fate of the wildlife of the Juan Fernandez islands where Robinson Crusoe was shipwrecked, and Mauritius, the idyllic setting of *Paul et Virginie*, provide sobering object lessons on how easily human interference can destroy the delicate balance within island ecosystems. On a confined landmass, habitat destruction can be total, and there is no retreat for the highly specialized plants and animals that have evolved without any defence against predation and more aggressive competition.

On oceanic islands, time, isolation and small area have led to the evolution of unique wildlife communities with high numbers of endemic plants and animals. These include the most bizarre and fascinating birds to be found anywhere in the world. To take one example, most of those birds that have lost the power of flight are, or sadly were, found only on islands. Island birds are high-risk species. No less than 200 of the 217 species or races of birds known to have become extinct in the last four centuries were island forms, and this alarming trend continues today: two-thirds of today's threatened species occur on islands.

For this reason, ICBP must take a special interest in these remarkable ecosystems. We recently analysed insular avifauna and found that the ranges of over ten percent of the world's bird species are limited to single islands only. ICBP has established an international island data bank for biological information vital for the conservation of island birds and ecosystems. Results of these efforts will be published in the Technical Publication series. The present volume will be followed by a list of the world's single island endemic bird species, and a review of all endemic birds in Madagascar.

For the most part, the struggle for survival of island birds in the face of human disturbance makes depressing reading. Historically, the major causes of extinction on islands have been predators and competitors intentionally or accidentally introduced by man. That is the main subject of this book.

As this book tells us, however, it is not all doom and gloom. Seemingly hopeless situations have led to some of the most imaginative and enterprising work in conservation management. Projects initiated out of despair have resulted in spectacular success and proved that, if the necessary resources, skills and dedication are available, we can still save many highly threatened island birds. The purpose of this book is to show what can be done and to encourage the dedicated conservationists who are facing those desperate situations, striving against time and terrible odds to put off the last word: extinction.

January 1985

EDITOR'S PREFACE

by P. J. Moors

This volume contains the papers presented at a symposium on island management held in Cambridge on 12 August 1982 as part of the XVIII World Conference of the International Council for Bird Preservation. The stimulus for the symposium was the 1981–82 ICBP Conservation Programme, which included a project to develop guidelines for the management of islands important for bird conservation. I accepted an invitation from Dr Christoph Imboden to organize the symposium and edit the resulting proceedings.

The symposium contributions deal with four topics in island conservation: processes affecting populations of island birds, regional surveys of the status of island birds, island conservation in action, and a programme for the protection of island ecosystems. Rather than attempt to obtain a comprehensive coverage of these subjects, I have sought contributions that will reveal what is actually being achieved in the field, or will provide information for future work and decision-making. Therefore virtually all the papers are by people actively studying or managing island birds. This has the pleasing additional benefit of allowing us to share in some of the excitement, achievements and innovative ideas which these endeavours generate. It was clear at the meeting, and remains so in the seventeen papers here, that there is a great reservoir of enthusiasm and commitment available for the conservation of islands—not just for the birds they harbour, but more importantly as healthy ecological systems.

Eleven papers were delivered to the meeting, five were presented as poster papers, and one (by R. J. Tomkins) was prepared specifically for this volume. The contributions by L. Calvopina and by M. C. Coulter, F. Cruz & T. Beach are published in the form of extended summaries. I have included them because both describe conservation and management activities which can be usefully applied on islands elsewhere. All the papers have been refereed, and revised where necessary. Most authors submitted their manuscripts at the meeting or shortly thereafter, but various delays—some avoidable, many not—have held up publication. However this has enabled many papers to be brought up to date with information from 1983 and 1984.

An island management workshop was held on the day after the symposium. The main subjects discussed were criteria for rating the priorities for action on important islands and endangered birds; the topics which should be covered in a planned ICBP handbook on island management; the grouping of islands into manageable regional units to enable easier collection of information and co-ordination of conservation action; and the preparation of an island inventory sheet to be completed by visitors to islands. The workshop participants made recommendations to ICBP on the establishment of an island advisory group, the development of a computerized data bank on islands, and the preparation of a standardized inventory sheet. The draft grouping of islands is included as Appendix 1 in the paper by C. B. Kepler & J. M. Scott.

I am most grateful to Sir Peter Scott for being the symposium chairman, to the authors for their contributions, to the referees for their prompt reviews of manuscripts, and to Dr Christoph Imboden for his Foreword and administrative support. I thank Mr Martyn Bramwell and Mrs Eve Imboden for shepherding the book through its publication stages.

P. J. MOORS

PART I
PROCESSES AFFECTING POPULATIONS OF ISLAND BIRDS

ISLAND BIRDS: WILL THE FUTURE REPEAT THE PAST?

WARREN B. KING

North Groton Road, Rumney, NH03266, USA

ABSTRACT

Although only a small percentage of the world's land and freshwater birds occur on oceanic islands, 93 percent of the 93 species and 83 subspecies that have become extinct since 1600 were island forms. Today island forms account for slightly more than half of the world's endangered birds, a large proportion of which are clearly destined to become tomorrow's extinctions. As deforestation accelerates in the continental tropics, the pendulum of extinction will swing increasingly in the direction of continental forms. Yet the same forces that caused avian extinction on islands over the last four centuries are threatening to precipitate new rounds of insular extinctions which, although not likely to keep pace with continental extinctions bird for bird, will probably outstrip continental extinctions relative to total species numbers for decades to come.

No island is so isolated as to be free of human disturbance. The single most important cause of extinction on islands has been predation by alien predators which have been introduced sometimes intentionally, sometimes inadvertently, by man. While this will remain a significant factor in extinctions for years to come, we are witnessing increasingly the gradual deterioration of many island habitats through the combined onslaught of selective browsing by introduced herbivores, excessive competition for space and light between native floras and vigorous introduced continental vegetation, and increased rates of utilization of trees for firewood and building materials by expanding human populations. Avian disease may play a more insidious role here than previously supposed.

Ironically, the limits of space inherent in island ecosystems (which are at the root of the vulnerability of insular forms) can be, and increasingly have been, used to advantage in the resurrection of lost island populations. Island habitats respond to management more readily than continental ones in much the same way that they can be destroyed more readily.

INTRODUCTION

The topic under discussion at this symposium, conservation problems of birds on islands, can be interpreted broadly to include birds in any habitats insulated from other similar patches of habitat, or more narrowly and traditionally to include only birds on islands surrounded by water barriers.

I would like to make the point at the outset that we should seek wherever possible to broaden the discussion to consideration of all islands, whether surrounded by water, desert, forest, wheat fields or pavement. There is a rich field of theoretical and, more recently, practical ecological investigation which has its foundations in the theory of island biogeography and the elucidation of the species–area relationship. These con-

3

cepts have added relevance to habitat islands on continents as the world's tropical forests become increasingly fragmented, and as problems of saving species become more and more a case of unattractive compromise—preserving a patch here while suffering a patch there to be destroyed because it has lesser biological wealth.

RATES OF AVIAN EXTINCTION

Since the seventeenth century, avian extinction has been largely an island phenomenon. Fully 93 percent of the 93 species and 83 subspecies of birds which have become extinct since 1600 have been island forms, and avian extinction on islands is far from a dead process. There are at this moment a dozen candidates for imminent extinction on islands, several of which will almost surely be lost before the end of the decade. The rate of avian extinction, roughly estimated in 1978 at one species or subspecies every 3.6 years (King 1980), will inevitably accelerate well beyond one extinction per year by the year 2000, in contrast to the presumed rate of extinction in the early Pleistocene of one species every 83.3 years (Fisher 1964; Brodkorb 1960).

The reason for this accelerated rate of extinction should be clear to everyone. Thus far extinctions have occurred most frequently where avian species diversity is lowest and where populations, already restricted by limited area, are especially prone to extinction because of demographic instability, inbreeding depression and, frequently, inclement environmental conditions (Wilcox 1980).

In contrast to the depauperate faunas on islands, the continental tropical forests contain the world's highest species diversity. Ninety percent of all species occur in the tropics, and tropical forests account for about 60 percent of the earth's avian species diversity (Soulé 1980; R. Pasquier & B. Beehler, pers. comm.). There is general agreement that by the year 2000 only remnants of once unbroken expanses of tropical forest will remain (e.g. Myers 1980; Whitmore 1980), and most reserves incorporating tropical forests will have been established. Assuming that the boundaries of these reserves will not be violated by operators hungry for forest products or by subsistence farmers and firewood gatherers, we shall be left with a series of forest archipelagos.

Estimates can already be made of the losses expected from a reserve or fragment of habitat of a given size. Species-area considerations tell us that the larger the habitat fragment the larger the proportion of the original complement of species which it will retain. Long-term figures have been derived from the relationship of the number of bird species on land-bridge islands to the number of species present on adjacent mainland areas, the difference being the predicted number of extinctions of island birds. For very large islands such as Sri Lanka (65,688km^2), 28 percent of the avifauna that was presumably present when it was in contact with India are now absent, and for smaller islands such as Fernando Po (2036km^2), the reduction of 64 percent is predictably larger (Terborgh & Winter 1980). The remnant forests of the future will surely be smaller than Sri Lanka, and probably all but a very few will be smaller than Fernando Po, so the outlook is bleak for the retention of complete assemblages of species in these forests.

Some examples of short-term extinction rates from much smaller remnants are available from the state of Sao Paulo, Brazil (Willis, in press). In a very few decades a 1400ha patch of forest lost 14 percent of its breeding birds, while a 21ha tract lost 62 percent. The well-publicized example of Barro Colorado Island in Gatun Lake, Panama, is also highly relevant. Estimates of the percentage of landbird species lost following creation of the 17km^2 island early in the twentieth century range between 8–28 percent (Willis & Eisenmann 1979; Karr 1982). Other evidence suggests that the selection of a reserve which can contain only a sample of species from the surrounding habitat will result in the *immediate* exclusion of 30 percent of the species of the surrounding community for each 10-fold reduction in area (Wilcox 1980).

These figures give us an idea of the extent of extinction we can expect under the most realistic circumstances. Samples of all major habitats will certainly not be preserved, nor will the design of those reserves which do become established be optimal. (What constitutes optimal design for reserves is subject to considerable debate: e.g. Simberloff & Abele 1975; Diamond 1976; Diamond & May 1976; Whitcomb *et al.* 1976; Terborgh 1976.) It seems to me entirely realistic that hundreds of bird species will become extinct in the next half century.

In light of this problem on an unprecedented scale, what is the significance of conservation of birds on islands of the traditional type? I believe that there are three major justifications, and as many minor ones as there are species on islands to save and people who want to do the work.

Firstly, the unifying theories that relate species number to area had their origins and original applications on islands, and these will continue to be the living laboratories from which data will come to help us better understand and manipulate populations on continents. The reduced complexity of islands compared with continental ecosystems permits quicker comprehension of ecological principles and processes.

Secondly, the techniques for manipulating small populations and their habitats are developed and applied most easily on islands, once again because of the relative simplicity of island habitats.

Thirdly, the fragmentation of tropical forests will leave only habitat islands *below* the minimum area required for autochthonous speciation (the division *in situ* of one species into two or more) to take place in higher vertebrates and plants. Therefore we will witness by the year 2000 the end of continental speciation of higher forms, the primary source of biological novelty in the world (Soulé 1980). While speciation by radiation or multiple invasion, which are typical of archipelagos (Mayr 1966), may continue on continental reserves, it is not only unlikely that man-created reserves will persist over the centuries required for speciation, but the higher rates of extinction that we can expect in these reserves will surely far out-balance any gains through speciation. Nevertheless, radiations and multiple invasions have taken place on islands in the past, and we may have to look to islands in the future as the primary—perhaps sole—source of speciation among higher vertebrates.

These reasons oblige us to take a closer look at islands, both to assess how they have fared in the recent past as bird habitats, and also how we can expect them to fare in the future.

HISTORY OF EXTINCTION OF BIRDS ON ISLANDS

There is mounting evidence that birds on islands suffered at the hand of man well before the exploration of the seas by European explorers. The fabled Moas of New Zealand were killed in large numbers by the Maoris, and by the time Captain James Cook arrived in 1770 they are thought to have disappeared. The remains of about 800 birds in one 170m^3 pit gives ample testimony to their heavy utilization by the Maoris (Duff 1952). In Hawaii the Polynesian population prior to western influence has been estimated at an impressively large 250,000–400,000 (Feher 1969), and the toll taken of birds, particularly those inhabiting the drier lowlands, must have been considerable. Subfossils and recent remains of seven species of geese, some flightless, two flightless ibises, and seven flightless rails suggest that these were foods for the Polynesians, as well as the species that survived to the present, such as the Nene (*Branta sandvicensis*) and several

Table 1:   Chronology of extinction of birds on islands (from King 1978).

| | Date of Extinction | | | | | | | |
Ocean	1601–1650	1651–1700	1701–1750	1751–1800	1801–1850	1851–1900	1901–1950	1951–present
Indian	2	2	4	4	4	5	0	0
Atlantic	0	1	1	4	0	12	9	0
Pacific	2	1	0	8	12	36	45	10
	4	4	5	16	16	53	54	10

seabirds. The discovery of recent fossil remains of several Hawaiian passerines on islands where even the earliest ornithologists did not record them points to significant environmental disturbance, almost certainly from human actions, probably in the form of burning and clearing of lowland forests (Olson & James 1982).

Since 1600 all extinctions except one have probably been the direct or indirect result of human activities. The exception, a bullfinch (*Loxigilla portoricensis grandis*) from St. Kitts, Lesser Antilles, was probably eliminated by two hurricanes which swept the island in 1899 (Raffaele 1977). Twenty-one birds have been lost from Indian Ocean islands, 27 from Atlantic islands including the Caribbean, and 113 from Pacific islands (King 1980). The chronology of these extinctions differs from ocean to ocean depending, it would seem, on the period during which European exploration and initial settlement took place (*Table 1*). Thus, the Indian Ocean took its losses disproportionately early, and has not yet lost a single species in the twentieth century. By comparison, extinctions in the Pacific Ocean have been recent, more having come in the first 50 years of this century than in any other 50-year period.

GEOGRAPHICAL CONSIDERATIONS

Assuming somewhat pessimistically that today's endangered birds will be tomorrow's extinct birds, we see that 53 percent (58 percent counting very large islands such as Madagascar, Taiwan and Borneo) of the 437 species and subspecies included in the second edition of ICBP's Red Data Book on birds (King 1978, 1981), is from islands. Of these, 57 percent (130 taxa) come from the Pacific, compared with 70 percent of extinct island forms known from that region; 27 percent (62 taxa) are from Atlantic islands, compared with 17 percent of extinct forms; and 16 percent (36 taxa) are from Indian Ocean islands, compared with 13 percent of extinct forms (*Table 2*). Increased threats to birds on Caribbean islands comprise the bulk of the difference for the Atlantic islands.

Among individual island groups, those which have suffered the most extinctions are the same ones that now harbour the lion's share of endangered birds (King 1978, 1981).

Table 2:   Incidence of extinct and endangered bird taxa from each ocean.

Ocean	Extinct island birds		Endangered island birds	
	Number of taxa	Percent	Number of taxa	Percent
Pacific	113	70	130	57
Atlantic	27	17	62	27
Indian	21	13	36	17

Hawaii leads the list with 24 extinct birds and 29 endangered birds. The Mascarenes have lost 22 birds and another 11 are endangered. New Zealand has lost 12 species and subspecies and 16 are endangered. Fourteen extinctions have occurred in the Antilles as a whole (and several more if one includes the 13 parrots known only from verbal descriptions), and an alarming 39 species or subspecies are endangered.

CAUSES OF ENDANGERMENT AND EXTINCTION

The causes of endangerment of island birds show some significant differences from the causes of extinction (*Table 3*). Habitat destruction or deterioriation is the most important cause of endangerment for island birds (King 1978; 1980), being implicated as either a primary or contributory cause in 58 percent of cases. By contrast, it has figured in only 19 percent of extinctions. On the other hand predation has not changed appreciably in its importance. It is a major factor for 40 percent of endangered birds on islands, whereas it has been a major cause of 42 percent of extinctions. Although threats from hunting have increased in frequency for endangered birds compared with extinct birds (26 percent vs. 15 percent), a case-by-case comparison suggests that, with certain major exceptions, hunting is now a contributory rather than a primary cause of endangerment.

Loss of habitat
Habitat destruction or deterioration is a convenient catch-all phrase that includes a considerable variety of problems. At one extreme lies the outright levelling of tracts of forest, often accompanied by replanting for agricultural or silvicultural purposes. This has happened over extensive areas, but seldom have all forests on an island been destroyed. One such case is the island of Cebu in the Philippines. Seven endemic subspecies—a fruit dove, hanging parakeet, grey-bird, bulbul, flowerpecker, white-eye and oriole—inhabiting these forests were lost by 1906. An exception is the Cebu Black Shama (*Copsychus niger cebuensis*), a few individuals of which have survived in brushy gullies (Vincent 1966). Fortunately, other races of all of these species occur elsewhere in the Philippines.

A second case, not carried to full completion, is the destruction of the tall tropical forests of Christmas Island, Indian Ocean, to mine the phosphate-rich soil for processing into fertilizer. This has been a classic case of direct confrontation between an exploitative industry and the survival of three endemic bird species, including Abbott's Booby (*Sula abbotti*), and three additional subspecies. As a result of lengthy negotiations those areas of forest will be spared which are the most important to boobies for nesting. However, lingering concern remains over the adequacy of rehabilitation of the mined areas, together with the fear that tall forest deprived of adequate buffer areas will succumb to the elements. A recently established park and the area reserved for booby nesting should protect the island's other endemic birds as well.

Table 3:   Relative occurrence of major causes of extinction and endangerment of island birds.

Cause	Percent of extinct island birds	Percent of endangered island birds
Habitat loss	19	58
Predation	42	40
Hunting	15	26

Most endangered and extinct species have been highly specialized and intolerant of changes in their habitat, but some are surprisingly tolerant. The native vegetation of Rodrigues Island, Mascarenes, has been almost totally destroyed, and has been replaced by thickets of jamrose (*Eugenia jambos*) which is itself subject to serious pressure from firewood gatherers. Although native plants can be found only in a few places on the island, two endemic birds, the Fody (*Foudia flavicans*) and the Brush Warbler (*Bebrornis rodericana*), have been sufficiently adaptable to persist in the remaining thickets of introduced plants, in spite of typhoons that periodically decimate their populations.

Habitat deterioration rather than outright destruction is far more frequently the situation faced by island birds. One form this deterioration can take is increasing encroachment of more vigorous introduced plants into native forests. For example, areas up to several thousand acres in extent are blanketed by an introduced passion fruit (*Passiflora* sp.) in Hawaii. Guava (*Psidium guajava*) is rapidly becoming the dominant vegetation in the small remaining area of so-called native forest on Mauritius. Lalang grass (*Imperata* sp.) has prevented re-establishment of forest on Lanyu, southeast of Taiwan, endangering a subspecies of the owl *Otus elegans*. Another form this deterioration can take is suppression of key plant species which are favoured foods for birds. The Hawaiian Crow (*Corvus tropicus*) is said to favour the 'ie'ie vine (*Freycinetia* sp.) which is eaten enthusiastically by pigs, and the fruits of which are taken by rats.

The extreme in plant suppression occurred on Laysan Island in 1923. European rabbits (*Oryctolagus cuniculus*) ate virtually every plant on the island, before themselves succumbing to their own lack of foresight, taking with them an endemic rail and a Hawaiian honeycreeper, but miraculously sparing the finch-bill *Psittirostra cantans* and the Laysan Duck (*Anas laysanensis*). The duck apparently survived the ultimate population bottle-neck when its population was reduced to one gravid female (Ely & Clapp 1973). Hares and rabbits have been introduced to many islands around the world, but nowhere else have they been such a serious problem to island avifaunas.

Overbrowsing by goats has created problems for birds in several parts of the world. Guadalupe Island off the west coast of Mexico has lost much of its vegetation. Regeneration of Cypress (*Cupressus guadalupensis*) and Pine (*Pinus radiata*)–Oak (*Quercus tomentella*) groves has been at a standstill for many years. A Kinglet (*Regulus calendula obscura*) and three other subspecies are at risk from this devegetation. California's Channel Islands, especially San Clemente, have too many goats, threatening two endemic subspecies, the shrike *Lanius ludovicianus mearnsi* and the sparrow *Amphispiza belli clementeae*. A similar situation exists on several islands in the Hawaiian group, and, until recently, on Round Island off Mauritius (from which the goats have now been removed), and on several islands in the Galapagos group. Goats are the single most destructive herbivore introduced to the islands of the world.

Sheep have also been a serious problem on certain islands. On Mangere Island, in the Chatham group, sheep caused the replacement of most of the native scrub forest by grass. This deforestation, and also predation by feral cats, resulted in the loss of the Chatham Island Snipe (*Coenocorypha aucklandica pusilla*), Chatham Island Pigeon (*Hemiphaga novaeseelandiae chathamensis*), Forbes' Parakeet (*Cyanoramphus auriceps forbesi*) and the Chatham Island Black Robin (*Petroica traversi*) from the island.

On the slopes of Mauna Kea, Hawaii, the Palila (*Loxioides bailleui*) occurs only in the high altitude Mamane (*Sophora chrysophylla*)–Naio (*Myoporum sandwicense*) forest that nearly encircles the volcano between 1830m and 2745m elevation. The Hawaii Division of Fish and Game has managed sheep there as a game species, and the resultant heavy browsing has caused the treeline of this forest to recede more than 150m in recent years. Regeneration of the forest has also been arrested, and many trees in it are overmature or dying. The fate of the Palila is directly tied to the health of this forest (Warner 1960; Van Riper 1981).

Competition for food by introduced animals, including man, is another form of habitat deterioration. In New Zealand, grazing by introduced Red Deer (*Cervus elaphus*) reduces the vigour and nutrient quality of alpine tussock grasses. This deprives the endangered Takahe (*Notornis mantelli*) of adequate supplies of its staple food (Mills & Mark 1977; Mills, pers. comm.). Human collection of the tree snail *Polymita* sp. on Cuba and Grenada contributes to the threats to two endemic subspecies of the Hook-billed Kite (*Chondrohierax uncinatus*) by depriving them of their food source.

Predation

Next in importance to habitat loss is predation. Rats (*Rattus* spp.) have been implicated in the greatest number of extinctions due to predators (54 percent; King 1980). Atkinson (1973; 1977; 1978; this vol.) has built strong cases from oftentimes circumstantial evidence for the significance of rat predation on island bird populations throughout the world, but particularly in New Zealand and Hawaii.

Of the three species which have shared blame for this record of predation, the Black or Roof Rat (*Rattus rattus*) has been the most serious problem, followed by the Norway or Brown Rat (*R. norvegicus*) and the Polynesian Rat (*R. exulans*). Each is said to take petrels whose weight is equal to or below that of the rat (Imber 1975), although the density of a petrel colony and the presence of other petrel species, particularly those with different breeding seasons, bear on the problem (Imber 1978). Even the smallest, the Polynesian Rat, can take eggs up to 55mm in length, and occasionally birds as large as albatrosses (Kepler 1967), and to be in general no less significant a predator gram for gram than the other two species (Atkinson 1978). Perhaps the most serious rat introduction in recent years was the establishment, in about 1964, of Roof Rats on Big South Cape Island, New Zealand (Bell 1978). This caused the local loss of three New Zealand endemic birds, and the complete extinction of two more, Stead's Bush Wren (*Xenicus longipes variabilis*) and the Stewart Island Snipe (*Coenocorypha aucklandica iredalei*).

Cats are the other significant predator, having caused 26 percent of island extinctions due to predators. The Socorro Dove (*Zenaida graysoni*) must now be added to the list of cat-caused extinctions, and the Socorro Mockingbird (*Mimodes graysoni*) will soon follow (Jehl & Parkes 1982).

Other predators of potential or actual importance to island birds include the Mongoose (*Herpestes auropunctatus*), feral dogs, Stoats (*Mustela erminea*), Pigs (*Sus scrofa*), Arctic Foxes (*Alopex lagopus*), and Monkeys (*Cercopithecus* and *Macaca*) (see also Moors & Atkinson, 1984). Ground-nesting birds, especially shearwaters and petrels, are particularly susceptible to predation from mongooses. Mongooses have presumably caused the extinction of the Jamaican Least Pauraque (*Siphonorhis americanus americanus*) and the Diablotin (*Pterodroma hasitata caribbea*), and threaten several others, including the Nene and the Dark-rumped Petrel (*Pterodroma phaeopygia sandwichensis*), both from Hawaii. Bryan (1908) found a mongoose nursing young in a petrel burrow on Molokai. The effect of mongoose predation can be seen indirectly in the restriction of several ground-nesting or ground-dwelling birds to relatively mongoose-free parts of otherwise infested islands. This is true of the Dark-rumped Petrel on Maui, the Whippoorwill (*Caprimulgus noctitherus*) on Puerto Rico, and probably also the Martinique and St. Lucia subspecies of the largely terrestrial White-breasted Thrasher (*Ramphocinclus brachyurus*). The recent invasion of mongooses into parts of the Zapata Swamp, Cuba, may already have caused the extinction of the endemic wren *Ferminia cerverai*, and increases the risk to the endemic rail *Cyanolimnas cerverai*.

Hunting

Hunting has been an important cause of extinction of island birds, and it continues to play a contributory role, but is now a serious factor in the decline of only a few species. The *Amazona* parrots of the Lesser and Greater Antilles have been hunted both for food and the pet trade. *Amazona imperialis* and *A. arausiaca* of Dominica suffer particularly from this problem at present. An exemplary conservation education programme concerning *A. versicolor* on St. Lucia has reduced the threat there considerably (Butler 1981).

Competition

Competition with introduced birds for food or space, including nest sites, has been an important factor in the decline of about 7 percent of native island birds. However, recent work on several New Zealand islands suggests that introductions took place only *after* introduced mammalian predators and browsers had decimated native species and altered the native forest. It was not competition from introduced birds that caused declines in native birds, but, conversely, that declines in native birds permitted establishment of introduced birds (Diamond & Veitch 1981).

Disease

The role of disease in causing extinction of birds on islands has recently come under increasing scrutiny (Warner 1968; Van Riper 1981, pers. comm.). Introduced mosquitos acting as vectors for malaria and bird pox are now seen to be rather more widespread altitudinally in Hawaii than previously thought. Mosquito-borne avian malaria has also been suggested to be linked to the reduction in range of the Tahiti Lorikeet (*Vini peruviana*) (King 1981). The massive problems afflicting virtually all the native birds of Guam may be in part related to susceptibility to disease. Until the deleterious effects of disease can be demonstrated, we should continue to think of disease as affecting birds only on the most isolated island groups, where the avifauna has evolved in the absence of disease vectors and thus has not had opportunity to develop immunity.

CONTROL MEASURES FOR INTRODUCED ANIMALS

A major problem facing those who would remove predators or browsers from selected islands of biological importance is that the size of the island, its accessibility and its topography place strict limitations on what can be accomplished. In general, larger animals can be controlled more effectively than smaller animals.

Goats have been the target of a major control campaign in the Galapagos (Calvopina, this vol.) and in two United States National Parks in Hawaii, but there are many islands around the world where goat control should be undertaken as a matter of priority.

Sheep removal from Mangere Island, Chatham group, has encouraged the gradual return of the native scrub forest to that island. To speed this process the New Zealand Wildlife Service planted large numbers of seedlings. Cats are no longer present, and Forbes' Parakeets have returned from adjacent Little Mangere Island. The New Zealand Wildlife Service transferred the tiny remnant population of Black Robins from Little Mangere to a small but rapidly regenerating patch of forest on Mangere in 1976 and 1977, with the expectation that the replanted areas will before long sustain Black Robins as well (Morris 1977).

On Hawaii the Sierra Club, National Audubon Society and Hawaii Audubon Society recently brought suit on behalf of the Palila against the Hawaii Department of Lands and Natural Resources to have sheep removed from Mauna Kea to permit regeneration of the Mamane-Naio forest. The judge decreed that the sheep were endangering the Palila and must be removed in compliance with the United States Endangered Species Act. The Department of Lands and Natural Resources quickly removed the sheep from Mauna Kea, but has now replaced them with Mouflon (*Ovis musimon*), a wild sheep species, thereby prolonging the deterioration of the Mamane-Naio habitat, and necessitating a follow-up law suit, currently being prepared.

The New Zealand Wildlife Service must be congratulated for its efforts to eradicate cats from several New Zealand islands (Veitch, this vol.), and from Frigate Island, Seychelles, where the Magpie Robin (*Copsychus sechellarum*) is now secure from cat predation.

The largest island from which rats have been removed in a control programme is Otata Island (22ha) in the Noises group, New Zealand (Moors, this vol.). A potential problem with rat control is the increasing resistance of rats to widely-used anticoagulant rodenticides such as 'Warfarin' (Wodzicki 1978), although the large amounts of poison, and the years required before resistance appears, are unlikely to be reached in most rodent control or eradication programmes on islands.

I know of no successful attempts to rid an island of mongooses. A programme to prevent the spread of mongooses on Kauai, where a lactating female and a number of sightings suggest that at least a foothold has been gained, has had equivocal results. Establishment of the mongoose on Kauai would mean the almost certain loss of the Koloa (*Anas wyvilliana*) and Newell's Shearwater (*Puffinus puffinus newelli*), both ground-nesting birds.

Pigs and foxes are more susceptible to control and have in fact been removed from sizeable islands, e.g. Malden Island, Line group, Central Pacific (King 1973), and Amchitka, Nizki and Alaid Islands, Aleutians, North Pacific (King 1981). Although the control of monkeys *Macaca fascicularis* is sorely needed on Mauritius, where they rob the nests of three of the world's most endangered birds, the Mauritius Kestrel (*Falco punctatus*), Pink Pigeon (*Nesoenas mayeri*) and Mauritius Parakeet (*Psittacula echo*), local religious beliefs prevent such measures.

SUSCEPTIBILITY TO EXTINCTION

One clear attribute of species with small populations is a high rate of extinction (Terborgh & Winter 1980; Diamond, this vol.). Many island birds have always had small populations which have often been reduced yet further by one or more of the factors just discussed. Thus, it should come as no surprise that extinction of island birds will continue, in spite of our best conservation efforts. Animal breeders and geneticists have developed a guideline that expresses the likelihood of survival of small populations, namely, that 'the expected number of generations to the extinction threshold is about 1.5 times the effective population size' (Soulé 1980). Although this guideline was developed for captive populations, the effects will be largely the same for small populations in the wild. Effective population size can be well below the total number of adults in a population once breeding structure, social inhibition, fluctuations in population size and overlapping of generations are taken into account. When we consider the impact on small island populations of random events, demographic instability and inbreeding we do not have much reason to be optimistic. Over the long term there seems little hope for the Chatham Island Black Robin, Kauai O'o (*Moho braccatus*), Mauritius Kestrel, Mauritius Parakeet, White-breasted Silver-eye (*Zosterops albogularis*) of Norfolk Island, Lord Howe Wood Rail (*Tricholimnas sylvestris*), Puerto Rican Parrot (*Amazona vittata*) or Seychelles Magpie Robin. There is already reason to believe that some of these may be suffering inbreeding effects. For example, the Mauritius Kestrel has shown an apparent genetic susceptibility to oviducal tumours, an otherwise highly unusual affliction in birds of prey (Cooper 1979). The effective population size of each of these and several other species of island birds is extremely small, and at a point where extinction is likely before the year 2000.

Why, then, should we expend time and effort to conserve these apparent lost causes? There are several good reasons. Firstly, predictability is not certainty. Even if we save one of these eight birds, I believe our efforts will have been well spent. Secondly, in the process we learn management techniques that can be applied, perhaps more successfully, to other healthier or more responsive species and their habitats. Thirdly, we can derive considerable educational and publicity value from the attempt, which should help to win over new converts to the cause of conservation, and should produce funds with which to wage other less futile battles.

CONCLUSIONS

There are certain practical considerations we cannot ignore. What are we presently able to do about the problems outlined here? I believe there is merit in looking carefully at the state of the world's islands and identifying which problems can be addressed and which are presently insoluble.

Important but often neglected inventories of biological resources on islands in the Pacific and Indian Oceans were undertaken under the auspices of the International Biological Programme (Douglas 1969; Elliott 1972). These inventories classified islands on the basis of the extent of man-caused modification. Obviously, islands with the least modification and with the most intact and most highly endemic flora and fauna are worthiest of conservation.

I recommend that an up-to-date inventory of the world's islands be undertaken as a matter of considerable priority. This inventory should record the presence of endemic organisms, unique or important habitats, introduced herbivores and predators, and other destabilizing factors. From such an inventory would emerge a clear plan of action for conserving birds on islands. The plan would be based on a solid set of priorities and also the knowledge of what can be accomplished and what cannot.

Preservation of intact or nearly intact island ecosystems is obviously the preferred kind of conservation action. Occasionally it involves intervention at the diplomatic level and nothing else, and achieves the most for the least effort. But in an era of increasing nationalistic pride, outsiders' interventions, however appropriate and well-intentioned, have less and less effect.

Habitat destruction on islands is largely an irreversible process, at least on any time scale which has significance for the preservation of bird populations. The rehabilitation of Mangere Island in the Chatham group by the New Zealand Wildlife Service following removal of sheep is one of the very few attempts at reversal of this destructive process, and it may or may not come in time to help the Chatham Island Black Robin. Many examples come to mind of habitat deterioration from invasion of vigorous exotic plants that *should* be reversed if the birds that inhabit the areas are to persist, but we have neither the resources nor the ability to undertake such rehabilitation. Habitat deterioration is the most significant present cause of endangerment to island birds, yet we are nearly helpless to deal with it. Captive breeding and labour-intensive manipulative techniques in the wild are futile gestures if we cannot assure the continued existence of sufficiently healthy and capacious habitat to permit the long-term survival of the species.

We can be slightly more optimistic about removal of herbivores and some predators, at least on carefully selected small islands. This is an area of activity where the international conservation community can and should increase its level of involvement. Even more important is the safeguarding of presently predator-free islands.

Control of hunting is another area in which the conservation community can be effective, for this is a problem that can be solved through political and educational approaches.

We have to make careful choices in committing our limited conservation resources. The temptation is to try to do everything, but this we can no longer do. We must commit our energies only to those activities which have a realistic chance of positively affecting the long-term survival of island ecosystems and species.

ACKNOWLEDGEMENTS

I would like to thank Cameron and Kay Kepler, and Phil Moors for their comments on this manuscript.

REFERENCES

ATKINSON, I. A. E. 1973. Spread of the Ship Rat (*Rattus rattus* L.) in New Zealand. *Journ. Royal Soc. New Zealand* **3**, 457–72.

ATKINSON, I. A. E. 1977. A reassessment of factors, particularly *Rattus rattus* L., that influenced the decline of endemic forest birds in the Hawaiian Islands. *Pac. Sci.* **31**, 109–33.

ATKINSON, I. A. E. 1978. Evidence of effects of rodents on the vertebrate wildlife of New Zealand islands. *In:* Dingwall, P. R., Atkinson, I. A. E. & Hay, C. (eds) The Ecology and Control of Rodents in New Zealand Nature Reserves. *Dept. Lands & Survey Information Series* No. 4: 7–30.

ATKINSON, I. A. E. (this vol.). The spread of commensal species of *Rattus* to oceanic islands and their effects on island avifaunas. *ICBP Tech. Pubn.* No. 3.

BELL, B. D. 1978. The Big South Cape Islands rat irruption. *In:* Dingwall, P. R., Atkinson, I. A. E. & Hay, C. (eds) The Ecology and Control of Rodents in New Zealand Nature Reserves. *Dept. Lands & Survey Information Series* No. 4: 33–40.

BRODKORB, P. 1960. How many species of birds have existed? *Bull. Fla. State Mus.* **5**, 41–53.

BRYAN, W. A. 1908. Some birds of Molokai. *B.P. Bishop Mus. Occas. Papers* **1**, 129–37.

BUTLER, P. 1981. The St. Lucia Amazon *Amazona versicolor*: its changing status and conservation. *In:* Pasquier, R. F. (ed.) Conservation of New World Parrots. *ICBP Tech. Pubn. No. 1:* 171–80.

CALVOPINA, L. (this vol.). The impact and eradication of feral goats on the Galapagos Islands. *ICBP Tech. Pubn.* No. 3.

COOPER, J. 1979. An oviduct adenocarcinoma in a Mauritius Kestrel *Falco punctatus*. *Avian Path.* **8**, 187–91.

DIAMOND, J. M. 1976. Island biogeography and conservation: strategy and limitations. *Science* **193**, 1027–9.

DIAMOND, J. M. (this vol.). Population processes in island birds: immigration, extinction and fluctuations. *ICBP Tech. Pubn.* No. 3.

DIAMOND, J. M. & MAY, R. M. 1976. Island biogeography and the design of nature reserves. *In:* May, R. M. (ed.) *Theoretical Ecology:* 163–86. Saunders, Philadelphia.

DIAMOND, J. M. & VEITCH, C. R. 1981. Extinctions and introductions in the New Zealand avifauna: cause and effect? *Science* **211**, 499–501.

DOUGLAS, G. 1969. Draft check list of Pacific Ocean islands. *Micronesica* **5**, 327–463.

DUFF, R. 1952. *Pyramid Valley.* Pegasus Press, Christchurch.

ELLIOTT, H. F. I. 1972. Island ecosystems and conservation with particular reference to the biological significance of islands of the Indian Ocean and the consequential research and conservation needs. *J. Mar. Biol. Assocn. India* **14**, 578–608.

ELY, C. A. & CLAPP, R. B. 1973. The natural history of Laysan Island, Northwestern Hawaiian Islands. *Atoll Research Bull.* **117**, 1–361.

FEHER, J. 1969. Hawaii: A Pictorial History. *B. P. Bishop Mus. Special Pub.* No. 58.

FISHER, J. 1964. Extinct birds. *In:* Thomson, A. L. (ed.) *A new dictionary of birds.* McGraw Hill, New York.

IMBER, M. J. 1975. Petrels and predators. *ICBP Bull.* **12**, 260–3.

IMBER, M. J. 1978. The effects of rats on breeding success of petrels. *In:* Dingwall, P. R., Atkinson, I. A. E. & Hay, C. (eds) The Ecology and Control of Rodents in New Zealand Nature Reserves. *Dept. Lands & Survey Information Series* No. 4: 67–71.

JEHL, J. & PARKES, K. C. 1982. The status of the avifauna of the Revillagigedo Islands, Mexico. *Wilson Bull.* **94**, 1–19.

KARR, J. R. 1982. Avian extinction on Barro Colorado Island, Panama: a reassessment. *Amer. Nat.* **119**, 220–39.

KEPLER, C. B. 1967. Polynesian Rat predation on nesting Laysan Albatrosses and other Pacific seabirds. *Auk* **84**, 426–30.

KING, W. B. 1973. Conservation status of birds of central Pacific islands. *Wilson Bull.* **85**, 89–103.

KING, W. B. 1978. Endangered birds of the world and current efforts toward managing them. *In:* Temple, S. A. (ed.) *Endangered Birds: Management Techniques for Preserving Threatened Species:* 9–17. Univ. of Wisconsin Press, Madison.

KING, W. B. 1980. Ecological basis of extinction in birds. *Proc. Berlin Internat. Ornith. Cong,* **17**, 905–11.

KING, W. B. 1981. *Endangered Birds of the World: The ICBP Bird Red Data Book.* Smithsonian Inst Press, Washington, D.C.

MAYR, E. 1966. *Animal Species and Evolution.* Harvard Univ. Press, Cambridge.

MILLS, J. A. & MARK, A. F. 1977. Food preferences of takahe in Fiordland National Park, New Zealand, and the effect of competition from introduced red deer. *J. Anim. Ecol.* **40**, 939–58.

MOORS, P. J. (this vol.). Eradication campaigns against *Rattus norvegicus* on the Noises Islands, New Zealand, using brodifacoum and 1080. *ICBP Tech. Pubn.* No. 3.

MOORS, P. J. & ATKINSON, I. A. E. (1984). Predation on seabirds by introduced mammals, and factors affecting its severity. *ICBP Tech. Pubn.* No. 2

MORRIS, R. B. 1977. Black Robin transfers. *Wildlife: A Review* **8**, 44–8.

MYERS, N. 1980. *Conversion of Tropical Moist Forests.* Nat. Acad. Sci./Nat. Research Council, Washington, D.C.

OLSON, S. L. & JAMES, H. F. 1982. Fossil birds from the Hawaiian Islands: evidence for wholesale extinction by man before western contact. *Science* **217**, 633–5.

RAFFAELE, H. 1977. Comments on the extinction of *Loxigilla portoricensis grandis* in St. Kitts, Lesser Antilles. *Condor* **97**, 389–90.

SIMBERLOFF, D. S. & ABELE, L. G. 1975. Island biogeography theory and conservation practice. *Science* **191**, 285–6.

SOULÉ, M. E. 1980. Thresholds for survival: maintaining fitness and evolutionary potential. *In:* Soulé, M. E. & Wilcox, B. A. (eds) *Conservation Biology: An Evolutionary–Ecological Perspective:* 151–69. Sinauer, Sunderland, Mass.

TERBORGH, J. W. 1976. Island biogeography and conservation: strategy and limitations. *Science* **193**, 1029–30.

TERBORGH, J. & WINTER, R. 1980. Some causes of extinction. *In:* Soulé, M. E. & Wilcox, B. A. (eds) *Conservation Biology: An Evolutionary–Ecological Perspective:* 119–33. Sinauer, Sunderland, Mass.

VAN RIPER, C. III. 1981. A breeding ecology of the endangered Palila (*Psittirostra baileui*) on Mauna Kea, Hawaii. *Coop. Nat. Pk. Resources Studies Unit, Univ. of Hawaii, Manoa, Tech. Rept.* 42.

VEITCH, C. R. (this vol.). Methods of eradicating feral cats from offshore islands in New Zealand. *ICBP Tech. Pubn.* No. 3.

VINCENT, J. 1966. *Red Data Book, Vol. II, Aves.* IUCN, Morges, Switzerland.

WARNER, R. E. 1960. A forest dies on Mauna Kea. *Pac. Discovery* **13**, 6–14.

WARNER, R. E. 1968. The role of introduced diseases in the extinction of the endemic Hawaiian avifauna. *Condcr* **70**, 101–20.

WHITCOMB, R. F., LYNCH, J. F., OPLER, P. A. & ROBBINS, C. S. 1976. Island biogeography and conservation: strategy and limitations. *Science* **193**, 1030–2.

WHITMORE, T. C. 1980. The conservation of tropical rain forest. *In:* Soulé, M. E. & Wilcox, B. A. (eds) *Conservation Biology: An Evolutionary–Ecological Perspective:* 303–18. Sinauer, Sunderland, Mass.

WILCOX, B. A. 1980. Insular ecology and conservation. *In:* Soulé, M. E. & Wilcox, B. A. (eds)

Biological Conservation: An Evolutionary–Ecological Perspective: 95–117. Sinauer, Sunderland, Mass.

WILLIS, E. O. (in press). The composition of avian communities in remanescent woodlots in southern Brazil. *Papeis Avulsos Museu Paulisto.*

WILLIS, E. O. & EISENMANN, E. 1979. A revised list of birds on Barro Colorado Island, Panama. *Smithsonian Contrib. Zool.* **291**, 1–31.

WODZICKI, K. 1978. A review of existing control methods. *In:* Dingwall, P. R., Atkinson, I. A. E. & Hay, C. (eds) The Ecology and Control of Rodents in New Zealand Nature Reserves. *Dept. Lands & Survey Information Series* No. 4: 195–205.

POPULATION PROCESSES IN ISLAND BIRDS: IMMIGRATION, EXTINCTION AND FLUCTUATIONS

JARED M. DIAMOND

Physiology Department, University of California Medical Center, Los Angeles, California 90024

ABSTRACT

This paper summarizes insular population processes that are important in bird conservation.

Although almost all birds *can* fly, not all birds *choose* to cross water gaps. As one approaches the equator, an increasing proportion of the mainland avifauna consists of species that are poor over-water colonists. This trend can be understood in terms of natural selection for and against dispersal. Low dispersal ability increases the risk of extinction for patchily distributed species.

Many modern extinctions of birds have been due to the catastrophic impact of man the hunter and his commensal mammals. However, habitat destruction and fragmentation are now becoming the main causes of extinction. Islands furnish models for the effect of habitat fragmentation. The risk of extinction for isolated populations decreases with the island's area and with the species' population density, and increases with the temporal coefficient of variation of population density. Some extinctions resulting from habitat fragmentation are mediated by loss of habitat diversity or by effects of competing species.

INTRODUCTION

Why do islands loom so large in discussions of bird conservation?

Part of the reason is that archipelagos of islands are models for what man is creating out of unmodified habitats on continents. Such habitats are becoming fragmented into patches surrounded by man-modified habitats. Island studies constitute a natural experiment on the fates of populations in the continents' shrinking habitat patches.

The other reason for our interest in islands is that a grossly disproportionate number of bird extinctions in the past century have involved island birds. At least four factors have made island populations so vulnerable. First, total population sizes are smaller on islands than on continents, and risk of extinction varies inversely with population size. Second, the small areas of islands compared to continents mean fewer sites for reserves or intact habitats. Third, the isolation of islands often means that they were not reached naturally by predators, diseases, and competitors with which mainland species evolved and became adjusted. The impact of arrival of these agents on island populations not previously exposed to the agents has often been rapid and catastrophic. Finally, islands are distinctive because they are separated by barriers to dispersal of the island birds themselves. As we shall see, fragmentation of range by dispersal barriers is one factor predisposing to extinction.

17

In this paper I shall review population processes operating on islands. I shall begin with immigration, continue with extinction, and conclude with the effects of habitat diversity and competition on island populations.

IMMIGRATION

That birds can fly is their most important characteristic, and also one of their most misleading ones. It is often inferred that the power of flight guarantees birds the ability to cross water gaps or expanses of alien habitat that act as barriers to flightless animals. In fact, the realization has been growing in recent years that many flying birds *choose* not to fly across barriers of water or alien habitat: they are psychologically flightless (Diamond 1981). As one expression of this, consider a mainland with nearby islands, and ask what fraction of the bird species breeding on the mainland have ever been recorded on the offshore islands. This fraction decreases as one moves from the poles towards the Equator. For example, about 99 percent of breeding British landbirds have been recorded from offshore islands near Britain, but the comparable percentage for southern California landbirds is 80 percent, and for New Guinea landbirds 40%.

Ability to disperse across barriers is important in bird conservation, because it determines whether one local population of a species can 'seed' itself on other islands, or into patches with suitable habitat. Any isolated population is subject to the risk of extinction. If a patchily distributed species is incapable of dispersing between patches, each isolated population is subject to the risk of extinction, and lights may wink out for these populations one after another until they are all gone. In contrast, if dispersal across barriers is possible, then any surviving population can provide emigrants to reverse extinctions in other patches, and it is unlikely that populations in all patches would happen to disappear simultaneously. Thus, all other things being equal, high dispersal ability protects a species against risk of extinction, and sedentary species are at greater risk of extinction than mobile species with the same total population size.

Why does dispersal ability decrease from the poles towards the equator? Even more surprisingly, why should a species 'choose' never to cross a water gap of even a few miles? Evidently, dispersal ability is subject to natural selection, just as are anatomy, physiology, reproductive characteristics, foraging behaviour, and other features of a species' biology. Dispersal offers potential benefits: the chance that a pair of colonists may find an unoccupied patch suitable for this species and be able to fill it with their progeny. But dispersal also involves costs and risks: the energetic costs of dispersal, the risks of dying en route, the risk of not finding a suitable habitat patch before energy reserves are exhausted, and the risk that the new-found habitat patch may be inferior to the natal one. The trade-offs between these costs and benefits are resolved by natural selection. Dispersal ability is lowest in stable habitats like tropical rainforest, where populations are rarely wiped out by succession or climatic extremes and where habitat patches unoccupied by the species rarely become available. Dispersal ability is highest in species of unstable habitats where unoccupied patches frequently become available. Thus, dispersal is high in species of successional habitats such as second-growth and temporary pools, and low in species of the forest interior. But the cost of dispersal also depends on whether the species already possesses the anatomical equipment for dispersing as part of its daily foraging machinery, or whether the power of flight is used mainly for dispersal and is debited in terms of costs mainly to the dispersal ledger. For example, hawks, swifts, and nomadic frugivores and nectarivores of the canopy need strong wings for their daily food foraging, while many species of the forest ground and understorey do not. Thus, it is not surprising that ground and understorey species tend to be much more sedentary and less likely to colonize empty patches, or to appear on previously unoccupied empty patches, or to appear on previously unoccupied islands. Even this generalization holds many surprises at the species-by-species level. For example, among the New Guinea bird species that have never been recorded from an island lacking a Pleistocene land-bridge to New Guinea are the New Guinea Harpy Eagle (*Harpyopsis novaeguineae*), the Dusky Lory (*Pseudeos fuscata*), and two New Guinea species of *Collocalia* swiftlets.

Rather than illustrate the conservation importance of dispersal ability by a confirmed past example, I shall instead stick my neck out and make a prediction that only the future can test. In 1976 the government of the Solomon Islands asked me to prepare an environmental impact report for Rennell Island. This remarkable island is one of the world's largest uplifted coral atolls, has one of the tropical Pacific's largest lakes occupying the former lagoon, and also has one of the Pacific's most distinctive avifaunas for an island of its size. Of Rennell's 42 breeding land and fresh-water bird species, five are endemic species, and 19 others are endemic subspecies. Rennell's lake contains numerous forested islands. While studying the lake and its islands, I was struck by the fact that I often saw some species flying over the lake but never saw others, and that some species occupied many or all of the lake islands while others occupied none, despite suitable habitat. I interpret these differences partly in terms of differences in each species' willingness to cross habitat barriers. Rennell is now covered largely by forest, but the forest risks fragmentation due to logging, mining, and an expanding population. I predict that species absent from islands in the lake will be the ones most at risk from forest fragmentation. In particular, at present the endemic flycatcher *Clytorhynchus hamlini* and the endemic subspecies of the whistler *Pachycephala pectoralis feminina* are among the most abundant forest bird species of Rennell, but their absence from forested lake islands seems to me to bode ill for their future as the forest becomes fragmented. Naturally, forest fragmentation is not the sole risk to Rennell birds, and dispersal ability is not their sole salvation. The sole rat now on Rennell is *Rattus exulans*. If *R. rattus* or *R. norvegicus* is inadvertently introduced there is likely to be an extinction wave similar to that which followed arrival of rats on Lord Howe Island and New Zealand's Big South Cape Island, correlating with susceptibility of nests to rat predation.

EXTINCTION

The regrettably large portfolio of case studies in avian extinction includes island avifaunas devastated after the arrival of Europeans in recent centuries. Prize examples are New Zealand, Hawaii, and the remote islands of the Indian and Atlantic Oceans. Another set of case studies is provided by recent discoveries of extinction waves accompanying the first arrival of humans (not just Europeans) on these same islands, such as the extinctions associated with arrival of Polynesians on Hawaii, New Zealand, and the Chathams, and of Indonesians on Madagascar (Olson & James 1982; see Diamond 1982 for summary). As is well known, the hands of Europeans and of pre-European colonists have fallen very unevenly on the island avifaunas that they encountered. Large bird species have been particularly susceptible to extinction because of their value as hunting targets, and also perhaps because of their low population densities and low reproductive potential. Flightless species have also been susceptible because of their exposure to man's commensal mammalian pests.

These patterns in catastrophic extinction waves are familiar, even if there remain many details that we do not understand. Much less familiar are the slower extinction waves accompanying 'insularization', the fragmentation of a formerly continuous habitat expanse into patches through man's activities such as clearing of forest. These extinction waves associated with habitat fragmentation occur on islands just as on continents. In addition, even pristine islands are already 'insularized' habitats, so that it seems to me that species distributions on islands can offer real insights into what can be expected of population fates in natural reserve systems on continents.

One set of natural experiments in insularization came at the end of the Pleistocene, when rising sea level flooded low-lying coastal plains throughout the world and cut off many land-bridge islands from their continents. Examples include the fragmentation of Borneo, Sumatra, and Java from the Sunda Shelf; of Trinidad from South America; of Fernando Po from Africa; of Sri Lanka and Hainan from Southeast Asia; of Tasmania from Australia; and of Aru, Japen, and the western Papuan Islands from New Guinea. Comparisons of modern species lists for these land-bridge islands with lists for comparable mainland areas make clear that such islands have lost numerous species since the end of the Pleistocene, when they were embedded in continents. It may seem far-fetched to transfer conclusions from these slow extinction waves that began 10,000 years ago to the extinction waves associated with forest fragmentation today. But a connection has been made through recent studies of avian extinctions in forest patches that have been fragmented from large forest patches within the past century. These modern fragmentation studies include the analyses by Willis (1974) for Barro Colorado Island and for Brazilian wood-lots, of Lovejoy and colleagues for forest patches in Amazonia, and by Whitcomb and colleagues for forest fragments in the eastern United States.

In all these studies it turns out that the extinction is selective in two senses. First, larger islands or patches lose species relatively more slowly than do smaller ones. Second, some species are much more susceptible to extinction following fragmentation than are other species. For example, on New Guinea's continental shelf some bird species survived on every fragment exceeding 100 square miles in area, while other species disappeared on every fragment other than New Guinea itself, even on islands up to 3000 square miles in area (Diamond 1972).

What patterns can be seen in this differential extinction of species?

Two main patterns emerge. First, risk of extinction varies inversely as the abundance of a species. This is the clearest pattern that Terborgh & Winter (1980) observed in analyzing Willis's data for bird extinctions in Brazilian wood-lots. It also explains many features of the differential extinction of mammals that Brown (1971) documented for mountains of the western North American Great Basin. The other, weaker pattern is that, for species of equal abundance, risk of extinction is greater for those species subject to greater fluctuations in abundance. This is the main pattern emerging from Karr's (1982) analysis of avian extinctions on Barro Colorado Island. Karr's discussion explicitly connects fluctuations in population size to habitat diversity and competition, thereby leading us to the remaining subject of this paper. I note in passing that these empirical studies of differential proneness to extinction in isolated populations agree well with predictions by theoretical population biologists (e.g. Leigh 1975). Leigh shows that rarity should be the best predictor of proneness to extinction in small populations; temporal variability the best predictor in large populations.

EFFECTS OF HABITAT DIVERSITY AND COMPETITION

Habitat diversity plays a two-fold role in extinction on islands. The smaller an island or mainland patch, the lower its habitat diversity is likely to be. The first consequence is that numerous species are habitat specialists and are obviously doomed to disappear on an island or patch on which their habitat is either lacking or present in only a very reduced area. More subtly, there are numerous species whose life cycles require several different habitats. All such habitats must occur on an island for the population to be safe. For example, New Guinea's birds of paradise and bowerbirds move altitudinally with age, living at higher altitudes as adults than as immatures. Wallace's Scrub-hen (*Megapodius wallacei*) of the Moluccas lives most of its life inland but nests on coastal beaches. Numerous bird species perform seasonal movements within a sufficiently large island, correlated with wet or dry seasons, availability of fruit, and flowering. On Barro Colorado Island one of the main modes of bird extinction recognized by Karr (1982) is that the island is too homogeneous in topography and microclimate to sustain populations of species that would survive by local population movements in a larger area. In particular, mainland species that escape the dry season in flat terrain by moving to the moister nearby hill forests have nowhere to retreat in the dry season on Barro Colorado Island. Such species show large fluctuations in abundance for local populations on the mainland, as these local populations can shift with conditions.

The population's coefficient of variation is also relevant to understanding effects of competition. Theory predicts that the more closely species are packed competitively, the greater will be the temporal variation in population numbers. Potentially, this means that members of ecologically similar pairs of species are at risk following habitat fragmentation. The overall significance of this factor awaits empirical testing. One anecdotal supporting example is that the New Guinea lowland forest avifauna includes two monarch flycatchers that are very similar morphologically and ecologically, *Monarcha manadensis* and *M. guttula*. The latter is much less sedentary than the former and has colonized nine islands with no recent land connections to New Guinea, while *M. manadensis* has colonized none. It is especially interesting that *M. manadensis* has also disappeared on every island connected to New Guinea by a Pleistocene land bridge, whereas *M. guttula* occurs on six of the seven largest land-bridge islands. A possible explanation is that their competitive similarity made both these species prone to extinction when the land-bridge islands were cut from the New Guinea mainland, and that the populations of *M. manadensis* disappeared on these islands one after another without the opportunity for subsequent refounding of the populations by overwater colonization, whereas *M. guttula* was able to reverse extinctions by dispersal across water.

REFERENCES

BROWN, J. H. 1971. Mammals on mountaintops: nonequilibrium insular biogeography. *Amer. Nat.* **105**, 467–78.

DIAMOND, J. M. 1972. Biogeographic kinetics: estimation of relaxation times for avifaunas of southwest Pacific islands. *Proc. Nat. Acad. Sci. USA* **69**, 3199–3203.

DIAMOND, J. M. 1981. Flightlessness and fear of flying in island species. *Nature* **293**, 507–8.

DIAMOND, J. M. 1982. Man the exterminator. *Nature* **298**, 787–9.

KARR, J. R. 1982. Avian extinction on Barro Colorado Island, Panama: a reassessment. *Amer. Natur.* **119**, 220–39.

LEIGH, E. G. 1975. Population fluctuations, community stability, and environmental variability. *In:* Cody, M. L. & Diamond, J. M. (eds) *Ecology and Evolution of Communities:* 51–73. Harvard University Press, Cambridge.

OLSON, S. L. & JAMES, H. F. 1982. Fossil birds from the Hawaiian islands: evidence for wholesale extinction by man before western contact. *Science* **217**, 633–4.

TERBORGH, J. W. & WINTER, B. 1980. Some causes of extinction. *In:* Soulé, M. E. & Wilcox, B. A. (eds) *Conservation Biology:* 119–34. Sinauer, Sunderland.

WILLIS, E. O. 1974. Populations and local extinctions of birds on Barro Colorado Island, Panama. *Ecol. Monogr.* **44**, 153–69.

ISLAND BIOGEOGRAPHIC THEORY IN BIRD CONSERVATION: AN ALTERNATIVE APPROACH

T. M. REED

Nature Conservancy Council, Northminster House, Peterborough, 1PU 1UA, England

ABSTRACT

The equilibrium theory of island biogeography (MacArthur & Wilson 1967) and its derivative, the species-area relationship, have increasingly assumed importance in conservation planning. The theory suggests that large areas should be favoured in the acquisition of nature reserves in order to retain maximum species diversity.

This paper examines the many shortcomings of the theory, especially the species–area relationship, using data from existing reserves for British island birds. Because of the many simplifying assumptions made by the theory, it is simplistic to use only one independent variable (area) to choose between potential reserves. The underlying premise that a constant number of bird species breeds on an island of a particular size is untenable given the unstable nature of bird populations. If reserve choice has to be based on regression analyses, it should include ecologically sensible variables such as habitat variety and proximity to colonizing sources, rather than area alone.

It is important that the dynamic component of bird populations is incorporated into conservation planning. Patterns of population turnover (immigrations and extinctions) are examined for British island birds by means of turnover triangles. Using this method for a series of islands highlights the importance of habitat requirements, threats to island populations, minimum population levels for establishment and long-term survival, and recolonization potentials.

INTRODUCTION

As the pressures upon existing natural and semi-natural habitats accelerate, the importance of islands and habitat islands as refuges for the remaining avifauna will increase. Because of this it is critical to try and assess some of the factors that influence the numbers of bird and other species that occur on islands, so that any conservation action that is taken will be as beneficial as possible.

Because of the nature of the task it is important that any theory that may purport to help with site selection is critically examined. In this paper I examine some of the shortcomings of the equilibrium theory of island biogeography (MacArthur & Wilson 1967), outline its limitations for practical conservation, and suggest several alternative approaches that can be used in its place in insular conditions.

EQUILIBRIUM THEORY

MacArthur and Wilson's theory is essentially very simple, its intuitive simplicity being one of its more beguiling aspects. The number of species on an island is a balance or

23

'equilibrium' between the rates of immigration and extinction. Immigration rates are inversely related to isolation from a colonizing source, whilst extinction rates are inversely related to population size and directly proportional to isolation.

The lessons for conservation from equilibrium theory appear to be simple: take large, non-isolated reserves to retain maximal species diversity. If reserve area is reduced, the number of species will reach a new equilibrium by 'relaxing' to a lower level consistent with the size and position of the site, so confirming the need to retain large areas as reserves.

EQUILIBRIUM THEORY REVISITED

If reviewed critically, the equilibrium theory can be shown to rest upon a series of convenient assumptions or untestable ideas. These are outlined in the following sections.

Species–area
Although great emphasis was placed on the relationship between species number (S) and area (A), this, like equilibrium, was a convenience necessary for the development of the theory. MacArthur & Wilson (1967: p. 8, 19, 20, 61, 65) realized that habitat diversity would be the major factor affecting S. They noted that area (A) was very much a second-best factor, yet proceeded to erect an hypothesis based on area alone. This by itself might not be so critical had the theory then not been so firmly constructed that increasingly precise statements and extrapolations were based on the species–area relationship.

The species–area relationship now dominates all considerations of reserve strategy to the exclusion of other factors that may be correlated with species number (Higgs 1981). The correlation between the two variables is taken as being absolute: that is, r = 1.0. This is never the case. Examining species–area correlations from 100 studies (Connor & McCoy 1979), Reed (1983) found that on average over half of the variance remained unaccounted for. This is an unpromising basis on which to erect any form of exacting theory. Choosing reserves purely on a single criterion is inefficient and biologically dubious, especially if the number of species can be predicted only with such a low degree of accuracy. This discrepancy between the observed and the theoretical species-area correlation is critical when 'relaxation' calculations are involved. These are becoming increasingly important as habitats are fragmented or reduced in area. This means that as an area of habitat is reduced in size one cannot realistically predict the number of species to be expected without a large error term—a very unsatisfactory position as far as conservation is concerned. Of course there is the further problem that one has no notion of which species will be kept and which will be lost. As will be seen later, if sites are to be chosen on the basis of regression plots (i.e. choosing sites which have more species than predicted by the regression equation), then biologically meaningful variables should be used, such as location, altitude and some index of habitat variety, rather than area alone.

Immigration and extinction
Immigration and extinction are the cornerstones of the concept of equilibrium. In the model, immigration is portrayed as a function of the number of species: high initially and finite once all the colonizing pool has arrived, provided there are no subsequent extinctions. These assumptions are simplistic. It is hard to define either the size or

position of the colonizing pools. Geographical ranges fluctuate within even short periods of time, so that a pool is an oscillatory rather than a fixed number. For many islands it is ecologically unreasonable to consider all species as potential colonists. MacArthur & Wilson were unable to define when a case of immigration had occurred, being unable to decide either how long a species would have to breed before it could be called 'established' or how large its new population would have to be. The rate of immigration as portrayed by MacArthur & Wilson (1967) was shown as a single smooth curve almost asymptotically approaching zero. As Sauer (1969, p. 589) noted, both immigration and extinction curves are 'artistic compromises between extremely wide possibilities'.

The roles of interference and competition are additional complicating factors. If a close competitor already occurs on an island, the immigration potential of a colonist is reduced and the immigration rate seriously affected. If the immigration rate is dependent upon the composition of the remaining pool of colonizing species, the immigration curve must at best be a broad blur. This brings into question the concept of a single equilibrium number and balance for an island of a given size.

Like immigration, extinction is seen purely as a function of the number of species present, which in turn is a function of area. Therefore both immigration and extinction rates at any time are merely loose probabilistic statements. What value these probabilities will have for each species, and for the colonizing pool as a whole, is not clear from the theory. As MacArthur (1972) noted, both composition and competition can quite drastically alter extinction rates. Furthermore, extinction is affected by habitat availability and location. These and other problems make extinction and immigration no more than probabilistic concepts affected by competition, species composition and habitat availability amongst other factors, and they are certainly not fixed as suggested by MacArthur & Wilson.

Equilibrium

If immigration and extinction are variable, equilibrium must be called into question. McArthur & Wilson (1967) admitted that equilibrium was a convenient concept rather than a reality, yet proceeded to erect a theory based on that assumption. However, MacArthur (1972, p. 100) has noted '. . . who is to say that the rate of extinction . . . is automatically equal to the rate of immigration?' Bearing in mind my reservations about immigration and extinction, equilibrium must also be a blur, its position changing with the same factors influencing the other two variables. It is not a simple function of time, distance, or the number of species in the colonizing pool.

Most islands lack long detailed records of breeding species. A list of species for one or two years is inappropriate for suggesting the presence of equilibrium, yet this often happens when fitting log:log plots of species to area. MacArthur & Wilson suggested that saturation (the exact prediction of the number of species for an island of a given area) implies equilibrium, with the species–area regression graph pre-supposing that the islands are in equilibrium. To calculate the degree of deviation from saturation assumes incorrectly that the species–area correlation is absolute. This means that the prediction that a given island will have a certain number of species must be false. Effectively the equilibrium number will range within a wide statistical confidence band, rather than be a single fixed number.

These and other points serve to show that the equilibrium theory is by no means the convenient water-tight model that is generally assumed (e.g. Diamond 1975; Diamond & May 1976; Wilson & Willis 1975). The limitations of the species–area approach in the choice of conservation reserves are illustrated in the following section.

COMPARISON OF SPECIES–AREA & STEPWISE REGRESSIONS

Species–area regressions include only one independent variable. This is inappropriate for conservation. Results from species-area regressions were compared with those from stepwise multiple regressions with five independent variables. The object was to see if factors other than area influence the numbers of breeding bird species on islands, and at the same time to increase the percentage variance which is explained (R^2), so that species number could be predicted with greater precision.

Data

Data were taken from a study of landbird populations on British islands (Reed 1981). Data were available from 61 islands throughout Britain for the number of species (S) known to have bred on each island, the data being drawn from observatory and similar records. This was the dependent variable used in the stepwise regression analyses. Data were available for five independent variables. Island area (A) was taken from Ordnance Survey maps and gazetteers. Maximum island elevation was extracted from 1:25,000 Ordnance Survey maps. Latitude in degrees and minutes north, and longitude in degrees and minutes west were taken for the geographical mid-point of each island on 1:25,000 Ordnance Survey maps. The number of habitats on an island during the period of available bird data was drawn from the same sources as the bird information, the only criterion being that the habitat exceeded an area of 0.2ha. Therefore all the variables were easily and cheaply obtained, and were the sort that might be used in any conservation programme.

Among the 61 islands, 33 were bird reserves. Each reserve was chosen on an ad-hoc basis rather than as part of a co-ordinated conservation strategy. Some reserves, such as Grassholm and Bass Rock, were chosen for their communities of rare birds. In the following analyses only the number of breeding landbird species on each island was considered.

Methods

Islands were analysed in two ways. As is usual with such data the log of species (S) and the log of island area (A) were plotted together. This was the species-area relationship for the sample. According to equilibrium theory the best sites for conservation purposes would be those above the regression line, containing more species than other islands of similar area.

In addition, the number of species was put into a stepwise regression programme (Dixon 1973) to identify factors that influence the number of breeding landbirds. The results from the stepwise regression program were plotted and, as with log S and log A, the scatter of islands compared to see if the islands which always had more species than predicted by the regression equation were reserves. If so then they would have been chosen correctly as reserves, in spite of their eclectic origins.

Results

Species–area. The log S − log A plot (r = 0.85, R^2 = 71.6 percent) indicated the scatter of reserves and other islands to be very similar (*Figure 1a*), but reserves tended to be above the regression line significantly more often than the other islands (X^2 = 3.98; p < 0.05). Furthermore, as can be seen from the regression intercepts (*Figure 1b*), when plotted separately the number of species per unit area is higher for reserves than for the other islands. The reserves were apparently species-rich, containing more species per unit area than the other islands, and were good for preserving bird communities.

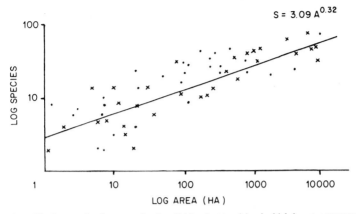

Figure 1a: The log species–log area plot for all islands. ✕ = island which is not a reserve, ● = reserve island.

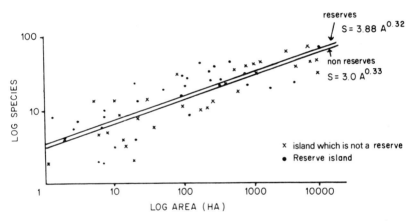

Figure 1b: The log species–log area plot with separate regression lines for reserves and non-reserves. ✕ = island which is not a reverve, ● = reserve island.

Table 1: The result of the stepwise regression of species number with six characteristics of 61 islands. (Area has been log transformed.)

Variable	Contribution to R^2	Total R^2	Significant at $p < 0.05$ (F test)
Habitat number	74.56	74.56	*
Distance to mainland	2.11	76.67	*
Area	4.73	81.40	*
Longitude	0.28	81.68	–
Elevation	0.15	81.83	–
Latitude	0.01	81.84	–

Stepwise regressions. The stepwise regression (*Table 1*) indicated that the number of bird species breeding on an island was positively correlated with the number of habitats and with island area, but was inversely correlated with distance ($R^2 = 81.8$ percent). Distance is significantly correlated with the number of species after allowing for linear dependence on habitat number, and area is similarly correlated after allowing for habitat number and distance to the mainland. Thus more species occur on large, varied islands near a source of colonists. Evidently area was not the best predictor of S for this sample of British islands. The percentage of explained variance was greater than that for log S − log A, meaning that one could predict the number of species to be expected with more certainty and at the same time identify which factors one should consider when trying to choose reserves. Reserves should be large, near the colonizing sources, and have a wide variety of habitats. Plotting the residuals from the stepwise regression against area (*Figure 2*) showed that the tendency for reserves to have more species than expected, and to fall above the regression line noted in the plot of log S − log A, was not repeated. Reserves fell almost equally above and below the regression line once factors other than area which might influence S were taken into consideration. The proportion of reserves above the line did not differ significantly from that for islands which are not reserves ($X^2 = 0.6$; $p < 0.05$).

Discussion
Over the last decade conservationists have tried to find a simple tool to help in choosing reserves. However, it must be recognized (e.g. Ratcliffe 1977; Adams & Rose 1978) that conservation and planning are based not on a single criterion, but on a series of criteria and decisions, thus making over-emphasis on species–area plots unrealistic. Ecological relationships can never be modelled or understood using only a single dimension.

The British island reserves illustrate one of the problems involved with assuming that species number and area are sufficient to identify suitable islands for conservation. Although area is significantly correlated with species number, it still leaves a large amount of the total variance unaccounted for. If reserves have to be chosen on the basis of regression results, the stepwise regression would be preferable, because it includes more biologically realistic variables than linear regression does, increases the explained R^2 substantially, and also identifies factors that may influence species number.

It is axiomatic in many studies that a significant log S:log A correlation is equivalent to verifying equilibrial theory (Gilbert 1980). It is impossible to know from a regression result that equilibrium is involved, especially when the data used are usually from single censuses, nor is it possible to infer that there is a significant distance effect when distance values are excluded from regressions. Until these and other fundamental objections are met, it is impossible to invoke an equilibrial interpretation of any set of biogeographical data (Reed, in prep.).

TURNOVER TRIANGLES

Perhaps one of the most critical problems with the species–area relationship (and equilibrium theory) is the working assumption that all species are equivalent. As can be seen in the span of data for the island of Steepholm (*Table 2*), species differ significantly in their capacity to colonize and remain on an island. In a conservation context this lack of equivalence is critical: few conservation programmes concentrate purely on the number of species, to the exclusion of the actual species involved. Species–area diagrams tell nothing of the conservation value of particular species, nor of population size, population dynamics and turnover rates that are essential for successful manage-

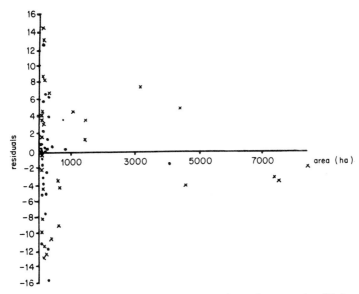

Figure 2: Plot of residuals from the 61 case stepwise regression against area: using all independent variables in the regression. × = island which is not a reserve, ● = reserve island.

ment and reserve acquisition. This lack of 'temporal accountability' can be countered by the use of turnover triangles (Reed 1980).

Turnover is the extinction or immigration of a species. In using turnover triangles for conservation purposes I am concerned only with extinction and immigration of individual species on individual islands. Turnover as used here is *not* related to MacArthur & Wilson's (1967) equilibrium theory.

Methods

The turnover triangle has two components: the ordinate, which is the rate of turnover per year (a turnover being an immigration or extinction from one breeding season to the next); and the abscissa, which is the percentage of the total years in which a species has bred at a particular site. Several basic requirements must be met in order to use the method effectively. Because percentage values are used, a run of as many years of data

Table 2: The number of breeding landbird species on Steepholm, England 1924–1977. The number of breeding species varies markedly from year to year. Although turnover (extinctions and immigrations) occurs, there is no evidence for a fixed equilibrium number of species.

Year	1924	'27	'28	'29	'30	'32	'34	'35	'36	'37	'38	'45	'47
Number of species	11	14	11	13	10	8	5	15	10	11	10	6	7
Year	1949	'50	'53	'54	'55	'57	'58	'59	'60	'61	'62	'63	'64
Number of species	7	9	7	8	8	7	8	8	9	8	8	8	11
Year	1965	'66	'67	'68	'69	'70	'71	'72	'73	'74	'75	'76	'77
Number of species	9	12	13	9	8	9	8	8	9	8	14	11	12

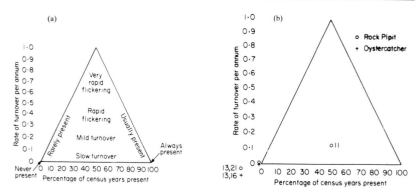

Figure 3a: The turnover triangle. Individual populations can easily be characterized by their position within the triangle and compared with other populations to identify factors affecting stability and long-term conservation prospects.

Figure 3b: Turnover triangles for two species whose requirements are met on nearly every island. Identification is given for islands with turnovers or always absent status.

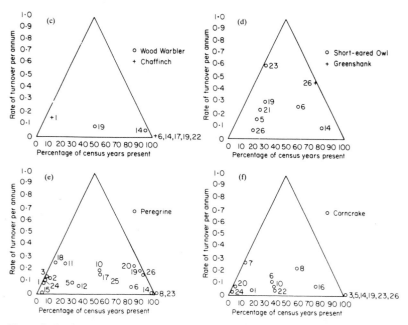

Figures 3c–f: (c, d) Turnover triangles for species with specialized requirements. (e, f) Turnover triangles for two man-influenced species. Identification is given only for islands with turnovers or always present status.

Note Numbers on graphs refer to the island numbers listed in *Table 3*.

Table 3: Islands and species used in turnover analysis. *denotes that a species has bred at least once on an island.

No.	Island	No. of years data	Size (ha)	A	B	C	D	E	F	G	H
1	Bardsey	16	179.7	*	*	*				*	*
2	Calf of Man	11	249.4	*	*			*			*
3	Cape Clear	10	639.8	*	*					*	*
4	Copeland	17	32.0	*	*						
5	Coll	10	7,415.4	*	*						*
6	Eigg	10	3,159.1	*	*	*		*		*	*
7	Faeroes	13	140,081.0	*	*					*	
8	Fair Isle	20	764.8	*	*					*	*
9	Farnes	29	32.4	*	*					*	
10	Foula	15	1,336.0	*	*					*	*
11	Grassholm	10	8.9	*	*						
12	Handa	11	310.1	*	*						*
13	Hilbre	14	6.5								
14	Isle of Man	37	57,191.5	*	*	*	*	*		*	*
15	Isle of May	37	48.6	*	*						*
16	Lindisfarne	13	541.7	*						*	
17	Lundy	28	451.8	*	*	*					*
18	North Rona	12	119.8	*	*						*
19	Rhum	11	10,688.2	*	*	*	*	*		*	*
20	St Kilda	13	853.0	*	*					*	*
21	Scolt Head	46	838.9		*			*			
22	Scilly	19	1,636.0	*	*	*				*	
23	Shetland	11	142,639.3	*	*			*		*	*
24	Skokholm	33	97.2	*	*					*	
25	Steepholm	37	19.0	*	*						*
26	Tiree	11	7,650.2	*	*			*	*	*	*

A = Rock Pipit (*Anthus spinoletta* Linnaeus); B = Oystercatcher (*Haematopus ostralegus* Linnaeus); C = Chaffinch (*Fringilla coelebs* Linnaeus); D = Wood Warbler (*Phylloscopus sibilatrix* Bechstein); E = Short-eared Owl (*Asio flammeus* Pontoppidan); F = Greenshank (*Tringa nebularia* Gunnerus); G = Corncrake (*Crex crex* Linnaeus); H = Peregrine (*Falco peregrinus* Tunstall).

as possible is required so that single years do not represent a high proportion of the total percentage. For this reason at least 10 years' data are necessary. Because turnovers chart year-to-year changes of status, any break in the records will lead to an underestimate of the real turnover rate because in-and-out sequences are missed (i.e. 'cryptoturnover' occurs, Lynch & Johnson 1974). The larger the gap the greater the underestimation. It is possible to divide the triangle (*Figure 3a*) into sections which characterize the population trends. Populations on the left of the triangle rapidly go extinct, populations on the right have long-term stability, and those in the centre repeatedly immigrate but fail to establish in the long-term. Whilst populations can be characterized on this basis, there is no single process describing all species or sites in any one position. The fate of each may be the result of a very different combination of circumstances, and historical data are needed to interpret them for each species and site. In order to understand the variations in positions within the triangle, and to use the triangle for individual species rather than for all species at one site, turnover values were calculated for eight landbirds breeding on 26 islands around the British coast (*Table 3*) (Reed 1980). Several species illustrate factors such as habitat availability, habitat area, range margins, food instability and human influence which affect turnover (*Figures 3b–f*).

Data
The Rock Pipit (*Anthus Spinoletta*) and Oystercatcher (*Haematopus ostralegus*) are

both species with simple, easily met habitat requirements. Both species are widespread, each being absent from only two islands (*Figure 3b*). The occurrence of the Chaffinch (*Fringilla coelebs*), by contrast, is both less frequent and less stable. Typically a bird of mature woodland and scrub edges, it occurs only on islands with such cover, and 'turns over' on Bardsey where the small area (0.5ha) of woodland is unable to support a sufficiently large population to prevent the species' extinction (*Figure 3c*). The Wood Warbler (*Phylloscopus sibilatrix*) is even more restricted in habitat, occurring only on the two islands with mature woodland cover; populations on both islands are too small to prevent turnover (*Figure 3c*). The Greenshank (*Tringa nebularia*) is at the southern margin of its breeding range in Britain, and its turnover rate is typical of a species constantly expanding and contracting its range (*Figure 3d*). The Short-eared Owl (*Asio flammeus*) is a food specialist, concentrating on the vole *Microtus agrestis* which tends to have cyclic populations. On no island in the sample does the owl breed annually. Instead, it seeks out areas of vole abundance, nesting for one or two years before moving on as prey numbers decrease (Reed 1979). Its turnover triangle reflects this (*Figure 3d*).

Raptors have small populations on all but the largest islands. When organochlorines became widely used in the 1950s the Peregrine (*Falco peregrinus*) declined rapidly, surviving only on a few scattered mainland localities (Ratcliffe 1980) and on the northernmost islands where organochlorines were introduced last and used for the shortest period (*Figure 3e*).

In Britain, agricultural change and rural depopulation have accelerated within the last century, especially on islands. As agriculture has changed, the avifauna associated with old farming practices has been forced to adapt or has gone extinct. The Corncrake *Crex crex* (*Figure 3f*) has been especially affected. Essentially a bird of late-cut meadowland, it has gone from islands that have been evacuated, such as St Kilda. As the area of late-cut hay has decreased and mechanized cutting increased, the Corncrake has become extinct over much of its former range. Now it breeds only on those islands retaining older methods and networks of small fields such as the Irish and Scottish outlying islands.

Discussion

The main advantage of the turnover triangle is that it incorporates much data omitted by other methods such as incidence curves (Diamond 1975). It is possible to identify distinct population variability between sites, and to incorporate ecological data which help identify the combinations of factors affecting turnovers and the islands on which a species occurs. These provide a much needed background for assessing the conservation potential of individual species both locally and over a wider region.

Future avenues

The next step will be to collate for individual species the data on population sizes and temporal continuity which are available from a large number of sites. This would give data not merely on presence or absence at sites, but also on population dynamics, population sizes needed for colonization to be successful and extinction unlikely, the effects of predation and competition on population sizes, and how these vary within and between species. This approach would allow the development of powerful probabilistic statements on population occurrence and variability which are increasingly needed in conservation.

CONCLUSION

The accolades given to equilibrium theory on its arrival and subsequent development in the conservation sphere are to a large degree unwarranted. Many of the cornerstones of the theory rest upon convenient assumptions, with undue and unwise emphasis on the species-area relationship. If regressions are to be used in conservation planning, they should be multiple rather than single. An active consideration of species and dynamics is needed if conservation is to make any significant advance in aiding the survival of individual bird species. It is vital therefore that conservation action takes account of as much information as possible. The turnover triangle is especially relevant here, because it provides a simple and practical framework within which to assess the rates and reasons for population changes. These assessments are needed when trying to safeguard island populations.

ACKNOWLEDGEMENTS

The majority of this work was carried out whilst holding a N.E.R.C. Research Studentship. I am grateful to F. J. Wright, P. J. Moors and a referee for their comments on a draft of this paper.

REFERENCES

ADAMS, W. M. & ROSE, C. I. (eds) 1978. The selection of reserves for nature conservation. *University College London Discussion Papers in Conservation*, No. 20.

CONNOR, E. F. & McCOY, E. D. 1979. The statistics and biology of the species-area relationship. *Amer. Nat.* **113**, 791–833.

DIAMOND, J. M. 1975. Assembly of species communities. *In* Cody, M. L. & Diamond, J. M. (eds) *Ecological Structure of Species Communities.* Belknapp Press, Harvard, Mass.

DIAMOND, J. M. & MAY, R. M. 1976. Island biogeographic theory and the design of natural reserves. *In* May, R. M. (ed) *Theoretical Ecology.* Blackwells, Oxford.

DIXON, W. J. (ed.) 1973. *Biomedical computer programs.* Univ. California Press, London.

GILBERT, F. S. 1980. The equilibrium theory of island biogeography: fact or fiction? *J. Biogeog.* **7**, 209–35.

HIGGS, A. J. 1981. Island biogeographic theory and nature reserves design. *J. Biogeog.* **8**, 117–24.

LYNCH, J. F. & JOHNSON, N. K. 1974. Turnover and equilibria in insular avifaunas, with special reference to the California Channel Islands. *Condor* **76**, 370–84.

MACARTHUR, R. H. 1972. *Geographival ecology.* Harper & Row, New York.

MACARTHUR, R. H. & WILSON, E. O. 1967. *The theory of island biogeography.* Princeton Univ. Press, Princeton, N.J.

RATCLIFFE, D. A. 1977. *Nature Conservation Review* vol. 1. Cambridge Univ. Press, London.

RATCLIFFE, D. A. 1980. *The Peregrine Falcon.* Poyser, Calton.

REED, T. M. 1979. Plantations and the birds of North Uist. *Heb. Nat.* **3**, 50–4.

REED, T. M. 1980. Turnover frequency in island birds. *J. Biogeog.* **7**, 329–35.

REED, T. M. 1981. The number of breeding landbird species on British Islands. *J. Anim. Ecol.* **50**, 613–25.

REED, T. M. 1983. The role of species-area relationships in reserve choice: a British example. *Biol. Cons.* **25**, 263–71.

SAUER, J. D. 1969. Oceanic islands and biogeographic theory. *Geog. Rev.* **59**, 582–93.

WILSON, E. O. & WILLIS, E. O. 1975. Applied biogeography. *In* Cody, M. L. & Diamond, J. M. (eds). *Ecological Structure of Species Community.* Belknapp Press, Harvard, Mass.

ICBP Technical Publication No. 3, 1985

THE SPREAD OF COMMENSAL SPECIES OF *RATTUS* TO OCEANIC ISLANDS AND THEIR EFFECTS ON ISLAND AVIFAUNAS

I. A. E. ATKINSON

Botany Division, Department of Scientific and Industrial Research, Lower Hutt, New Zealand

ABSTRACT

The spread of commensal species of *Rattus* to oceanic islands is traced for the past 3000 years. Until AD1000 the principal species involved was the Pacific Rat (*R. exulans*). The Ship Rat (*R. rattus*) became the most commonly dispersed species from AD1000 to AD1700. Then for 130–150 years the Norway Rat (*R. norvegicus*) became the rat most frequently carried to islands. Since AD1850 *R. rattus* (most commonly) and *R. norvegicus* have both been dispersed to further islands. Commensal rats have now reached 82 percent of the world's major islands and island groups, though rat-free islands remain within some of these groups.

Different effects of commensal rats on birds reflect behavioural differences among the three species. Behaviour and size of the birds preyed upon may also determine whether a rat–bird relationship leads to coexistence (the most common case) or decline of the bird population.

The avifaunas of some islands have suffered drastically from predation by rats. The effects are amplified when rats become food for larger predators, which in turn prey on birds. On a few islands the proportion of bird species that have declined or become extinct following the introduction of *R. rattus* is so great that the term catastrophe is appropriate. Rat-induced catastrophes have occurred most frequently on islands in the temperate zone.

On islands within the tropical and subtropical zone there is sometimes little to suggest that introduced rats have had much effect on the avifaunas. One possible explanation which requires further study centres on the presence of land crabs within this warmer zone. These animals are sometimes predators of birds and thus may have functioned as a selective force on island birds, resulting in populations having attributes that reduce crab predation. Birds with such attributes would be more likely to coexist with rats than would those without them.

Enough is known about rats and their effects to identify those island avifaunas now at greatest risk from rat invasions. This information should be related to the other faunal and floral values of rat-free islands. Islands with only one species of commensal rat also need protection against further invasions. A broadly-based protection plan for both these and other biologically important islands of the world should be implemented.

INTRODUCTION

This paper outlines the history of the spread of commensal rats by man to oceanic islands, discusses the different effects they have had on island avifaunas, and shows that

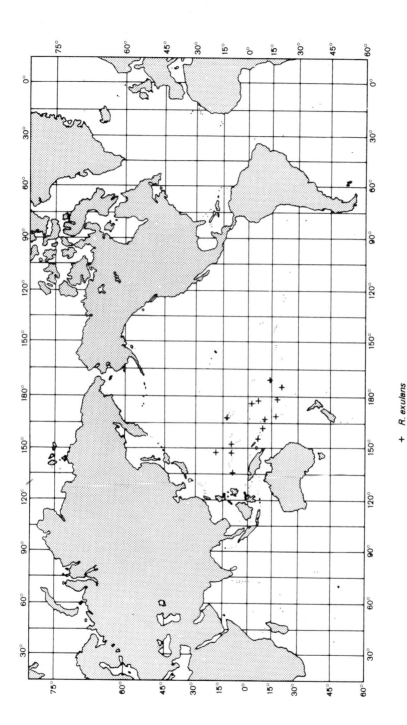

+ *R. exulans*

Figure 1: Probable distribution of *R. exulans* on oceanic islands in 1100BC. Data from *Table 1*.

the avifaunas of the world's remaining rat-free islands may not be equally vulnerable to rats.

Commensal species of rats are those commonly associated with man, although the three species discussed can live in completely unmodified habitats. They are the Pacific or Polynesian Rat (*Rattus exulans*), the Ship or Black Rat (*R. rattus*) and the Norway or Brown Rat (*R. norvegicus*). Other species of commensal rodent occur but, apart from mice (*Mus musculus*), they have seldom spread to oceanic islands. *R. rattus* may consist of more than one species as Yosida (1980) and his co-workers have shown that there are at least two widespread karyotypic forms of this rat: the Asian type with a diploid chromosome number of 42, and the Oceanian type with 38. On present evidence it is the 38-chromosome Oceanian type that has been spread widely to oceanic islands. Equally, the predation by *R. rattus* quoted in this paper relates mainly, if not entirely, to the Oceanian type. The name *R. rattus* as used here includes the slate-coloured 'black' colour morph sometimes referred to as '*R. r. rattus*', the brownish-grey colour morph with white underparts ('*R. r. frugivorus*'), and the colour morph with grey back and slaty underparts ('*R. r. alexandrinus*'). These colour morphs are known to interbreed freely (Johnson 1962), and therefore the use of these subspecific epithets is not justified.

It is essential to know when a rat species arrived on an island before its impact on the biota can be separated from that of other introduced animals or other environmental changes. A primary aim of this study has been to determine the arrival time of each species of rat present on an island. The method has been to search relevant scientific papers, historical accounts and some unpublished documents for information on the presence and behaviour of rats on each of the world's major oceanic islands. A few island groups of continental shelves have also been included because of their biological interest. The species of rat present, if not reliably identified, can sometimes be inferred from the description of its behaviour. Where no arrival time for a rat species has been published, it is sometimes possible to compare historical comments and infer the most likely period when it established. The results are summarized in *Tables 1, 2* and *3* based on data compiled between 1977 and 1983. Islands with inferred arrival dates for rats have been distinguished from those where published dates are available, but with the inferred dates space has precluded any detailed argument. It is hoped that publication of this compilation will encourage others to fill gaps in our knowledge of rat arrivals or refine known arrival times where appropriate.

SPREAD OF RATS TO ISLANDS DURING THE LAST 3000 YEARS

Before 1500BC to *c.* AD1000

R. exulans is presumed to have evolved somewhere in the Indo-Malayan region (Tate 1935). Its movement eastward into the Pacific basin probably began more than 3000 years ago. At that time the Lapita people, a seafaring race named from their distinctive Lapita pottery, were voyaging eastwards from the Bismarck Archipelago north of New Guinea (Bellwood 1979); Archaeological studies have shown that *R. exulans* was often associated with Lapita settlements (e.g. Green 1979). In the absence of precise information the ^{14}C dates for the earliest known occupation of particular islands by the Lapita people can be used to indicate the likely arrival times of *R. exulans* on those islands (*Table 1*). These dates show that by 1100BC *R. exulans* is likely to have spread with the Lapita people as far east as Samoa, Tonga and Fiji (*Figure 1*). The colonizers of eastern Micronesia are also likely to have been Lapita people (Bellwood 1980) and they probably took *R. exulans* to that part of the Pacific as well. Archaeologists regard the Lapita people as proto-Polynesians ancestral to the Polynesian race as we now know it (e.g. Bellwood 1979, Green 1979).

Table 1: Dates of introduction of *R. exulans*, *R. norvegicus* and *R. rattus* to islands in the Pacific Ocean. The dates given indicate the most likely period during which the species was first introduced.
* Indicates that one or more rat-free islands of high biological value were known to be present in the group as recently as 1960.

Island or island group	*R. exulans*		*R. norvegicus*		*R. rattus*	
	Presence and time of earliest known settlement[1]	Source of information	Time of introduction	Source of information	Time of introduction	Source of information
EAST PACIFIC						
Clipperton I.*	Not present	—	Not present	Sachet 1962	Not present	Sachet 1962
Cocos I.	Not present	—	Pre-1899	Coll. 1899, J. Schonewald, in litt. 1979, Snodgrass & Heller 1902	Pre-1906	Coll. 1905, J. Schonewald, in litt. 1979
Desventurados Is	Not present	—	Probably not present	Requires confirmation	Probably not present	Requires confirmation
Galapagos Is*	Not present	—	Pre-1900; Santiago I. only	Coll. 1899, J. Schonewald, in litt. 1979	1684–c. 1710 (Santiago) and subsequently to other islands	Patton et al. 1975
Guadelupe I.	Not present	—	Not recorded	Anthony 1925	Not recorded	Anthony 1925
Juan Fernandez Is	Not present	—	Present, introduction time unknown	Torres & Aguayo 1971	After 1590	Torres & Aguayo 1971
Malpelo I.	Not present	—	Probably not present	Requires confirmation	Probably not present	Requires confirmation
Revilla Gigedo Is*	Not present	—	Not recorded	McLellan 1926	Present	McLellan 1926
POLYNESIA						
Austral Is (incl. Rapa I.)	Present; AD1050 but probably settled earlier	Aitken 1930; J. Davidson, pers. comm. 1982	?	—	Pre-1922	Coll. in 1921–2, A. C. Ziegler, in litt. 1973
Cook Is	Present; AD950 but probably settled earlier	Williams 1839; J. Davidson, pers. comm. 1982	1850–85	Gill 1885	Pre-1963	Alicata & McCarthy 1964
Easter I.	Formerly present, possibly persists; AD400	Metraux 1940; Jennings 1979	Pre-1934	Metraux 1957	Not recorded	—
Gambier Is	Present; c. AD1200 but probably settled earlier	Douglas 1969; J. Davidson, pers. comm. 1982	?	—	?	—
Hawaii*	Present; AD500	Tomich 1969; Jennings 1979	1825–35	Atkinson 1977	1840–80, most probably 1870–80	Atkinson 1977

Howland and Baker Is	Possibly still present on Howland I.	Greenway in Howland 1955, King 1973	Pre-1887 (Baker I. only)	Inferred from Ellis 1936, Bryan 1942	Not recorded	—
Johnston Atoll	Not present	Kirkpatrick 1966	Not present	Kirkpatrick 1966	1940–62	Kirkpatrick 1966
Line Is (Kiribati)	Present	King 1973	Not recorded	—	Pre-1924	Herms 1926
Marquesas Is	Present, AD300	Heyerdahl 1940; Sinoto 1979	Pre-1915	Inferred from 1929 copy of notes of M. Le Bronnec held by M-H. Sachet	c. 1915	Inferred from 1929 copy of notes of M. Le Bronnec held by M-H. Sachet
Niue I.	Present; AD120 but probably settled earlier	Wodzicki 1971; J. Davidson, pers. comm. 1982	Not present	K. Wodzicki, pers. comm. 1975	1902–25	Smith 1902; Wodzicki 1971
Phoenix Is (Kiribati)	Present	Bryan 1942	1828–40? (Gardner I. only)	Wilkes 1845	1885 (Sydney I. only)	Ellis 1936
Pitcairn Is.	Present; AD1160 but probably settled earlier	Williams 1960; J. Davidson, pers. comm. 1982	?	—	?	—
Samoa	Present; 1030 ± 80BC	Marples 1955; Green 1979	1845–1923	Inferred from Stair 1897 and Buxton & Hopkins 1927	1845–1922	Inferred from Peale 1848, Stair 1897, Buxton & Hopkins 1927
Society Is	Present; AD600	Peale 1848; Jennings 1979	1767–1921	Coll. 1921, S. Anderson, in litt. 1978; Inder 1977	Pre-1920	Coll. in 1920, S. Anderson, in litt. 1978
Tokelau Is	Present; no archaeological work done	Wodzicki 1972	Unconfirm. introd. 1979–81, Atafu I. only	K. Wodzicki, pers. comm. 1982	Not present	Wodzicki 1972
Tonga	Present; 1100BC	Twibell 1973; Jennings 1979	Pre-1973	Twibell 1973	Pre-1973	Twibell 1973
Tuamotu Is.	Present; probably before AD800 but no C$_{14}$ dates	Peale 1848; J. Davidson, pers. comm. 1982	Pre-1955	Dumbleton 1955	1855–75	Inferred from Morrison 1954
Tuvalu (Ellice Is)	Present; 1100–1000BC	Hedley 1897; Jennings 1979	1850–96	Inferred from Waite 1897 and J. M. Williams, in litt. 1982	1922; two later invasions 1940–5	J. M. Williams, in litt. 1982
Wallis and Futuna Is	Not recorded ?	Tate 1935	Pre-1932 (Futuna)	Tate 1935	Not recorded	Tate 1935
MICRONESIA						
Bonin Is	Not present	—	Rats present: species unknown (Greenway 1967)		Pre-1932	
Caroline Is	Present; 1300BC	Marshall 1962; Marck 1975	Pre-1932	Koroia 1934; Marshall 1962	Pre-1932	Koroia 1934; Johnson 1962
Gilbert Is (Kiribati)	Present; 1300BC	Smith 1968; Marck 1975	Not present	J. M. Williams, in litt. 1982	1940–5	Smith 1968; J. M. Williams, in litt. 1982

(continued)

Table 1: Continued

Island or island group	R. exulans		R. norvegicus		R. rattus	
	Presence and time of earliest known settlement[1]	Source of information	Time of introduction	Source of information	Time of introduction	Source of information
Marcus I.	Not present	Sakagami 1961	Not present	Sakagami 1961	1897–1951	Inferred from Kuroda 1954 and Sakagami 1961
Mariana Is	Present; pre-1000BC	Marshall 1962; Bellwood 1979	Pre-1819	Inferred from Quoy & Gaimard 1824, and Freycinet 1824	Not recorded	Johnson 1962
Marshall Is	Present; 1300BC	Marshall 1962; Marck 1975	Not recorded	—	Pre-1932	Koroia 1934
Nauru I. Ocean I.	Present ?	Williams 1979 —	Not observed ?	Williams 1979 —	Present 1900–69	Williams 1979 Inferred from Smith 1970 and Derrick 1951
Palau Is	Present; pre-1000BC	Marshall 1962; Bellwood 1979	Pre-1931	Koroia 1934	Not recorded	Johnson 1962
Volcano Is Wake I.	Not present present	— Peale 1848	Rats present; species unknown (Greenway 1967) Not recorded	—	1923–51	Inferred from Bryan 1943, Fosberg 1959 and King 1973
MELANESIA Coral Sea Is	?	—	?	—	?1845	Hindwood 1964
Fiji Is	Present; 1590BC	Pernetta & Watling 1978; Green 1979	1830–76	Inferred from Moseley 1879 and Derrick 1951	1840–76	Inferred from Moseley 1879, Wilkes 1945 and Peale 1848
Gt. Barrier Reef Is	Recorded by Moulton 1961 from Heron I. Not confirmed	—	Not recorded	—	Pre-1964	J. Kikkawa, in litt. 1982
Loyalty Is	Present	Tate 1935	Pre-1912	Revilliod 1913	Pre-1912	Revilliod 1913
New Caledonia (and associated is.)	Present; 900BC	Revilliod 1913; Green 1979	Pre-1944	Warner 1948	Pre-1912	Revilliod 1913
New Hebrides (incl. Banks and Torres Is)	Present; 1300BC	Tate 1935; Green 1979	Pre-1975	Medway & Marshall 1975	Pre-1922	Coll. 1922 (Brit Mus.) M. Levitt, in litt. 1979
Rennell and Bellona Is	Present	Hill 1956	Not recorded	Hill 1956	Not recorded	Hill 1956
Rotuma I.	Present	Allardyce 1886	Pre-1974	Williams 1974	Not recorded	—

		Green 1976, 1979	Either or both R. norvegicus and R. rattus present (Green 1976)		Pre-1920	
Santa Cruz Is (incl. Reef Is)	Present although recent records appear lacking; 1400BC					
Solomon Is	Present; 1500BC	Johnson 1946; White in Jennings 1979	?		—	Coll. in 1920, 1921; J. Schonewald, in litt. 1979
NONTROPICAL PACIFIC OCEAN						
Aleutian Is	Not present	—	Pre-1782	Brechbill 1977	Not recorded	—
Antipodes Is*	Not present	—	Not present	Warham & Johns 1975	Not present	Warham & Johns 1975
Auckland Is*	Not present	—	Not present[2]	Taylor 1975	Not present[2]	Taylor 1975
Bounty Is*	Not present	—	Not present	Atkinson 1978	Not present	Atkinson 1978
Campbell I.*	Not present	—	1810–67	Inferred from Armstrong in Hector 1869	Not recorded	Bailey & Sorensen 1962
Chatham Is*	Formerly present	Coll. 1892, J. E. Hill, in litt. 1971	Pre-1870	Travers 1870	Pre-1978	Atkinson 1978
Commander Is	Not present	—	1883–1938	Stejneger 1883; Barabash-Nikiforov 1938	Not recorded	Barabash-Nikiforov 1938
Diego Ramirez Is*	Not present	—	Not observed 1921	Hough 1975	Not observed	Hough 1975
Kermadec Is*	Present	Watson 1961	Not recorded	Watson 1961	Not present	Merton 1970
Lord Howe I.*	Formerly present; no known pre-European settlement	Hindwood 1940			1918	Hindwood 1940
Macquarie I.	Not present	—	Not present	Jones 1977	1880–1908	Inferred from Cumpston 1968. R. A. Falla, pers. comm. 1977
New Zealand*	Present; AD800	Watson 1956; Jennings 1979	1770–1820	Atkinson 1973	1858–65	Atkinson 1973 and unpub.
Norfolk I.*	Present; possibly AD900–1100	Coll. 1978, Atkinson, unpub.; Specht 1978	Not recorded	—	Pre-1977	Coll. 1978, Atkinson unpub.
Pribilof Is*	Not present	—	Introduced many times but do not persist	Murie in Kenyon 1961	Not recorded	—
Snares I.*	Not present	—	Not present	Fineran 1964	Not present	Fineran 1964
St Lawrence I.*	Not present	—	Not present	L. Colwell, in litt. 1982	Not present	L. Colwell, in litt. 1982
St Mathew Is	Not present	—	Not recorded	Hanna 1920	Not recorded	Hanna 1920

[1] ^{14}C errors are not included in this table.
[2] Reports of unidentified species of rats mentioned by Falla (1965) have not been confirmed.

Table 2: Dates of introduction of *R. rattus* and *R. norvegicus* to islands in the Indian Ocean.
The dates given indicate the most likely period during which the species was first introduced.
* Indicates that one or more rat-free islands of high biological value were known to be present in the group as recently as 1960.

Island or island group	*R. rattus*		*R. norvegicus*	
	Time of introduction	Source of information	Time of introduction	Source of information
NORTH INDIAN OCEAN				
Andaman Is	Pre-1900	Lloyd 1909; Chasen & Kloss 1927	Not recorded	Chasen & Kloss 1927
Laccadive Is	Pre-1898	Palmer 1898	?	—
Maldive Is	Pre-1886	Rosset 1886	Not recorded	—
Nias I. (off Sumatra)	Pre-1927	Chasen & Kloss 1927	Not recorded	Chasen & Kloss 1927
Nicobar Is	Pre-1888	Blanford 1888, 1891	Not recorded	Chasen & Kloss 1927
Simeulue Is (off Sumatra)	Pre-1927	Chasen & Kloss 1927	Not recorded	Chasen & Kloss 1927
SOUTH INDIAN OCEAN				
Agalega I.	1891	Cheke & Lawley, in press	Not present	Cheke & Lawley, in press
Aldabra I.	Pre-1893	Abbott 1893; Fryer 1911	Not present	Recorded in error by Abbott 1893
Amirante Is	Present, introduction time unknown	Stoddart & Poore 1970a	Not recorded	—
Amsterdam I.	1795–c. 1900	Inferred from Peron 1824, Dorst & Milon 1964	Not recorded	Dorst & Milon 1964
Assumption I.	Rats introduced before 1906; Nicoll quoted by Stoddart *et al.* 1970; species unknown			
Astove I.	Rats introduced before 1895. Bayne *et al.* 1970; species unknown			
Cargados Carajos Is	?	Stoddart 1971	Present; time of arrival unknown	Newlands 1975
Chagos Archipelago	Pre-1840		Not recorded	—
Christmas I.	1898–1908	Inferred from Andrews 1899, 1909	1908–38	Inferred from Andrews 1909 and Gibson-Hill 1947a
Cocos Keeling Is	1878	Gibson-Hill 1948, Tate 1950	Not present; recorded in error by Waterhouse 1839 and Wood-Jones 1912	Tate 1950
Comoro Is	Rats present, Benson 1960; species unknown			
Cosmoledo I.	Rats introduced before 1895, Baty 1895; species unknown			
Crozet Is*	c. 1822–1900 (Possession I. only)	Inferred from Goodridge 1843 and Dorst & Milon 1964	Not recorded	Dorst & Milon 1964
Enggano I.	Pre-1927	Chasen & Kloss 1927	Not recorded	Chasen & Kloss 1927
Europa I.	Pre-1904	Voeltzkow 1902–5; Malzy 1966	Not recorded	Malzy 1966
Farquhar Is	Not observed	Stoddart & Poore 1970b; C. J. Feare, in litt. 1977	Not observed	Stoddart & Poore 1970; C. J. Feare, in litt. 1977
Gloriosa I.	Rats introduced before 1883, Coppinger 1883; species unknown			
Heard and McDonald Is*	Not present	Johnstone 1982	Not present	Johnstone 1982

Houtman Abrolhos Is., Western Australia*	?pre-1840 (on Rat I. only but not confirmed)	Fuller & Burbidge 1981	Not recorded	—
Kerguelen Is*	1949–56	Lesel & Dérenne 1975	Possibly introduced but apparently have not persisted	Inferred from Holdgate & Wace 1961 and R. A. Falla, pers. comm. 1977
Mauritius I.*	1568–1606	Inferred from Barnwell 1948 and Cheke, in press	1730–50	Cheke, in press
Mentawai Is (off Sumatra)	Not recorded	Chasen & Kloss 1927	Not recorded	Chasen & Kloss 1927
Prince Edward Is* (Prince Edward; Marion)	Not present	Williams et al. 1979	Not present	Williams et al. 1979
Province Is* (incl. Cerf and St Pierre)	Pre-1801, probably pre-1760	Grant 1801	Not observed	C. J. Feare, in litt. 1977
Réunion I.	c. 1680	Cheke, in press	1735	Cheke, in press
Rodriguez I.	1507–1691	Inferred from Leguat 1708, Milne-Edwards 1873; Cheke, in press	Present; time of arrival unknown	Cheke, in press
Seychelles Is*	Pre-1773; Bird I. 1967	Barre 1773; Feare 1979	Not recorded	Seychelles Dept. of Agriculture 1952
St Paul I.	1795–1874; probably 1822–74	Inferred from Peron 1824, Goodridge 1843 and Vélain 1877	Not present	Dorst & Milon 1964; recorded probably in error by Vélain 1877
Tromelin I.	Not recorded	Staub 1970	Pre-1953	Staub 1970

Table 3: Dates of introduction of R. rattus and R. norvegicus to islands in the Atlantic Ocean. The dates given indicate the most likely period during which the species was first introduced.
* Indicates that one or more rat-free islands of high biological value were known to be present in the group as recently as 1960.

Island or island group	R. rattus		R. norvegicus	
	Time of introduction	Source of information	Time of introduction	Source of information
NORTH ATLANTIC OCEAN				
Azores Is	Present, introduction time unknown	Millais 1905; specimens in Brit. Mus. (Nat. Hist.)	?	—
Bermuda Is	1613	Lefroy 1877–9; specimens in Amer. Mus. Nat. Hist.	'end of the eighteenth century'	Jones 1884; specimens in Am. Mus. Nat. Hist.
Canary Is	?	—	1700–1835. Coll. 1910 (Brit. Mus.)	Inferred from Barker-Webb & Berthelot 1835
Cape Verde Is	Rats present; species unknown			
Faeroe Is*	Pre-1750; disappeared after 1768	Barrett-Hamilton & Hinton 1912; Landt 1800	1768	Landt 1800
Iceland*	1905–19 but earlier introductions possible; does not persist	Millais 1905; Saemundsson 1939	Sometime around or before 1850; Flatey I.: 1800–20 and 1896–1900, now exterminated	A. Petersen, in litt. 1978, 1979; Petersen 1979
Jan Mayen I.*	Not present	B. Jensen, in litt. 1980	Not present	B. Jensen, in litt. 1980
Madeira Is	Present, introduction time unknown	Specimens in Brit. Mus. (Nat. Hist.)	?	—
Príncipe	Rats present; species unknown			
Sable I.	Not present	F. Scott, in litt. 1982	Pre-1802, no longer present	MacDonald 1883, Wright, in litt. 1982, F. Scott, in litt. 1982
Sao Tomé I.	Rats present; species unknown			
Shetland Is*	Pre-1650	Berry & Johnston 1980	Present, introduction time unknown	Barrett-Hamilton & Hinton 1912
Svalbard (Spitzbergen)	Never observed	O. Lönö, in litt. 1980	Occ. introductions, some probably after 1905; further introductions since 1945; does not persist outside buildings	O. Lönö, in litt. 1980
West Indies (incl. Bahama Is)	1492–1654	Inferred from Allen 1911 and historical accounts	1700–1866	Inferred from Allen 1911

SOUTH ATLANTIC OCEAN

Annobón I.*	Rats present; species unknown (Fry 1961)			
Ascension I.*	1656–1754, possibly 1701	Inferred from Temple & Anstey 1936, La Caille 1763 and Osbeck 1771	Not present; recorded in error by Duffey 1964	Davis, unpub. 1966; E. Duffey, in litt. 1978
Falkland Is*	Not recorded	Woods 1975	1725–1833	Inferred from Darwin 1839 and Woods 1975
Fernando de Noronha I.	Pre-1890	Ridley 1890; S. Olson, in litt. 1982	Not recorded	Ridley 1890; S. Olson, in litt. 1982
Gough I.*	Not present	Wace & Holdgate 1976	Not present	Wace & Holdgate 1976
Martin Vaz. I.	Probably not present	Requires confirmation	Probably not present	Requires confirmation
South Georgia*	Not present	Pye & Bonner 1980	c. 1800	Murphy 1917
St Helena I.	1513–1665	Inferred from Gosse 1938	Present; probably 1730–1800	Duffey 1964; inferred from historical accounts
Trindade I.*	Not present	Olson 1981	Not present	Olson 1981
Tristan da Cunha Is*	1882	Brander 1940	Not present; recorded in error by Elton 1958	Wace & Holdgate 1976

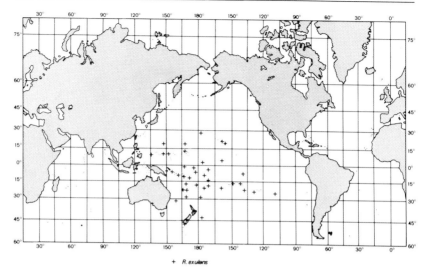

Figure 2:   Probable distribution of *R. exulans* on oceanic islands in AD1000. Data from *Table 1*.

Judged by the available radiocarbon evidence, there was a long interval after 1100BC before any significant movement of people, and hence rats, occurred further eastwards. The earliest settlement date of any island group east of Samoa and Tonga is AD300 for the Marquesas Islands (Sinoto 1979). This leaves a gap of 1400 years that may be narrowed as more carbon dates become available.

Following colonization of the Marquesas, there appears to have been a relatively rapid spread of Polynesians and thus *R. exulans* to most of the major island groups in the Pacific. By AD800, *R. exulans* had probably reached as far as the Hawaiian Islands in the north and Easter Island in the east. By AD1000 New Zealand may also have been reached (*Figure 2*). The time when Polynesians first colonized the latter country is not certainly known, but Davidson (1979) remarks: 'The colonization of New Zealand by the rat . . . appears to have been at least as rapid as its colonization by man.'

There are some island groups in the Pacific without *R. exulans* (*Table 1*). However there appear to be no island groups reached by the early Polynesians that were not also colonized by *R. exulans*. These people apparently carried this rat with them, by choice or by chance, whenever they undertook long sea voyages. Any interpretation of the impact of *R. exulans* on the floras and faunas of Pacific Islands must consider changes that began 1000 to 3000 years ago.

From *c.* AD1000 to *c.* AD1500

Movement of *R. exulans* in the Pacific Ocean during this period was probably restricted to further spread within island groups already colonized. Outside the Pacific most oceanic islands remained undiscovered and thus unaffected by commensal rats. However, throughout this period and earlier, exploration and trading by Asian, Arabian and European peoples would have dispersed rats, particularly *R. rattus*, from Europe, the Middle East and Asia to islands of the continental shelves.

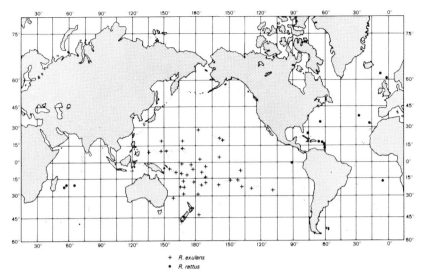

+ *R. exulans*
• *R. rattus*

Figure 3:   Known distribution of commensal rats on oceanic islands in AD1700. Data from *Tables 1–3.*

From *c.* AD1500 to *c.* AD1700

The voyage of Columbus to America in 1492 began a new era of rat spread. During the following 200 years, *R. rattus* was carried by trading vessels to islands in the Indian and Atlantic Oceans (*Tables 2 and 3, Figure 3*). It is likely that *R. rattus* was more widespread by AD1700 than shown in *Figure 3*, but reliable evidence is so far lacking. However, its almost complete absence from islands in the Pacific Ocean reflects the fact that many Pacific islands had not then been discovered by Europeans. An exception is Santiago Island, Galapagos group, where English buccaneers established a base towards the end of the 17th century (Patton *et al.* 1975).

In theory, *R. rattus* could have reached a number of Pacific islands discovered by the Spanish, Portuguese or Dutch during the 16th and 17th centuries. Magellan's ships, for example, are known to have carried rats (Pigafetta 1906). However, most explorers had no proper means nor desire to tie their ships to the shore of a newly discovered island with unknown inhabitants. Contact with the shore was usually by means of small open boats in which the risk of rat carriage was low. Only where settlements were established by the European explorers, as in the Philippines, Guam and New Hebrides, is it likely that *R. rattus* was able to establish during 1500–1700. In the Philippines *R. rattus* has difficulty in establishing where other closely related species or subspecies of *R. rattus* are already present (Johnson 1962). On other islands where subspecies of *R. rattus* already occurred there must remain doubt as to whether the rats carried by early Spanish expeditions were able to establish.

From *c.* AD1700 to *c.* AD1830

At some time after 1700—but probably not later than 1716—an ecological event occurred in Europe that changed the whole trend of rat spread to oceanic islands. This was the movement of *R. norvegicus* from the region north of the Caspian Sea into western Europe, where it largely displaced *R. rattus* (Barrett-Hamilton & Hinton 1912).

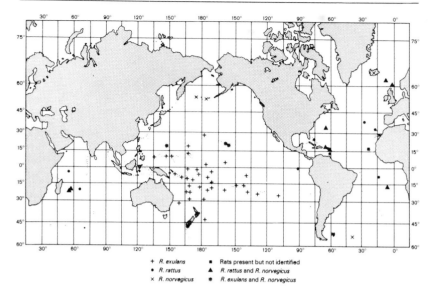

+ *R. exulans*   ■ Rats present but not identified
● *R. rattus*   ▲ *R. rattus* and *R. norvegicus*
× *R. norvegicus*   ✻ *R. exulans* and *R. norvegicus*

Figure 4: Known distribution of commensal rats on oceanic islands in AD1850. Data from *Tables 1–3.*

So complete was this displacement, both in Britain and other parts of Europe, that some naturalists of the eighteenth and early nineteenth centuries encountered *R. rattus* only once or twice in a lifetime (e.g. Waterton 1836). Despite suggestions that *R. norvegicus* was already present in western Europe during Mediaeval times (Heinrich 1976), the evidence so far has been equivocal. If *R. norvegicus* was present then or earlier, some mechanism must have maintained the dominance of *R. rattus* because all indications are that it was the only common rat in Europe prior to the 1700s.

The displacement of European *R. rattus* by *R. norvegicus* during the 1700s resulted in dominance by *R. norvegicus* at ports. Its presence at wharves and warehouses soon extended to countries beyond Europe, including ports along the north Atlantic seaboard of the United States (Donaldson 1924). As a result, *R. norvegicus* replaced *R. rattus* as the common rat aboard European and American sailing ships, so that for a century or more after 1700 rat invasions of oceanic islands involved mainly *R. norvegicus* (*Tables 1–3, Figure 4*). The spread of *R. rattus* was curtailed from approximately 1700 to 1830, and probably to 1850 in some parts of the world (*Figure 5*). Rats aboard ships are seldom identified, and thus the number of records is extremely small in relation to the total number of voyages. Is it possible that the time-gap in the spread of *R. rattus* is an artifact of sampling?

The question can be answered by taking an island country, such as New Zealand, which experienced frequent contact with Europe during part of the time in question. Whalers and sealers frequently visited New Zealand, sometimes establishing shore bases, from 1792 onwards. Major settlements were established by Europeans after 1840. Many rat-infested ships must have visited the country between 1790 and 1850, yet although there are records of the presence of *R. norvegicus*, there is no reliable evidence of *R. rattus* having reached New Zealand during that time (Atkinson 1973). Other

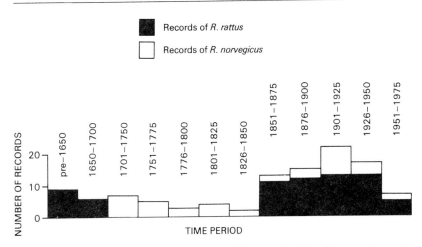

Figure 5: Changes in the proportions of *R. rattus* and *R. norvegicus* aboard ocean-going vessels between 1500 and 1975 (n = 109 records). This histogram combines available dated records of identified rat species reaching islands (*Tables 1–3*) with a smaller number of dated records of identified rats aboard ships (Atkinson, unpub. compilation).

islands in the Pacific including Hawaii (Atkinson 1977), the Tuamotu, Marquesas, Samoan and Fiji Islands (*Table 1*) have somewhat similar rat histories. Available data strongly suggest that *R. rattus* did not arrive on islands in the Pacific until the second half of last century or later. In the Indian and Atlantic Oceans, islands settled by Europeans were usually already colonized by *R. rattus* if settlement had taken place prior to 1700. But if settlement occurred later than this, as for example on Cocos Keeling, Indian Ocean, and Tristan da Cunha, Atlantic Ocean, the arrival of *R. rattus* was delayed until after 1850.

Thus the gap in records of *R. rattus* on ships (*Figure 5*) appears to be a real hiatus in its spread. Whether it was a complete cessation of the movement of *R. rattus* throughout the world is not established. For example, *R. rattus* reached Mauritius before 1607 (*Table 2*), and this island could then have become a secondary dispersal centre from which rats spread along trade routes to other islands in the Indian Ocean (e.g. the Seychelles) until well into the eighteenth century. Nevertheless, on islands in the Pacific Ocean the arrival of *R. norvegicus* commonly preceded that of *R. rattus*—the reverse of what has generally been accepted for this ocean (e.g. Greenway 1967: 52).

From *c.* AD1830 to AD1980
The most puzzling feature of *Figure 5* is the comparatively sudden reappearance of *R. rattus* on ships during the 1850s when it became, as now, the most common shipboard rat. This change remains to be explained. There was at the same time a marked increase in records of identified rats aboard ships (*Figure 5*), reflecting both an increase in shipping and the greater accessibility of recent records. The presence on ships of both *R. rattus* and *R. norvegicus* during the last 150 years has resulted in many island groups of the Atlantic and Indian Oceans being invaded by both species, while in the Pacific Ocean there are now many island groups with three species of commensal rat (*Figure 6*). Of the

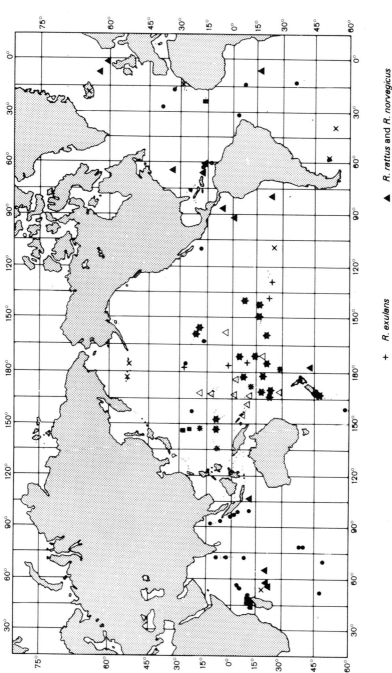

Figure 6: Known distribution of commensal rats on oceanic islands in AD 1980. Data from *Tables 1–3.*

+   *R. exulans*

●   *R. rattus*

×   *R. norvegicus*

■   Rats present; not identified

◀   *R. rattus* and *R. norvegicus*

✳   *R. exulans* and *R. norvegicus*

△   *R. exulans* and *R. rattus*

✷   *R. exulans, R. norvegicus* and *R. rattus*

Table 4:   Distribution of commensal rats among major islands and island groups.

Rat species present	Number of islands or island groups			
	Pacific Ocean	Indian Ocean	Atlantic Ocean	Total
R. exulans alone	2	—	—	2
R. rattus alone	6	17	3	26
R. norvegicus alone	4	1	5	10
R. exulans + *R. rattus*	7	—	—	7
R. exulans + *R. norvegicus*	6	—	—	6
R. rattus + *R. norvegicus*	4	4	5	13
R. exulans + *R. rattus* + *R. norvegicus*	15	—	—	15
One or more unidentified species of commensal rat present	9	7	6	22
Free or probably free of commensal rats	12	5	5	22
TOTAL	65	34	24	123

123 major island groups included in this study, only 22 (18 percent) are probably without rats, although confirmation is required in some cases (*Table 4*). But in at least 20 of the 101 island groups affected there remain biologically valuable islands that are at present rat-free (*Tables 1–3*).

Records of rats reaching islands during the past 140 years are sufficient to estimate a minimum rate of 6.5 island invasions every 20 years (*Figure 7*). The real rate must exceed this. The rate of spread peaked during 1941–60 as a result of the establishment of military bases on Pacific islands during World War II. The decreased rate since 1960 is not statistically significant. The spread of rats to islands is continuing.

DIFFERENCES AMONG RAT SPECIES IN THEIR EFFECTS ON BIRDS

Rats affect island biotas primarily by preying on birds (Fleet 1972), small mammals (Brosset 1963), tortoises (MacFarland *et al.* 1974), lizards (Whitaker 1973), large insects (Ramsay 1978), land molluscs (Meads *et al.*, 1984) and plant seeds and seedlings (Clark 1981). The magnitude of these effects depends on both the behaviour of the rat species and of the prey. Differences in behaviour among the three commensal rats are particularly important in relation to their effects on birds.

R. norvegicus is the largest of the three rats, with adult weights of 350–450g. It excavates and nests in burrows much more frequently than the other two species, but appears to climb trees less frequently. Thus birds nesting on or near the ground or in burrows are more likely to be preyed upon by *R. norvegicus* than birds nesting in the higher parts of trees. Seabirds frequently nest in sites vulnerable to these rats, and 27 of the 53 birds listed as prey of *R. norvegicus* are seabirds (*Table 5*).

R. rattus usually weighs 100–180g, commonly nests in trees and is the most agile climber of the three rats. Almost any bird's nest can potentially be reached, but those of larger birds usually escape predation. Fewer species of seabird are known to be preyed on by *R. rattus* than by *R. norvegicus*, and 25 of the 39 prey species and subspecies listed in *Table 6* are perching birds.

R. exulans seldom exceeds 130g in weight, and commonly nests in vegetation near or on the ground or in short burrows. It also is an agile climber, but fewer species are preyed on compared with the other two rats (*Table 7*). Although *R. exulans* is the smallest of the three species, the records include predation on adult Laysan Albatross (*Diomedea immutabilis*) and Great Frigatebird (*Fregata minor*), larger birds than any recorded as prey of the other rats.

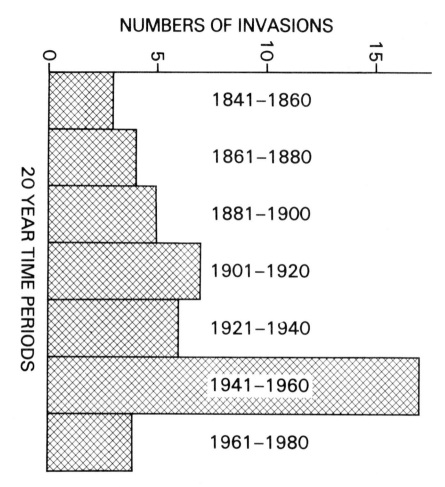

Figure 7:   Changes in the rate of rat invasions to islands during the past 140 years. The mean rate is 6.57 invasions/20 year period. Assuming that rat invasions follow a stationary Poisson process, i.e. are randomly distributed in time, the only statistically significant difference from the mean is that for the period 1941–1960. Data from *Tables 1–3*, together with published information on times of rat invasions for a few additional islands of continental shelves.

Table 5: Predation by *R. norvegicus* on birds.
Only one example of predation is included for each species.

Bird species	Family	Locality	Usual nest station	Stage of life-cycle preyed upon[1]	Effect on population	Source of information
Eudyptes crestatus (Rockhopper Penguin)	Spheniscidae	Campbell I.	ground surface	eggs (67 × 51mm)	unknown	Westerskov 1960
Pterodroma cahow (Cahow)	Procellariidae	Bermuda	burrows	circumstantial evidence that all stages can be eaten	local elimination from one island	D. B. Wingate, pers. comm. 1982
Pterodroma macroptera (Grey-faced Petrel)	Procellariidae	Whale I., New Zealand	burrows	eggs (66 × 49) chicks	'less than 10–35% of chicks per year'	Imber 1976
Pterodroma neglecta (Kermadec Petrel)	Procellariidae	Raoul I., Kermadec Is	ground surface	eggs	'heavy predation'	Davison *in* Merton 1970
Halobaena caerulea (Blue Petrel)	Procellariidae	South Georgia	burrows	adult	continuing coexistence with rats	Pye & Bonner 1980
Pachyptila desolata (Antarctic Prion)	Procellariidae	South Georgia	burrows	adults	probable major effect	Murphy 1936, Lönnberg 1906
Procellaria aequinoctialis (White-chinned Petrel)	Procellariidae	South Georgia	burrows	chicks	continuing coexistence with rats	Pye & Bonner 1980
Puffinus griseus (Sooty Shearwater)	Procellariidae	Whale I., New Zealand	burrows	chicks	probably significant	Imber 1975; M. J. Imber, pers. comm. 1978
Puffinus l'herminieri (Audubon's Shearwater)	Procellariidae	Bermuda	burrows	adults	minor	D. B. Wingate, pers. comm. 1982
Puffinus puffinus (Manx Shearwater)	Procellariidae	Small islands off British coast	burrows	unknown	continuing decline	Parslow 1973
Puffinus tenuirostris (Short-tailed Shearwater)	Procellariidae	Griffiths I., Victoria, Australia	burrows	chicks, adults	apparently no long-term effect	Bowker 1965
Pelagodroma marina (White-faced Storm Petrel)	Hydrobatidae	Noises Is., New Zealand	burrows	adults	heavy mortality	D. V. Merton, pers. comm. 1978
Pelecanoides georgicus (South Georgian Diving Petrel)	Pelecanoididae	South Georgia	burrows	adults	not assessed	Lönnberg 1906, Murphy 1936
Phaethon lepturus (Whitetailed Tropic-bird)	Phaethontidae	Castle Harbour Is., Bermuda	holes and crevices in cliffs	eggs, adults	temporary minor effect	F. T. Hall, unpub. 1945 (D. B. Wingate, pers. comm. 1982)
Anas georgicus (South Georgia Pintail)	Anatidae	South Georgia	ground surface beneath tussocks	unknown	restriction to rat-free habitat	Pye & Bonner 1980
Anas platyrhynchos (Mallard)	Anatidae	Manawatu, New Zealand	ground surface	eggs (60 × 42)	probable 'significant effect'	Balham 1952

(*continued*)

Table 5: Continued

Bird species	Family	Locality	Usual nest station	Stage of life-cycle preyed upon[1]	Effect on population	Source of information
Falco peregrinus (Peregrine Falcon)	Falconidae	Amchitka I., Alaska	ground surface	?chicks	major effect in one year	White *in* Jones & Byrd 1979
Gallus gallus (Common Fowl)	Phasianidae	Britain	ground surface	eggs (57 × 43)	not studied in the wild	Barnett 1976
Perdix perdix (Grey Partridge)	Phasianidae	Britain	ground surface	eggs (36 × 27)	4% of nests destroyed during study (n = 1232)	Middleton 1935
Rallus longirostris[3] (Clapper Rail)	Rallidae	California, USA	ground surface	eggs	not assessed	de Groot 1927
Rallus philippensis (Banded Rail)	Rallidae	Hawkes Bay, New Zealand	ground surface	eggs (38 × 29)	75% of nests destroyed in study area	Guthrie-Smith 1925
Fulica atra (Coot)	Rallidae	Britain	near water surface	eggs (47 × 34)	not assessed	Coward 1914
Gallinula chloropus (Moorhen)	Rallidae	Britain	near water surface, <3m	eggs (41 × 31)	not assessed	Cott 1952
Haematopus ostralegus (Oystercatcher)	Haematopodidae	Nordercoog I., Germany	ground surface			Steinger 1948 (quoted by Norman 1975)
Pluvialis apricaria (Golden Plover)	Charadriidae	Norderoog I., Germany	ground			Steinger 1948 (quoted by Norman 1975)
Vanellus vanellus (Lapwing)	Charadriidae	Denmark	ground surface	adults	minor	Moller 1983
Burhinus oedicnemus (Stone Curlew)	Scolopacidae	England	ground surface	eggs (54 × 38)	not assessed	Ticehurst 1932
Calidris ferruginea (Curlew Sandpiper)	Scolopacidae	Norderoog I., Germany	ground surface			Steinger 1948 (quoted by Norman 1975)
Numenius arquata (Curlew)	Scolopacidae	Norderoog I., Germany	ground surface			Steinger 1948 (quoted by Norman 1975)
Tringa totanus (Redshank)	Scolopacidae	Denmark	ground surface	adults	minor	Moller 1983
Recurvirostra avosetta (Avocet)	Recurvirostridae	England	ground surface	eggs (50 × 35)	extinction in the absence of man's intervention	Brown 1949, Watson 1953
Larus canus (Common Gull)	Laridae	Denmark	ground surface	eggs (58 × 41), chicks, adults	minor	Moller 1983
Larus ridibundus (Black-headed Gull)	Laridae	Denmark	ground surface	eggs (52 × 37), chicks, adults	'excessive mortality' in some years	Moller 1983
Rissa tridactyla (Kittiwake)	Laridae	Denmark	ground surface	eggs (57 × 41), chicks	minor	Moller 1983
Sterna nilotica (Gull-billed Tern)	Laridae	Denmark	ground surface	eggs (53 × 38)	minor	Moller 1983

Species	Family	Location	Nesting site	Prey taken	Effect	Reference
Sterna albifrons (Least Tern)	Laridae	Cape Cod, USA	ground surface	eggs (31 × 24) chicks, adults	major effects some years, minor others	Austin 1948
Sterna dougalli (Roseate Tern)	Laridae	Cape Cod, USA	ground surface	eggs (42 × 30) chicks, adults	major effects some years, minor others	Austin 1948
Sterna fuscata (Sooty Tern)	Laridae	Puits-a-Eaux, Cargados Carajos Is	ground surface	eggs (54 × 37), chicks	almost 50% of eggs and chicks taken in 1975	Newlands 1975
Sterna hirundo (Common Tern)	Laridae	Cape Cod, USA	ground surface	eggs, chicks, adults	major effects some years, minor others	Austin 1948
Sterna paradisea (Arctic Tern)	Laridae	Cape Cod, USA	ground surface	eggs, chicks, adults	major effects some years, minor others	Austin 1948
Sterna sandvicensis (Sandwich Tern)	Laridae	Minsmere (Brit.) and Denmark	ground surface	eggs, chicks, adults	no young fledged one year	Axell 1973; Moller 1983
Anous stolidus (Common Noddy)	Laridae	Dry Tortugas Is, Florida, USA	ground surface	eggs (53 × 36), chicks	up to 90% of eggs and young destroyed some years	Russel *in* Sprunt 1948
Cepphus grylle (Black Guillemot)	Alcidae	Flatey I, Iceland	ground surface	eggs (58 × 39), chicks	decline	Petersen 1981
Fratercula arctica (Puffin)	Alcidae	Britain	burrows	eggs, chicks	unknown	Campbell 1892
Nestor meridionalis (North Island Kaka)	Nestoridae	Kapiti I., New Zealand	ground surface, branches >3m	chick	unknown	Lovegrove 1982[2]
Riparia riparia (Bank Swallow)	Hirundinidae	USA	burrows			Stoner 1937
Anthus antarcticus (Antarctic Pipit)	Motacillidae	South Georgia I.	ground surface; tussocks <3m	unknown	restriction to rat-free habitat	Pye & Bonner 1980
Troglodytes troglodytes (Winter Wren)	Troglodytidae	Amchitka I., Aleutian Is	branches, often <3m	unknown	major decline	Kenyon 1961
Erithacus rubecula (English Robin)	Muscicapidae	England	cavities, branches, often <3m	eggs	continuing coexistence with rats	Wayne 1849 quoted by Cott 1952
Petroica australis longipes (North Island Robin)	Muscicapidae	Kapiti I., New Zealand	cavities, branches often <3m	eggs, chicks	continuing coexistence with rats	Wilkinson & Wilkinson 1952
Melospiza melodia (Song Sparrow)	Emberizidae	Amchitka I., Aleutian Is	branches, often <3m	unknown	major decline	Kenyon 1961
Lonchura punctulata (Spice Finch)	Estrildidae	Mauritius	branches >3m	chicks	unknown	C. Jones, pers. comm. 1982
Philesturnus carunculatus (North Island Saddleback)	Callaeatidae	Kapiti I., New Zealand	ground surface; cavities <3m	eggs (29 × 22), chicks, adults	major decline	Lovegrove 1982[2]

[1] Egg-sizes from Oliver 1955, Murphy 1936, Cramp 1980, 1983, P. J. Moors, pers. comm.

[2] Lovegrove makes no assumptions about the species of rat involved in this predation. However, at the time of the study *R. norvegicus* was common, whereas *R. exulans*, the other rat present on the island, was not seen or trapped in the study area.

[3] Nomenclature of rails follows Ripley 1977.

Table 6: Predation by *R. rattus* on birds.
Only one example of predation is included for each species.

Bird species	Family	Locality	Usual nest station	Stage of life-cycle preyed upon[1]	Effect on population	Source of information
Diomedea immutabilis (Laysan Albatross)	Diomedeidae	Midway I., Hawaii	ground surface	chicks	continuing coexistence with rats	Fisher 1975 (reported rat incorrectly as *R. norvegicus*)
Pterodroma brevirostris (Kerguelen Petrel)	Procellariidae	Possession I., Crozet Is.	burrows	chicks	loss of all chicks in some years	Mougin 1969, 1975
Pterodroma hypoleuca (Bonin Petrel)	Procellariidae	Midway I., Hawaii	burrows	eggs, chicks	major decline	Grant *et al.* 1981
Pterodroma phaeopygia phaeopygia (Galapagos Dark-rumped Petrel)	Procellariidae	Santa Cruz I., Galapagos Is.	burrows	eggs, chicks	contributing to decline	Harris 1970, Tomkins, this vol., Coulter *et al.*, this vol.
Pterodroma phaeopygia sandwichensis (Hawaiian Dark-rumped Petrel)	Procellariidae	Maui, Hawaii	burrows	chicks	nearly 40% of eggs and chicks destroyed during 2-year study	Larson *in* Berger 1981
Pachyptila vittata (Broad-billed Prion)	Procellariidae	Amsterdam I., Indian Ocean	burrows	adults	decline	Jouanin & Paulian 1960
Procellaria aequinoctialis (White-chinned Petrel)	Procellariidae	Possession I., Crozet Is	burrows	chicks	substantial numbers of chicks in some years	Mougin 1969, 1975
Calonectris diomedea (Cory's Shearwater)	Procellariidae	Iles Marseillaises, off France, Mediterranean	hollows or burrows	chicks	high mortality rate	Fernandez 1979
Phaethon lepturus (White-tailed Tropicbird)	Phaethontidae	Bermuda	holes and crevices in cliffs	eggs	continuing coexistence with rats	Gross 1912
Porzana palmeri[2] (Laysan Rail)	Rallidae	Midway I., Hawaii	ground surface	unknown	extinction	Johnson 1945
Coenocorypha aucklandica (Stewart Island Snipe)	Scolopacidae	Big South Cape I., New Zealand	ground surface	unknown	extinction	Atkinson & Bell, 1973
Sterna fuscata (Sooty Tern)	Laridae	Bird I., Seychelles	ground surface	eggs (54 × 37) chicks	'small losses of eggs and chicks'	Feare 1976, 1979
Gygis alba (White Tern)	Laridae	Midway I., Hawaii	branches, often <3m	eggs suspected; chicks	not measured	Grant *et al.* 1981; Alsatt *in* Munro 1945
Synthliboramphus antiquus (Ancient Murrelet)	Alcidae	Langara I., British Columbia	burrows	eggs, possibly chicks and adults	small effect in some years; may cause reduction in others	Campbell 1968, Sealy 1976, Vermeer *et al.*, in press
Geopelia striata (Barred Dove)	Columbidae	Hawaii	branches often <3m	chicks	unknown	Schwartz & Schwartz 1950
Cyanoramphus auriceps (Yellow-crowned Parakeet)	Psittacidae	Big South Cape I., New Zealand	cavities, often >3m	unknown	major decline	Atkinson & Bell 1973

Species	Family	Location	Nest site	Stage	Effect	Reference
Cyanoramphus novaezelandiae (Red-crowned Parakeet)	Psittacidae	Big South Cape I., New Zealand	cavities, often <3m	unknown	major decline	Atkinson & Bell 1973
Chalcites lucidus (Shining Cuckoo)	Cuculidae	Wellington, New Zealand, c. 1950	branches >3m	chick	single observation	R. A. Falla, pers. comm. 1978
Acanthisitta chloris (Rifleman)	Acanthisittidae	Kaikoura, New Zealand	cavities <3m	eggs	continuing coexistence with rats	Moors 1983; P. J. Moors, pers. comm.
Xenicus longipes (Stead's Bush Wren)	Acanthisittidae	Big South Cape I., New Zealand	on or near ground	unknown	extinction	Atkinson & Bell 1973
Coracina typica (Mauritius Cuckoo-shrike)	Campephagidae	Mauritius	branches >3m	chicks	unknown but species is endangered	C. Jones, pers. comm. 1982
Bowdleria punctata (Stewart I. Fernbird)	Sylviidae	Big South Cape I., New Zealand	low bushes, reeds or grasses	unknown	extinction	Atkinson & Bell 1973
Finschia novaeseelandiae (Brown Creeper)	Sylviidae	Kaikoura, New Zealand	foliage >3m	eggs (19 × 14)	continuing coexistence with rats	Moors 1983; P. J. Moors, pers. comm.
Gerygone igata (Grey Warbler)	Sylviidae	Kaikoura, New Zealand	branches <3m	eggs (17 × 12), chicks	major cause of mortality with *Mustela erminea*	Gill 1983
Gerygone insularis (Lord Howe Warbler)	Sylviidae	Lord Howe I.	branches	unknown	extinction	Hindwood 1940
Rhipidura cervina (Lord Howe Fantail)	Muscicapidae	Lord Howe I.	branches, often <3m	unknown	extinction	Hindwood 1940
Rhipidura f. fuliginosa (South Island Fantail)	Muscicapidae	Kaikoura, New Zealand	branches <3m	eggs (16 × 12)	continuing coexistence with rats	Moors 1983; P. J. Moors, pers. comm. 1982
Petroica a. australis (South Island Robin)	Muscicapidae	Kaikoura, New Zealand	branches >3m	eggs (25 × 18), chicks, adult females	up to 13% of nests predated by rats in some years	Flack & Lloyd 1978, Moors 1983
Petroica a. rakiura (Stewart I. Robin)	Muscicapidae	Big South Cape I., New Zealand	branches <3m	eggs (25 × 19), chicks, adults	extinction	Atkinson & Bell 1973
Turdus merula (Blackbird)	Turdidae	Kaikoura, New Zealand	branches <3m	eggs (29 × 21) chicks	continuing coexistence with rats	Moors 1983; P. J. Moors, pers. comm.
Turdus xanthopus vinitinctus (Vinous-tinted Thrush)	Turdidae	Lord Howe I.	ground surface	unknown	extinction	Hindwood 1940
Zosterops strenua (Robust Silvereye)	Zosteropidae	Lord Howe I.	branches	unknown	extinction	Hindwood 1940
Anthornis melanura (Bellbird)	Meliphagidae	Big South Cape I., New Zealand	cavities, often >3m	unknown	major decline	Atkinson & Bell 1973
Telespyza cantans (Laysan Finchbill)	Drepanididae	Midway I., Hawaii	on or near ground	unknown	extinction	Johnson 1945

(continued)

Table 6: Continued

Bird species	Family	Locality	Usual nest station	Stage of life-cycle preyed upon[1]	Effect on population	Source of information
Himatione sanguinea (Apapane)	Drepanididae	Kilauea, Hawaii	branches >3m	chicks, adults	unknown	Berger 1981
Fringilla coelebs (Chaffinch)	Fringillidae	Kaikoura, New Zealand	branches >3m	eggs (20 × 14)	continuing coexistence with rats	Moors 1983; P. J. Moors, pers. comm.
Serinus canaria (Canary)	Fringillidae	Midway I., Hawaii	branches >3m	unknown	major decline	Alsatt *in* Munro 1945; Berger 1981
Aplonis fuscus hullianus (Lord Howe Starling)	Sturnidae	Lord Howe I.	cavities and hollows <3m	unknown	extinction	Hindwood 1940
Philesturnus carunculatus (South Island Saddleback)	Callaeatidae	Big South Cape I., New Zealand	cavities, often <3m	probably all stages	extinction	Atkinson & Bell 1973

[1] Egg-sizes from Oliver 1955, P. J. Moors, pers. comm.
[2] Nomenclature of rails follows Ripley 1977.

Table 7: Predation by *R. exulans* on birds.
Only one example of predation is included for each species.

Bird species	Family	Locality	Usual nest station	Stage of life-cycle preyed upon[1]	Effect on population	Source of information
Diomedea immutabilis (Laysan Albatross)	Diomedeidae	Kure Atoll, Hawaii	ground surface	chicks, adults	coexistence with rat; significant predation only in some seasons	Kepler 1967, Woodward 1972
Diomedea nigripes (Black-footed Albatross)	Diomedeidae	Kure Atoll, Hawaii	ground surface	chicks	minor	Woodward 1972
Pterodroma cooki (Cook's Petrel)	Procellariidae	Little Barrier I., New Zealand	burrows	eggs (52 × 40), chicks	continuing coexistence with rats	Imber 1975
Pterodroma hypoleuca (Bonin Petrel)	Procellariidae	Kure Atoll, Hawaii	burrows	eggs, chicks	no young raised in some years	Kepler 1967, Woodward 1972
Pterodroma neglecta (Kermadec Petrel)	Procellariidae	Raoul I., Kermadec Is	ground surface	chicks	contributing factor to major decline	Bell *in* Merton 1970
Puffinus pacificus (Wedge-tailed Shearwater)	Procellariidae	Kure Atoll, Hawaii	burrows	eggs (66 × 44), ?chicks	minor	Woodward 1972
Pelecanoides urinatrix (Northern Diving Petrel)	Pelecanoididae	Mercury Is, New Zealand	burrows	eggs (36 × 29)	not measured	Thoresen 1967
Phaethon rubricauda (Red-tailed Tropicbird)	Phaethontidae	Kure Atoll, Hawaii	ground surface	eggs (68 × 48), chicks	up to 65% and 100% losses of eggs and chicks respectively in some years	Fleet 1972
Fregata minor (Great Frigatebird)	Fregatidae	Kure Atoll, Hawaii	branches <3m	adults	minor	Woodward 1972
Sterna fuscata (Sooty Tern)	Laridae	Kure Atoll, Hawaii	ground surface	eggs (54 × 37), chicks	continuing coexistence with rats	Kepler 1967, Wirtz 1972
Sterna lunata (Grey-backed Tern)	Laridae	Kure Atoll, Hawaii	ground surface	eggs, chicks	all young destroyed in one year	Woodward 1972
Anous stolidus (Common Noddy)	Laridae	Kure Atoll, Hawaii	ground surface	eggs (53 × 36), chicks	continuing coexistence with rats	Kepler 1967, Wirtz 1972
Petroica australis (South Island Robin)	Muscicapidae	Motuara I., New Zealand	branches >3m	eggs (25 × 18), chicks	26% of nests preyed on in year of observation	Flack & Lloyd 1978, J. A. D. Flack, pers. comm.
Petroica longipes (North Island Robin)	Muscicapidae	Little Barrier I., New Zealand	branches >3m	eggs (23 × 18)	continuing coexistence with rats	Guthrie-Smith 1925
Prosthemadera novaeseelandiae (Tui)	Meliphagidae	Chetwode Is, New Zealand	branches >3m	eggs, chicks	unknown	Stead 1936 (reported incorrectly as *R. rattus*)

[1] Egg-sizes from Oliver 1955. P. J. Moors, pers. comm.

Tables 5–7 bring together the most reliable examples of predation by identified species of rats on particular birds that I have been able to find. The examples come mainly from islands, but probably represent only a small fraction of the species preyed upon by rats. The nest stations quoted are those usually used and not necessarily the particular stations of the birds recorded as predated. This information is shown in *Figure 8* to illustrate the effects of each rat species on birds nesting at different heights. The height criterion of 3m used to separate higher from lower nest positions is an arbitrary level chosen to emphasize the differences in climbing frequency of *R. norvegicus* and *R. rattus*. *R. norvegicus* does sometimes climb to 3m or greater (e.g. Hill *et al.* 1983), but *R. rattus*, perhaps because of its tree-nesting habits, frequently forages in trees well above 3m. No information is available on the frequency with which nests in particular positions are preyed upon, and thus only a qualitative picture emerges. This indicates the high percentage of ground-nesting species among the prey of *R. norvegicus* and the vulnerability of all nest positions to *R. rattus*. The lack of records of *R. exulans* preying on nests in vegetation higher than 3m is presumed to be an artifact related to the small sample size. It is apparent that the three species cannot be treated as equals in their effects on birds. Therefore an island of conservation importance that already has one species of rat still requires precautions against the entry of further species (cf. Atkinson 1978).

Apart from size and behavioural differences among the three species, other variables influence rat predation. One of these is the number of rats present which will depend on habitat and food supply. When rats reach a hitherto rodent-free island their numbers often irrupt to high levels, presumably a result of food abundance. This happened on Big South Cape Island, New Zealand, in the 1960s (Atkinson & Bell 1973). The high rat numbers are likely to increase the incidence of bird predation above that which can be observed after rat numbers have subsequently fallen to sustainable levels.

Seasonal changes in food availability also influence rat numbers and thus the incidence of predation on birds, even though they are often only a minor part of the rats' diet. An inverse functional effect can also occur where, because of a seasonal failure of preferred foods, the rats switch to birds as a major alternative prey. An example is Fleet's (1972) study of the nesting success of Red-tailed Tropicbirds (*Phaethon rubricauda*) on Kure Atoll.

Although as yet little studied, there is the possibility that spatial or temporal differences in severity of predation can result from certain rats in a population learning to prey on eggs, chicks or adult birds. Possible examples are given in the studies of Woodward (1972) on Kure Atoll and Grant *et al.* (1981) on Midway Atoll.

DIFFERENCES AMONG BIRD SPECIES THAT AFFECT THEIR VULNERABILITY TO RATS

Nest position is only one of a number of prey features that determine the frequency and severity of predation by rats. Other features of importance are the bird's size—larger birds being less vulnerable—and behaviour in the presence of predators. For example, although adult Laysan Albatrosses are sometimes killed by *R. exulans* on Kure Atoll (Kepler 1967), there are no records of this occurring with the more aggressive Black-footed Albatross (*Diomedea nigripes*) which breeds on the same island. Birds with either long incubation or long fledging periods, such as members of the Hawaiian Honeycreeper family (Berger 1981), run greater risk of predation than those with short periods. If breeding coincides with seasonal peaks in rat numbers then predation is again more likely. The near-extinct New Zealand Kakapo Parrot (*Strigops habroptilus*),

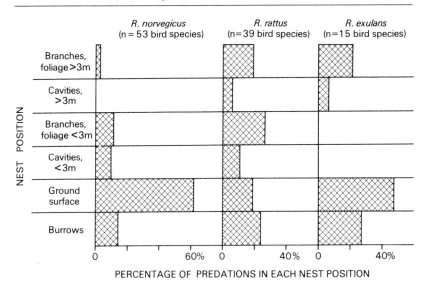

Figure 8: Nest position in relation to predation by commensal rats. The common nesting stations of the bird species recorded as preyed upon by rats in *Tables 5–7* have been placed in position-classes relative to ground level. For each rat species the histogram shows the proportions of each of these position-classes as a percentage of all species predations recorded. This allows a qualitative comparison of the ways in which the three rat species affect nesting success.

which nests on the ground and is thus already potentially vulnerable to rats, has a fledging period of about ten weeks (Merton *et al.* 1984). The timing of this period in late summer coincides with seasonal peaks in rat numbers, thus increasing the risk of predation. Birds which do not re-nest after losing a brood, or which normally raise only one brood in a season, are also more vulnerable to predation than those which behave otherwise. Recently Lovegrove (1983) has demonstrated that overnight roosting sites that are on or close to the ground can also make a bird vulnerable to predation. How often and for how long the parents leave their chicks unattended may also be important with seabirds. Some of these factors are discussed in detail by Moors & Atkinson (1984).

Egg size and shell thickness must also affect a bird's vulnerability to predation, with the larger and stronger species of rat being able to prey on larger and more robust eggs. Egg sizes are included in *Tables 5–7* where available. The data are still too limited to suggest what the upper limits of egg size and shell thickness are for each species of rat.

Indigenous avian predators are present on some islands, but anti-predator behaviours developed in response to these are not always effective in protecting a bird against rats.

The examples of predation listed in *Tables 5–7* range in severity from those where there was no significant effect on the bird population to extinction of species. When rats reach an island the level of predation experienced by each species of bird will be governed by the various predator and prey factors discussed above. These factors, acting with the birds' food supply, disease, and other predators, will influence breeding success and adult survival, and thus determine whether a particular rat–bird relationship is one of coexistence (the most common situation), decline or extinction of the bird.

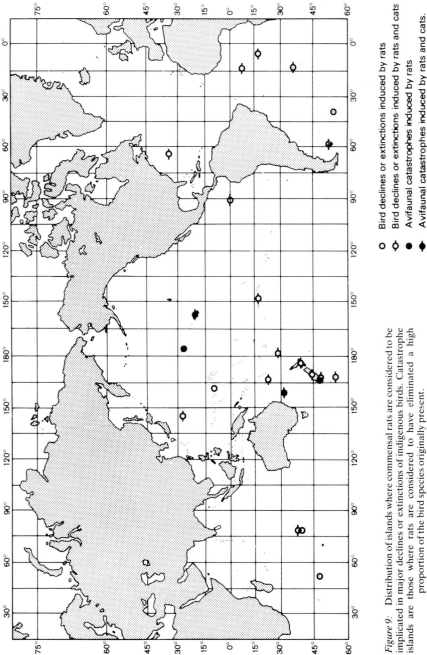

Figure 9:   Distribution of islands where commensal rats are considered to be implicated in major declines or extinctions of indigenous birds. Catastrophe islands are those where rats are considered to have eliminated a high proportion of the bird species originally present.

○ Bird declines or extinctions induced by rats
⌀ Bird declines or extinctions induced by rats and cats
● Avifaunal catastrophes induced by rats
◆ Avifaunal catastrophes induced by rats and cats.

RAT-INDUCED DECLINES AND EXTINCTIONS OF ISLAND BIRDS

Reliability of the evidence

Reliable observations of rats preying on birds are known in addition to those listed in *Tables 5–7*, but they have not been included because identification of the rat was not possible. The predominantly nocturnal habits of rats make both their identification and observation of their predatory behaviour difficult. In all probability the incidence of rat predation is higher than yet realized. The great variation in effects of rats on different bird populations has, however, misled some people into believing that rat predation on birds has been overemphasized in relation to other factors (e.g. Norman 1975). As pointed out by Bourne (1981) and Moors & Atkinson (1984), even a low frequency of rat predation can have a severe effect if for other reasons there are few birds. There were no contemporary observers of many declines and extinctions of island birds. Of the 23 examples of rat-induced declines in island birds contained in *Table 8* and *Figure 9*, bird mortality was measured in only three (Galapagos, Kermadec and Crozet Islands). In a fourth example (New Caledonia) there are direct observations but no mortality estimates. With Lord Howe, Midway and Big South Cape Islands the circumstantial evidence from contemporary observers leaves little doubt that rats were responsible; hence the inclusion of the species affected in the predation tables (*Tables 5–7*). The largest group of 11 examples in *Table 8* are mainly retrospective studies of circumstantial evidence made some time after the event; these vary in quality according to the amount of evidence available. In the remaining six examples, there is weak circumstantial evidence worthy of inclusion only because more likely explanations are lacking at present.

Rats and cats

Rats may sometimes exert indirect effects on island bird populations by becoming prey to larger predators—usually cats. Cats may thence maintain higher numbers than would otherwise be possible, and cat predation on birds increases. Cats were present, if not actually involved, during at least 15 of the declines or extinctions cited in *Table 8*. For example, *R. rattus* and cats had both become established on St Helena Island by 1665. Rats repeatedly reached very high numbers in the period 1666 to 1742 (as well as subsequently), and cats were described in 1715 as being present in 'vast numbers' (Gosse 1938). This indirect adverse effect of rats where cats are present has been particularly devastating for seabirds. Outside the breeding season such birds may be absent for several months, but cats sustain their own numbers on rats as an alternative food source until the seabirds return to breed (Moors & Atkinson, 1984). A similar effect can be expected where rats are present on an island with mongooses or mustelids.

The human influence

The circumstances under which rats reached the islands listed in *Table 8* are sometimes known even though details are usually lacking. In at least 11 examples the arrival of rats coincided with settlement by people. Construction of substantial wharves to which ocean-going vessels moored probably allowed rats to reach the shore, although occasionally rats may have become established prior to wharf construction. Ship-borne rats are commonly associated with carriage of bulk foodstuffs, particularly grains (Atkinson, unpub.). Whenever an island settlement had to import food from continental countries the chances of commensal rats also arriving were thus increased.

A second major cause of rats reaching islands is man's exploitation of local resources such as fish, seals, whales or birds, even though there may be no permanent settlement. At least five cases in *Table 8* may have resulted from this cause. For example, *R. norvegicus* reached South Georgia when seal-hunting along the island's shores was at its height.

Table 8: Islands where rats have been implicated in major declines or extinctions of birds.

Island	Rat spp. present[1]	Other introduced terrestrial predators[2]	Effects on avifauna and nature of evidence
Galapagos Is: Floreana I. San Cristóbal I. Santa Cruz. I. Santiago I.	*R. rattus* *R. rattus* *R. rattus* *R. rattus*, *R. norvegicus*	cats, dogs, pigs cats, dogs, pigs cats, dogs?, pigs cats, pigs	Harris (1970) found evidence of *R. rattus* as a cause of the very low breeding success of Dark-rumped Petrels in the Galapagos Islands. Subsequent studies by Tomkins (this vol.) and Coulter *et al.* (this vol.) have confirmed that *R. rattus* is a major predator of this endangered petrel, although cats, dogs and pigs are also contributing to losses of both adults and young.
Society Is	*R. exulans*, *R. norvegicus*, *R. rattus*	cats, dogs, pigs	Thibault (1973) presumed that rats were implicated in the extinctions during the late 18th and early 19th centuries of the Tahitian Rail *Rallus pacificus*, the Tahitian Sandpiper *Prosobonia leucoptera* and two species of parakeets, *Cyanoramphus zealandicus* and *C. ulietanus*.
Hawaiian Is: Kauai, Oahu, Molokai, Lanai, Maui and Hawaii	*R. exulans*, *R. norvegicus*, *R. rattus*	cats, dogs, mongooses, pigs	Although various causes of bird declines operated throughout the historic period in Hawaii, Atkinson (1977) concluded from circumstantial evidence that *R. rattus* was responsible for the accelerated declines or extinctions of many species of forest birds that occurred on all the main islands between 1870 and 1930. For the prehistoric period, Olson & James (1982) concluded that *R. exulans* was a contributing factor to the massive extinctions of Hawaiian bird species that they demonstrated took place during the Polynesian occupation.
Midway Is.	*R. rattus*		Populations of the Laysan Rail and Laysan Finch became extinct within 18 months of the arrival on Midway in 1943 of *R. rattus* (Johnson 1945, Fisher & Baldwin 1946).
Bonin Is: Peel I.	Rats present	cats, dogs	Greenway (1967) presumed that cats and rats may have caused the extinction of the Bonin I. Thrush *Zoothera terrestris* between 1828 and 1899.
Volcano I.	Rats present	cats	Momiyama (1930) presumed the extinction of the Iwo Iima Rail *Porzana cinerea brevipes* to be due to introduced rats and cats.
Kusaie I., Caroline Is.	*R. exulans*, *R. rattus*	?	Rats are suggested by Greenway (1967) as a possible cause for the extinction of the Kusaie I. Starling *Aplonis corvina* and Kusaie I. Rail *Porzana monasa* between 1828 and 1880.
New Caledonia	*R. exulans*, *R. norvegicus*, *R. rattus*	cats, dogs, pigs	Warner (1948) concluded from his field observations that the decline of the Kagu *Rhynochetos jubatus* was in part related to predation and food competition by rats, particularly *R. rattus*.
Lord Howe I.	*R. rattus* (*R. exulans*)	cats	Five species of indigenous landbirds became extinct following the arrival of *R. rattus* in 1918 (Hindwood 1940, Recher & Clark 1974).
Raoul I., Kermadec Is.	*R. exulans*, *R. norvegicus*	cats	Merton (1970) concluded from his bird survey that the virtual extinction of the Kermadec Petrel on Raoul I, which had occurred since 1914 could be attributed to the combined predation of cats and rats. Taylor (1979) concluded from counts of predated chicks that predation by rats and cats could be destroying the colony of Sooty Terns on the island.
Campbell I.	*R. norvegicus*	cats	Study of published accounts suggests that predation by rats and cats has eliminated the Campbell I. Teal *Anas aucklandica nesiotis* and small petrels from the main island, as well as greatly reducing the large population of Sooty Shearwaters formerly present (cf. Bailey & Sorensen 1962).

	R. species	Predators[2]	
New Zealand: Big South Cape I.	R. rattus	wekas	Eight species of indigenous landbirds were either greatly reduced or became extinct immediately following the arrival of R. rattus about 1962 (Atkinson & Bell 1973).
North, South and Stewart Is.	R. exulans, R. norvegicus, R. rattus	cats, stoats, weasels, ferrets, hedgehogs, pigs	Several authors (e.g. Buller 1888, Oliver 1955, Atkinson 1973) have suggested that declines or extinctions of certain indigenous birds in the 19th century can be attributed primarily to rats. The importance of rats relative to other causes of declines has yet to be evaluated for any particular species.
Tromelin I.	R. norvegicus	—	The breeding of smaller seabirds has been greatly reduced by rats (Bourne in Morris 1964).
Possession I., Crozet Is.	R. rattus		Mougin's (1969) study of the Kerguelen Petrel on Possession I. showed that R. rattus causes heavy losses of chicks in some years, but not in others. He concluded that rats threaten the survival of the species in the Crozet Islands.
Amsterdam I.	R. rattus	cats (pigs)	From their study of bones and other remains on the island, Jouanin & Paulian (1960) concluded that major declines of small petrels, particularly Broad-billed Prions, could be related primarily to predation by R. rattus.
St Paul I.	R. rattus	(cats) (pigs)	Using circumstantial evidence, Segonzac (1972) concluded that major declines in Broad-billed Prions and possibly also White-bellied Storm Petrels Fregetta grallaria could be attributed to predation by R. rattus.
Bermuda Is	R. rattus, R. norvegicus	cats, pigs	Breeding of Cahow, Black-capped Petrel P. hasitata and Audubon's Shearwater has become restricted to small islands off the main island partly as a result of predation by cats and rats (D. B. Wingate, pers. comm. 1982).
Ascension I.	R. rattus	cats	The Ascension I. Rail Atlantisia elpenor was probably eliminated by R. rattus before the arrival of cats (Kinnear 1935, Olson 1973).
St Helena I.	R. rattus, R. norvegicus	cats, dogs, pigs	Bones of 21 species of non-passerine birds no longer present on the island have been described by Olson (1975). It seems probable that the extinctions of at least a few of these species, as well as that of unrecorded forest passerines, can be attributed to predation by cats and rats during the first 150 years of European contact.
Tristan da Cunha I.	R. rattus	(cats), dogs	Massive reductions of Storm Petrels Pelagodroma marina and Prions Pachyptila forsteri on this island can be attributed to predation by cats and R. rattus. These predators may also have been involved in the extinction of the Tristan Finch Nesospiza acunhae (Olson 1973, Wace & Holdgate 1976).
Falkland Is	R. norvegicus	cats, pigs, Patagonian Fox	Breeding of the Tussock Bird Cinclodes antarcticus and the Southern House Wren Troglodytes aedon has become restricted to cat and rat-free islands. Reduction of small petrels, including the Antarctic Prion Pachyptila desolata, has occurred on rat-inhabited islands (Tickell 1962, Woods 1975).
South Georgia	R. norvegicus		Breeding of Antarctic Pipits and South Georgia Pintails has become restricted to rat-free habitats (Pye & Bonner 1980).

[1] Data from Tables 1–3 of present paper.

[2] Predators bracketed are believed to have been eliminated.

With the issuing of permits in 1982 by the New Zealand Department of Lands and Survey allowing fishing boats to moor directly to the main Snares Island, one of the world's least modified forested islands is now at risk from rats.

Shipwrecks have taken rats to four of the islands where major bird declines have occurred. Proximity of an island to continents or major trade routes increases the chances of shipwreck, as does exploitation of natural resources (oil, minerals, fish) in the vicinity of an island. Establishment of naval, military or air force bases also increases the risk of rat invasions, as occurred for example with the military base on Midway Island during World War II.

At first sight many of these rat invasions of oceanic islands would have been difficult to avoid. However, it is well established that not all ships have rats aboard, even those of earlier centuries. The Auckland Islands, for example, have so far escaped rats in spite of several major shipwrecks in the group and a temporary settlement last century. The incidence of rats reaching oceanic islands could be significantly reduced if there were more effective regulations to exclude rodents from all ocean-going vessels and better inspection of cargoes during loading.

Rat-induced catastrophes

On a few islands rat-induced extinctions of birds have affected such a high proportion of the island's avifauna that the term catastrophe is appropriate. The earliest well documented case is that of Lord Howe Island, where in 1918 *R. rattus* came ashore from the grounded steamship S.S. *Makambo*. Within a few years five species of endemic forest bird had become extinct—more than 40 percent of the indigenous species of landbird (Hindwood 1940; Recher & Clark 1974). Cats and mice had already been present for some time, and the accounts quoted by Hindwood indicate that *R. exulans* was also present prior to 1918, although no specimens or subsequent sight records are known.

In 1943 *R. rattus* came ashore with cargo at the military base on Midway Island, and within 18 months two species of landbird had been eliminated (Johnson 1945; Fisher & Baldwin 1946). These were Laysan Rails (*Porzana palmeri*) (introduced earlier from Laysan Island where they subsequently became extinct) and introduced Laysan Finches (*Psittirostra c. cantans*) (a species that still survives on Laysan Island). No other indigenous landbirds are known to breed on Midway Island. Mice are also present, but no predator other than *R. rattus* is known to have played any significant part in these extinctions.

About 1962 *R. rattus* established on Big South Cape Island, off the southwest coast of Stewart Island, New Zealand. Within three years of their arrival, major declines or extinctions occurred in eight species of landbird, comprising more than 40 percent of the island's landbird fauna (Blackburn 1965; Atkinson & Bell 1973). No rodents or other introduced predators apart from the rail *Gallirallus australis* were present prior to the invasion.

These three islands are the best-documented examples of rat-induced catastrophes to island avifaunas. In each case there are sufficient observations to conclude that the arrival of *R. rattus* was the only major ecological change that occurred at the time when the bird declines began.

A fourth case may have occurred in the Hawaiian Islands. Here there is circumstantial evidence that more than 50 percent of the declines or extinctions of endemic forest birds which occurred late last or early this century could be attributed to *R. rattus* (Atkinson 1977). It had earlier been argued that disease, particularly avian malaria and birdpox, could explain these changes (Warner 1968). A recent study by van Riper *et al.* (1982) has shown that the malarial parasite *Plasmodium relictum* ssp. *capistranoae* is unlikely to have become permanently established in the islands until after 1900, thus removing it as a likely cause of the late nineteenth century Hawaiian bird declines. Atkinson (1977) suggested a stepwise spread of *R. rattus* from island to island as wharves were constructed to service settlements. For this reason the declines and extinctions were not synchronized between islands, but extended over a period of nearly 60 years. *R. norvegicus*, *R. exulans*, *Mus musculus* and cats were already well established prior to the arrival of *R. rattus*, but no catastrophic decline in the avifauna was observed between European discovery and the late nineteenth century. Indeed, a number of Hawaiian birds were unknown until the 1890s. Had the major declines occurred earlier, some of these species would never have been seen by Europeans, as is the case with the many bird species described by Olson & James (1982) which became extinct as a result of Polynesian settlement. There can be little doubt that further studies will recognize the past occurrence of rat-induced catastrophes on other islands.

The possible influence of endemic rats
While some islands have suffered rat induced catastrophic changes to their avifaunas others have not. A notable example is the Galagapos Islands. Although *R. rattus* reached Santiago Island in the late seventeenth or early eighteenth centuries, other large islands in the group were not invaded until the nineteenth or twentieth centuries (Patton *et al*. 1975). Apart from the adverse effect of rats on Dark-rumped Petrels (*Pterodroma phaeopygia*) (*Table 6*), no other declines or extinctions attributable to rats have been described from these islands (Harris 1970, 1973).

Christmas Island, Indian Ocean, was reached by both *R. rattus* and *R. norvegicus* between 1898 and 1938 (*Table 2*). From the accounts of the birds given by Andrews (1900) and Gibson-Hill (1947b) there is nothing to suggest any effect of introduced rats on the avifauna.

Both Christmas Island and the Galagapos Islands formerly had endemic species of rats. The two species of endemic *Rattus* on Christmas Island disappeared following the arrival of *R. rattus* (Andrews 1909). Both species were originally very numerous, particularly *R. macleari* which climbed tree-trunks and lianes with ease (Gray 1981). Seven endemic species of cricetine rodents are known from the Galagapos Islands (Orr 1966; Steadman & Ray 1982), and the extinction of at least two of them followed the arrival of *R. rattus* on particular islands (Heller 1904; Brosset 1963). The two surviving species are on islands that have so far escaped invasion by *R. rattus*. Brosset's study demonstrated a close similarity between the feeding and other behaviour of one of these endemic rodents, *Oryzomys bauri*, and that of *R. rattus*.

The avifaunas of both Christmas and the Galapagos Islands had probably been preyed on by endemic rats for many thousands of years prior to the arrival of commensal rats. If so, one might not expect any catastrophic effect from the new arrivals. A similar selection pressure may have operated in the West Indies, Fernando de Noronha, the Andaman and the Nicobar Islands. In all these islands endemic rats were present prior to the arrival of commensal species (Simpson 1956; Olson 1981; Miller 1902). However, few oceanic islands either have or have had endemic rodents.

The possible influence of land crabs
There are a number of island groups lacking endemic rodents which apparently sustained no substantial losses to their avifaunas following the arrival of commensal rats. For example, the avifaunas of Fiji, Samoa, Tonga and the Marquesas Islands were all moderately well known prior to the arrival of *R. rattus*, although not necessarily before the arrival of *R. norvegicus*. If *R. rattus* affected the avifaunas, particularly the forest birds, of these islands to any major extent, the effect should be detectable. Rats may be implicated in the disappearance of a few species, such as the Wood Rail (*Gallinula pacifica*) of Samoa and the Barred-wing Rail (*Rallus poecilopterus*) of Fiji, but evidence

for a more extensive effect of rats on these islands seems lacking. In the Marquesas Islands, which *R. rattus* did not reach until about 1915 (*Table 1*), none of the nine species of endemic landbird have become extinct, a fact that Greenway (1967) commented on as surprising.

These island groups with avifaunas apparently less vulnerable to rat predation occur within an equatorial zone bounded by latitudes 15° N and 20° S, although the real width of the zone may be broader. The reduced effect of rats on island avifaunas in this zone may result from the presence of land crabs, both terrestrial Hermit Crabs (*Birgus latro*, *Coenobita* spp.) and terrestrial Brachyuran Crabs (particularly *Gecarcinus* spp.).

The Coconut or Robber Crab (*Birgus latro*) is widely distributed in tropical and subtropical islands of the Indian and Pacific Oceans (Yaldwyn & Wodzicki 1979), but is absent from the Atlantic Ocean (Reyne 1939). Hermit Crabs of the genus *Coenobita* have a worldwide tropical and subtropical distribution (Page & Willason 1982). Species of *Gecarcinus* are widespread on islands in both the Atlantic and Pacific Oceans (Dodson & Fitzgerald 1980; Olson 1981).

Predation by land crabs on birds, particularly seabirds, has been observed. Robinson, quoted by Sprunt (1948: 14), describes thousands of Hermit Crabs (probably *Coenobita diogones*) eating newly-hatched chicks of Sooty Terns (*Sterna fuscata*) in the Dry Tortugas Keys, although Sprunt himself subsequently found *C. diogones* to be uncommon. Amerson (1969) stated that both *Coenobita rugosa* and *B. latro* eat eggs and young birds, but gave no details of the bird species affected. *Coenobita perlitus* has been reported to prey on ground-nesting birds at Christmas Island, Line group (King 1973). Hermit Crabs in large numbers (species not stated) have been seen preying on both Sooty Terns and Frigatebirds on Enderbury Island in the Phoenix group (King 1973). D. B. Wingate (pers. comm. 1982) has observed *Gecarcinus laterallus* preying on chicks of Common Terns (*Sterna hirundo*) in Bermuda and on one occasion an attempted predation of a small passerine. Predation by *Gecarcinus planatus* on chicks of Masked Boobies (*Sula dactylatra*) has been photographed on Clipperton Island by Jacques Cousteau (P. J. Moors, pers. comm. 1982). Dodson & Fitzgerald (1981) observed mainly the nests of Brown Boobies (*Sula leucogaster*) on the same island and thought that chicks left unattended would probably quickly succumb to land crabs. On Tromelin Island in 1856 E. L. Layard noted predation by a Hermit Crab (*Pagurus* sp.) on chicks of Masked Boobies (Brooke 1981). Rockwell (1932) stated that *Gecarcinus lagostomus* destroys eggs and young of White Terns (*Gygis alba*) on Isla da Trindade, Atlantic Ocean.

The presence of *Gecarcinus* land crabs in the South Atlantic was suggested by Olson (1981) as having prevented many burrowing or ground-nesting petrels from colonizing Fernando de Noronha, Ascension and Trindade Islands. On St Helena, where these land crabs are absent, he has shown that at least seven species of burrowing petrels were formerly present (Olson 1975).

Although land crabs are usually considered to be scavengers and grazers, these observations show that eggs and chicks of seabirds, and probably also those of terrestrial landbirds, are eaten when the opportunity arises. Whether they would also prey on arboreal nests of landbirds would depend on their climbing ability. *Birgus latro* is a good climber, but some other species also climb well, e.g. *Coenobita brevimana* and *Sesarma gardineri* (Yaldwyn & Wodzicki 1979), *C. perlata* (Cohic 1957), *Pagurus* sp. (Layard in Brooke 1981) and *Geograpsus grayi* (Sakagami 1961). The last author reports that on Marcus Island *G. grayi* climbs *Messerschmidia* and *Pisonia* trees 'to fairly high twigs'. Remembering that land crabs search for potential food, including that in tree cavities, as they climb, it is likely that any birds nesting or roosting within climbing range of the crabs are at risk.

Land crabs on high oceanic islands

Land crabs could thus be an under-rated factor in influencing the avifaunas of coral atolls and other islands of low relief in the equatorial zone. It becomes crucial to know whether land crabs formerly inhabited the inland and higher slopes of high volcanic islands in the same zone. Unfortunately *Birgus latro* and some other species of land crab are much sought after as food by local inhabitants. The present numbers and distribution of these animals may therefore bear little resemblance to that of pre-settlement times.

On Christmas Island, Indian Ocean, Andrews (1899) reported land crabs (*Gecarcoidea natalis*) 'living in burrows all over the island'. He found *Birgus latro* also very numerous and stated it could be found 'anywhere in the forest'. The plateau of Christmas Island averages about 240m above sea level and rises to the highest point at 381m. Gray (1981) reports that *B. latro* is still plentiful on most parts of the island from the shore terrace to the highest plateau areas, and that the endemic *G. natalis* is astonishingly abundant with a similar distribution.

On Easter Island T. Heyerdahl collected *Geograpsus crinipes* from a hole 250m above sea level (Garth 1973). Bright & Hogue (1972) record *Gecarcinus ruricola* at altitudes up to 500m above sea level on 'island mountains'. Land crabs are frequently nocturnal and there seems to be little information about their inland distribution on high islands. Stair (1897), describing Samoa in the period 1838 to 1845, comments that 'gigantic land-crabs' were present in many parts of the island. He was presumably referring to *Birgus latro*.

If the former coexistence or partial coexistence of land crabs with forest birds on high islands can be demonstrated, then many of these birds may have attributes or behaviours that reduce crab predation. As the avifauna of such an island developed through immigration and autochthonous evolution, only those birds with the appropriate anti-predator characteristics would survive. The group of birds remaining after this selection could well include many that were capable of coexisting with rats, at least to a greater extent than species never exposed to land crab predation.

Rat species involved in major declines or extinctions

R. rattus is the most frequent rat identified with bird declines and rat-induced catastrophes on islands (*Table 8*). More complete documentation of other examples, Campbell Island for instance, may well show that *R. norvegicus* has also caused catastrophic changes to some island avifaunas.

Whether *R. exulans* has caused major declines or extinctions is less clear, mainly because its major impact is prehistoric and some birds possibly affected are now extinct. Their habits can be inferred from their size and bone morphology and the distribution of subfossil remains, but such inferences are inconclusive evidence of vulnerability to predation. In New Zealand both large and very small birds became extinct following the arrival of Polynesians with *R. exulans*. The disappearance of the larger birds including Moas can be attributed to a combination of hunting by man and habitat destruction (Fleming 1962). However, following Kepler's (1967) observations of *R. exulans* killing adult Laysan Albatrosses on Kure Atoll, Fleming (1969) suggested that *R. exulans* may have contributed to the decline of the Moas by predation on chicks or adults. But Laysan Albatrosses on Kure continue to coexist with *R. exulans*, apparently because predation occurs only in years when there is a failure of the limited plant foods usually eaten by the rats as a result of late winter and spring storms (Woodward 1972; Fleet 1972). Such special conditions of food supply would not have operated on the New Zealand mainland. Even on islands around the New Zealand coast, populations of larger petrels coexist with sometimes very abundant numbers of *R. exulans*. For example, Imber (1975) found no evidence of *R. exulans* preying on young or adult Black Petrels (*Procellaria parkinsoni*) on Little Barrier Island.

The disappearance or reduced numbers of some small passerines in New Zealand during the Polynesian period cannot be attributed satisfactorily to either hunting or habitat destruction. However, any small bird that nests on or near the ground may be vulnerable to rats. Circumstantial evidence from the island distribution of New Zealand Wrens (*Xenicus; Acanthisittidae*) and the subantarctic Snipe (*Coenocorypha aucklandica*), all of which were ground-living birds, suggests these birds may have been eliminated from the mainland by *R. exulans* (Atkinson 1978). The Bush Wren (*Xenicus longipes*) was seen by Europeans in a few mainland localities prior to its extinction (Oliver 1955), but the Snipe is known only as subfossil material from the mainland (e.g. Medway 1971). More recently, the extinct Stephens Island Wren (*Xenicus lyallii*), which was seen alive only on Stephens Island, has been shown by Millener (1981 and pers. comm.) to have occurred in both the North and South Islands. This bird seldom if ever flew, at least on Stephens Island (Oliver 1955), so that its elimination from the mainland by *R. exulans* must be considered a distinct possibility.

Bird groups involved in major declines or extinctions

The studies quoted in *Table 8* show that rat-induced declines and extinctions are most frequent among perching birds. This can be linked to the importance of *R. rattus* in causing extinctions and is presumably related to its efficient climbing ability. Seabird populations are sometimes vulnerable to rats, but they are not dependent on the land for food, and breeding can continue on isolated islets and stacks free of predators. Nevertheless, local reductions or extinctions of Gadfly Petrels (*Pterodroma* spp.), Prions (*Pachyptila* spp.), Storm Petrels (Hydrobatidae) and Diving Petrels (Pelecanoididae) appear to be rather widespread. Among ground birds, rails are clearly one of the most vulnerable groups, but some species of island rails coexist with rats, e.g. the White-throated Rail (*Canirallus cuvieri*) with *R. rattus* on Aldabra (Penny & Diamond 1971).

CONCLUSION

Human factors above all else determine the chances of commensal rats reaching an island. The presence of other rodents and the presence of rat predators may sometimes affect the chances of rats establishing on an island (Taylor 1978). Once rats have established, the risk to the avifauna is dependent in some unknown way on its geographical position, with the avifaunas of temperate islands appearing to be most vulnerable. Within any particular avifauna, whatever its geographical position, some birds are more vulnerable than others. These include small endemic landbirds not previously exposed to mammalian predators, those that nest on or near the ground or in burrows, and those that nest in tree cavities. If mammalian predators capable of using rats as food are also present, such as cats or mongooses, the impact on the avifauna is likely to be greater. The former presence of endemic rats and the presence of land crabs living inland may explain the reduced vulnerability of island avifaunas in the tropical and subtropical zones. But these are working hypotheses that should not be used as management guidelines unless substantiated. Island avifaunas are more likely to suffer declines and extinctions if *R. rattus* is introduced than if other commensal rats become established. These various factors, affecting both the risk of rats establishing on islands and the vulnerability of their avifaunas, are summarized in *Table 9*.

The spread of commensal rats to oceanic islands began more than 3000 years ago and continues today. Nevertheless there are still a number of sizeable oceanic islands that are rat-free, and, where not unduly modified in other ways, these islands are of

Table 9:   Factors affecting rat establishment on islands and the vulnerability of their avifaunas.

Factor	High risk of rats establishing	Lower risk of rats establishing
Human influence	Permanent settlement Wharves large enough for ocean-going vessels Foodstuffs, particularly cereals, imported Exploitation of natural resources of the island or its surrounding waters, e.g. sealing, whaling, fishing, birding, mining, oil exploration and drilling Establishment of military bases Proximity to continents or major trade routes; shipwrecks	No permanent settlement No large wharves Settlement self-sufficient for food No exploitation of natural resources No bases for armed forces Isolated and distant from continents and major trade routes; no shipwrecks
	High risk to avifauna	**Lower risk to avifauna**
Geographical position of island	Outside the tropical and subtropical zone bounded approximately by latitudes 15°N and 20°S	Within the tropical and subtropical zone bounded approximately by latitudes 15°N and 20°S
Avifaunal characteristics	Endemic landbirds and seabirds present Many species of small birds Many species without anti-predator behaviours Many burrow-, ground and hole-nesting species	Seabirds only Few species of small birds Many species with anti-predator behaviours Few burrow-, ground and hole-nesting species
Other predators present	Cats or mongooses present as well as rats No endemic rats originally present No land crabs living away from the shoreline	No mammalian predators apart from rats ?Endemic rats originally present ?Land crabs living away from the shoreline
Species of rats introduced	*R. rattus, R. norvegicus*	*R. exulans*

inestimable value for conservation and scientific study. They include Gough Island in
the Atlantic Ocean (Wace & Holdgate 1976), Prince Edward Island in the Indian Ocean
(Williams *et al*. 1979), and Clipperton, Auckland and Snares Islands in the Pacific Ocean
(Sachet 1962; Taylor 1975; Fineran 1964). Within the many island groups that have
commensal rats there remain smaller islands of high biological value that are rat-free.
Examples are St Kilda in the British Isles (Fisher 1948), Inaccessible and Nightingale
Islands in the Tristan da Cunha group (Wace & Holdgate 1976), Frigate Island in the
Seychelles group (Elliott 1972), Cochons and East Islands in the Crozet group (Derenne
& Mougin 1976; Despin *et al*. 1972), Nihoa and Laysan Islands in the Hawaiian group
(King 1973), Fernandina and Santa Fe Islands in the Galapagos group (Eckhardt 1972),
Pitt Island in the Chatham group (Atkinson 1978) and Poor Knights and Stephens
Islands in New Zealand (Atkinson & Bell 1973). Of the numerous islands in the Pacific
that have *R. exulans* but which lack the other two commensal rats, some are of great
conservation and scientific value. A few examples are Rennell Island in the Solomon
region (Hill 1956), Rose Island in the Samoan group (King 1973), Henderson Island in
the Pitcairn group (Bourne & David 1983), and Little Barrier and Codfish Islands in
New Zealand (Atkinson & Bell 1973).

Judged by the island histories examined, the avifaunas of these various islands are not
equally at risk should they suffer future rat invasions. Although the reasons for this are
not fully understood, many of the avifaunas at greatest risk can be identified; that of the
Snares Islands is an example. All such islands should now be listed and the particular
precautions likely to be most effective in preventing rat entry should be spelt out and
implemented in each case. A necessary further step is to integrate this information into
a broadly based conservation plan for protecting the indigenous biotas and communities
of all of the world's biologically important islands. This plan needs to be presented in a
practical and unambiguous manner so that it can be acted upon by the appropriate
governments and controlling authorities.

ACKNOWLEDGEMENTS

I am indebted to Mrs J. E. Davin and her library staff at Soil Bureau, NZDSIR, for their
patient work in locating and obtaining many of the references quoted in this paper.
Numerous people helped with unpublished information about individual islands, but I
would particularly like to thank Drs Anthony Cheke and Chris Feare, Mr David Todd
and Dr J. Morgan Williams. Earlier drafts of the paper were improved as a result of
critical comments received from Pamela J. Atkinson, and Drs Phil Cowan, John Flux
and Phil Moors.

REFERENCES

Abbott, W. L. 1893. Notes on the natural history of Aldabra, Assumption & Glorioso Islands,
    Indian Ocean. *Proc. U.S. National Mus.* **16**, 759–64.
Aitken, R. T. 1930. Ethnology of Tubuai. *Bernice P. Bishop Mus. Bull.* **70**.
Alicata, J. E. & McCarthy, D. D. 1964. On the incidence and distribution of the rat lungworm
    Angiostrongylus cantonensis in the Cook Islands, with observations made in New Zealand and
    Western Samoa. *Canad. J. Zool.* **42**, 605–11.
Allardyce, W. L. 1886. Rotooma and the Rotoomans. *Queensland Geographical Jour.* **1**, 130–44.
Allen, G. M. 1911. Mammals of the West Indies. *Bull. Mus. Comp. Zoology* **54**, 175–263.
Amerson, A. B. 1969. Ornithology of the Marshall and Gilbert Islands. *Atoll Res. Bull.* **127**, 1–348.
Andrews, C. W. 1899. A description of Christmas Island (Indian Ocean). *J. Roy. Geog. Soc.* **13**,
    17–39.

ANDREWS, C. W. 1900. *A monograph of Christmas Island (Indian Ocean)*. British Museum of Natural History, London.
ANDREWS, C. W. 1909. On the fauna of Christmas Island. *Proc. Zool. Soc.* **1909**, 101–3.
ANTHONY, A. W. 1925. Expedition to Guadelupe Island, Mexico, in 1922. The birds and mammals. *Proc. Calif. Acad. Sci.* **XIV**, 277–320.
ATKINSON, I. A. E. 1973. Spread of the ship rat (*Rattus r. rattus* L.) in New Zealand. *J. of the Roy. Soc. N.Z.* **3**, 457–72.
ATKINSON, I. A. E. 1977. A reassessment of factors, particularly *Rattus rattus* L., that influenced the decline of endemic forest birds in the Hawaiian Islands. *Pac. Sci.* **31**, 109–33.
ATKINSON, I. A. E. 1978. Evidence for the effects of rodents on the vertebrate wildlife of New Zealand islands. *In:* Dingwall, P. R., Atkinson, I. A. E. & Hay, C. (eds) The ecology and control of rodents in New Zealand Nature Reserves. *N. Z. Dept. Lands and Survey Information Series* **4**, 7–30.
ATKINSON, I. A. E. & BELL, B. D. 1973. Offshore and outlying islands. *In:* Williams, G. R. (ed.) *The Natural History of New Zealand:* 372–92. A. H. and A. W. Reed, Wellington.
AUSTIN, O. L. 1948. Predation by the Common Rat (*Rattus norvegicus*) in the Cape Cod colonies of nesting terns. *Bird Banding* **19**, 60–5.
AXELL, H. E. 1973. Minsmere (Part II). *In: Manual of Wetland Management*, International Waterfowl Research Bureau, Game Biology Station, Kalo, DK 8410, Runde, Denmark.
BAILEY, A. M. & SORENSEN, J. H. 1962. *Subantarctic Campbell Island*. Proc. No. 10 of the Denver Museum of Natural History. Dist. by A. H. and A. W. Reed, Wellington.
BALHAM, R. W. 1952. Grey and Mallard Ducks in the Manawatu distrtict, New Zealand. *Emu* **52**, 163–91.
BARABASH-NIKIFOROV, I. 1938. Mammals of the Commander Islands and the surrounding sea. *J. Mammal.* **19**, 423–9.
BARKER-WEBB, P. & BERTHELOT, S. 1835. *Histoire Naturelle des Iles Canaries*. Vol. II. Zoologie. Béthune, Paris.
BARNETT, S. A. 1976. *The Rat. A study in behaviour*. Revised ed. Australian National University Press, Canberra.
BARNWELL, P. J. 1948. *Visits and Dispatches (Mauritius 1598–1948)*. The Standard Printing Establishment, Port Louis, Mauritius.
BARRÉ, BRAYER DU 1773. Description de l'Isle Seychelles. *In:* Fauvel, A. A. 1909. *Unpublished documents on the history of the Seychelles Islands anterior to 1810:* 215. Seychelles Government. (Held by Public Library: Mahé, Seychelles.)
BARRETT-HAMILTON, G. E. H. & HINTON, M. A. C. 1912. *A History of British Mammals, Vol. 2.* Gurney & Jackson, London.
BATY, G. C. E. 1895. *Report on the Aldabra group of islands*. Crown Lands Department, Mahé, Seychelles.
BAYNE, C. J., COGAN, B. H., DIAMOND, A. W., FRAZIER, J., GRUBB, P., HUTSON, A., POORE, M. E. D., STODDART, D. R. & TAYLOR, J. D. 1970. Geography and ecology of Astove. *Atoll Res. Bull.* **136**, 115–20.
BELLWOOD, P. S. 1979. The oceanic context. *In:* Jennings, J. D. (ed.) *The Prehistory of Polynesia:* 6–26. Harvard University Press, Cambridge, Mass.
BELLWOOD, P. S. 1980. The Peopling of the Pacific. *Sci. Amer.* **243**, 138–47.
BENSON, C. W. 1960. The birds of the Comoro Islands: results of the British Ornithologists' Union Centenary Expedition 1958. *Ibis* **103b**, 5–106.
BERGER, A. J. 1981. *Hawaiian Birdlife* 2nd ed. University Press of Hawaii, Honolulu.
BERRY, R. J. & JOHNSTON, J. L. 1980. *The Natural History of Shetland*. Collins, London.
BLACKBURN, A. 1965. Muttonbird Islands diary. *Notornis* **12**, 191–207.
BOURNE, W. R. P. 1981. Rats as avian predators: discussion. *Atoll Res. Bull.* **255**, 69–72.
BOURNE, W. R. P. & DAVID, A. C. F. 1983. Henderson Island, central South Pacific, and its birds. *Notornis* **30**, 233–52.
BOWKER, G. 1965. Predators of the Mutton-birds. *Emu* **65**, 290.
BRANDER, J. 1940. *Tristan da Cunha, 1506–1902*. Allen and Unwin, London.
BRECHBILL, R. A. 1977. Status of the Norway rat. *In:* Merritt, M. L. & Fuller, R. G. (eds) *The environment of Amchitka Island, Alaska*. U.S. Energy Research and Development Administration, Washington.

BRIGHT, D. B. & HOGUE, C. L. 1972. A synopsis of the burrowing land crabs of the world and list of their arthropod symbionts and burrow associates. *Contributions in Science of the Los Angeles County Natural History Museum* **220**, 1–58.

BROOKE, R. K. 1981. Layard's bird hunting visit to Tromelin or Sandy Island in December 1856. *Atoll Res. Bull.* **255**, 73–82.

BROSSET, A. 1963. Statut actuel des mammifères des îles Galapagos. *Mammalia* **27**, 323–38.

BROWN, P. E. 1949. The breeding of avocets in England, 1948. *British Birds* **42**, 2–13.

BRYAN, E. H. 1942. *American Polynesia and the Hawaiian Chain.* Tongg Publishing Co., Honolulu.

BULLER, W. L. 1888. *A History of the Birds of New Zealand* (2nd ed.) 2 vols. The author, London.

BUXTON, P. A. & HOPKINS, G. E. H. 1927. Researches in Polynesia and Melanesia. *London School Hyg. trop. Med. Mem.* **1**.

CAMPBELL, J. M. 1892. On the appearance of the brown rat (*Mus decumanus* Pallas) on the Ailsa Craig. *Ann. Scot. Nat. Hist.* **1**, 132–4.

CAMPBELL, R. W. 1968. Alexandrian Rat predation on Ancient Murrelet eggs. *Murrelet* **49**, 38.

CHASEN, F. N. & KLOSS, C. B. 1927. Spolia Mentawiensia—Mammals. *Zool. Soc. of London Proc.* **53**, 797–840.

CHEKE, A. (in press). An ecological history of the Mascarene Islands, with particular reference to the extinction and introduction of land vertebrates. *In:* Diamond, A. W. (ed.) *Studies of Mascarene Island Birds, Chap. 1.* Cambridge University Press, Cambridge.

CHEKE, A. S. & LAWLEY, J. C. (in press). The biological history of Agalega (Indian Ocean), with special reference to birds and other land vertebrates. *Atoll Res. Bull.*

CLARK, D. A. 1981. Foraging patterns of black rats across a desert-montane forest gradient in the Galapagos Islands. *Biotropica* **13**, 182–94.

COHIC, F. 1959. Report on a visit to the Chesterfield Islands, September 1957. *Atoll Res. Bull.* **63**, 1–11.

COULTER, M. C., CRUZ, F. & BEACH, T. (this vol.). A programme to save the Dark-rumped Petrel, *Pterodroma phaeopygia* on Floreana Island, Galapagos, Ecuador.

COPPINGER, R. W. 1883. *Cruise of the 'Alert'. Four years in Patagonia, Polynesia and Mascarene waters (1878–82).* W. Swan Sonnenschein, London.

COTT, H. B. 1952. The palatability of birds eggs; illustrated by three seasons experiments (1947, 1948 and 1950) on the food preferences of the rat (*Rattus norvegicus*). *Proc. Zool. Soc. Lond.* **122**, 1–54.

COWARD, T. A. 1914. Faunal survey of Rostherne Mere. II. Vertebrata. *Mem. Proc. Mench. lit. phil. Soc.* **58**, 1–37.

CRAMP, S. (ed.) 1980. *Handbook of the Birds of Europe, the Middle East and North Africa. Vol. II.* Oxford University Press, London.

CRAMP, S. (ed.) 1983. *Handbook of the Birds of Europe, the Middle East and North Africa. Vol. III.* Oxford University Press, London.

CUMPSTON, J. S. 1968. *Macquarie Island.* Antarctic Division, Dept. Ext. Affairs, Australia.

DARWIN, C. 1839. *The Zoology of the Voyage of H.M.S. Beagle during the years 1832–1836.* Smith, Elder, London.

DAVIDSON, J. 1979. New Zealand. *In:* Jennings, J. D. (ed.) *The Prehistory of Polynesia:* 222–48. Harvard University Press, Cambridge, Mass.

DE GROOT, D. S. 1927. The Californian Clapper Rail, its nesting habits, enemies and habitat. *Condor* **29**, 259–70.

DERENNE, P. & MOUGIN, J. L. 1976. Données écologiques sur les mammifères introduits de l'isle aux Cochons, Archipel Crozet (46° 06′ S 50° 14′ E). *Mammalia* **40**, 21–53.

DERRICK, R. A. 1951. *The Fiji Islands.* Govnt. Printing Dept. Suva, Fiji.

DESPIN, B., MOUGIN, J. L. & SEGONZAC, M. 1972. Oiseaux et mammifères de l'isle de l'Est, archipel Crozet (46° 25′ S 52° 12′ E). *Comité National Français des Recherches Antarctiques* **31**, 1–106.

DODSON, J. J. & FITZGERALD, G. J. 1980. Observations on the breeding biology of the boobies (Sulidae) at Clipperton Island, eastern Pacific. *Le Naturaliste Canadien* **107**, 259–67.

DONALDSON, H. H. 1924. *The Rat. Data and reference tables for the Albino Rat* (Mus. norvegicus albinus) *and the Norway Rat* (Mus norvegicus). 2nd ed. revised. Published by the author, Philadelphia.

DORST, J. & MILON, PH. 1964. Acclimatation et conservation de la nature dans les îles Subantarctiques Françaises. *In:* Carrick, R. *et al.* (eds) 1ᵉʳ Symposium de Biologie antarctique: 579–88.

Douglas, G. 1969. Draft check list of Pacific Oceanic Islands. *Micronesica* 5, 332–463.

Duffey, E. 1964. The terrestrial ecology of Ascension Island. *J. Applied Ecol.* 1, 219–51.

Dumbleton, L. J. 1955. Rat poisoning in French Oceania. *Quart. Bull. South Pacific Commission* 5, 15–16.

Eckhardt, R. C. 1972. Introduced plants and animals in the Galapagos Islands. *Bio-Science* 22, 585–90.

Elliott, H. F. I. 1972. Island ecosystems and conservation with particular reference to the biological significance of islands of the Indian ocean and consequential research and conservation needs. *J. Mar. Biol. Assoc. India* 14, 578–608.

Ellis, A. F. 1936. *Adventuring in Coral Seas*. Angus & Robertson, Sydney.

Elton, C. S. 1958. *The Ecology of Invasions by Animals and Plants*. Methuen, London.

Falla, R. A. 1965. Birds and mammals of the subantarctic islands. *Proc. N.Z. Ecol. Soc.* 12, 63–8.

Feare, C. J. 1976. The exploitation of Sooty Tern eggs in the Seychelles. *Biol. Conserv.* 10, 169–81.

Feare, C. J. 1979. Ecology of Bird Island, Seychelles. *Atoll Res. Bull.* 226, 1–29.

Fernandez, O. 1979. Observations sur le puffin cendré *Calonectris diomedea* nicheur sur les iles Marseillaises. *Alauda* 47, 65–72.

Fineran, B. A. 1964. An outline of the vegetation of the Snares Islands. *Trans. Roy. Soc. N.Z. (Botany)* 2, 229–36.

Fisher, J. 1948. St Kilda. A natural experiment. *New Nat.* 1, 91–108.

Fisher, H. I. 1975. Mortality and survival in the Laysan Albatross *Diomedea immutabilis*. *Pacific Sci.* 29, 279–300.

Fisher, H. I. & Baldwin, P. H. 1946. War and the birds on Midway Atoll. *Condor* 48, 3–15.

Flack, J. A. D. & Lloyd, B. D. 1978. The effects of rodents on the breeding success of the South Island Robin. *In:* Dingwall, P. R., Atkinson, I. A. E. & Hay, C. (eds) The ecology and control of rodents in New Zealand Nature Reserves. *N.Z. Dept. Lands and Survey Information Series* 4, 59–66.

Fleet, R. R. 1972. Nesting success of the red-tailed tropicbird on Kure Atoll. *Auk* 89, 651–9.

Fleming, C. A. 1962. The extinction of moas and other animals during the Holocene period. *Notornis* 10, 113–17.

Fleming, C. A. 1969. Rats and moa extinction. *Notornis* 16, 210–11.

Fosberg, F. R. 1959. Notes on rats and pest control on Wake Island, 1952. *In:* Bryan, E. H. Notes on the geography and natural history of Wake Island. *Atoll Res. Bull.* 66, 7–8.

Freycinet, L. De 1824. Voyage autour du monde, exécuté sur les corvettes de S. M. l'Uranie et la Physicienne, pendant les années 1817, 1818, 1819 et 1820. Historique Vol. II, pt. 1.

Fry, C. H. 1961. Notes on the birds of Annobon and the other islands in the Gulf of Guinea. *Ibis* 103a, 267–76.

Fryer, J. C. F. 1911. The structure and formation of Aldabra and neighbouring islands—with notes on their flora and fauna. *Trans. Linn. Soc. London. Second Series—Zoology* 14, 397–442.

Fuller, P. J. & Burbidge, A. A. 1981. *The birds of Pelsart Island, Western Australia*. Dept. Fisheries & Wildlife Report No. 44. Western Australian Wildlife Research Centre. Wanneroo, W.A.

Garth, J. S. 1973. The brachyuran crabs of Easter Island. *Proceedings of the California Academy of Sciences* 39, 311–36.

Gibson-Hill, C. A. 1947a. A note on the mammals of Christmas Island. *Bull. Raffles Mus.* 18, 166–7.

Gibson-Hill, C. A. 1947b. Notes on the birds of Christmas Island. *Bull. Raffles Mus.* 18, 87–165.

Gibson-Hill, C. A. 1948. Notes on the Cocos-Keeling Islands. *J. Malayan Branch Royal Asiatic Soc.* 20, 140–202.

Gill, W. W. 1885. *Jottings from the Pacific*. Religious Tract Society. London.

Gill, B. J. 1983. Breeding habits of the grey warbler. *Notornis* 30, 137–65.

Goodridge, C. M. 1843. *Narrative of a voyage to the South seas and the shipwreck of the 'Princess of Wales' cutter with an account of two years residence on an uninhabited island*. 5th ed. C. M. Goodridge, Exeter.

Gosse, P. 1938. *St Helena, 1502–1938*. Cassell & Co., London.

Grant, C. 1801. *The history of Mauritius or the isle of France and the neighbouring islands, from their first discovery to the present time; composed principally from the papers and memoirs of Baron Grant, who resided twenty years in the island*. G. and M. Nichol, London.

GRANT, S. G., PETTIT, T. N. & WHITTOW, G. C. 1981. Rat predation on Bonin Petrel eggs on Midway Atoll. *J. Field Ornith.* **52**, 336–8.

GRAY, H. 1981. *Christmas Island—Naturally—The natural history of an isolated oceanic island.* Howard Gray, Geraldton, Western Australia.

GREEN, R. C. 1976. Lapita sites in the Santa Cruz group. *In:* Green, R. C. & Cresswell, M. M. Southeast Solomon Islands Culture History. *Roy. Soc. N.Z. Bull.* **11**, 245–65.

GREEN, R. C. 1979. Lapita. *In:* Jennings, J. D. (ed.) *The Prehistory of Polynesia:* 27–60. Harvard University Press, Cambridge, Mass.

GREENWAY, J. C. 1967. Extinct and Vanishing Birds of the World. *Amer. Comm. Int. Wildl. Prot. Spec. Pub.* **13**.

GROSS, A. O. 1912. Observations on the Yellow-billed Tropicbird (*Phaethon americanus* Grant) at the Bermuda Islands. *Auk* **29**, 49–71.

GUTHRIE-SMITH, H. 1925. *Bird Life on Island and Shore.* William Blackwood & Sons, Edinburgh and London.

HANNA, G. D. 1920. Mammals of the St Matthew islands, Bering Sea. *J. Mammalogy* **1**, 118–22.

HARRIS, M. P. 1970. The biology of an endangered species, the dark-rumped petrel (*Pterodroma phaeopygia*), in the Galapagos Islands. *Condor* **72**, 76–84.

HARRIS, M. P. 1973. The Galapagos avifauna. *Condor* **75**, 265–78.

HECTOR, J. 1869. Notes on the geology of the outlying islands of New Zealand; with extracts from official reports. *Trans. N.Z. Inst.* **2**, 176.

HEDLEY, C. 1897. The ethnology of Funafuti. *Mem. Aust. Mus.* **3**, 229–304.

HEINRICH, D. 1976. Bemerkungen zum mittelalterlichen Vorkommen der Wanderratte (*Rattus norvegicus* Berkenhout, 1769) in Schleswig-Holstein. *Zool. Anz. Jena* **196**, 273–8.

HELLER, E. 1904. Mammals of the Galapagos archipelago, exclusive of the Cetacea. *Proc. Calif. Acad. Sci. Ser. 3. Zoology* **3**, 233–51.

HERMS, W. B. 1926. *Diocalandra taitensis* (Guerin) and other coconut pests of Fanning and Washington Islands. *Philip. J. Sci.* **30**, 243–74.

HEYERDAHL, T. 1940. Marquesas Islands. *Proc. Sixth Pac. Sci. Cong. of the Pac. Sci. Assoc.* **IV**, 543–6.

HILL, J. E. 1956. The mammals of Rennell Island. *In: The Natural History of Rennell Island, British Solomon Islands* **1**, 73–84. Danish Science Press, Copenhagen.

HILL, D. A., ROBERTSON, H. A. & SUTHERLAND, W. J. 1983. Brown Rats (*Rattus norvegicus*) climbing to obtain sloes and blackberries. *J. Zool. Lond.* **200**, 302.

HINDWOOD, K. A. 1940. The birds of Lord Howe Island. *Emu* **40**, 1–86.

HINDWOOD, K. A. 1964. Birds of the Coral Sea isles. *Australian Natural History* **14**, 305–11.

HOLDGATE, M. W. & WACE, N. M. 1961. The influence of man on the floras and faunas of southern islands. *Polar Record.* **10**, 475–93.

HOUGH, R. 1975. Islands beyond Cape Horn. *Geog. Mag.* **47**, 561–6.

HOWLAND, L. 1955. Howland Island, its birds and rats, as observed by a certain Mr Stetson in 1854. *Pacific Sci.* **9**, 95–106.

IMBER, M. J. 1975. Petrels and predators. *XII Bulletin of the International Council for Bird Preservation:* 260–3.

IMBER, M. J. 1976. Breeding biology of the Grey-faced Petrel *Pterodroma macroptera gouldi. Ibis* **118**, 51–64.

INDER, S. 1977. *Pacific Islands Yearbook 12th ed.* Pacific Publications, Sydney.

JENNINGS, J. D. (ed.) 1979. *The Prehistory of Polynesia.* Harvard University Press, Cambridge, Mass.

JOHNSON, M. S. 1945. Rodent control on Midway Islands. *U.S. Nav. Med. Bull.* **45**, 384–98.

JOHNSON, D. H. 1946. The rat population of a newly established military base in the Solomon Islands. *U.S. Naval Med. Bull.* **46**, 1628–32.

JOHNSON, D. H. 1962. Rodents and other Micronesian mammals collected. *In:* Storer, T. I. (ed.) Pacific Island Rat Ecology. *Bernice P. Bishop Mus. Bull.* **225**, 21–38.

JOHNSTONE, G. W. 1982. Zoology. *In:* Veenstra, C. & Manning, J., Expedition to the Australian territory of Heard and McDonald Islands 1980. *Dept. National Development & Energy Tech. Report* **31**, 33–9.

JONES, J. M. 1884. The mammals of Bermuda. *Bull. U.S. nat. Mus.* **25**, 145–61.

JONES, E. 1977. Ecology of the feral cat, *Felis catus* (L.) (Carnivora: Felidae) on Macquarie Island. *Australian Wildlife Research* **4**, 249–62.

JONES, R. D. & BYRD, G. V. 1979. Interrelationships between seabirds and introduced mammals. *In:* Bartonek, C. J. & Nettleship, D. N. (eds) Conservation of marine birds of northern North America. *U.S. Fish and Wildl. Serv. Res. Rep.* **11**, 221–6.

JOUANIN, C. & PAULIAN, P. 1960. Recherches sur des ossements d'oiseaux provenant de l'île Nouvelle-Amsterdam (océan Indien). *12th Int. Ornithological Congress, Helsinki, 1958* **1**, 368–72.

KENYON, K. W. 1961. Birds of Amchitka Island, Alaska. *Auk* **78**, 305–26.

KEPLER, C. B. 1967. Polynesian Rat predation on nesting Laysan Albatrosses and other Pacific seabirds. *Auk* **84**, 426–30.

KING, W. B. 1973. Conservation status of birds of central Pacific islands. *Wilson Bulletin* **85**, 89–103.

KING, W. B. 1981. *Endangered Birds of the World.* The ICBP Bird Red Data Book. Smithsonian Institution Press, Washington.

KINNEAR, N. B. 1935. Zoological notes from the voyage of Peter Mundy, 1655–56 (a) Birds. *Proc. Linn. Soc. 1934–1935:* 32–3.

KIRKPATRICK, R. D. 1966. Mammals of Johnston Atoll. *J. Mammal.* **47**, 728–9.

KOROIA, N. 1934. (Rodents of the South Sea Islands in the collection of Marquis Yamashina). *Botany and Zoology, theoretical and applied (Tokyo)* **2**, 1012–20.

KURODA, N. 1954. Report on a trip to Marcus Island with notes on the birds. *Pac. Sci.* **8**, 84–93.

LA CAILLE, N. L. 1763. Journal Historique des Voyages Fait au Cap de Bonne-Espérance. Guillyn, Paris.

LANDT, G. 1800. *Forsog til en Beskrivelse over Faeroerne.* Copenhagen. (Reprinted as *A Description of the Feroe Islands,* London, 1810.)

LEFROY, J. H. 1877–1879. *Memorials of the discovery and early settlement of the Bermudas or Somers Islands 1515–1652. Compiled from the Colonial Records and other original sources.* Vol. 1 and 2. Longmans, Green & Co., London.

LEGUAT, F. 1708. *Voyage et Adventures.* D. Mortier, London.

LESEL, R. & DERENNE, P. 1975. Introducing animals to Iles Kerguelen. *Polar Record* **17** (110), 485–94.

LLOYD, R. E. 1909. The races of Indian rats. *Rec. Indian Mus.* **3**, 1–100.

LÖNNBERG, E. 1906. Contributions to the fauna of South Georgia. I. *K. svenska Vetensk Akad. Handl.* **40**, no. 5.

LOVEGROVE, T. G. 1982. *Report to the District Office of the Lands and Survey Department, Wellington, on the effects of the re-introduction of North Island Saddlebacks* (Philesturnus carunculatus rufusater) *to Kapiti Island Nature Reserve.* Unpub. report, March 1982.

LOVEGROVE, T. G. 1983. *Report to the District Office of the Lands and Survey Department, Wellington, on the re-introduction of North Island Saddlebacks* (Philesturnus carunculatus rufusater) *to Kapiti Island Nature Reserve.* Second Annual Report. Unpub. report, July 1983.

MACDONALD, S. D. 1883 [1886]. Notes on Sable Island. *Proc. and Trans. Nova Scotia Inst. Nat. Science* **VI**, 12–33.

MACFARLAND, C. G., VILLA, J. & TORO, B. 1974. The Galapagos Giant Tortoises (*Geochelone elephantopus*). Part 1: Status of the Surviving populations. *Biol. Conserv.* **6**, 118–33.

MALZY, P. 1966. Oiseaux et mammifères de l'île Europa. *Mémoires Séries A Zoologie—Museum National d'Histoire Naturelle (Paris)* **41**, 23–7.

MARCK, J. C. 1975. *On the origin and dispersal of the proto-nuclear Micronesians.* Unpub. thesis. Univ. of Iowa.

MARPLES, R. R. 1955. *Rattus exulans* in Western Samoa. *Pac. Sci.* **9**, 171–6.

MARSHALL, J. T. 1962. Geographic distribution and colour phases of Micronesian rodents. *In:* Storer, T. I. (ed.) Pacific Island Rat Ecology. *Bernice P. Bishop Mus. Bull.* **225**, 39–44.

MCLELLAN, M. E. 1926. Expedition to the Revillagigedo Islands, Mexico, in 1925, VI. The birds and mammals. *Proc. Calif. Acad. Sciences* (4th Series) **15**, 279–322.

MEADS, M. J., WALKER, K. J. & ELLIOTT, G. P. (1984). Status, conservation and management of the land snails of the genus *Powelliphanta* (Mollusca: Pulmonata). *New Zealand J. Zool.* **11**, 277–306.

MEDWAY, D. G. 1971. Sub-fossil avian remains from the Awakino-Mahoenui area. *Notornis* **18**, 218–19.

MEDWAY, LORD & MARSHALL, A. G. 1975. Terrestrial vertebrates of the New Hebrides: origin and distribution. *Phil. Trans. Roy. Soc. Lond. B.* **272**, 423–65.

MERTON, D. V. 1970. Kermadec Islands Expedition reports: a general account of birdlife. *Notornis* **17**, 147–99.
MERTON, D. V., MORRIS, R. B. & ATKINSON, I. A. E. (1984). Lek behaviour in a parrot: the Kakapo *Strigops habroptilus* of New Zealand. *Ibis.* **126**, 277–83.
METRAUX, A. 1940. Ethnology of Easter Island. *Bernice P. Bishop Mus. Bull.* **160**, 1–432.
METRAUX, A. 1957. *Easter Island a stone age civilization of the Pacific.* (Transl. by M. Bullock.) A Deutsch, London.
MIDDLETON, A. D. 1935. Factors controlling the population of the Partridge (*Perdix perdix*) in Great Britain. *Proc. Zool. Soc. Lond.* (1935): 795–815.
MILLAIS, J. G. 1905. *The Mammals of Great Britain and Ireland.* Vol. II. Longmans, Green & Co., London.
MILLENER, P. R. 1981. *The Quaternary avifauna of the North Island, New Zealand.* Unpublished Ph.D thesis, University of Auckland.
MILLER, G. S. 1902. The mammals of the Andaman and Nicobar Islands. *Proc. U.S. Nat. Mus.* **24**, 751–95.
MILNE-EDWARDS, A. 1873. Recherches sur la faune ancienne des Iles Mascareignes. *Ann. Sci. Nat. Zool.* (5), 19 art. 3: 1–31.
MOLLER, A. P. 1983. Damage by rats *Rattus norvegicus* to breeding birds on Danish islands. *Biol. Conserv.* **25**, 5–18.
MOMIYAMA, T. T. 1930. On the birds of Bonin and the Iwo-Islands. *Bull. Bio-Geogr. Soc. Japan* **1**, 89–186.
MOORS, P. J. 1983. Predation by mustelids and rodents on the eggs and chicks of native and introduced birds in Kowhai Bush, New Zealand. *Ibis* **125**, 137–54.
MOORS, P. J. & ATKINSON, I. A. E. 1984. Predation on seabirds by introduced animals and factors affecting its severity. *ICBP Tech. Pubn.* No. 2.
MORRIS, R. O. 1964. The birds of some islands in the Indian Ocean. *Sea Swallow* **16**, 68–79.
MORRISON, J. P. E. 1954. Animal ecology of Raroia Atoll, Tuamotus. *Atoll Res. Bull.* **34**, 1–26.
MOSELEY, H. N. 1879. *Notes by a Naturalist. An account of observations made during the Voyage of H.M.S. 'Challenger' round the world in the years 1872–1876.* Werner, London.
MOUGIN, J. L. 1969. Ecological notes on the Kerguelen Petrel *Pterodroma brevirostris* of Possession Island (Crozet Archipelago). *L'Oiseau et la Revue Française d'Ornithologie* **39**, 58–81.
MOUGIN, J. L. 1975. Ecologie comparée des Procellariidae antarctiques et subantarctiques. *Comité National Français des Recherches Antarctiques* No. **36**.
MOULTON, J. M. 1961. Some observations on the Heron Island fauna. *Atoll Res. Bull.* **82**, 15–16.
MUNRO, G. C. 1945. Tragedy in bird life. *Elepaio* **5**, 48–51.
MURPHY, R. C. 1917. Faunal conditions in South Georgia. *Science* **46**, 112–13.
MURPHY, R. C. 1936. *Oceanic Birds of South America* (2 volumes). American Museum of Natural History, New York.
NEWLANDS, W. A. 1975. *St Brandon: Fauna conservation and management.* Unpub. report to the Ministry of Agriculture and the Environment, Mauritius.
NORMAN, F. I. 1975. The murine rodents *Rattus rattus, exulans*, and *norvegicus* as avian predators. *Atoll Res. Bull.* **182**, 1–12.
OLIVER, W. R. B. 1955. *New Zealand Birds* (2nd ed.). A. H. and A. W. Reed, Wellington.
OLSON, S. L. 1975. Paleornithology of St Helena Island, South Atlantic Ocean. *Smithsonian Contributions to Paleobiology* **23**, 1–49.
OLSON, S. L. 1981. Natural history of vertebrates on the Brazilian islands of the mid south Atlantic. *National Geographic Society Research Reports* **13**, 481–92.
OLSON, S. L. & JAMES, H. F. 1982. Prodromus of the fossil avifauna of the Hawaiian Islands. *Smithsonian Contributions to Zoology* **365**, 1–59.
ORR, R. T. 1966. Evolutionary aspects of the mammalian fauna of the Galapagos. *In:* Bowman, R. I. (ed.) *The Galapagos: Proceedings of the Symposia of the Galapagos International Scientific Project:* 276–81. University of California Press, Berkeley.
OSBECK, P. 1771. *A Voyage to China and the East Indies.* Vol. 2. Transl. from the German by J. R. Forster. Benjamin White, London.
PAGE, H. M. & WILLASON, S. W. 1982. Distribution patterns of terrestrial hermit crabs at Enewetak Atoll, Marshall Islands. *Pac. Sci.* **36**, 107–17.

PALMER, T. S. 1898. The danger of introducing noxious animals and birds. *U.S. Dept. of Agriculture Yearbook* **1898**, 87–110.

PARSLOW, J. 1973. *Breeding birds of Britain and Ireland.* T. & A. D. Poyser, Berkhamsted.

PATTON, J. L., Yang, S. Y. & Myers, P. 1975. Genetic and morphologic divergence among introduced rat populations (*Rattus rattus*) of the Galapagos Archipelago, Equador. *Syst. Zool.* **24**, 296–310.

PEALE, T. E. 1848. *United States Exploring Expedition.* Vol. 8. Mammalia and Ornithology. Lea and Blanchard, Philadelphia.

PENNY, M. J. & DIAMOND, A. W. 1971. The White-throated Rail *Dryolimnas cuvieri* on Aldabra. *Phil. trans. Roy. Soc. Lond. B.* **260**, 529–48.

PERNETTA, J. C. & WATLING, D. 1978. The introduced and native terrestrial vertebrates of Fiji. *Pac. Sci.* **32**, 223–44.

PÉRON, E. 1824. *Memoires du Capitaine Peron sur ses voyages.* 2 vols. Bressot-Thivars, Paris.

PETERSEN, A. 1979. The breeding birds of Flatey and some adjoining islets, in Breidafjordur, N.W. Iceland (English summary). *Natturufraedingurinn* **49**, 229–56.

PETERSEN, A. 1981. *Breeding biology and feeding ecology of black guillemots.* Unpub. D.Phil. thesis, University of Oxford.

PIGAFETTA, A. 1906. *Magellan's Voyage Around the World.* Transl. and edit. by J. A. Robertson. 3 vols. Cleveland.

PYE, T. & BONNER, W. N. 1980. Feral brown rats, *Rattus norvegicus*, in South Georgia (South Atlantic Ocean). *J. Zool., Lond.* **192**, 237–55.

QUOY, J. R. C. & GAIMARD, J. P. 1824. Voyage autour du monde, exécuté sur les corvettes de S. M. l'Uranie et la Physicienne, pendant les années 1817, 1818, 1819 et 1820. Vol. 4. Zoologie. Paris, Chez Pillet.

RAMSAY, G. W. 1978. A review of the effect of rodents on the New Zealand invertebrate fauna. *In:* Dingwell, P. R., Atkinson, I. A. E. & Hay, C. (eds) The ecology and control of rodents in New Zealand Nature Reserves. *N.Z. Dept. Lands & Survey Information Series* **4**, 89–95.

RECHER, H. F. & CLARK, S. S. 1974. A biological survey of Lord Howe Island with recommendations for the conservation of the island's wildlife. *Biol. Conserv.* **6**, 263–73.

REVILLIOD, P. 1913. Les mammifères de la Nouvelle Caledonie et des isles Loyalty. *In:* Sarasin, F. & Roux, J. *Nova Caledonia:* A Zoologie. Vol. 1, 341–65. Forschunger in Neu-Caledonier und auf der Loyalty Inseln. Berlin, C. W. Kriedets Verlag.

REYNE, A. 1939. On the food habits of the coconut crab (*Birgus latro* L.) with notes on its distribution. *Archives Neerlandaises de Zoologie* **III**, 283–320.

RIDLEY, H. N. 1890. Notes on the zoology of Fernando Noronha. *Lin. Soc. London (Zoology)* **20**, 473–570.

RIPLEY, S. D. 1977. *Rails of the World.* Godine, Boston.

ROCKWELL, R. H. 1932. Southward through the doldrums. *Natural History* **32**, 424–36.

ROSSET, C. W. 1886. [Remarks on the Maldive Islands] *Proc. Zool. Soc. London* 1886: 295–6.

SACHET, M-H. 1962. Geography and land ecology of Clipperton Island. *Atoll Res. Bull.* **86**, 1–115.

SAEMUNDSSON, B. 1939. Mammalia. *Zoology of Iceland* **4**(76), 1–52.

SAKAGAMI, S. F. 1961. An ecological perspective of Marcus Island, with special reference to land animals. *Pac. Sci.* **15**, 82–104.

SCHWARTZ, C. W. & SCHWARTZ, E. R. 1950. Breeding habits of the Barred Dove in Hawaii with notes on weights and sex ratios. *Condor* **52**, 241–6.

SEALY, S. G. 1976. Biology of nesting Ancient Murrelets. *Condor* **78**, 294–306.

SEGONZAC, M. 1972. Données recentes sur la faune des îles Saint-Paul et Nouvelle Amsterdam. *L'Oiseau et R.F.O.* **42**, special no.: 3–68.

SEYCHELLES DEPARTMENT OF AGRICULTURE 1952. *Annual Report.*

SIMPSON, G. G. 1956. Zoogeography of West Indian mammals. *American Museum Novitates* **No. 1759**, 1–28.

SINOTO, Y. H. 1979. The Marquesas. *In:* Jennings, J. D. (ed.) *The Prehistory of Polynesia:* 110–34. Harvard University Press, Cambridge, Mass.

SMITH, S. P. 1902. Niue Island and its people. (Pt 1). *J. Polyn. Soc.* **11**, 80–106.

SMITH, F. J. 1968. Rat damage to coconuts in the Gilbert and Ellice Islands. *In: Rodents as factors in disease and economic loss.* Proceedings of a conference. Asia-Pacific Interchange, Honolulu, Hawaii: 55–7.

SMITH, F. J. 1970. La recherche sur les rats dans les atolls. *Oleagineux* **25**, 147–52.
SNODGRASS, R. E. & HELLER, E. 1902. The birds of Clipperton and Cocos Islands. *Proc. Wash. Acad. Sci.* **4**, 501–20.
SPECHT, J. 1978. The early mystery of Norfolk Island. *Australian Natural History* **19**, 218–23.
SPRUNT, A. 1948. The tern colonies of the Dry Tortugas Keys. *Auk* **65**, 1–19.
STAIR, J. B. 1897. *Old Samoa or Flotsam and Jetsam from the Pacific Ocean.* Religious Tract Society. London.
STAUB, F. 1970. Geography and ecology of Tromelin Island. *Atoll Res. Bull.* **136**, 197–209.
STEAD, E. F. 1936. *Unpublished letter to the Commissioner of Crown Lands, Blenheim.* Copy held by the New Zealand Wildlife Service, Dept. of Internal Affairs, Wellington.
STEADMAN, D. W. & RAY, C. E. 1982. The relationships of *Megaoryzomys curioi*, an extinct cricetine rodent (Muroidea: Muridae) from the Galapagos Islands, Ecuador. *Smithsonian Contributions to Paleobiology* **51**, 1–23.
STEINIGER, F. 1948. Biologische Beobachtungen an freilebenden Wanderratten auf Hallig Norderoog. *Zool. Anz.*, Suppl. **13**, 152–6.
STEJNEGER, L. 1883. Contributions to the history of the Commander Islands. No. 1. Notes on the natural history, including descriptions of new cetaceans. *Proc. U.S. Nat. Mus.* **6**, 58–89.
STODDART, D. R. 1971. Terrestrial fauna of Diego Garcia and other Chagos atolls. *Atoll Res. Bull.* **149**, 163–70.
STODDART, D. R., BENSON, C. W. & PEAKE, J. F. 1970. Ecological change and effects of phosphate mining on Assumption Island. *Atoll Res. Bull.* **136**, 121–145.
STODDART, D. R. & POORE, M. E. D. 1970a. Geography and ecology of Desroches. *Atoll Res. Bull.* **136**, 155–65.
STODDART, D. R. & POORE, M. E. D. 1970b. Geography and ecology of Farquhar Atoll. *Atoll Res. Bull.* **136**, 7–26.
STONER, D. 1937. The house rat as an enemy of the bank swallow. *J. Mammal.* **18**, 87–9.
TATE, G. H. H. 1935. Rodents of the genera *Rattus* and *Mus* from the Pacific Islands, collected by the Whitney South Sea Expedition, with a discussion of the origin and races of the Pacific Island Rat. *Bull. Amer. Mus. Nat. Hist.* **68**, 145–78.
TATE, G. H. H. 1950. The Muridae of the Cocos-Keeling Islands. *Bull. Raffles Mus.* **22**, 271–277.
TAYLOR, R. H. 1975. The distribution and status of introduced mammals on the Auckland Islands, 1972–73. *In:* Yaldwyn, J. C. (ed.) Preliminary results of the Auckland Islands expedition 1972–1973. *N.Z. Dept. of Lands and Survey Reserves Series* 1975/3.
TAYLOR, R. H. 1978. Distribution and interactions of rodent species in New Zealand. *In:* Dingwall, P. R., Atkinson, I. A. E. & Hay, C. (eds) The ecology and control of rodents in New Zealand Nature Reserves. *N.Z. Dept. of Lands and Survey Information Series* **4**, 135–141.
TAYLOR, R. H. 1979. Predation on Sooty Terns at Raoul Island by rats and cats. *Notornis* **26**, 199–202.
TEMPLE, R. C. & ANSTEY, L. M. (eds) 1936. *The Travels of Peter Mundy in Europe and Asia 1608–1667.* Vol. 5. Second series: 78. Hakluyt Society, London.
THIBAULT, J. C. 1973. Remarques sur l'appauvrissement de l'avifaune Polynesienne. *Societé des Etudes Océaniennes Bulletin* **15**, 262–70.
THORESEN, A. C. 1967. Ecological observations on Stanley and Green Islands, Mercury group. *Notornis* **14**, 182–200.
TICEHURST, C. B. 1932. *A History of the Birds of Suffolk.* Gurney & Jackson, London.
TICKELL, W. L. N. 1962. The Dove Prion, *Pachyptila desolata* Gmelin. *Falkland Islands Dependency Survey Sci. Rep.* **33**.
TOMICH, P. Q. 1969. Mammals in Hawaii: a synopsis and notational bibliography. *Spec. Pub. Bernice P. Bishop Mus.* **57**.
TOMKINS, R. J. (this vol.). Breeding success and mortality of dark-rumped petrels in the Galapagos, and control of their predators.
TORRES, D. & AGUAYO, A. 1971. Algunas observaciones sobre la fauna del archipelago de Juan Fernandez. Mammals. *Boletin de la Universidad de Chile* **112**, 34–5.
TRAVERS, H. H. 1870. On the Chatham Islands. *Trans. N.Z. Inst.* **1**, 119–27.
TWIBELL, J. 1973. The ecology of rodents in the Tonga Islands. *Pac. Sci.* **27**, 92–8.
VAN RIPER III, C., VAN RIPER, S. G., LEE GOFF, M. & LAIRD, M. 1982. The impact of malaria on birds in Hawaii Volcanoes National Park. *Cooperative National Park Resources Studies Unit University of Hawaii at Manoa Technical Report* **47**.

VÉLAIN, CH. 1877. Passage de Vénus sur le soleil (9 decembre 1874). Expédition française aux îles Saint-Paul et Amsterdam. Zoologie. Observations générales sur la faune des deux îles suivies d'une description des Mollusques. *Arch. Zool. Exp. et Gen.* **16**, 1–144.

VERMEER, K., SEALY, S. G., LEMON, M. & RODWAY, M. (1985). Effects of predation and potential environmental perturbances on nesting Ancient Murrelets in British Columbia. *ICBP Tech. Pubn.* No. 2.

VOELTSKOW, A. and others, 1902–1905. Wissenschaftliche Ergebisse der Reisen in Madagaskar und Ostafrika. *Abh. Senckenb. naturforsch. Ges.* **27**, 1–392.

WACE, N. M. & HOLDGATE, M. W. 1976. *Man and nature in the Tristan da Cunha Islands.* IUCN Monograph No. 6. International Union for Conservation of Nature and Natural Resources, Morges, Switzerland.

WAITE, E. R. 1897. The mammals, reptiles and fishes of Funafuti. *Aust. Mus. Memoir* **3**, 165–201.

WARHAM, J. & JOHNS, P. M. 1975. The University of Canterbury Antipodes Island expedition 1969. *J. Roy. Soc. N.Z.* **5**, 103–31.

WARNER, W. 1948. The present status of the Kagu, *Rhynochetos jubatus*, on New Calendonia. *Auk* **65**, 287–288.

WARNER, R. E. 1968. The role of introduced diseases in the extinction of the endemic Hawaiian avifauna. *Condor* **70**, 101–120.

WATERHOUSE, G. R. 1839. Mammalia. *In:* Darwin, C. *Zoology of the Voyage of H.M.S. Beagle.* Part 2.

WATERTON, C. 1836. Notes on the history and habits of the Brown, or Grey, Rat (*Mus decumanus*). *Magazine of Natural History* **9**, 1–6.

WATSON, J. S. 1953. Aliens in the forest. 3. The rat. *Forest and Bird*, August 1953: 10–12.

WATSON, J. S. 1956. The present distribution of *Rattus exulans* (Peale) in New Zealand. *N.Z. J. Sci. Tech.* **37**, 560–70.

WATSON, J. S. 1961. Rats in New Zealand: a problem of interspecific competition. *Proc. Ninth Pac. Sci. Cong. 1957* **19**. Zoology. Bangkok 1961.

WAYNE, R. 1849. Blackbird's eggs sucked by a rat. *Zoologist* **7**, 2495.

WESTERSKOV, K. 1960. *Birds of Campbell Island.* N.Z. Dept. of Internal Affairs, Wellington.

WHITAKER, A. H. 1973. Lizard populations on islands with and without Polynesian rats, *Rattus exulans* (Peale). *Proc. N.Z. Ecol. Soc.* **20**, 121–30.

WILKINSON, A. S. & WILKINSON, A. 1952. *Kapiti Bird Sanctuary.* Masterton Printing Co., Masterton.

WIRTZ, W. O. 1972. Population ecology of the Polynesian rat, *Rattus exulans*, on Kure Atoll, Hawaii. *Pac. Sci.* **26**, 433–64.

WILKES, C. 1845. *Narrative of the United States Exploring Expedition during the years 1838, 1839, 1840, 1841, 1842, under the command of Charles Wilkes.* 5 vol. and atlas. Lea & Blanchard, Philadelphia.

WILLIAMS, J. 1839. *A Narrative of Missionary Enterprises in the South Seas.* J. Snow, London.

WILLIAMS, G. R. 1960. The birds of the Pitcairn Islands. *Ibis* **102**, 58–70.

WILLIAMS, J. M. 1974. *The ecology and behaviour of Rattus species in relation to the yield of coconuts and cocoa in Fiji.* Unpub. Ph.D. thesis, University of Bath.

WILLIAMS, J. M. 1979. *Report on the rat situation in Nauru.* Unpub. N.Z. Ministry of Agriculture & Fisheries Report.

WILLIAMS, A. J., SIEGFRIED, W. R., BURGER, A. E. & BERRUTI, A. 1979. The Prince Edward Islands: a sanctuary for seabirds in the southern ocean. *Biol. Conserv.* **15**, 59–71.

WODZICKI, K. A. 1971. The birds of Niue Island, South Pacific: an annotated checklist. *Notornis* **18**, 291–304.

WODZICKI, K. A. 1972. Effect of rat damage on coconut production on Nukunonu Atoll, Tokelau Islands. *Oleagineux* **27**, 309–14.

WOOD-JONES, F. 1912. *Corals and Atolls.* Levell Reeve, London.

WOODS, R. W. 1975. *The Birds of the Falkland Islands.* Anthony Nelson, Oswestry, Shropshire.

WOODWARD, P. W. 1972. The natural history of Kure Atoll, northwestern Hawaiian Islands. *Atoll Res. Bull.* **164**, 1–318.

YALDWYN, J. C. & WODZICKI, K. 1979. Systematics and ecology of the land crabs (Decapoda: Coenobitidae, Grapsidae and Gecarcinidae) of the Tokelau Islands, Central Pacific. *Atoll Res. Bull.* **235**, 1–53.

YOSIDA, T. H. 1980. Cytogenetics of the Black Rat. Karyotype evolution and species differentiation. University of Tokyo Press, Tokyo.

PART II
REGIONAL SURVEYS OF THE STATUS OF ISLAND BIRDS

ICBP Technical Publication No. 3, 1985

THE CONSERVATION OF LANDBIRDS ON ISLANDS IN THE TROPICAL INDIAN OCEAN

A. W. DIAMOND

*Edward Grey Institute of Field Ornithology, Zoology Department, South Parks Rd.,
Oxford OX1 3PS, England
(Present address: Canadian Wildlife Service, Environment Canada, Ottawa
K1A 0E7, Canada)*

ABSTRACT

Islands in this region hold 29 taxa listed in the Red Data Book, including some of the smallest and most desperately threatened populations in the world. Apart from Hawaii, more island birds have become extinct, or are close to doing so, in the Mascarenes and Seychelles alone than on any other islands in the world. Islands range from densely forested archipelagos still at an early stage of development, through densely populated modern states to rocks stripped bare by guano mining.

Low coral islands had naturally depauperate avifaunas, lacking endemics and sometimes with no native breeding landbirds at all. Isolated high islands were often diverse with high endemicity (Mascarenes), while others even more isolated had puzzlingly poorly-differentiated avifaunas (Seychelles). Recent human history has dominated the fortunes of the avifaunas but needs to be seen against the long-term evolutionary background.

Conservation problems are reviewed in each major archipelago or island. Threatened species are listed and their status briefly reviewed. Pleas are made for urgent research on the status of birds in poorly-known archipelagos (especially Andamans, Nicobars and Comores), and for conservation to be directed towards the island as an ecosystem, rather than to individual species.

INTRODUCTION

The islands of the tropical Indian Ocean hold 29 taxa listed in the most recent ICBP Red Data Book (King 1981) and include some of the smallest and most desperately threatened bird populations in the world. More island birds have become extinct in historical times, or are close to doing so, in the Mascarenes and Seychelles than on any other islands in the world except for the Hawaiian archipelago.

This review attempts to identify present threats and predict future ones, and to suggest suitable strategies to counter likely hazards. The islands concerned range from densely forested archipelagos, still at a very primitive stage of development, through densely-populated and highly developed modern states, to remote islands stripped almost bare by guano mining. Almost all the causes of extinction of island birds are active in the region, which therefore can serve as a microcosm illustrating the general principles involved in conserving island birds.

The geographical, evolutionary, historical and ecological factors involved in shaping the avifaunas of the islands need to be outlined very briefly. Each island or archipelago has its own characteristic bird conservation problems which result from differences in these influences, and these need to be appreciated if effective strategies for conservation are to be designed and implemented. Unfortunately some of the islands are very poorly treated in the literature, so coverage is uneven; it is also influenced by my own field experience which is confined to the western part of the region (Mascarenes westward) south of the equator.

ISLAND TYPES

Three main geological types of island are represented in the region:

- – 'Low' islands: coral atolls and sand-banks. These are geologically very recent and in their present size and position, at least, date from the rise in sea-level which accompanied the end of the last major glacial epoch 8–12,000 years ago. Sand-banks are often ephemeral, changing topography, size and even location, and sometimes disappearing and reappearing according to changes in wind and sea conditions from year to year.
- – Raised limestone islands. These are former coral islands or atolls elevated much higher above sea level than low islands by either tectonic activity or a drop in sea-level, or both.
- – 'High' islands. These usually, though not necessarily, reach greater altitudes than raised islands, and are of volcanic (or exceptionally, in the Seychelles, granitic) origin.

The series from low to high islands corresponds with an increasing range of available habitats and with increasing age of the biota, to the extent that a high island is less vulnerable than a low one to the changes in sea level that have accompanied the glaciations of the last 2.5 million years. These changes in sea level have not only successively drowned and re-exposed a number of banks, ridges and islands, but have drastically altered their areas (Peake 1971; Taylor et al. 1979).

The islands considered here are oceanic rather than continental, i.e. they have never been connected to a continental land mass. The granitic Seychelles are of very ancient continental origin and represent a detached fragment of 'Gondwanaland' (the ancient continent comprising present-day Africa, India, Madagascar and Australia), but the Seychelles' connection with other continents was broken too long ago to affect its present avifauna. The continental islands fringing the region and surrounding Madagascar are not considered here. All the islands discussed can therefore be taken as having been colonised by birds over water rather than by dispersal over land.

A further property of an island that needs to be taken into account is whether it is a single isolate, or part of an archipelago with a number of near neighbours; opportunities for speciation, and for resisting extinction, are clearly very different in the two situations.

HUMAN INFLUENCE IN THE ISLANDS

A feature of the region is the large number of its islands which were uninhabited when they were first discovered by Europeans in the late fifteenth, sixteenth and seventeenth centuries. The myriads of tiny coralline and sand islands of the Amirantes, Chagos, and Cargados Carajos were perhaps understandably empty, but the larger high islands of the Seychelles and Mascarenes, and the raised Christmas Island in the east, were thickly

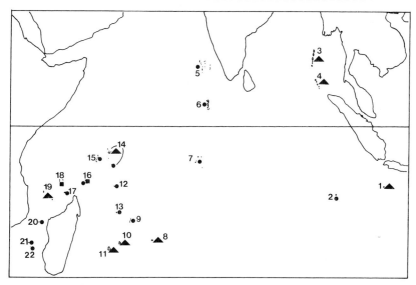

Figure 1: Map of the oceanic islands of the tropical Indian Ocean. ▲ = high islands; ■ = raised islands; ● = low islands.
1—Christmas. 2—Cocos-Keeling. 3—Andamans. 4—Nicobars. 5—Laccadives. 6—Maldives. 7—Chagos. 8—Rodrigues. 9—Cargados Carajos. 10—Mauritius. 11—Réunion. 12—Agalegas. 13—Tromelin. 14—Seychelles. 15—Amirantes. 16—Farquhars. 17—Gloriosa. 18—Aldabras. 19—Comores. 20—Juan de Nova. 21—Bassas da India. 22—Europa.

vegetated and for the most part well-watered so their lack of indigenous inhabitants is surprising. Even Madagascar was not colonised until about fifteen hundred years ago (from Indonesia). Only the Andamans and Nicobars appear to have been inhabited by aboriginal human populations; elsewhere, apart from passing Arab traders or Indonesian migrants, the island avifaunas have had to adapt to human settlement in only the last few hundred years.

ANNOTATED LIST OF ISLANDS

The islands and archipelagos of the region are listed in geographic order from east to west, starting with the northernmost (*Figure 1*). The current administrative authority is given immediately after the island name. Geographic and avifaunal data are taken chiefly from Elliott (1972) and Snow (1970), supplemented by more recent information where cited.

Christmas Island (Australia)
Technically a raised coral island but, with three peaks over 365m, Christmas is higher than many 'high' islands; it is also larger than many (135km^2). It is noted especially for its seabirds (see Feare, 1985) but of its seven native landbirds, two (the Imperial Pigeon (*Ducula whartoni*) and the Silver-eye (*Zosterops natalis*)) are endemic species and the others are racially distinct. The pigeon is listed as 'vulnerable' in the Red Data Book, and two other landbirds—the Brown Goshawk and the Owl—as 'rare'. Forshaw (in litt.)

found the owl calling regularly, even near the settlement, in December 1980. The island is biologically one of the most interesting in the world, with a high proportion of endemics throughout its biota. It currently has a human population of over 3000, involved in guano mining on an industrial scale. This involves clear-felling large areas of the dense forest cover and stripping the soil bare. Most of the considerable conservation efforts have centred on the endemic Abbott's Booby (*Sula abbotti*), but all the forest biota are threatened by this large-scale exploitation. The island is now administered by Australia as one of its Indian Ocean Territories. In 1980 a National Park of 1600ha was declared, in the southwestern corner of the island (J. M. Forshaw, in litt.), but it is not clear what proportion of the avifauna will be effectively protected by the park. Mining operations are expected to cease by the end of the 1980s, but how much native habitat will remain is not clear. The large human population also represents a direct threat through hunting and introduced pets and other aliens; a management plan for conserving the biota as a whole (and not just the Booby) is an urgent priority for this unique island.

Cocos-Keeling (Australia)
Cocos-Keeling comprises a coral atoll about 5.5km across, containing 26 small islands around a large lagoon, and the isolated island of North Keeling about 24km to the north. Total land area is about 14km^2, of which North Keeling makes up 1.1km^2 (Stokes *et al.* 1984). North Keeling has not been settled and has suffered least change, retaining much native vegetation and lacking the feral cats, rats and mice which abound elsewhere. It holds large seabird colonies and a population of the endemic Cocos Buff-banded Rail (*Rallus philippensis andrewsi*) which is the only landbird native to the group. It was apparently introduced to North Keeling at the end of the nineteenth century (Gibson-Hill 1949); this was a wise precaution because Stokes *et al.* 1984 found none on the main atoll in January 1982 and believed it extinct there. It remains common on North Keeling; as an endemic taxon confined to a single small island, it surely merits Red Data Book status; Stokes described it as 'certainly endangered' and recommended that North Keeling be declared a National Park or Nature Reserve in view of the increasing activities of seabird hunters from the main atoll.

No native landbirds remain on the main atoll, and most of the Christmas Island landbirds introduced there in the late nineteenth century have disappeared; only the Christmas Island Silver-eye (*Zosterops natalis*) remains. (The record of *Ducula whartoni* on West Island—quoted in King 1981—is challenged by Stokes.) The atoll was settled in 1825 and developed as a coconut plantation and fishing settlement; almost all the native vegetation has been converted to coconuts and the people hunt birds extensively.

Andamans (India)
This group contains 204 high islands with a total area of about 6400km^2, forming a southward continuation of the Arakan Yoma mountains of Burma. The natural vegetation is mainly tropical forest, much of which apparently still remains. The small aboriginal population of negroid people is now greatly outnumbered by settlers from India. The avifauna is rich, with about 80 breeding species; five are endemic to the group, and another three to the Andamans and Nicobars together. (Snow (1970) quoted six species endemic to the Andamans and two more shared with the Nicobars, but this seems to be an error as the Starling (*Sturnus erythropygius*), which Snow listed as an Andaman endemic, is also shared with the Nicobars—Abdulali 1965.) There are 41 endemic subspecies and 14 more shared only with the Nicobars.

The islands' avifauna has been described regularly by Abdulali (1965, 1967, 1969, 1971, 1974, 1978). Since 1972, large areas of forest have been cleared and settled with immigrants from mainland India, and in Little Andaman elephants have been introduced to help the logging operations that precede the establishment of oil palm plantations (S. A. Hussein, in litt.). Introduced species of bird may also pose a long-term threat; Indian Mynas (*Acridotheres tristis*) and 'Sparrows' are now well established in the central Andamans (S. A. Hussein, in litt.).

An up-to-date assessment of the conservation status of this fascinating archipelago is needed. Apparently only one species is confined to a single island (the Hornbill, *Rhyticeros (plicatus) narcondami*, on Narcondam); its population was last estimated (in 1902) as 200 (Snow 1970). Any species confined to such a small island (area 11km², altitude 710m) is vulnerable, and there is surely a good case for listing the Narcondam Hornbill as either Rare or Vulnerable (depending on investigation of its current status) in the Red Data Book.

The indigenous peoples of the Andamans have such a fearsome reputation that until recently they have effectively discouraged settlement in many parts of the archipelago. While the biota is fairly well known taxonomically, it seems not to have been very thoroughly investigated ecologically; the undisturbed nature of much of the group offers outstanding research opportunities of conservation as well as general scientific interest. Very few tropical archipelagos are in as pristine a state as the Andamans; the Indian government should be encouraged to capitalise on their unique opportunities for research and conservation. It is encouraging that four wildlife sanctuaries were declared in 1977, on Narcondam (680ha), Barren Island (810ha), North Reef Island (350ha) and South Sentinel (160ha) (J. Harrison, in litt.), but it is not clear what proportion of the native biota is contained within these sanctuaries.

Nicobars (India)

Approximately equidistant (130–150km) from the southern Andamans and northwest Sumatra, the 22 islands of the Nicobars cover about 1900km² total land area. They are structurally 'high' islands (maximum altitude 639m) but the northern group of volcanic and metamorphic rocks is higher than the southern, where sedimentary rocks predominate. The biota is less well known than that of the Andamans, and only Abdulali's (1978) popular account of a recent visit has appeared since his earlier reviews (Abdulali 1965, 1967, 1969). About 50 bird species probably breed including two endemics (a parakeet and a bulbul), and three others are shared only with the Andamans. Subspecific differentiation is rather more marked than in the Andamans (29 subspecies are endemic), some species having more than one race within the group; concern has been expressed for the status of some of these (Abdulali 1967), but there is an urgent need for an up-to-date assessment. The native vegetation has been more extensively altered by Indian settlers than is the case in the Andamans—the aboriginal Shompens apparently being less ferocious than the Jerwa and Onges of the Andamans—and although there may still be substantial areas of intact forest in the interior of Great Nicobar (Snow 1970), large areas have been felled in the last decade (S. A. Hussein, in litt.).

The Andamans and Nicobars are by far the richest and least spoiled islands left in the entire Indian Ocean, and indeed are of world-wide interest on both counts; although recent information is inadequate, there seems every chance that vigorous conservation measures taken now could ensure the preservation of many of the remaining habitats and species, alongside the aboriginal peoples of these remarkable islands.

Laccadives or Lakshadweep Islands (India)

These 24 small coral atolls, with a total land area of about 28km², have only a few common Indian landbirds, which Elliott (1972) implied were all introduced. These islands are close to the Indian mainland and were no doubt settled so long ago that no traces remain of any endemic landbirds.

Maldives (Independent)
Of the 2500 or so islands in this archipelago of atolls, about 220 are permanently
inhabited; total land area is about 298km^2. The vegetation was apparently entirely of
Indian origin; most has now been replaced by food-plants or other introduced species.
The four native breeding landbirds include two endemic races, of the Indian House
Crow (*Corvus splendens*) and the rail (*Amaurornis phoenicurus*) and all are reported as
being reasonably abundant (Snow 1970). An up-to-date assessment of the status of the
endemic subspecies is needed.

Chagos (Britain)
This extremely remote group (*c*. 1500km south of India) contains four main atolls and
many coral islands, with a total land area of about 65km^2. Its landbirds are almost all
introduced, but the origins of some are still obscure. The Green Heron (*Butorides
striatus*) has been described as an endemic race *albolimbatus*; this decision was
supported by Ripley (1969) but challenged by Bourne (1971). This illustrates a common
problem in deciding conservation priorities; in cases such as this, of an isolated
population, the decision of the taxonomist can be crucial in deciding whether or not
conservation action needs to be taken. Fortunately in this case the bird concerned is
widespread throughout the archipelago and probably in no need of special protective
measures.
      The status of the resident race of the Madagascar Turtle Dove (*Streptopelia picturata
chuni*) is also in doubt. Certainly it was native, as it was recorded in 1842 (Bourne 1971);
but the native form may have gone extinct and been replaced by introduced birds of
another race. Benson (1970a) thought they might be hybrids of the Madagascar and
Comoro forms, but Ripley (in Bourne 1971) believed them to be an endemic form.
Bourne's (1971) suggestion that their characteristics might be 'the result of recent
evolution of typical birds imported from Mauritius' seems the least likely explanation.
Hutson's (1975) descriptions and measurements of live birds led him to conclude that the
present stock is probably derived from introduced *S. p. picturata*, perhaps with some *S.
p. comorensis*; he found them abundant on Diego Garcia, but they are found nowhere
else in the Chagos (M. J. D. Hirons, pers. comm.). The identity—and indeed the
existence—of the 'Moorhen' reported to various visitors to Diego Garcia remains to be
established, though Hutson (1975) decided that none could still be surviving.
      There are no reserves in the group, whose main conservation importance lies in its
seabird colonies. The United States military base on Diego Garcia must pose some
threat to conservation, but to what extent is not clear.

Rodrigues (Mauritius)
The easternmost of the Mascarene Islands is volcanic, rising to 396m and covering
108km^2. The extraordinary native landbird fauna (Cheke, in press a) is reduced to the
pathetic remnant of struggling populations of the Rodrigues Fody (*Foudia flavicans*)
and the Rodrigues Brush Warbler (*Acrocephalus (Bebrornis) rodericanus*). These are
described in detail by Cheke; in brief, both are confined to small wooded areas and are
vulnerable to natural catastrophes such as cyclones (which occur frequently) as well as
the pressures exerted by a burgeoning human population. Fewer than 60 pairs of the
Fody, and 10 of the Warbler, remained in 1982 (Cheke, in press a). Rodrigues, which is
a dependency of the independent state of Mauritius, has a much larger human
population than its own resources can support; habitat destruction by cutting and
overgrazing, and hunting for food and sport have brought the native biota (which
includes the rarest Fruit Bat in the world) to the brink of extinction. Cheke (in press b)
has discussed the ecological history of the island in detail and has made specific

conservation recommendations for it (Cheke 1979b, 1980) and for the Mascarenes as a whole (Cheke 1979a).

Cargados Carajos or St. Brandon (Mauritius)

An archipelago of reefs, shoals and low coral and sand islands, the group has a total land area that varies with sea conditions but averages about 300ha on some 19 islands. No landbirds, native or otherwise, have been recorded, but the islands are important breeding stations for seabirds (Staub 1970).

Mauritius (Independent)

Mauritius is a large ($1840km^2$), high (904m) volcanic island, sharing many elements of its biota with the other Mascarene Islands (Rodrigues and Réunion). Its exceptional native avifauna has been reviewed by Cheke (in press b,c), who also describes in detail the current status of its remnants. Mauritius has the unfortunate distinction of harbouring several of the most critically endangered species in the world; five full species and two subspecies are included in the Red Data Book. The past decade has seen vigorous efforts to conserve several of these—notably the Mauritius Kestrel (*Falco punctatus*), Pink Pigeon (*Nesoenas mayeri*) and Echo Parakeet (*Psittacula echo*). The island is one of the most densely populated states in the world; the few remaining fragments of native vegetation are penetrated by invasive alien plants, grossly overstocked with deer for hunting, rife with feral pigs and rats (*Rattus rattus*), and plagued by feral monkeys (*Macaca fascicularis*) which plunder the nests of native birds. Introduced Ring-necked Parakeets (*Psittacula krameri*) threaten the five or so remaining native Parakeets, and international 'aid' agencies have recently subsidised and encouraged the destruction of the pathetic remnants of native vegetation (Procter & Salm 1975; Owadally 1980). Conservation of the three species named above is now a matter of last-ditch captive breeding programmes, with all their attendant difficulties of inbreeding, disease and dietary problems. ICBP has maintained an active programme there since 1972, and the Jersey Wildlife Preservation Trust has co-operated fully in the captive breeding programme in recent years (Jones 1980). Ultimately it is intended that captive-bred birds be re-introduced into the wild, but until the future of their destined habitat is better assured it is unlikely that such re-introductions will succeed.

Réunion (France)

Of all the Mascarenes, Réunion (a French Overseas Department) has most native vegetation and the most intact avifauna; it also lacks the monkeys, pigs and mongooses (*Herpestes edwardsii*) that have done so much damage elsewhere in the Mascarenes. Its ecological history and the state of its native birds are described in detail by Cheke (in press b,d respectively). Only one landbird—the Réunion Cuckoo-Shrike (*Coracina newtoni*)—is endangered; its range is very restricted but is included in a proposed new reserve (J. Harrison, in litt.). Cheke (in press b) has suggested that introduced diseases, resembling those implicated in the extinction of Hawaiian birds (Warner 1968), may account for the otherwise mysterious restriction of range of several of the native landbirds. Cheke also drew attention to the possible dangers attending the introduction of alien birds such as the Red-whiskered Bulbul (*Pycnonotus jocosus*) which can be a serious predator on the nests of small birds. So long as the island remains at least as free of introduced aliens and retains as much suitable habitat as it does now, Réunion could well play an important role in conserving birds from the other Mascarene Islands by accepting translocations of species gravely threatened on their native islands (Cheke 1980).

Agalegas (Mauritius)

These twin coral islands have a combined land area of about 21km² and a maximum altitude of 15m (Cheke & Lawley, in press). They were settled in 1808, 299 years after their discovery (Scott 1961). The only known native landbird is the Glossy Ibis (*Plegadis falcinellus*), whose population has declined precipitously in the last 30 years and is now around 20 birds (Cheke & Lawley, in press). This population must have been isolated for a long time and may be distinct taxonomically; if it is, it would at once merit 'endangered' status. The local population of Turtle Doves (*Streptopelia picturata*) is also of unknown taxonomic status. There are no known specimens of either species, and the birds' taxonomic status should be determined from live-caught birds and not by collecting specimens.

Tromelin (France)

This isolated, low (6m), small coral island (175ha) has no native landbirds; an airstrip serves the meteorological station, and rats, rabbits and mice have been introduced (Staub 1970).

Seychelles (Independent)

This is the world's only oceanic archipelago of granitic origin apart from the minute St. Paul's Rocks in the South Atlantic. Most are high islands, up to 912m; all are small, the total land area of about 404km² being divided among 90 or so islands. Some of the central group are low coral islands, and the political unit of Seychelles also includes the outlying coral islands of the Amirantes and the raised islands of the Farquhar, Providence and Aldabra groups, which are here listed separately purely for convenience. The native avifauna of the Seychelles contains none of the ancient, bizarre or flightless elements that characterise the Mascarenes, though the Seychelles are geologically much older; the Seychelles avifauna, unlike that of its amphibia and reptiles, is strikingly young, with no endemism above the species level. The history and biogeography of the avifauna is covered most recently by Diamond & Feare (1980) for the central (chiefly granitic) group and Diamond (1984) for the whole of political Seychelles. More Red Data Book taxa occur here than on any archipelago outside Hawaii; in the central group, nine taxa are threatened, though one of these is listed rashly as 'out of danger'. As in the Mascarenes, this desperate situation attracted ICBP's attention some years ago; beginning with the outright purchase of Cousin Island and its management as a nature reserve (Diamond 1975, 1980), most of the threatened taxa have been studied since (reviewed by Watson, 1984). On the main island of Mahe the Scops Owl (*Otus insularis*) is known from several localities and the Kestrel (*Falco araea*) is probably as abundant as its territorial requirements will allow, but the White-eye (*Zosterops modesta*) remains known from only very few sites and must give the most concern. On Praslin, the Black Parrot (an endemic race of *Coracopsis nigra* of the Comores) holds its own, as do the remaining more widespread endemics such as the Sunbird (*Nectarinia dussumieri*), Bulbul (*Hypsipetes crassirostris*) and Blue Pigeon (*Alectroenas pulcherrima*). On Cousin, the Warbler (*Acrocephalus sechellensis*) and the Fody (*Foudia sechellarum*) have increased numbers dramatically (Diamond, this vol.), but the remnant population of the Seychelles race *rostrata* of the Turtle Dove (*Streptopelia picturata*) is almost certainly now extinct through hybridisation with the introduced nominate race. A thorough check on the neighbouring island of Cousine would probably be wise before this bird is definitely pronounced extinct.

The species causing most concern are the Magpie Robin (*Copsychus sechellarum*) and the Paradise Flycatcher (*Terpsiphone corvina*). The Robin survives on Frégate, where an increase in feral cats wiped out one season's production of young and threatened the adults. Prompt action in 1981–2 through the Seychelles Government and ICBP brought expert help from New Zealand to trap cats and train local staff in appropriate techniques, which brought the cat population close to zero and the robins back to normal strength. However the only cat whose death really counts is of course the last one, and continued vigilance and precautions will be necessary to ensure the bird's future. Attempts to transfer birds to Aride Island were at first successful, leading to at least one pair breeding, but all but one bird disappeared shortly afterwards and further trans-locations have been suspended until proper arrangements can be made for release and subsequent monitoring. The possibility of using Cousin as an alternative breeding site for such vulnerable Seychelles species is being seriously considered.

The Paradise Flycatcher is more abundant, and in addition to the main population on La Digue it has recently been found at several sites on Praslin. A fenced reserve has been set up on La Digue specifically for the birds and is wardened by the government with help from the Royal Society for Nature Conservation. The bird's population appears to be stable.

Seychelles has excellent conservation legislation and a vigorous government conser-vation department. The active involvement over more than a decade of ICBP and the Royal Society for Nature Conservation has helped to foster an awareness of bird conservation in the general public, and the prospects for all these birds are generally good. However no birds with such low and geographically restricted populations can ever be considered safe, and a long-term strategy for their conservation will need to aim at establishing alternative breeding populations and an adequate system for monitoring all these threatened birds.

Amirantes (Seychelles)
Although politically part of the Seychelles, the Amirantes are sufficiently distant and different to justify separate treatment here. They are 18 scattered coral islands, atolls and sandbanks, important for seabirds but with few surviving native landbirds. The possibility that the endemic race *S. p. saturata* (= *aldabrana*) of the Turtle Dove (*Streptopelia picturata*) survives on St. Joseph needs to be assessed. One was seen there in 1967 together with the introduced Madagascar race which has exterminated the endemic Seychelles race on the granitic islands (see above) (Benson 1970b). Magpie Robins were introduced to Alphonse and survived until wiped out by feral cats. With proper precautions against such disasters some of these islands could well be very useful for future translocations.

Farquhars (Seychelles)
This remote group includes Farquhar itself, an atoll containing seven islands with a land area of about 7km^2; St. Pierre, a small raised-limestone island; and Providence Banks, a low sandy island. No native landbirds survive on any of them, and the only known species was a small species of Blue Pigeon *Alectroenas* on Farquhar and Providence (Stoddart & Benson 1970).

Gloriosa (France)
Glorioso, Gloriosa or Iles Glorieuses comprises two islands connected by a sandbank with a total land area of about 6km^2. None of the surviving native landbirds is endemic, and all seem to be reasonably abundant (Benson *et al.* 1975).

Aldabra (Seychelles)
The Aldabra group consists of three raised atolls: Aldabra itself, Cosmoledo and Astove, and the raised island of Assumption.

Aldabra is much the largest (land area 155km^2) and has a rich and distinctive biota which has been studied intensively since 1967 (Stoddart & Westoll 1979). Of the 15 native landbirds, two are endemic species and 12 endemic subspecies (Benson & Penny 1971). Some species, such as the Kestrel (*Falco newtoni*), are probably naturally scarce; others, such as the Fody (*Foudia eminentissima aldabrana*), may be seriously affected by nest predation by introduced rats (Frith 1976). The most threatened species is the endemic Warbler (*Nesillas aldabranus*) discovered only in 1967 and then, as now, one of the world's rarest birds. Prys-Jones (1979) found only five birds in two years and put the maximum possible population at 25. He recommended total protection for its habitat, including keeping out goats and giant tortoises which would affect the vegetation, and investigation of the last remaining possible site for the species. This area has since been investigated but no warblers were found (C. Huxley, pers. comm.). Captive breeding and translocation may have to be considered if the species shows no signs of increase or is not found elsewhere on the atoll.

The endemic flightless race of the rail *Dryolimnas cuvieri* is abundant on several islands of the atoll, but may be vulnerable to feral cats if they should become abundant on those islands (Penny & Diamond 1971). The establishment of a captive population, or translocation to a nearby island such as Cosmoledo, would be sensible precautions to take to assure the future of the last of the Indian Ocean's famous flightless birds.

Aldabra is now run as a reserve by the Seychelles Islands Foundation, and in late 1982 was declared a World Heritage Site by UNESCO. As a site it needs no further protective measures, but extra steps may still have to be taken for critically threatened taxa such as the Brush Warbler, for which habitat protection and lack of disturbance may not be enough to prevent extinction. A very serious threat, which Aldabra's own protected status is powerless to counter, is posed by introductions of exotic species to Assumption island only 27km away. These were documented by Prys-Jones et al. (1981) who point out forcefully that such introductions are the first to the entire group and, including as they do potential competitors to the native Aldabran avifauna as well as possible carriers of disease, represent a potentially disastrous threat to Aldabra. Assumption, like Aldabra, is politically part of the Seychelles, where such introductions are illegal, but it is in practice managed from Mauritius whence these introductions have come. Firmer management on Assumption must become part of the conservation management of Aldabra.

Assumption itself (land area 10.5km²) has been devastated by phosphate mining, which still continues. Little remains of the native biota, and the sunbird (*Nectarinia sovimanga abbotti*) is the only surviving native landbird. Birds there are still killed for food. Prys-Jones et al. (1981) described the avifauna and its history, and made detailed conservation recommendations.

Cosmoledo Atoll consists of eight main islands and many islets with a total land area of about 5.2km². The sunbird (*Nectarinia sovimanga buchenorum*) is a race shared with Astove, and the White-eye is possibly an endemic race (*Zosterops maderaspatana menaiensis*) (Benson 1970c). Benson thought the Turtle Dove (*Streptopelia picturata*) likely to be extinct, but Dr. J. Mortimer has shown me colour slides of two birds taken on South Island in 1982, so a relict population may survive there. Its taxonomic status is unknown.

Astove has a land area of about 4.25km²; none of its remaining three to four native landbirds is endemic (Benson 1970d).

Comores (Independent, except Mayotte (France))
The four main volcanic islands range in area from 216km² (Moheli) to 950km² (Grand Comore). Since Benson's (1960) detailed report, little has been done (though see Forbes-Watson 1969). The avifauna is rich, diverse and well-differentiated. There is one endemic genus (a Flycatcher, *Humblotia*), 8 endemic species and 46 endemic races. Many species are differentiated on different islands. The islands themselves retain

surprisingly large areas of forest, especially on Moheli, and many of the endemics are abundant. However, more remains to be discovered, not only about status (which is poorly known for many taxa) but even taxonomically. In a brief visit to the Grand Comore forest in 1975 I saw a warbler that was certainly not of the only genus recorded (*Nesillas*). In view of the large number of island endemics in the group, and recent political changes giving independence to three of the four main islands, a detailed survey of the status of landbirds throughout the group is strongly recommended. Currently only three breeding taxa, all subspecies, are listed in the Red Data Book, but it is very likely that more than these will merit conservation measures. Forest clearance has accelerated alarmingly since independence in 1975, and the forest around the summit of Anjouan had shrunk by 1974 to one third of its size in 1968 (Cheke & Dahl 1981). The islands are small enough to be very vulnerable and deserve urgent attention.

Islands in the Mozambique Channel (France)

Europa, Bassas da India and Juan de Nova are small low islands—coralline or sandy—with possibly important seabird colonies but apparently no native landbirds. Europa now has nature reserve status (Hughes & Batchelor 1974).

DISCUSSION

Tables 1 and *2* summarize the species numbers, endemism and Red Data Book entries of the islands of the region. Several general points stand out.

- The poverty of the low islands, which is partly natural (they offer few ecological niches and are often small and remote (Diamond, 1984)) but also a function of their extreme vulnerability to human interference.
- The striking concentration of Red Data Book entries in only two states—the Seychelles (including Aldabra) and Mauritius. This partly reflects real conservation problems, but also raises the suspicion that states outside the British sphere of influence may be under-represented for reasons not related to the extent of their conservation problems. The Andamans and Nicobars, and the Comores, have such rich and differentiated avifaunas that on grounds of probability alone it seems most unlikely that between them they really have only three taxa—all subspecies—in need of conservation. Early field assessment of the true conservation situation on all three of these groups must surely be a major priority in the region. An up-to-date assessment of the status of all the Christmas Island

Table 1:   Atolls, coral and sand islands ('low' islands)

Name	Native landbirds	Endemic species	Endemic subspecies
AGALEGA	1 (?2)	0	?
AMIRANTES	1	0	1
BASSAS DA INDIA	0	—	—
CARGADOS CARAJOS	0	—	—
CHAGOS	1?	0	1?
COCOS-KEELING	1	0	1
EUROPA	0	—	—
FARQUHAR	0	0	0
JUAN DE NOVA	0	—	—
LACCADIVES	c. 4	0	0
MALDIVES	4	0	2
PROVIDENCE	0	—	—
TROMELIN	0	—	—

Table 2: Raised and 'high' islands

Name	Native landbirds	Endemic genera	Endemic species	Endemic subspecies	Endangered Sp.	Endangered Sub.	Vulnerable Sp.	Vulnerable Sub.	Rare Sp.	Rare Sub.
a) Raised coral-limestone										
ALDABRA GROUP	15	0	2	12	0	0	1	3	0	0
CHRISTMAS ISLAND	7	0	2	5	0	0	1	0	0	2
ST. PIERRE	1	0	0	0	0	0	0	0	0	0
b) High (volcanic or granitic) islands										
ANDAMANS	c. 80	0	5 }+3	41 }+14	0	0	0	0	0	0
NICOBARS	c. 50	0	2 }	29 }	0	0	0	0	0	0
COMORES	47	1	8	46	0	2	0	0	0	0
MAURITIUS	11	0[1]	7 }+2	2 }+2	4	0	1	1	0	1
REUNION	9	0[1]	4 }	3 }	2	0	0	0	1	0
RODRIGUES	2	0[1]	2	0	2	0	0	0	0	0
SEYCHELLES	13	0	9	4	2	2	3	0	1[2]	0

Notes: Numbers to the right of brackets (}+) refer to endemic taxa shared by the bracketed islands or archipelagos.
[1] Surviving taxa only; several endemic genera are long extinct.
[2] Not including *Acrocephalus sechellensis*, which merits 'rare' status but was listed as 'out of danger' by King (1981).

endemics should also be a priority, which could well be included in the ornithological research programme about to begin there (J. B. Nelson, pers. comm.).
– A point which has arisen repeatedly is the importance of taxonomic decisions in defining conservation needs. This is particularly striking in a region such as this, where there are many isolated populations that may be only poorly differentiated. If such populations can be shown to differ from all others, they automatically become endemic taxa, and qualify for conservation measures if they are threatened. If, on the other hand, they are merely representatives of widespread taxa, they are of no conservation interest (in a regional context, at least) unless the taxon as a whole becomes endangered. This curious situation is of course a function of the species approach to conservation which is embodied in the Red Data Book concept; an ecosystem approach would pay as much attention to a taxon in a system whatever its taxonomic status. However, despite the prodigious efforts of Benson and others, there do still remain some taxonomic problems that affect conservation priorities within ICBP's current (species-oriented) approach to bird conservation (see summary).

A REGIONAL CONSERVATION STRATEGY

An ambitious attempt by Temple (1981) to apply biogeographic theory to bird conservation problems in the western Indian Ocean (not the whole ocean as the paper's title suggests) demands comment. Temple used a regression analysis of species number against island area to show that the Seychelles are richer than the present area of the islands would lead one to expect, and to show that they, and the fragments of forest remaining on Mauritius, are 'super-saturated' with more landbird species than they can hold. He did not give the data on which he based his regression analysis, but in any case the analysis is invalid because it assumes unrealistic source regions and combines three ecologically different types of island—low, raised and high in my terminology—in an analysis which assumes area to be the important variable influencing species number. In fact isolation is also important and in the outlying coralline islands is unfortunately correlated with area (Diamond & Feare 1980; Diamond, 1984). Temple's conclusion—that Seychelles have a disproportionately high number of breeding landbirds because the avifauna is still 'relaxing' from a size appropriate to the much larger land mass it would have occupied before the post-glacial rise in sealevel—may well be correct qualitatively, though I question the quantitative details. But his application of this point to bird conservation problems in Mauritius is contrived and, more importantly, quite unnecessary. It is perfectly obvious that insufficient native forest survives on Mauritius to support the native birds, without recourse to theories of supersaturated avifaunas. Temple's analysis of Mascarene conservation problems purely in terms of island biogeography theory is extraordinary because it completely ignores the factors which are actually threatening the species today, notably nest predation by introduced monkeys and mongooses, habitat degradation by feral stock and deer, and competition from an introduced congener (Cheke, in press b): these receive a passing mention but their effect is otherwise ignored.

Temple's practical suggestions for conserving the threatened birds of Mauritius boil down to translocating them to Réunion. In general this remains an idea worth pursuing seriously (Cheke 1975), but at a much more rigorous level than shown by Temple. It will be necessary, for example, to take into account that the Réunion Harrier (*Circus maillardi*) is not at all a close ecological equivalent of the Mauritius Kestrel, and to realize that the kestrel's staple food, far from being White-eyes (*Zosterops* spp.) as Temple suggests, is actually diurnal geckos (Jones, in press). It would also be madness without a public education programme to introduce large and succulent Pink Pigeons (*Nesoenas mayeri*) to an island populated by avid hunters who have already wiped out most of the indigenous shootable birds.

Translocation between islands of the region, nonetheless, remains my main suggestion for a regional conservation strategy for species conservation. It should be applied only to those species for which there can be no realistic hope of survival in the wild on their native islands, and those with a small population on a single island; and it should be preceded by a rigorous ecological appraisal of both the recipient island and the orphan species, and accompanied and followed by intensive monitoring.

A plea should also be entered for less lip-service and more real commitment to be paid to the concept of conserving total island ecosystems. The taxonomic approach inherent in the Red Data Book concept is inadequate and outdated, and leads to ridiculous anomalies such as assessment of conservation status on purely taxonomic grounds. Does the Chagos Island Green Heron really merit protection more if it is accorded subspecific rank than if it is not? Is it not playing the same role in its island ecosystem whatever a taxonomist's opinion of its degree of differentiation? There are still some island systems in the tropical Indian Ocean which closely approach a reasonably natural state: some of the Andamans and Nicobars perhaps, the interior of Réunion (Mascarenes) and Moheli (Comores), North Keeling and Aldabra. Others—Cousin in the Seychelles is a spectacularly successful case in point (Plunkett 1977), and probably Cousine, Aride and others—could still be restored to a near-natural state. Is it not, in the long term, better to re-create or conserve representatives of distinctive island systems, rather than concentrate piecemeal on minute and probably ultimately doomed populations of dubious distinction?

SUMMARY OF RECOMMENDATIONS

- Assessments of the true status of endemic taxa on the Andamans, Nicobars and Comores, and less urgently on Christmas Island, are needed in the near future.
- Resolution of several taxonomic problems may affect the conservation status of several forms, notably:
     the 'Waterhen,' Turtle Dove and Green Heron on Diego Garcia;
     the Glossy Ibis on Agalega;
     the Turtle Dove on the Amirantes;
     the Turtle Dove and the White-eye on South and Menai Islands,
          respectively, of Cosmoledo.
- Introductions of alien birds to Assumption represent a very serious threat to the integrity of the otherwise well-protected biota of Aldabra, and may in general become a major threat throughout the region now that most islands have already suffered habitat destruction and introduction of alien predators. The widespread extinction by hybridization of island races of Turtle Doves (*Streptopelia picturata*) resulting from introductions of the nominate Madagascar race, are a graphic example of the threat posed by such introductions.
- More consideration may need to be given to translocation and captive breeding— on nearby islands where possible—to increase the long-term safety of many small, single-island populations, especially in the Seychelles and Mascarenes.
- Nature reserve status for North Keeling is urgently recommended to conserve the endemic rail.
- A re-assessment of the philosophy of conservation to be applied to island biotas is urged, and a plea made for a truly integrated strategy rather than the piecemeal taxonomic approach which has dominated the conservation scene in the region to date.

ACKNOWLEDGEMENTS

I thank J. Forshaw for recent information on Christmas Island; J. Harrison of IUCN's Protected Areas Data Unit for information on protected areas on the Andamans, Nicobars and Réunion; and S. A. Hussein for recent information on the Andamans and Nicobars. Anthony Cheke made very useful suggestions for improving the paper.

REFERENCES

ABDULALI, H. 1965. The birds of the Andaman and Nicobar Islands. *J. Bombay Nat. Hist. Soc.* **59**, 281–3.

ABDULALI, H. 1967. The birds of the Nicobar Islands, with notes on some Andaman birds. *J. Bombay Nat. Hist. Soc.* **61**, 483–571.

ABDULALI, H. 1969. The birds of the Nicobar Islands with notes on some Andaman birds. *J. Bombay Nat. Hist. Soc.* **64**, 139–90.

ABDULALI, H. 1971. Narcondam Island and notes on some birds from the Andaman Islands. *J. Bombay Nat. Hist. Soc.* **68**, 385–411.

ABDULALI, H. 1974. The fauna of Narcondam Island—I. *J. Bombay Nat. Hist. Soc.* **71**, 496–505.

ABDULALI, H. 1978. The birds of Great and Car Nicobars with some notes on wildlife conservation in the islands. *J. Bombay Nat. Hist. Soc.* **75**, 744–72.

BENSON, C. W. 1960. The birds of the Comoro Islands: Results of the British Ornithologists' Union centenary expedition 1958. *Ibis* **103b**, 5–106.

BENSON, C. W. 1970a. The systematic status of the form of *Streptopelia picturata* on Diego Garcia. *Bull. Br. Orn. Club* **90**, 32–5.

BENSON, C. W. 1970b. An introduction of *Streptopelia picturata* into the Amirantes. *Atoll Res. Bull.* **136**, 195–6.

BENSON, C. W. 1970c. Land (including shore) birds of Cosmoledo. *Atoll Res. Bull.* **136**, 67–82.

BENSON, C. W. 1970d. Land (including shore) birds of Astove. *Atoll Res. Bull.* **136**, 83–100.

BENSON, C. W. & PENNY, M. J. 1971. The land birds of Aldabra. *Phil. Trans. Roy. Soc. Lond.* B **260**, 417–528.

BENSON, C. W., BEAMISH, H. H., JOUANIN, C., SALVAN, J. & WATSON, G. E. 1975. The birds of the Iles Glorieuses. *Atoll Res. Bull.* **176**, 1–34.

BOURNE, W. R. P. 1971. The birds of the Chagos Group, Indian Ocean. *Atoll Res. Bull.* **149**, 175–207.

CHEKE, A. S. 1975. Proposition pour introduire a La Réunion des oiseaux rares de l'Ile Maurice. *Info-Nature, Ile Réunion* **12**, 25–9.

CHEKE, A. S. 1979a. Recommendations pour la conservation des vertèbres des Iles Mascareignes. *Info-Nature, Ile Réunion* **16**, 69–83.

CHEKE, A. S. 1979b. The Rodrigues Fody *Foudia flavicans*. A brief history of its decline, and a report on the 1978 expedition. *Dodo* **15**, 12–19.

CHEKE, A. S. 1980. Urgency and inertia in the conservation of endangered island species, illustrated by Rodrigues. *Proc. 4th Pan-Afr. orn. Congr.* 355–9.

CHEKE, A. S. (in press, a). Observations on the surviving endemic birds of Rodrigues. *In:* Diamond, A. W. (ed.) *Studies of Mascarene Island birds.* Cambridge University Press, Cambridge.

CHEKE, A. S. (in press, b). An ecological history of the Mascarene Islands. *In:* Diamond, A. W. (ed.) *Studies of Mascarene Island birds.* Cambridge University Press, Cambridge.

CHEKE, A. S. (in press, c). The surviving native landbirds of Mauritius. *In:* Diamond, A. W. (ed.) *Studies of Mascarene Island birds.* Cambridge University Press, Cambridge.

CHEKE, A. S. (in press, d). The ecology of the surviving native landbirds of Reunion. *In:* Diamond, A. W. (ed.) *Studies of Mascarene Island birds.* Cambridge University Press, Cambridge.

CHEKE, A. S. & DAHL, J. S. 1981. The status of bats on western Indian Ocean islands, with special reference to *Pteropus*. *Mammalia* **45**, 205–38.

CHEKE, A. S. & LAWLEY, J. C. (in press). The biological history of Agalega (Indian Ocean), with special reference to birds and other land vertebrates. *Atoll Res. Bull.*.

DIAMOND, A. W. 1975. *Cousin Island Nature Reserve Management Plan 1975–79.* ICBP (British Section), London.

DIAMOND, A. W. 1980. *Cousin Island Nature Reserve Management Plan Revision 1980–84.* ICBP (British Section), London.

DIAMOND, A. W. (this vol.). Multiple use of Cousin Island nature reserve, Seychelles.

DIAMOND, A. W. 1984. Biogeography of Seychelles land birds. *In:* Stoddart, D. R. (ed.) *Biogeography and ecology of the Seychelles islands.* 487–504. Junk, The Hague.

DIAMOND, A. W. & FEARE, C. J. 1980. Past and present biogeography of central Seychelles birds. *Proc. 4th Pan-Afr. orn. Congr.* 89–98.

ELLIOTT, H. F. I. 1972. Island ecosystems and conservation with particular reference to the biological significance of islands of the Indian Ocean and consequential research and conservation needs. *J. Mar. Biol. Assocn. India* 14, 578–608.

FEARE, C. J. 1985. Seabird Status and Conservation in the Tropical Indian Ocean. *ICBP Technical Pubn. No. 2.*

FORBES-WATSON, A. D. 1969. Notes on birds observed in the Comoros on behalf of the Smithsonian Institution. *Atoll Res. Bull.* 128, 1–23.

FRITH, C. B. 1976. A twelve month field study of the Aldabra Fody *Foudia eminentissima aldabrana. Ibis* 118, 155–78.

GIBSON-HILL, C. A. 1949. The birds of the Cocos-Keeling Islands (Indian Ocean). *Ibis* 91, 221–42.

HUGHES, G. & BATCHELOR, G. 1974. Birds of the islands. *African Wildlife* 28, 17–20.

HUTSON, A. M. 1975. Observations on the birds of Diego Garcia, Chagos archipelago, with notes on other vertebrates. *Atoll Res. Bull.* 175, 1–25.

JONES, C. G. 1980. Parrot on the way to extinction. *Oryx* 15, 350–4.

JONES, C. G. (in press). Observations on the biology and life history of the Mauritius Kestrel. *In:* Diamond, A. W. (ed.) *Studies of Mascarene Island birds.* Cambridge University Press, Cambridge.

KING, W. B. 1981. *Endangered birds of the world.* Smithsonian Inst./ICBP, Washington, D.C.

OWADALLY, W. 1980. Some forest pests and diseases in Mauritius. *Rev. Agric. Sucr. Ile Maurice* 59, 76–94.

PEAKE, J. F. 1971. The evolution of terrestrial faunas in the western Indian Ocean. *Phil. Trans. Roy. Soc. Lond.* B 260, 581–610.

PENNY, M. J. & DIAMOND, A. W. 1971. The White-throated Rail *Dryolimnas cuvieri* on Aldabra. *Phil. Trans. Roy. Soc. Lond.* B 260, 529–48.

PLUNKETT, R. L. 1977. Integrated management of endangered birds: a review. *In:* Temple, S. A. (ed). *Endangered birds:* 387–96. Croom Helm, London.

PROCTER, J. & SALM, R. 1975. *Conservation in Mauritius 1974.* IUCN, Morges.

PRYS-JONES, R. P. 1979. The ecology and conservation of the Aldabran brush warbler *Nesillas aldabranus. Phil. Trans. Roy. Soc. Lond.* B 286, 211–24.

PRYS-JONES, R. P., PRYS-JONES, M. S. & LAWLEY, J. C. 1981. The Birds of Assumption Island, Indian Ocean: past and future. *Atoll Res. Bull.* 248, 1–16.

RIPLEY, S. D. 1969. Comment on the Little Green Heron of the Chagos archipelago. *Ibis* 111, 101–2.

SCOTT, R. 1961. *Lemuria: the lesser dependencies of Mauritius.* Oxford University Press, London.

SNOW, D. W. 1970. The eastern Indian Ocean islands. *In: IUCN Eleventh Technical Meeting, papers and proceedings* 1: 212–23. IUCN Publications new series No. 17.

STAUB, F. 1970. Geography and ecology of Tromelin Island. *Atoll Res. Bull.* 136, 197–210.

STODDART, D. R. & BENSON, C. W. 1970. An odd record of a Blue Pigeon *Alectroenas* species on Farquhar and Providence. *Atoll Res. Bull.* 136, 35–6.

STODDART, D. R. & WESTOLL, T. S. (EDS) 1979. The terrestrial ecology of Aldabra. *Phil. Trans. Roy. Soc. Lond.* B 286, 654pp.

STOKES, T., SHEILS, W. & DUNN, K. 1984. Birds of the Cocos (Keeling) Islands, Indian Ocean. *Emu* 84: 23–8.

TAYLOR, J. D., BRAITHWAITE, C. J. R., PEAKE, J. F. & ARNOLD, E. N. 1979. Terrestrial faunas and habitats of Aldabra during the late Pleistocene. *Phil. Trans. Roy. Soc. Lond.* B 286, 47–66.

TEMPLE, S. A. 1981. Applied island biogeography and the conservation of endangered island birds in the Indian Ocean. *Biol. Cons.* 20, 147–161.

WARNER, R. E. 1968. The role of introduced diseases in the extinction of the endemic Hawaiian avifauna. *Condor* 70, 101–120.

WATSON, J. 1984. Land birds: endangered species on the granitic Seychelles. *In:* Stoddart, D. R. (ed.) *Biogeography and ecology of the Seychelles islands.* 513–27 Junk, The Hague.

THREATS TO BIRDS ON SUBANTARCTIC ISLANDS

G. W. JOHNSTONE

Antarctic Division, Department of Science and Technology, Kingston, Tasmania, 7150, Australia

ABSTRACT

Populations of breeding birds on subantarctic islands vary greatly in size. Small populations are not necessarily endangered. To identify a population as endangered one should be able to demonstrate a decline in breeding numbers or breeding success and identify the agent responsible. Because subantarctic islands are remote and either unoccupied or sparsely populated, the required information is not often available.

The past and present distribution on subantarctic islands of man and his introduced vertebrates is summarized. Bird populations known to be endangered are identified and the causes of their decline discussed. Past exterminations can provide useful information for interpreting current dangers and for predicting future trends; the chain of events on Macquarie Island is outlined. Introduced predators, particularly cats, constitute the most serious threat, especially when introduced prey such as rabbits and rodents are present to provide alternative food at times of year when the bird prey may be absent. Alteration of the structure of vegetation resulting from grazing by introduced herbivores can also affect breeding numbers of some birds.

At some islands, research has been followed by the initiation of management procedures aimed at controlling introduced species. This is difficult and slow but may have spectacular results. Other management practices such as strict quarantine measures and the use of islands free of introduced predators as refuges for endangered species are discussed. A common approach to conservation by the six nations with subantarctic territory is most desirable.

INTRODUCTION

The subantarctic zone is the name usually given to that part of the Southern Ocean bounded by the Antarctic convergence in the south and the subtropical convergence in the north. The islands in this zone are the subantarctic islands. However, in this paper I also include islands south to 60°S and in the north the Tristan da Cunha group, Ile Amsterdam and Ile Saint Paul, which are usually considered to be slightly north of the subtropical convergence, as well as the Chatham Islands which effectively straddle it. The subtropical convergence does strange things in the eastern Pacific Ocean and the western Atlantic Ocean, sweeping north up the western and eastern coasts of South America. In the New Zealand region it is usually drawn between the North Island and the South Island. All islands and island groups are shown in *Figure 1*. The vegetation of these islands ranges from the stunted trees and woody shrubs of the 'fern bush' of islands north of the subtropical convergence through the tussock grassland, herb fields and feldmark of the true subantarctic islands to the relatively barren and often ice-capped islands south of the Antarctic convergence, where the flora of tussock grassland, cushion

101

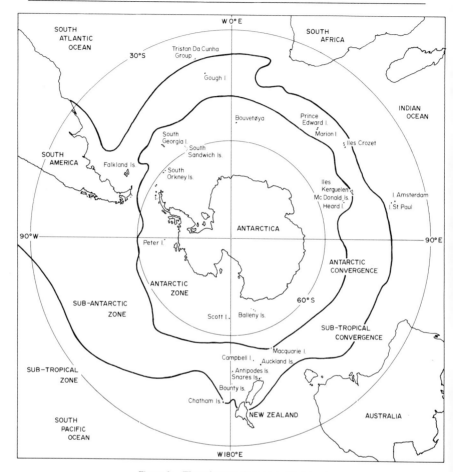

Figure 1:   The subantarctic zone and its islands.

plants and mosses becomes progressively depauperate of species with increasing latitude.

RED DATA BOOK BIRDS

The ICBP/IUCN Red Data Book, Volume 2, Aves (King 1981) has been my prime resource of information on endangered birds. For the subantarctic islands it lists seven endangered species, all breeding only in the Chatham Islands (two petrels, two waders, a pigeon, a parakeet and a passerine). Another three species are listed as vulnerable, two of which breed in the Falkland Islands and the third in the New Zealand region. In the third Red Data Book category, rare but at risk, are the New Zealand Snipe

Table 1: Endangered, vulnerable and rare species of birds on subantarctic islands (summarized from King 1981 with additions).
CE = critically endangered; E = endangered; V = vulnerable; R = rare; I = indeterminate status

Falkland Islands	V	*Chloephaga rubidiceps*	Ruddy-headed Goose
	V	*Falco peregrinus*	Peregrine Falcon
Tristan da Cunha group	R	*Nesocichla eremita eremita*	Tristan Starchy (Thrush)
	R	*Nesospiza wilkinsi*	Grosbeak Bunting (Big Bill Canary)
Campbell Island	V	*Anas aucklandica nesiotis*	Campbell Island Teal
Auckland Islands	V	*Anas aucklandica aucklandica*	Auckland Island Teal
	I	*Rallus pectoralis muelleri*	Auckland Island Rail
	R	*Coenocorypha aucklandica aucklandica*	Auckland Island Snipe
Antipodes Island	R	*Coenocorypha aucklandica meinertzhagenae*	Antipodes Island Snipe
Snares Islands	R	*Coenocorypha aucklandica huegeli*	Snares Island Snipe
Chatham Islands	E	*Pterodroma axillaris*	Chatham Island Petrel
	E	*Pterodroma magentae*	Chatham Island Taiko (Magenta Petrel)
	E	*Haematopus chathamensis*	Chatham Island Oystercatcher
	E	*Thinornis novaeseelandiae*	New Zealand Shore Plover
	R	*Coenocorypha aucklandica pusilla*	Chatham Island Snipe
	CE	*Hemiphaga novaeseelandiae chathamensis*	Chatham Island Pigeon
	E	*Cyanoramphus auriceps forbesi*	Chatham Island Yellow-crowned Parakeet
	CE	*Petroica traversi*	Black Robin

(*Coenocorypha aucklandica*) and two passerines from the Tristan da Cunha group. In a fourth category, indeterminate, is the Auckland Island Rail (*Rallus pectoralis muelleri*). *Table 1* lists these species by locality, and brief notes are given in Appendix 1 (summarized from King (1981) with additions). These Red Data Book species are the contemporary candidates in a continuing process of extinction of birds on subantarctic islands. For example, of the 67 species recorded at the Chatham Islands, 29 had become extinct in pre-European times and eight since European settlement (Atkinson & Bell 1973). The significance of these figures is reinforced when it is realized that 16 of the 38 taxa of indigenous birds still breeding there are endemic. Extinctions have occurred at many other subantarctic islands, but information is incomplete for most of them.

It is important to note that since most subantarctic islands are widely scattered around the Southern Ocean there is little gene flow between island populations of birds. Penguins and petrels dominate the avifauna, and both groups display a strong tendency to return to breed at the island where they fledged. Thus insular forms have evolved and the taxonomy of some groups, such as albatrosses, giant petrels and prions, is difficult. There is an associated tendency to see every island population of a species as taxonomically distinct, which results in a perhaps exaggerated concern for the protection of small populations.

The Heard Island Shag (*Phalacrocorax atriceps nivalis*) is an island race of the Blue-eyed Shag, one of the two circumpolar species (the other being the King Shag *P. albiventer*) which have recently been merged with *P. atriceps* as the Emperor Shag (Devillers & Terschuren 1978). In 1950 the breeding population on Heard Island was confined to two colonies, one with about 20 pairs and the other with about seven pairs (Downes *et al.* 1959). However, this small population appears to be highly successful, and with a normal clutch of four eggs this shag produces a large crop of young birds each year. In 1980 they were at least as common as in 1950, and the larger colony may have increased somewhat (Johnstone 1982). This example illustrates that a small population need not necessarily be endangered. Far larger populations give grounds for greater concern if their numbers or productivity are declining.

Table 2: Man and introduced vertebrates on islands in the Southern Ocean between the subtropical convergence and 60°S. Sealers probably visited and stayed on most islands for varying periods during the 19th century. Areas and sizes of human populations are approximate.

Island	Area (km²)	Human popn.	Date of occupation	Introduced vertebrates[1,2]	References[3]
1. ISLANDS CLOSE TO SUBTROPICAL CONVERGENCE					
Chatham Is	960	500	c. 1100–	Cattle, goat, sheep, horse, poultry, brush-tailed possum *Trichosurus vulpecula*, *R. norvegicus*, *R. rattus*, cat, dog (all P). *R. exulans* (E)	4
Tristan da Cunha group					
Inaccessible I.	18	Nil		Cattle, sheep, goat, pig (all E. –1960s), dog (E); F	27
Nightingale I.	2	Nil		Sheep (E); F	27
Tristan I.	95	300	1810–	Cattle, sheep, cat, dog (all P, 1817–), goat (E, C18–1951), donkey (P, 1860–), horse (E), pig (E), poultry (P, 1810–), *R. rattus* (P, 1882–), house mouse (P, 1830–)	27
Gough I.	57	10	Station 1955–	Sheep (E, 1958), poultry, dog (both E), house mouse (P)	27
Falkland Is	12,030	1,800+	1764–	Cattle, goat, horse, pig (all P, 1764–), sheep (P, early C19–), rabbit (P, C18–), hare *Lepus capensis* (P), guanaco* *Lama guanacoe* (P, 1862–), poultry, cat, Patagonian fox* *Dusicyon griseus*, *R. norvegicus*, house mouse (all P)	5, 2, 30
I. Amsterdam	55	Nil	Station 1950–	Cattle (P, 1871–), house mouse, cat, *R. rattus* (all P, C19–), pig (E, C19), goat, sheep (both P), *R. norvegicus* (?P)	22
I. Saint Paul	7	Nil		Pig (E, C19), cat (E, C19– pre 1874), rabbit (P, post 1874–), goat (E), sheep (E, –1958), house mouse, *R. rattus* (both P, C19–), *R. norvegicus* (?P)	22
2. NEW ZEALAND SUBANTARCTIC ISLANDS					
Antipodes I.	20	Nil		Cattle, goat (both E), sheep (E, 1885–1895), house mouse (P)	3,13,25
Auckland Is		Nil	Intermittent 1841–1945		28
Adams I.	120	Nil		F	26
Auckland I.	460	Nil		Cattle (E, 1895), goat (P, 1888–), sheep (E, intermittent 1840–1900), horse (E, 1850), brush-tailed possum (E), dog (E), house mouse (P, 1820–), pig (P, 1807–), cat (P, 1840–)	26
Enderby I.	6	Nil		Cattle (P, 1850, 1897–), sheep (E, 1850, 1897), goat (E, 1864–1889), pig (E, 1842–1887), dog (E), rabbit (P, 1840, 1864–), house mouse (P, 1850–)	26
Bounty Is		Nil		F	21
Campbell I.	109	10	Farm 1890–1931, Station 1941–	Cattle (E, –1984), goat, dog, pig (all E), sheep (P, 1895–), cat (P, post 1916–), *R. norvegicus* (P)	11
Snares Is	22	Nil		F	

3. ISLANDS CLOSE TO ANTARCTIC CONVERGENCE

Island			Station	Introduced vertebrates	Refs
Is Crozet					
I. des Apotres	7			F	
I. aux Cochons	60			Rabbit (P. 1850–), pig (E. 1820–1860), cat (P. 1887–), house mouse (P. C19–)	10
I. de l'Est	130			Rabbit (P)	
I. des Pingouins	3			F	
I. de la Possession	400		Station 1962–	Goat (E), sheep (E. 1969–1981), house mouse (P. C19–), *R. rattus* (P. C19–)	18
Is Kerguelen	7,000	90	Station 1949–	Cattle (E), mule (E. 1949–53), sheep (P. 1909–1932, 1952–), mouflon* *Ovis musimon* (P. 1956–), reindeer *Rangifer tarandus* (P. 1955–), rabbit (P. 1874–), poultry (P), pig (E. C19; some now in captivity), dog (E. 1903–1928), mink* *Mustela vison* (E. 1956–1963), cat (P. 1800–50, 1952–), house mouse (P. C19–), *R. rattus* (P. 1956–)	9, 17, 19
Macquarie I.	112	20	Station 1911–1915, 1948–	Cattle, horse, donkey, goat, sheep, pig, dog, poultry (all E), rabbit (P. 1870s–), cat (P. 1812–), house mouse (P. 1890–), *R. rattus* (P. 1910–), weka *Gallirallus australis* (P. 1867–)	7, 8, 14
Marion I.	290	15	Station 1948–	Sheep (E. 1947–1967), poultry (E. 1950–1967), cat (P. 1949–), house mouse (P. C19–)	1, 2
Prince Edward I.	44	Nil		F	23, 29

4. ISLANDS SOUTH OF ANTARCTIC CONVERGENCE

Island			Station	Introduced vertebrates	Refs
Bouvetoya	50	Nil		F	
Heard I.	460	14	Station 1947–1955	Dog (husky) (E. 1947–1955), sheep (E. 1950); F	12
McDonald Is	3	Nil		F	15
South Georgia	5,000		Sealers, whalers 1796–1965	Sheep, dog (both E), cat (almost E), horse (E. 1905), rabbit (E. 1872), reindeer (P. 1911–), house mouse (P. 1850–), *R. norvegicus* (P. 1800–)	6, 16, 20
Bird I.	10		Station 1965–	F	
South Sandwich Is	400	4	Station 1963, 1982–	F	

Notes: 1. Symbols: P = species now present; E = species now extinct; F = island free of introduced vertebrates; C18, C19 = 18th and 19th centuries; * = not on main island of group. + = Population has increased significantly since the 1982 UK/Argentina conflict

2. Dates are often not known precisely; those given are based on the best available information. A dash after a year indicates that the species has been present continuously since then.

3. 1. Anderson & Condy 1974; 2. Anon. 1980; 3. Atkinson 1978; 4. Atkinson & Bell 1973; 5. Bauer 1973; 6. Berry *et al.* 1979; 7. Carrick 1957; 8. Cumpston 1968; 9. Derenne 1976; 10. Derenne & Mougin 1976; 11. Dilks 1979; 12. Downes *et al.* 1959; 13. Falla 1965; 14. Jenkin *et al.* 1982; 15. Johnstone 1982; 16. Leader-Williams 1978; 17. Lesel & Derenne 1975; 18. Mougin 1969; 19. Pascal 1982; 20. Pye & Bonner 1980; 21. Robertson & van Tets 1982; 22. Segonzac 1972; 23. Skinner *et al.* 1978; 24. Strange 1972; 25. Taylor 1975; 26. Taylor 1968; 27. Wace & Holdgate 1976; 28. Warham & Bell 1979; 29. Williams *et al.* 1979; 30. Woods 1975.

THE FATAL IMPACT

The history of man's involvement with subantarctic islands is well documented. Three major island groups were colonized by man and they retain settled human populations to this day: the Chatham Islands, first colonized by the Maori people about 1100; the Falkland Islands where the first settlement was established in 1764; and Tristan da Cunha where, although sealing started in 1780, the first settlers did not arrive until 1811 (Wace & Holdgate 1976). During the nineteenth century most of these islands were visited in pursuit of fur seal skins and, later, oil from elephant seals, penguins and whales. Many of these visits lasted several years, and the men frequently but unintentionally brought rats and mice with them. Cats and dogs were brought too in some instances, both for companionship and also to control the rats and mice. Because shipping services were unreliable, local supplies of food were often required. Penguins and albatrosses and their eggs were exploited for this purpose, and seal meat was also eaten. However, alternative and more palatable meat could be obtained from imported sheep, cattle and goats if there was suitable vegetation for grazing and browsing. Rabbits and, on Macquarie Island, Wekas (*Gallirallus australis*) were introduced for the same purpose, and also as food for the survivors of shipwrecks.

The flora and fauna of the subantarctic islands have evolved in the absence of terrestrial mammalian herbivores and predators. The only exception is at the Falkland Islands, where the Falkland Island Fox (*Dusicyon antarcticus*) was endemic. It was exterminated by 1876, but has since been replaced on some of the West Falkland Islands by the introduced Patagonian Grey Fox (*D. griseus*). The only significant indigenous land predator is the Southern or Antarctic Skua (*Catharacta antarctica*) which occurs at all the southern islands. One or both species of Giant Petrel, the northern *Macronectes halli* and the southern *M. giganteus*, breed at most islands. Both occasionally prey upon smaller petrels and penguin chicks, but on land they are principally scavengers rather than predators (Johnstone 1977). The ecological impact on these island ecosystems of the introduction of terrestrial mammals was therefore likely to be profound.

Table 2 summarizes information about the introduction of vertebrates other than fish to the subantarctic islands. For the Falkland Islands, Strange (1972) lists ibis, parrot, rhea, otter and skunk in addition to those in *Table 2*, but no further details are available. Though primarily vegetarian, some species (e.g. pigs) have their major impact as carnivores as a result of their occasional predation of birds. House Mice (*Mus musculus*) are usually classed as herbivores, though they occasionally take eggs of small birds such as storm petrels and pipits on Antipodes Island (P. J. Moors, pers. comm.).

Macquarie Island: a case history of one subantarctic island

Macquarie Island can be used as an example of how the indigenous fauna of a subantarctic island has responded to man and the animals that he has introduced. The story has been told elsewhere (e.g. Carrick 1957; Taylor 1979; Jenkin *et al.* 1982), but it is worth summarizing here (*Table 3*). Many important details are contained in the fascinating history of the island compiled by Cumpston (1968). Macquarie Island was discovered in 1810, and by 1835 virtually no fur seals (*Arctocephalus* sp.) remained. Over the next 40 years there was little sealing activity, but in the 1870s the oil gangs returned. King Penguins (*Aptenodytes patagonicus*), Royal Penguins (*Eudyptes schlegeli*) and Southern Elephant Seals (*Mirounga leonina*) were then harvested annually until about 1918. Since then Royal Penguins and Elephant Seals have recovered their former abundance. King Penguins are still increasing (Rounsevell & Copson 1982), but their elimination from the isthmus near the north end of the island, where they bred last century (Debenham 1945), has not yet been made good. Cats were introduced soon after the island's discovery and had become feral by 1820 (Debenham

Table 3:   A brief history of man's impact on Macquarie Island.

	Human Affairs		Changes in Fauna
1800	Pre-1810: shipwrecks and castaways?		
	1810 Island discovered: hectic exploitation of fur seals	c. 1812	Cats introduced
1820		1820	Feral dogs and cats reported
		1835	Fur seals exterminated
1840			
1860		1867	Stewart Island Weka introduced
	1870s Oil gangs renew activity: Elephant Seals, King Penguins, Royal Penguins exploited	1870s	Rabbit introduced
1880		1880s	Parakeet and Banded Rail become extinct
		1890	First report of house mice
1900	1911–15 AAE* Station	1910	First report of Rattus rattus
	1918 Last oil season	1911	King Penguins reduced to 5000 birds
1920			
	1933 Declared a Wildlife Sanctuary		
1940		1940s	King Penguins steadily increasing
	1948 ANARE** Station established		
1960		1968	First rabbit fleas introduced
	1971 Proclaimed a Tasmanian Nature Reserve	1970s	Small breeding colonies of Blue Petrels, Fairy Prions and Diving Petrels discovered on coastal stacks
		1979	First annual introduction of myxoma virus
1980		1980	King Penguin population c. 250,000
2000		2000	No rabbits, cats or wekas remain?

* Australasian Antarctic Expedition.
** Australian National Antarctic Research Expeditions.

1945). Dogs followed the same pattern, but evidently died out sometime after 1820 (Debenham 1945; Mawson 1943). House mice were first reported in 1890 and *R. rattus* in 1910 (Cumpston 1968). Stewart Island Wekas (*Gallirallus australis scotti*) were introduced in 1872 (Falla 1937) and the European Rabbit (*Oryctolagus cuniculus*) in the 1870s (Scott 1882). Sometime between 1880 and 1891 the ground-nesting Macquarie Island Parakeet (*Cyanoramphus novaezelandiae erythrotis*) became extinct (Hamilton 1894), and the Macquarie Island Banded Rail (*Rallus philippensis macquariensis*) had disappeared by 1894 (Vestjens 1963). One can only speculate how these two endemic ground-dwelling birds survived for 70 years after cats arrived. Taylor (1979) has suggested that during this period there was only a small population of cats which relied on burrow-nesting petrels and beach scavenging for food, and that the subsequent introduction of rabbits brought about a great increase in cats and wekas and predation on the birds.

It is certain that the numbers of species and individuals of burrow-nesting petrels on Macquarie Island were originally far greater than they are today. Jones (1980) conducted a survey of the island's populations based on the remains of kills by skuas and cats. Brothers (1984) in the last few years has surveyed the present breeding colonies of petrels, and his results in general agree with Jones' findings. The Antarctic Prion (*Pachyptila desolata*) is the most common species, occurring mainly on the inland plateau above 180m; it is absent in winter for five months. The White-headed Petrel (*Pterodroma lessoni*) is also common but may be decreasing; it breeds on dense tussock-clad slopes as well as on higher parts with less vegetation, and leaves the island for only two months. Sooty Shearwaters (*Puffinus griseus*) are less common and probably decreasing; they breed only on tussock-covered slopes and are absent for five months. Brothers has also explored the coastal stacks inaccessible to rats, cats and Wekas, and has found small breeding populations of Blue Petrels (*Halobaena caerulea*), Fairy Prions (*Pachyptila turtur*) and Common Diving Petrels (*Pelecanoides urinatrix*). Blue Petrels and Diving Petrels were known to breed on the main island in large numbers in the 1890s (Campbell 1900), but the original status of the Fairy Prion is not known. All three species visit their burrows in winter. The Grey Petrel (*Procellaria cinerea*), a winter breeder, used to nest on the island (Campbell 1900), but no longer does so. The status of the Grey-backed Storm Petrel (*Garrodia nereis*) and Thin-billed Prion (*Pachyptila belcheri*), both of which have been found in burrows, is not known (Rounsevell & Brothers, 1984).

It is difficult to define the separate roles of cats, rats and wekas in bringing about the extinction of the rail and parakeet and the extirpation of burrow-nesting petrels from the main island. Jones (1977) found that the cats' diet consisted mainly of rabbits, most of which were less than 10 weeks old. Antarctic Prions and White-headed Petrels were also common foods. The sparse population of Antarctic Terns (*Sterna vittata*) has almost certainly been depressed as a result of predation by cats. Jones estimated that the population of about 375 cats annually ate 56,000 rabbits, 47,000 Antarctic Prions and 11,000 White-headed Petrels. A few rats, mice and wekas were also eaten. An important conclusion was that availability of food in winter was limiting the cats' numbers. Skira (1978) showed that rabbits on Macquarie Island did not breed from April to August. In consequence no young rabbits were present during winter, so forcing the cats to subsist on other foods. Cats can kill larger rabbits with difficulty, and apparently do so only occasionally. Other winter food included beach carrion (e.g. Elephant Seals) and wekas. In the nineteenth century winter-visiting Blue Petrels, Diving Petrels, Grey Petrels and (perhaps) Fairy Prions would also have been available. It is not surprising then that these are the species that appear to have suffered most.

There is little evidence that *R. rattus* is a significant predator of birds on Macquarie Island. The rats are largely confined to tussock, and their diet is primarily vegetarian with some invertebrate material (Jenkin *et al.* 1982). However, Brothers (1984) found that breeding failure of Sooty Shearwaters and White-headed Petrels mainly occurred at or soon after hatching, and although direct evidence was lacking he thought rats were responsible. He also found abandoned eggs which had been gnawed by rats. Of 10 faecal pellets of rats collected in 1982, two contained small feathers (T. Pye, pers. comm.), but these could have been the result of either scavenging or predation.

Similarly, there is little direct evidence of predation by wekas. Brothers (1984) found no avian remains in the guts of wekas, but other observations indicated that they do prey to a small extent on both Sooty Shearwaters and White-headed Petrels. They also take very young rabbits. Blackburn (1968) reported heavy predation by Stewart Island Wekas on burrow-nesting petrels on Codfish Island, the wekas having been introduced from nearby Stewart Island.

The most common indigenous predator of small petrels at Macquarie Island is the Southern Skua. It is largely absent from May until August. Jones & Skira (1979) showed a strong correlation existed between the occurrences of rabbits and nesting skuas on the plateau, but not on the coastal terrace. On the plateau the skuas' diet consisted mainly of young rabbits, Antarctic Prions and White-headed Petrels, but near the coast they took few rabbits and depended largely on killing penguin chicks and occasionally wounded adults, and scavenging penguin and seal carcasses.

Thus it appears that the presence of rabbits has significantly boosted the population of skuas, with the result that the skua predation upon small petrels has also increased. The cats, similarly dependent on rabbits, must now be far more numerous than when rabbits were absent. Wekas also eat some very small rabbits, but are certainly less dependent on them than are skuas and cats. Another effect of the rabbits is to have greatly reduced the area where the tussock *Poa foliosa* grows. Sooty Shearwaters nest only in tussock areas and so do many White-headed Petrels. Antarctic Prions, which now nest mostly on the tussock-free plateau, may have benefited in the past from the ground cover of tussock and are now much more exposed to predation outside their burrows. The only possible benefit conferred by the grazing effect of rabbits is that wekas and rats are largely confined to the reduced areas of tussock. Cats, however, range over all habitats. It appears, then, that the introduction of rabbits was the single factor that spelt doom for so many small and medium-sized birds on Macquarie Island. The introduction in itself would have been less damaging had cats and wekas not also been present.

EFFECTS OF ALIEN VERTEBRATES

Domestic stock
The continuing threats to birds on Macquarie Island are a legacy from the events of last century and generally this is true for many other subantarctic islands. At the more northern islands where domestic stock were able to thrive on the relatively lush vegetation the result was severe modification of the habitat. This is exemplified by the Chatham Islands where the original lowland forest survives only in the south of the main island, the steep dissected terrain there being virtually impenetrable to domestic stock. If current land-use continues the outlook for forest-dwelling birds there is bleak.

Further south at islands near the Antarctic convergence, cattle and sheep have persisted on Campbell Island (*Table 2*) where a sheep station was established in 1895. It proved uneconomic and was abandoned in 1931, leaving behind 4000 sheep and a few cattle. In 1970 a fence was constructed across the narrow middle of the island, and all the sheep on the northern half were destroyed. The situation has been regularly monitored (Dilks & Wilson 1979; Wilson 1979). The vegetation has regenerated spectacularly, but there has apparently been little change in the island's large population of Southern Royal Albatrosses (*Diomedea epomophora epomophora*) (c. 4000 pairs breed each year), whose large nests remain dispersed over most of the island on both sides of the fence. In 1984 a new fence was erected confining the sheep to a smaller western part of the island.

Sheep are also on some islands of the Kerguelen archipelago, but the present population stems from stock imported in 1952. Reindeer (*Rangifer tarandus*) and Moufflon (*Ovis musimon*) were also introduced to Iles Kerguelen in the 1950s (Lesel & Derenne 1975). The staple diet of the Reindeer on South Georgia is the tussock *Poa flabellata*, and their numbers have been increasing (Bonner 1980). The destruction of tussock deprives ground-nesting birds of cover and cryptic nesting sites. This together with the trampling and collapsing of underground nest-burrows is the main effect of large herbivores on the bird populations. Cattle still run free on Ile Amsterdam as they have done for more than a century (Petit 1977) and a small herd remains on Enderby Island, Auckland Islands group. The few feral cattle on Campbell Island were removed in 1984.

Rabbits
Rabbits have survived on many of the subantarctic islands to which they have been introduced (*Table 2*). As shown for Macquarie Island, their ecological effects are twofold: firstly, their grazing dramatically alters the structure of the vegetation which with their scraping and burrowing increases erosion; and secondly, by acting as food for predators they maintain populations of the predators at a higher level than otherwise, with severe consequences for burrow-nesting petrels and other birds which are preyed on.

Rats

There has been some contention about the extent to which rats are predators of seabirds. Three species are involved: the Black or Ship Rat (*Rattus rattus*), the Brown or Norway Rat (*R. norvegicus*) and the Polynesian Rat (*R. exulans*), of which the first two have been introduced to a number of subantarctic islands (*Table 2*). Norman (1975) considered that the predatory capabilities of rats were the result mainly of supposition rather than direct observations or studies of their diet. However recent extensive reviews by Atkinson (1978, this vol.) and Moors & Atkinson (1984) confirm their depredatory activities and provide many examples. Atkinson (1978) acknowledged that evidence of rat predation is often circumstantial, but pointed out that this is to be expected because rats are nocturnal feeders. There is no doubt that on subantarctic islands both *R. rattus* and *R. norvegicus* do take unguarded eggs and young chicks of burrow-nesting petrels.

In the New Zealand region Imber (1975) has shown that *R. norvegicus* and *R. exulans* take eggs and small chicks of Cook's Petrels (*Pterodroma cooki*) and Grey-faced Petrels (*P. macroptera gouldi*). These observations together with correlations between the occurrences of Diving Petrels (Pelecanoididae) and Storm Petrels (Hydrobatidae) on islands with and without these rats have led Imber to propose that a petrel colony is endangered if it is invaded by a species of rat whose maximum weight is close to or exceeds the adult weight of the petrel. *R. exulans* has an average weight of 60–100g, *R. norvegicus* ranges from 200–450g and *R. rattus* is intermediate, about 125–200g.

Rats were apparently reported from the main Auckland Island earlier this century (Falla 1965), but they were not found in 1972–3 (Taylor 1975) and there is reason to think that the original source was referring to house mice, which do occur there (R. H. Taylor, pers. comm.). At Iles Kerguelen Falla (1937) noted rats (believed to have been *R. norvegicus*; I. A. E. Atkinson, pers. comm.) and mice at the old Jeanne d'Arc Whaling Station on the southeastern peninsula of Grande Terre in the summer of 1929–30. However, evidently they did not spread: after the scientific station was established in 1949 some 100km away at Port aux Français, the first rat—a *R. rattus*—was found there only in 1956.

There is indirect evidence from Ile Amsterdam and Ile Saint Paul that within 50 years or so of its introduction early last century *R. rattus* had caused a heavy reduction in the breeding populations of Broad-billed Prions (*Pachyptila vittata*) and perhaps also White-bellied Storm Petrels (*Fregetta grallaria*) (Segonzac 1972). At Iles Kerguelen, *R. rattus* has been blamed for a major decline in the breeding populations of Antarctic Prions and Blue Petrels (Dorst & Milon 1964). On Ile de la Possession, Iles Crozet, Mougin (1969) recorded two periods of a few days each in 1968 when *R. rattus* killed and ate chicks of Kerguelen Petrels (*Pterodroma brevirostris*) (1–5 December) and chicks of White-chinned Petrels (*Procellaria aequinoctialis*) (late January). He speculated that these were times when the rats' usual foods had become temporarily scarce. According to B. Despin (pers. comm.) these rats also prey upon nestlings of Antarctic Terns and Kerguelen Terns (*Sterna virgata*), as well as Soft-plumaged Petrels (*Pterodroma mollis*), Blue Petrels, Antarctic Prions, Salvin's Prions (*Pachyptila vittata salvini*), Common Diving Petrels and South Georgian Diving Petrels (*Pelecanoides georgicus*). On Ile de ia Possession, Prions and Diving Petrels are found in small numbers and only above 500m, whereas on Ile de l'Est, rat-free and only 20km away, these seabirds are abundant and nest from sea-level to above 500m.

The most southern rat population to have been studied is that of *R. norvegicus* on South Georgia (Pye & Bonner 1980). Although these rats eat mainly plant matter, invertebrates and carrion, there is some evidence that birds are taken. Pye & Bonner reported a negative correlation between the distribution of rats and that of breeding Antarctic Pipits (*Anthus antarcticus*) and South Georgia Pintails (*Anas georgicus*).

Antarctic Prions, Blue Petrels and Diving Petrels were thought to be taken by the rats, though the only evidence was a Blue Petrel skull in a rat burrow and some feathers in rat faecal pellets. Rats were also seen eating newly hatched chicks of White-chinned Petrels.

Pigs

Well known as omnivores, pigs are listed in *Table 2* as predators even though their diet is probably largely vegetarian. A study of their diet on Auckland Island, the only subantarctic island where they occur today, found avian remains in five of the sixteen stomachs sampled (Challies 1975). One contained most of a Yellow-eyed Penguin (*Megadyptes antipodes*) and two others contained remains of Antarctic Prions. Pigs have been known to dig up the burrows of petrels and have also been accused of taking eggs and young of penguins, albatrosses and shags.

Cats

Cats pose a greater threat to birds than any other animal introduced to the subantarctic islands. Those on Marion Island have been the subject of intensive research during the last decade (Anderson & Condy 1974, Skinner *et al.* 1978, van Aarde 1978, 1979, 1980, van Aarde & Skinner 1982, Williams 1978). Five were introduced in 1949 to control house mice at the meteorological station established the previous year. In 1951 one cat was seen 12km from the station, and by 1965 feral cats were established around the periphery of the island, giving a dispersal rate of 2km per year. Analysis of prey (van Aarde 1980) showed that the Broad-billed Prion was the species taken most frequently; Soft-plumaged, Kerguelen, Great-winged (*Pterodroma m. macroptera*) and White-chinned Petrels were also commonly eaten, with Blue Petrels, Diving Petrels and Lesser Sheathbills (*Chionis minor*) being occasional prey. The frequency of mice (16 percent) was second only to that of Broad-billed Prions, but the mice provided a much smaller proportion by weight of the total diet. Adults, chicks and eggs of most petrels were vulnerable, and cats were even seen entering the small burrows of prions. Diving Petrels used to be common in the early 1950s, but no nests have been found since 1965. However this species is abundant on neighbouring Prince Edward Island, which has no introduced mammals. Storm Petrels are similarly rare on Marion but abundant on Prince Edward. Van Aarde (1979) estimated the cat population to be 2137 in 1975–6. He estimated that each cat killed 213 birds per year, giving a total for the entire cat population of about 455,120 birds (van Aarde 1980).

On Iles Kerguelen the diet of cats is similar to that on Macquarie Island (Derenne 1976). Rabbits are eaten in all months of the year, and birds comprise most of the rest of the diet. Adult seabirds weighing less than 250g are taken outside their burrows, which are apparently too small for Kerguelen cats to enter: these include Blue Petrels, prions (particularly Antarctic Prions) and Common and South Georgian Diving Petrels. These species have declined markedly since 1950 near Port aux Français, where cats were released in 1952. Medium-sized birds dig burrows large enough for cats to enter and prey upon the occupant, whether egg, chick or adult. Soft-plumaged and White-headed Petrels are both in this category, as is the winter-breeding Great-winged Petrel, which faces the same fate as the winter-breeding Grey Petrel on Macquarie Island. The Kerguelen Petrel is apparently safe because it nests in wet areas which cats avoid. The large Grey and White-chinned Petrels also nest in wet sites and can defend themselves, and they appear seldom to be taken by cats. Derenne had no evidence of cats preying upon surface-nesting Kerguelen Teal (*Anas eatoni*), Lesser Sheathbills, Kelp Gulls (*Larus dominicanus*), Antarctic Terns or Kerguelen Terns. Pascal (1980) estimated that 1.2 million birds were killed each year by cats on Iles Kerguelen.

On Ile aux Cochons, Iles Crozet, cats and rabbits have coexisted for nearly 100 years (Derenne & Mougin 1976). Strangely, rabbits are seldom eaten, but instead mice provide the staple prey. Limited information indicates that Broad-billed Prions are the cats' favourite avian food.

Cats have not survived on every island to which they have been introduced, and it is instructive to examine the situations in which they have failed to persist. They have been present on South Georgia but have probably not survived in a feral state. The combined effects of a scarcity of winter food and the severe climate may have been responsible. Though still present there, they have probably survived only by partial dependence on man. At least during the 1970s, a few persisted in a semi-feral state in the region of the British Antarctic Survey station at Grytviken. Their diet included *Rattus norvegicus* and Antarctic Prions. The last breeding record was in summer 1973–4 (T. Pye, pers. comm.). In 1982 only two individuals were thought to remain (Headland 1982). On Iles Kerguelen they were present during the first half of last century but died out about 1850 and were re-introduced in 1952. In the meantime rabbits had been released in 1874 and the cats are now flourishing despite a shooting campaign begun in 1973 (Pascal 1980). On Ile Amsterdam they have survived in low numbers, but on Ile Saint Paul they died out before 1874.

From the pattern of survivals and extinctions in *Table 2* I conclude that cats are able to persist on subantarctic islands in the following situations:

  – For 50 years or so where populations of burrow-nesting petrels are large and have not been subject to the depredations of other introduced predators.
  – Where another introduced mammal (normally the rabbit or House Mouse) provides an alternative food source once the petrel populations have been reduced.
  – Where both petrels and alternative mammalian prey are present when cats first become established.

Table 4 illustrates this. Examples of the first situation are Iles Kerguelen, Ile Saint Paul and Macquarie Island prior to the introduction of rabbits at all three islands. Examples of the second situation are Ile Amsterdam (mice), Ile aux Cochons (mice and rabbits), Auckland Island (mice) and Macquarie Island since the 1870s (mice and rabbits). The conditions on Marion Island and on Iles Kerguelen after the 1952 cat introduction exemplify the third situation. If unrelieved by the introduction of suitable prey as an alternative to birds, the first situation terminates when the stock of winter-breeding or winter-visiting petrels has been reduced below the level required for cats to over-winter.

Table 4: Occurrence of mice, rabbits and rats on subantarctic islands where cats have been introduced.

Island	Mouse	Rabbit	Rattus norvegicus	Rattus rattus	Date of introduction of cat	Comment
Amsterdam	×		?	×	early 19C	
Auckland	×				c. 1840	Also pigs
Campbell			×		after 1916	Very scarce
Chatham	×		×	×	?	
Crozet (I. aux Cochons)	×	×			1887	
Falkland	×		×		?	
Kerguelen (Grande Terre)	×	×	?	×	c. 1800–1850; 1952	
Macquarie	×	×		×	c. 1812	Also weka
Marion	×				1949	
St. Paul	×	×		×	early 19C	Died out before 1874
Trista da Cunha	×			×	c. 1817	

This apparently happened last century on Iles Kerguelen and also on Ile Saint Paul despite the probable presence of mice. The second and third situations will come to an end only when the numbers of prey or of cats are reduced by some means to a level where either the prey are too scarce to support cats or there are too few cats to maintain a viable population.

The situation on Campbell Island is of particular interest because it varies from the general pattern. Cats were introduced after 1916 probably in the hope of controlling *R. norvegicus*. Very few cats are present now (Dilks 1979). Dilks collected cat scats during three summers in the 1970s and showed that rats were the most common prey, occurring in 19 out of 20 samples. Fifteen samples contained insects. Remains of birds were found in only seven samples, the species mostly being introduced landbirds (Silvereye, *Zosterops lateralis*; Redpoll, *Acanthis flammea*; and Hedge-sparrow, *Prunella modularis*). Remains of a 'prion-sized seabird' were found in one sample. The Pipit (*Anthus novaezeelandiae*) is absent from the main Campbell Island, but occurs on several small offshore islands free of rats and cats, as does a local flightless race of the New Zealand Brown Teal (*Anas aucklandica*) at Dent Island (Appendix 1). There is no information on the winter food of cats on Campbell Island; presumably they get by on a diet of rats augmented by insects and scavenging.

MANAGEMENT

Six nations administer subantarctic islands: Australia (Macquarie Island, Heard Island, McDonald Islands), France (Ile Amsterdam, Iles Crozet, Iles Kerguelen, Ile Saint Paul), New Zealand (Antipodes Islands, Auckland Islands, Bounty Islands, Campbell Island, Chatham Islands, Snares Islands), Norway (Bouvetoya), South Africa (Marion Island, Prince Edward Island) and the United Kingdom (Falkland Islands, Gough Island, Tristan da Cunha group, South Georgia, South Sandwich Islands).

A review of the management of subantarctic islands could occupy an entire symposium. I shall restrict my comments in this paper to management aimed at conserving or protecting the indigenous avifauna from man and his agents.

Use of predator-free islands as refuges
Despite the widespread introduction of vertebrates to the subantarctic region many islands within particular groups fortunately still remain predator-free. These places, usually offshore 'satellite' islands (Wingate, this vol.), provide vital refuges for many birds. Their importance for seabirds at Macquarie Island has already been described. Bird Island near South Georgia and Adams Island in the Auckland Islands group are especially valuable refuges of this type.

Predator-free islands also offer opportunities for active management, an approach which has been used most effectively in New Zealand. There are two well-known examples from the Chatham Islands. After South East Island was declared a Reserve in 1954 all sheep and cattle were removed and the island continues as the home of the only known breeding population of the Chatham Island Petrel (*Pterodroma axillaris*). The tiny population of Black Robins (*Petroica traversi*) has been successfully translocated from rapidly deteriorating habitat on Little Mangere Island to regenerating forest on Mangere Island, and more recently to South East Island (Appendix 1).

Management of populations of introduced vertebrates
The exciting experiment of the fence across Campbell Island has already been referred to. Two programmes aimed at reducing, if not eliminating, introduced vertebrates have been under way for several years on Macquarie and Marion Islands.

Rabbit control was started at Macquarie Island in 1968 (Brothers *et al*. 1982) and is now being conducted by the Tasmanian National Parks and Wildlife Service. Studies had shown that shooting and poisoning were ineffective, and that myxomatosis offered the only hope. However, there were no suitable blood-sucking parasites in the rabbit population to spread the disease, and the first ten years of the programme were devoted to introducing the Rabbit Flea (*Spilopsyllus cuniculi*). By 1978 the flea was widely distributed and the first introduction of myxoma virus was made. Impressive local kills resulted and fresh introductions of virus have continued each summer. The virus can survive the subantarctic winter and retains its viability into the next summer. The role of the rabbit in providing food for cats has already been stressed, and the cats may have increased temporarily with the new availability of dead and dying rabbits. The cat population should fall as rabbits become scarcer and methods for reducing it still further are now being considered. In the meantime some control of cats is effected by shooting (Rounsevell & Brothers, in prep.). Wekas will also be controlled by shooting, and there is a chance that they can be totally eliminated.

The major management on Marion Island concerns the elimination of cats. Feline panleucopaenia virus (FPL) was introduced in 1977 and by mid-1980 the cat population had been reduced by about 60 percent from a winter level of 2000–3000 (P. R. Condy, pers. comm.). FPL is evidently still active and there are no signs of immunity having developed. A new three-year programme of research and fieldwork was initiated in 1981 as part of the South African Antarctic Program. It involves continued monitoring of the effect of FPL on the cat population. Research on the dynamic relationship between the cats and their prey continues, with assessment of hunting cats in summer as a further method to reduce the population. The decline in cats achieved between 1977 and 1980 gives hope that FPL may be an effective control method for other subantarctic islands.

A campaign to eradicate cats at Iles Kerguelen started in 1973 and is continuing (Pascal 1980). In each of the five summers 1973–7 between 447 and 685 cats have been shot. Until the mid-1970s the cats were confined to Peninsule Courbet on the eastern side of Grande Terre, but in 1975, 1976 and 1977 their faeces were found at places to the south and west, indicating a westward spread. Pascal (1980) comments that any let-up in the campaign will result in a population explosion with colonization of new areas and the destruction of bird populations. Nevertheless, shooting has not prevented cats from dispersing into new areas and at best the campaign is only slowing their expansion. It appears that effective control will have to rely on biological control of both rabbits and cats: the examples of Macquarie Island and Marion Island indicate the feasibility and likely effectiveness of such an approach.

Prevention of disease

Introduced poultry are not known to have directly affected the indigenous avifauna of any subantarctic islands. Wace & Holdgate (1976), however, pointed out that the small flock of fowls once kept at the meteorological station on Gough Island involved the risk of introducing avian diseases. Recent research by Morgan *et al*. (1981) has demonstrated the presence of antibodies to Newcastle disease virus (NDV), a poultry disease, in the serum of 6 percent of 499 Royal Penguins on Macquarie Island. Antibodies to a flavivirus and an avian paramyxovirus were detected in King Penguins, Royal Penguins and Rockhopper Penguins (*Eudyptes chrysocome*), but not Gentoo Penguins (*Pygoscelis papua*). Isolates of several paramyxoviruses, one being NDV, were obtained from cloacal swabs of Royal and King Penguins (I. R. Morgan, pers. comm.). Antibodies to avian influenza virus, NDV and avian paramyxoviruses were found in 162 adults and 98 chicks of Adelie Penguins (*Pygoscelis adeliae*) in colonies near the Australian Antarctic Station at Casey, and at the now-abandoned Wilkes Station nearby as well as near the French Station at Dumont d'Urville (Morgan & Westbury 1981). In one colony with a relatively high incidence of antibodies to avian influenza virus and paramyxovirus there had been a heavy mortality of 4–5 week-old chicks, but the cause was not known. In summer 1981–2 a similar survey of Adelie Penguins was conducted near the Australian Station at Davis, together with a few Emperor Penguins (*Aptenodytes forsteri*) from the colony at Amanda Bay, 87km southwest of Davis. Three isolates of paramyxovirus (not NDV) were obtained from swabs from Adelie Penguins, but the serological studies are not yet complete (I. R. Morgan, pers. comm.). NDV has also been isolated from Adelie Penguins collected near the United States Station at McMurdo Sound (Pierson & Pfow 1975).

These findings indicate that penguins may risk infection with viruses which cause diseases in domestic poultry. The serological evidence shows that some individuals have recovered, but the low incidence of antibodies suggests that some infections may be lethal and that a large proportion of the populations remains susceptible to future infections. An avirulent strain of NDV is widespread and endemic in poultry throughout Australia. While there is not yet conclusive evidence that penguins have contracted the viruses from poultry or poultry products taken to subantarctic and Antarctic stations, it would be wise to minimize this risk. Under the Agreed Measures for the Conservation of Antarctic Fauna and Flora (Article IX of the Antarctic Treaty), no exotic bird species may be introduced into Antarctica (south of 60°S) without a permit. No such international agreement applies to the subantarctic islands. However, Australia (and possibly some other nations) applies the substance of the Agreed Measures to her subantarctic stations, and all poultry wastes (e.g. carcasses, egg shells) are incinerated. The introduction of cage birds—parrots in particular—and live poultry to subantarctic islands should be prohibited.

CONCLUSION

The history of man's ecological involvement with the subantarctic islands is generally deplorable. This review has been confined to the effects on birds, but the wholesale butchery of seals, particularly fur seals, last century was so thorough that some island populations are still recovering. Similarly the botanical damage wrought by introduced herbivores has drastically altered the physical structure of the vegetation and its floristic composition and accelerated erosion. Introduced salmonid fishes at Iles Kerguelen are changing the composition of the aquatic fauna of at least seven river systems in Grande Terre and at Iles Crozet at least two rivers on Ile de la Possession are similarly affected (Davaine & Beall 1982).

Compared with the ecological changes that have occurred on the populated continents and more hospitable islands the changes on subantarctic islands, even Iles Kerguelen, are relatively minor. At the Falkland Islands, Tristan da Cunha and the Chatham Islands, the three permanently-settled island groups covered by this review, man's continuing presence as an exploiter of the environment contrasts with his presence on the other subantarctic islands where he is essentially a visitor supplied with food, shelter and clothing produced elsewhere. The establishment and maintenance of buildings on these latter islands inevitably has a disruptive environmental impact. Intelligent siting of buildings and roads can minimize this impact. For example, a proposal to drive a road through a colony of King Penguins between the French station on Ile de la Possession, Iles Crozet, and the most convenient beach for the landing of supplies has been a cause of concern (B. Despin, pers. comm.). The drastic environmental impact that human affairs can wreak on these ecologically simple, and hence vulnerable, island ecosystems was amply demonstrated in 1982 by the war in the Falkland Islands.

The most southern islands experience such an extreme climate that few alien species can survive and breed. House Mice, *Rattus norvegicus* and Reindeer have managed to cope with conditions on the coastal plains of South Georgia, but an attempt to establish rabbits was unsuccessful (Holdgate & Wace 1961) and cats have probably never become feral. The other islands south of the Antarctic convergence are free of introduced mammals.

Other than small satellite islands in archipelagos, Prince Edward is the only island in the true subantarctic zone which remains free of introduced mammals. Williams *et al.* (1979) have stressed its importance as a breeding station and sanctuary for birds. Among the New Zealand subantarctic islands, Adams Island in the Auckland Islands group and the smaller Snares and Bounty Islands are virtually unmodified. Of the islands near the subtropical convergence, both Inaccessible and Nightingale Islands in the Tristan da Cunha group now have a chance to recover their former natural glory.

Twenty years ago Carrick (1964) predicted 'Conservation of the living resources of the Antarctic and subantarctic will be satisfactorily achieved when internationally-agreed legislation ensures that the impact of human activities on this environment and its marine and terrestrial fauna and flora does not cause avoidable impairment of them'. The Agreed Measures for the Conservation of the Antarctic Fauna and Flora (Third Antarctic Treaty Consultative Meeting, 1964) afford protection for the Antarctic south of 60°S, but no such internationally-agreed protection exists for the subantarctic islands. Keage (1981) considered ways in which the environment of the Australian Territory of Heard Island and the McDonald Islands could be given appropriate legal protection. He concluded that the extension of the (Australian) Antarctic Treaty (Environmental Protection) Act 1980 to include these Islands would be the most desirable of several options.

All six nations with subantarctic territory are also signatories to the Antarctic Treaty. The legal obstacles may be formidable, but in principle at least a logical way of giving environmental protection to the subantarctic islands would be for each country to extend its current legislation for the protection of Antarctic wildlife to include its subantarctic territory. A precedent has recently been set with the Convention for the Conservation of Antarctic Marine Living Resources prepared by the Antarctic Treaty nations in 1980, which applies to the ocean from the Antarctic continent to the region of the Antarctic convergence. Additional protection with international support would be gained by listing outstanding and substantially unmodified islands (e.g. Prince Edward Island, Heard Island, the McDonald Islands, the Snares Islands and Adams Island) as World Heritage Sites under the International Convention concerning the Protection of the World Cultural and Natural Heritage.

It is encouraging to see that the subantarctic conservation programmes mounted by South Africa, New Zealand and Tasmania are proving effective, and generally receive continuing government support. We must ensure that other governments realize the unique importance of their subantarctic territories and initiate long-term programmes of conservation and conservation-oriented research. Priorities should be:

– Prohibition of the introduction of alien fauna and flora.
– Application of strict quarantine controls for personnel and imported materials.
– Control (and preferably eradication if possible) of introduced animals, particularly cats and rabbits.

A united approach by the six nations involved is ultimately the only way that existing threats to birds on subantarctic islands can be reduced and even eliminated in some cases.

APPENDIX 1

NOTES ON RED DATA BOOK BIRD SPECIES
SUMMARIZED FROM KING (1981) WITH ADDITIONS

Chatham Island Petrel (*Pterodroma axillaris*) **Endangered**
Known only from South East Island (220ha). Vegetation had been reduced by sheep and cattle, which were removed in 1961; vegetation now recovering dramatically. Popuation 100–200 birds. Black-winged Petrel (*P. nigripennis*) nests on high parts of same island and may be competing. No introduced predators.

Chatham Island Taiko or Magenta Petrel (*Pterodroma magentae*) **Endangered**
Rediscovered in 1978; 23 birds banded after capture at lights set up near the Tuku River, southern part of main Chatham Island. No nests found yet. Forest deteriorating due to possums, cattle, sheep, pigs; there are also cats, rats and wekas.

New Zealand Brown Teal (*Anas aucklandica*) **Vulnerable**
A. a. aucklandica: flightless; common on those islands in Auckland group which lack cats. *A. a. chlorotis:* strong flier, formerly abundant; breeds only in a few places on the North Island, in Fiordland and on Great Barrier and possibly Stewart Islands. *A. a. nesiotis:* flightless; only on predator-free Dent Island, 1.6km off Campbell Island.

Ruddy-headed Goose (*Chloephaga rubidiceps*) **Vulnerable**
Mainland population in northern Tierra del Fuego, Chile and Argentina migrates in winter to grasslands of southern Argentina. Falkland population sedentary, widely distributed and said to compete with sheep. Unprotected: bounties paid in Tierra del Fuego and Falklands.

Peregrine Falcon (*Falco peregrinus*) **Vulnerable**
Falkland Islands race is *F. p. cassini*. Quite common.

Auckland Island Rail (*Rallus pectoralis muelleri*) **Indeterminate**
Most recent record from one individual captured on Adams Island in 1966. Nine other subspecies found outside New Zealand. Only the Auckland Island subspecies is at risk.

Chatham Island Oystercatcher (*Haematopus chathamensis*) **Endangered**
Only on Chatham Island. Total population *c*. 60 birds, possibly slowly increasing.

New Zealand Shore Plover (*Thinornis novaeseelandiae*) **Endangered**
Now only on predator-free South East Island in the Chathams group; formerly widespread on mainland New Zealand and Chatham Islands. About 40 breeding pairs. Very vulnerable to mammalian predators.

New Zealand Snipe (*Coenocorypha aucklandica*) **Rare**
C. a. aucklandica: extirpated from main Auckland Island but still on Ewing, Disappointment, Enderby and Adams Islands. *C. a. huegeli:* only on Snares Island. *C. a. meinertzhagenae:* only on the Antipodes Islands. *C. a. pusilla:* Chatham Islands (Pitt, South East, Mangere Islands). Extirpated from Pitt and Mangere before 1900 by cats, but successfully reintroduced to Mangere Island after cats died out; has also colonized nearby Star Keys. *C. a. iredalei:* was on Big South Cape and Jacky Lee Islands off Stewart Island. Extirpated on Jacky Lee by introduced weka in the early 1900s and from Big South Cape when *Rattus rattus* colonized and reached plague proportions in 1964. Probably extinct.

Chatham Island Pigeon (*Hemiphaga novaeseelandiae chathamensis*) **Critically endangered**
Only *c*. 50 remain, main factors being habitat destruction by stock and predation by man and cats. Now only on Chatham and also South East Islands, where 4 birds translocated in 1984.

Chatham Island Yellow-crowned Parakeet (*Cyanoramphus auriceps forbesi*) **Endangered**
Formerly on Mangere and Little Mangere Islands. Mangere was deforested, and parakeet then
confined to Little Mangere. As Mangere revegetates *C. a. forbesi* is recolonizing and increasing,
but hybridizes sometimes with the local race of the Red-crowned Parakeet *C.
novaeseelandiae chathamensis*, which is not at risk and is being removed. Population *c.* 80 birds.

Tristan Starchy (*Nesocichla eremita eremita*) **Rare**
Occurs on Tristan da Cunha despite predation by cats and *R. rattus. N. e. gordoni* on Inaccessible
Island and *N. e. procax* on Nightingale Island are abundant; both islands lack mammalian
predators.

Chatham Island Black Robin (*Petroica traversi*) **Critically endangered**
Originally on several of the Chatham Islands, but disappeared when cats arrived. Survived only on
cat-free Little Mangere Island until 1976–7, when all 7 birds translocated to Mangere Island by New
Zealand Wildlife Service; 5 birds transferred from Mangere to nearby South East Island in 1983. In
early 1984 total of 8 birds on Mangere and 12 on South East.

Grosbeak Bunting (*Nesospiza wilkinsi*) **Rare**
Only on Tristan da Cunha group. *N. w. wilkinsi* on Nightingale Island, *N. w. dunnei* on Inaccessible
Island. Depends on *Phylica* woodland, which was reduced on Inaccessible by stock until their
removal in the 1960s. Main threat is risk of introducing cats and *R. rattus* from Tristan Island.

ACKNOWLEDGEMENTS

This paper was prepared with the help of several people including Harry Burton, John
Langford and my wife Kate, and I am most grateful to them. In particular I thank Dr P.
J. Moors for his invaluable help in producing the final version of the paper. I also
acknowledge with thanks the following people who allowed me to quote their unpublished information: Dr I. A. E. Atkinson, N. P. Brothers, Dr P. R. Condy, Dr B.
Despin, Dr P. J. Moors, Dr I. R. Morgan, T. Pye and R. H. Taylor. My attendance at
the ICBP Conference was funded by Antarctic Division, Australian Department of
Science and Technology, and I thank the then Director, Mr C. G. McCue, and the
Deputy Director (Research), Dr P. G. J. Quilty, for their support.

REFERENCES

ANDERSON, G. D. & CONDY, P. R. 1974. A note on the feral house cat and house mouse on Marion
Island. *S. Afr. J. Antarct. Res.* **4**, 58–61.
ANON. 1980. *The cats at Marion Island.* Press release, Council for Scientific and Industrial
Research, Pretoria.
ATKINSON, I. A. E. 1978. Evidence for effects of rodents on the vertebrate wildlife of New Zealand
islands. *In:* Dingwall, P. R., Atkinson, I. A. E. & Hay, C. (eds) The ecology and control of
rodents in New Zealand nature reserves. *N. Z. Dept. Lands & Survey Information Series* **4**, 7–30.
ATKINSON, I. A. E. (this vol.). The spread of commensal species of *Rattus* to oceanic islands and
their effects on island avifaunas.
ATKINSON, I. A. E. & BELL, B. D. 1973. Offshore and outlying islands. *In:* Williams, G. R. (ed.)
The natural history of New Zealand: 372–92. A. H. & A. W. Reed, Wellington.
BAUER, E. A. 1973. The Falklands. *Sea Frontiers* **19**, 279–89.
BERRY, R. J., BONNER, W. N. & PETERS, J. 1979. Natural selection in House Mice (*Mus musculus*)
from South Georgia (South Atlantic Ocean). *J. Zool.* **189**, 385–98.
BLACKBURN, A. 1968. The birdlife of Codfish Island. *Notornis* **15**, 51–65.
BONNER, W. N. 1980. British biological research in the Antarctic. *Biol. J. Lin. Soc.* **14**, 1–10.
BROTHERS, N. P. 1984. Breeding, distribution and status of burrow-nesting petrels at Macquarie
Island. *Aust. Wildl. Res.* **11**, 113–31.

BROTHERS, N. P., EBERHARD, I. E., COPSON, G. R. & SKIRA, I. J. 1982. Control of rabbits on Macquarie Island by myxomatosis. *Aust. Wildl. Res.* **9**, 477–85.

CAMPBELL, A. J. 1900. *Nests and eggs of Australian birds.* 1974 edn. Wren Publishing, Melbourne.

CARRICK, R. 1957. The wild life of Macquarie Island. *Aust. Museum Mag.* **12**, 255–60.

CARRICK, R. 1964. Problems of conservation in and around the Southern Ocean. *In:* Carrick, R., Holdgate, M. & Prevost, J. (eds) *Biologie Antarctique:* 589–98. Hermann, Paris.

CHALLIES, C. N. 1975. Feral pigs (*Sus scrofa*) on Auckland Island: status, and effects on vegetation and nesting sea birds. *New Zeal. J. Zool.* **2**, 478–90.

CUMPSTON, J. S. 1968. *Macquarie Island.* Australian National Antarctic Research Expeditions Sci. Rep. Ser. A(1), Publ. No. 93, Melbourne.

DAVAINE, P. & BEALL, E. 1982. Introductions de salmonides dans les Terres Australes et Antarctiques Françaises. *In:* Colloque sur les écosystèmes subantarctiques, Paimpont, 1981. *Comité National Français des Recherches Antarctiques* No. 51: 289–300.

DEBENHAM, F. (ed.) 1945. *The voyage of Captain Bellingshausen to the Antarctic seas, 1819–1821.* Vol. 2. Hakluyt Society, London.

DERENNE, P. 1976. Notes sur la biologie du chat haret de Kerguelen. *Mammalia* **40**, 531–95.

DERENNE, P. & MOUGIN, J. L. 1976. Données écologiques sur les mammifères introduits de l'Ile aux Cochons, Archipel Crozet (46°06′S, 50°14′E). *Mammalia* **40**, 21–52.

DEVILLERS, P. & TERSCHUREN, J. A. 1978. Relationships between the blue-eyed shags of South America. *Gerfaut* **68**, 53–86.

DILKS, P. J. 1979. Observations on the food of feral cats on Campbell Island. *New Zeal. J. Ecol.* **2**, 64–6.

DILKS, P. J. & WILSON, P. R. 1979. Feral sheep and cattle and royal albatrosses on Campbell Island: population trends and habitat changes. *New Zeal. J. Zool.* **6**, 127–39.

DORST, J. & MILON, P. 1964. Acclimatation et conservation de la nature dans les îles subantarctiques françaises. *In:* Carrick, R., Holdgate, M. & Prevost, J. (eds) *Biologie Antarctique:* 579–88. Hermann, Paris.

DOWNES, M. C., EALEY, E. H. M., GWYNN, A. M. & YOUNG, P. S. 1959. *The birds of Heard Island.* Australian National Antarctic Research Expeditions Sci. Rep. Ser. (B) *1*, Publ. No. 51, Melbourne.

FALLA, R. A. 1937. Birds. *British, Australian & New Zealand Antarctic Research Expedition Rep. Ser. B*, **2**, 1–288.

FALLA, R. A. 1965. Birds and mammals of the subantarctic islands. *Proc. New Zeal. Ecol. Soc.* **12**, 63–8.

HAMILTON, A. 1894. Notes on a visit to Macquarie Island. *Trans. New Zeal. Inst.* **27**, 560–79.

HEADLAND, R. K. 1982. *South Georgia: a concise account.* British Antarctic Survey, Cambridge.

HOLDGATE, M. W. 1970. Conservation in the Antarctic. *In:* Holdgate, M. W. (ed.) *Antarctic Ecology, Vol. 2:* 924–45. Academic Press, London.

HOLDGATE, M. W. & WACE, N. M. 1961. The influence of man on the floras and faunas of southern islands. *Polar Rec.* **10**, 475–93.

IMBER, M. J. 1975. Petrels and predators. *Bull. Int. Council Bird Presvn.* **12**, 260–3.

JENKIN, J. R., JOHNSTONE, G. W. & COPSON, G. R. 1982. Introduced animal and plant species on Macquarie Island. *In:* Colloque sur les écosystèmes subantarctiques, Paimpont, 1981. *Comité National Français des Recherches Antarctiques* No. 51: 301–13.

JOHNSTONE, G. W. 1977. Comparative feeding ecology of the Giant Petrels *Macronectes giganteus* (Gmelin) and *M. halli* Matthews. *In:* Llano, G. (ed.) *Adaptations within Antarctic ecosystems. Proc. 3rd SCAR Symp. Antarct. Biol.:* 647–68. Smithsonian Institution, Washington.

JOHNSTONE, G. W. 1982. Zoology. *In:* Veenstra, C., Manning, J. *et al. Expedition to the Australian Territory of Heard Island and McDonald Islands* 1980: 33–9. Tech. Rep. 31, Divn. National Mapping, Dept. National Development & Energy, Canberra.

JONES, E. 1977. Ecology of the feral cat, *Felis catus* (L.) (Carnivora: Felidae) on Macquarie Island. *Aust. Wildl. Res.* **4**, 249–62.

JONES, E. 1980. A survey of burrow-nesting petrels at Macquarie Island based upon remains left by predators. *Notornis* **27**, 11–20.

JONES, E. & SKIRA, I. J. 1979. Breeding distribution of the Great Skua at Macquarie Island in relation to numbers of rabbits. *Emu* **79**, 19–23.

KEAGE, P. K. 1981. *The conservation status of Heard Island and the McDonald Islands.* Occasional Paper No. 13, Centre for Environmental Studies, University of Tasmania.

KING, W. B. 1981. *Endangered birds of the world. ICBP Bird Red Data Book.* Smithsonian Institution, Washington.

LEADER-WILLIAMS, N. 1978. The history of the introduced reindeer of South Georgia. *Deer* 4, 256–61.

LESEL, R. & DERENNE, P. L. 1975. Introducing animals to Iles Kerguelen. *Polar Rec.* 17, 485–94.

MAWSON, D. 1943. Macquarie Island: its geography and geology. *Australasian Antarctic Expedition (1911–1914) Sci. Rep.* (A) 5.

MOORS, P. J. & ATKINSON, I. A. E. 1984. Predation on seabirds by introduced animals, and factors affecting its severity. *ICBP Tech. Pubn.* No. 2.

MORGAN, I. R. & WESTBURY, H. A. 1981. Virological studies of Adelie Penguins (*Pygoscelis adeliae*) in Antarctica. *Avian Diseases* 25, 1019–26.

MORGAN, I. R., WESTBURY, H. A., CAPLE, I. W. & CAMPBELL, J. 1981. A survey of virus infection in sub-Antarctic penguins on Macquarie Island, Southern Ocean. *Aust. Vet. J.* 57, 333–5.

MOUGIN, J. L. 1969. Notes écologiques sur le pétrel de Kerguelen *Pterodroma brevirostris* de l'Ile de la Possession (Archipel Crozet). *Comité National Français des Recherches Antarctiques, Rev. fr. Ornith. L'Oiseau et RFO* 39 (no. spécial): 58–81.

NORMAN, F. I. 1975. The murine rodents *Rattus rattus, exulans* and *norvegicus* as avian predators. *Atoll Res. Bull.* 182, 1–13.

PASCAL, M. 1980. Population structure and dynamics of feral cats on Kerguelen Is. *Mammalia* 44, 161–82.

PASCAL, M. 1982. Les espèces mammaliennes introduites dans l'archipel des Kerguelen (Territoires des T.A.A.F.). Bilan des recherches entreprises sur ces espèces. *In:* Colloque sur les écosystèmes subantarctiques, Paimpont, 1981. *Comité National Français des Recherches Antarctiques* No. 51: 269–88.

PETIT, J. P. 1977. Adaptations des bovins a l'écosystème constitué par l'Ile d'Amsterdam. *In:* Llano, G. A. (ed.) *Adaptations within Antarctic ecosystems. Proc. 3rd SCAR Symp. Antarct. Biol.:* 1203–10. Smithsonian Institution, Washington.

PIERSON, G. P. & PFOW, C. J. 1975. Newcastle disease surveillance in the United States. *J. Amer. Vet. Med. Ass.* 167, 801–3.

PREVOST, J. & MOUGIN, J. L. 1970. *Guide des oiseaux et mammifères des Terres Australes et Antarctiques Françaises.* Delachaux & Niestlé, Neuchâtel, Switzerland.

PYE, T. & BONNER, W. N. 1980. Feral Brown Rats *Rattus norvegicus* in South Georgia (South Atlantic Ocean). *J. Zool.* 192, 237–55.

ROBERTSON, C. J. R. & VAN TETS, G. F. 1982. The status of birds at the Bounty Islands. *Notornis* 29, 311–36.

ROUNSEVELL, D. E. & BROTHERS, N. P. The status and conservation of seabirds at Macquarie Island. *ICBP Tech. Pubn.* No. 2

ROUNSEVELL, D. E. & COPSON, G. R. 1982. Growth rate and recovery of a King Penguin (*Aptenodytes patagonicus*) population after exploitation. *Aust. Wildl. Res.* 9, 519–25.

SCOTT, J. H. 1982. Macquarie Island. *Trans. New Zeal. Inst.* 15, 484–93.

SEGONZAC, M. 1972. Données recentes sur la faune des Iles St-Paul et Nouvelle Amsterdam. *L'Oiseau et RFO* 42 (no. special): 3–68.

SKINNER, J. R., CONDY, P. R., VAN AARDE, R. J., BESTER, M. N. & ROBINSON, T. J. 1978. The mammals of Marion Island: a review. *S. Afr. J. Antarct. Res.* 8, 35–8.

SKIRA, I. J. 1978. Reproduction of the rabbit, *Oryctolagus cuniculus* (L.) on Macquarie Island, Subantarctic. *Aust. Wildl. Res.* 5, 317–26.

STRANGE, I. J. 1972. *The Falkland Islands.* David & Charles, Newton Abbot, England.

TAYLOR, R. H. 1968. Introduced mammals and islands: priorities for conservation and research. *Proc. New Zeal. Ecol. Soc.* 15, 61–7.

TAYLOR, R. H. 1975. The distribution and status of introduced mammals on the Auckland Islands, 1972–1973. *In:* Yaldwyn, J. C. (ed.) *Preliminary results of the Auckland Islands Expedition 1972–1973:* 233–43. Dept. Lands & Survey, Wellington, New Zealand.

TAYLOR, R. H. 1979. How the Macquarie Island Parakeet became extinct. *New Zeal. J. Ecol.* 2, 42–5.

VAN AARDE, R. J. 1978. Reproduction and population ecology in the feral house cat *Felis catus* on Marion Island. *Carniv. Genet. Newsl.* 3, 288–316.

VAN AARDE, R. J. 1979. Distribution and density of the feral house cat *Felis catus* on Marion Island. *S. Afr. J. Antarct. Res.* 9, 14–19.

VAN AARDE, R. J. 1980. The diet and feeding behaviour of feral cats *Felis catus* at Marion Island. *S. Afr. J. Wildl. Res.* **10**, 123–8.

VAN AARDE, R. J. & SKINNER, J. D. 1982. The feral cat population at Marion Island: characteristics, colonization and control. *In:* Colloque sur les écosystèmes subantarctiques, Paimpont, 1981. *Comité National Français des Recherches Antarctiques* No. 51: 281–8.

VESTJENS, W. J. M. 1963. Remains of the extinct Banded Rail at Macquarie island. *Emu* **62**, 248–50.

WACE, N. M. & HOLDGATE, M. W. 1976, *Man and nature in the Tristan da Cunha Islands*. IUCN Monograph No. 6. Morges, Switzerland.

WARHAM, J. & BELL, B. D. 1979. The birds of Antipodes Island, New Zealand. *Notornis* **26**, 121–69.

WATSON, G. E. 1975. *Birds of the Antarctic and Sub-Antarctic*. Am. Geophys. Union, Washington.

WILLIAMS, A. J. 1978. Mineral and energy contributions of petrels (Procellariiformes) killed by cats, to the Marion Island terrestrial ecosystem. *S. Afr. J. Antarct. Res.* **8**, 49–53.

WILLIAMS, A. J., SIEGFRIED, W. R., BURGER, A. E. & BERRUTI, A. 1979. The Prince Edward Islands: a sanctuary for seabirds in the Southern Ocean. *Biol. Conserv.* **15**, 59–71.

WILSON, P. R. 1979. Inter-relationships of feral stock, sea birds and vegetation on Campbell Island. *New Zeal. J. Ecol.* **2**, 92–3.

WINGATE, D. B. (this vol.). The restoration of Nonsuch Island as a living museum of Bermuda's pre-colonial terrestrial biome.

WOODS, R. W. 1975. *The birds of the Falkland Islands*. Anthony Nelson, Oswestry, England.

PART III
ISLAND CONSERVATION IN ACTION

METHODS OF ERADICATING FERAL CATS FROM OFFSHORE ISLANDS IN NEW ZEALAND

C. R. VEITCH

NZ Wildlife Service, Department of Internal Affairs, PO Box 13, Papakura, New Zealand

ABSTRACT

Cats (*Felis catus*) were probably introduced to New Zealand early last century. Feral populations became established on offshore islands between about 1840 and 1931. Information is given on the impact they have had on island birdlife. Cats have subsequently been eliminated from eight islands, and the methods used in three recent operations are summarized. The main habits and field sign of feral cats are described. The choice of management options (extermination, control, or no action) for island cats are considered, and the general approach and planning for eradication are discussed. Proven eradication methods (introduction of disease, poisons, cage traps, gin traps and dogs) are described in detail, and possible methods (humane traps, male sterilization and others) discussed. Compound 1080 poison and Lanes Ace gin traps are the best methods. Fresh fish is the most efficient bait. Methods to reduce capture of non-target species are described.

INTRODUCTION

Domestic cats (*Felis catus*) have been associated with man and human habitation for thousands of years. Cats were probably brought to New Zealand on the ships of seal hunters about 1800, or by the earliest European settlers about 1840 (*Anon.* 1981). They reached some of our offshore islands (*Figure 1*) in a similar manner during the period 1840 to 1931, and in many places became feral. The introduction of cats to these islands has resulted in the eradication of many species of bird (*Table 1*). The subsequent eradication of cats from several islands in the New Zealand region (*Table 1*) has allowed birds to increase in both numbers and species diversity (e.g. Mangere and Cuvier Islands). However, systematic data on bird numbers before and after cat eradication have been gathered only on Little Barrier Island, where Stitchbirds (*Notiomystis cincta*) in particular have increased significantly since cat eradication (Veitch, in prep.). Changes in bird numbers on other islands have often been additionally affected by habitat changes which took place at a similar time to the introduction of cats. The effects of these two changes cannot always be readily separated.

The eradication methods described in this paper have evolved during work on the islands listed in *Table 1* and on Frigate Island, Republic of the Seychelles, and are recommended for use on islands. Except for very special circumstances, I do not recommend their use on mainland areas because of the risk to humans and domestic

Table 1: Islands from which cats have been removed.

Island	History of cats and other changes	Birds affected and current status	
Stephens 180ha	Cats introduced about 1892 at the time of lighthouse construction. Reached high numbers. Killed out by lighthouse keepers in 1925. At same time most of the forest destroyed and whole island grazed up to 1952, when fence was erected to restrict stock to 1/3 of the island. Tree planting by Wildlife Service is assisting forest regeneration. No rodents.	Yellow-crowned Parakeet	—locally extinct
		Stephens Island Wren	—extinct
		South Island Thrush	—extinct
		South Island Robin	—locally extinct
		Yellow-breasted Tit	—locally extinct
		Tui	—locally extinct
		Bellbird	—locally extinct
		South Island Kokako	—extinct
		South Island Saddleback	—locally extinct
Putahina 135ha	Very little data. Muttonbirders reports only. Cats now gone. *Rattus exulans* present.	Early records lacking. Snipe. Saddleback. Wren. Robin, Fernbird obvious absentees.	
Kapiti 2023ha	Cats never numerous; eradicated by caretaker by 1934. *R. norvegicus*, *R. exulans*, possums, wekas present.	Early records lacking. Saddlebacks locally extinct; re-introduced 1981. No petrels except Sooty Shearwaters.	
Mangere (Chathams) 130ha	Cats introduced late last century to deal with rabbits. They apparently did so effectively, and died out themselves in the 1950s. No rodents.	White-faced Storm Petrel	—not present 1924; now recolonizing
		Grey-backed Storm Petrel	—not present 1968; now recolonizing
		Southern Diving Petrel	—not present 1900; now recolonizing
		Chatham Island Rail	—extinct 1900
		N.Z. Shore Plover	—locally extinct; last seen 1898
		Chatham Island Snipe	—last seen 1871, re-introduced 1972
		Chatham Island Pigeon	—locally extinct
		Chatham Island Parakeet	—locally extinct; now re-colonizing
		Chatham Island Yellow-crowned Parakeet	—re-colonized since 1970—rare
		Chatham Island Fernbird	—extinct 1900
		Black Robin	—locally extinct 1900; re-introduced 1976
		Chatham Island Tui	—locally extinct; now re-colonizing
		Chatham Island Bellbird	—extinct
Herekopare 28ha	Cats introduced between 1926 and 1931. Wildlife Service removed the entire population of 33 cats in 1970. Wekas and goats introduced and subsequently removed. Vegetation modified by muttonbirders. No rodents.	Broad-billed Prion	—rare
		Fairy Prion	—greatly reduced
		Diving Petrel	—greatly reduced
		Banded Rail	—locally extinct
		Stewart Island Snipe	—extinct
		Yellow-crowned Parakeet	—locally extinct
		Brown Creeper	—locally extinct
		Stewart Island Fernbird	—locally extinct
		Grey Warbler	—greatly reduced
		South Island Robin	—locally extinct
Cuvier 194ha	Following establishment of a lighthouse in 1889 cats became feral. Wildlife Service destroyed entire population of 12 cats between 1960 and 1964. Goats exterminated 1959–61. Fence erected in 1963 to exclude lighthouse keepers' stock from forest. *R. exulans* present.	Grey-faced Petrel	—reduced
		Red-crowned Parakeet	—locally extinct; re-introduced 1974
		Pied Tit	—locally extinct
		Tui	—locally extinct, now re-colonizing
		North Island Saddleback	—locally extinct, re-introduced 1968

Little Barrier 2817ha — Cats present from about 1870 to 1980. Eradication achieved by Wildlife Service between 1977 and 1980. *R. exulans* present.

Grey-faced Petrel	—locally extinct
Cook's Petrel	—heavily preyed on
Black Petrel	—heavily preyed on
Fluttering Shearwater	—rare
Stitchbird	—greatly reduced, now increasing
North Island Saddleback	—locally extinct; re-introduced 1984

Motuihe 160ha — Cats probably introduced last century. Flora totally modified. Estimated 50 cats removed by Hauraki Gulf Maritime Park staff during rabbit control work 1978–9.

No data available on birds present before modification of habitat. No native passerines present now.

Table 2: Important islands for wildlife where cats are still present.

Island	History of cats and other changes	Birds affected and current status
Main and Masked (Auckland Group) 45975ha	Cats present on the main island and Masked Island of the Auckland Group from early 1840s as a result of sealing, whaling and farming; described as 'fairly numerous'. Mice, pigs and goats present on the main island.	Prions —found only in inaccessible areas Storm petrels —locally extinct Flightless Teal —locally extinct Auckland I. Merganser —extinct Auckland I. Rail —locally extinct Auckland I. Snipe —locally extinct Red-crowned Parakeet —rare
Campbell 11400ha	Cats probably reached this island when it was farmed (1908). Cats are now in low numbers and do not seem to affect remaining birdlife. *Rattus norvegicus* present.	Campbell I. Flightless Teal —locally extinct (exists on Dent I.) Breeding Petrels rare, smaller species absent. No account of other predation.
Mayor 1277ha	Cats present in low numbers since European occupation. *R. norvegicus, R. exulans* and pigs present.	Grey-faced Petrel —rare, declining White-faced Storm Petrel —rare, declining Inadequate records of other species.
Raoul (Kermadec) 2900ha	Cats introduced about 1850. N.Z. Forest Service eradicated goats 1984. *R. exulans* present. *R. norvegicus* introduced 1918.	Kermadec Petrel —locally extinct Black-winged Petrel —locally extinct White-naped Petrel —locally extinct Wedge-tailed Shearwater —locally extinct Red-tailed Tropic Bird —rare Banded Rail —locally extinct Spotless Crake —locally extinct Sooty Tern —heavily preyed on Grey Ternlet —locally extinct White-capped Noddy —locally extinct White Tern —rare Kermadec Parakeet —locally extinct

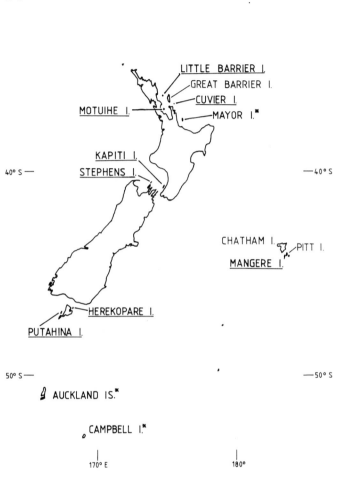

Figure 1: Offshore islands inhabited by feral cats, either in the past or at present. Islands from which they have been eradicated are underlined, and those from which eradication may be feasible are marked with an asterisk.

non-target species. Care should be taken to ensure that eradication methods are in accordance with local laws, and meet with the approval of interested organizations.

IMPACT OF CATS ON NEW ZEALAND AVIFAUNA

Cats and other mammalian predators (three species of mustelid and two species of rat, but not including *Rattus exulans*) reached mainland New Zealand between 1780 and

1880 (Atkinson 1973, Wodzicki 1950). The dispersal of these animals through New Zealand was uneven, and there is a paucity of bird records for this period so it is often not possible to determine a single cause for the extermination of birds. However, on some offshore islands (e.g. Cuvier, Little Barrier; *Table 1*) cats were the only introduced predator apart from *R. exulans*, which were introduced by the Maori people hundreds of years earlier. On other islands the time of introduction of cats is clearly separated from predators other than *R. exulans* (e.g. Raoul; *Table 2*). However, on most islands there has been some habitat modification at a similar time to predator introduction and in many instances this alone could have caused the extinction of some or all of the birds (e.g. Stephens, Mangere).

RESUMÉ OF RECENT CAT ERADICATION PROJECTS

Cuvier Island
The entire population of 12 cats was eradicated during four months' work in the years 1960–4 (Merton 1970). Cage traps were used but caught no cats, two cats were shot and the remainder were caught in Oneida Victor No I gin traps, mostly baited with fish-flavoured tinned domestic cat food.

Herekopare Island
Up to 118 Lane Ace gin traps, baited with fresh fish, were used during this six-week project in 1970. Thirty cats were trapped and one was shot during the first four days of hunting. Twelve days later an adult female was cornered by a dog and shot. The last cat, an adult male, was found dead, apparently due to an abscess extending from its teeth into its right eye (Fitzgerald & Veitch, in prep.).

Little Barrier Island
Eradication was achieved during a four-year project from 1977 to 1980 involving 128 people in 3880 man-days of work. Up to 950 Lanes Ace gin traps, usually baited with fresh fish, were used. Some 27,000 pieces of fish poisoned with compound 1080 were spread along tracks. Dogs were used, but failed to find any cats. One hundred and fifty one cats are known to have been killed (Veitch, in prep.).

THE HABITS AND SIGN OF FERAL CATS

Feral cats are solitary predators capable of hunting both by night and day, depending on the abundance of prey. Their home range may consist of a well-frequented core area and an outer area consisting of a network of tracks linking favoured places (Leyhausen 1979). The home ranges of neighbouring individuals overlap, and they mark within their home ranges with urine and droppings. The home ranges of males are considerably larger than those of females (Macdonald & Apps 1978). Within the core area cats attempt to cover their droppings, but not to a degree that this sign cannot be observed; outside the core area droppings are usually left exposed (Panaman 1981). Cats prefer dry places to rest in, and need a reliable year-round food supply. They need fresh water only when food is scarce; at other times they get all the water they need from their food (Prentiss *et al.* 1959). In an unmodified feral population they may live 7–8 years. Females may have two litters annually averaging 4 kittens per litter, but in a stable population most kittens will die before reaching maturity (Pascal 1980). On Little Barrier and Raoul Islands the average litter size was 3 (n = 9).

The density of a cat population is probably determined by its food supply. Their first preference for food may appear to be the largest available item (e.g. seabirds or rabbits),

but in some places they seem to prefer a better habitat with smaller food items. For example, on Little Barrier Island when cat numbers were reduced they lived on the lower, drier slopes with *R. exulans* for food, in preference to the higher, wetter areas with the apparently larger seasonal food source of Black (*Procellaria parkinsoni*) and Cook's (*Pterodroma cooki*) Petrels and lower numbers of *R. exulans*. The highest densities recorded for feral populations have been firstly on 0.25km^2 Cousine Island, Republic of the Seychelles, with equivalent to at least 220 cats/km^2 (D. M. Todd, pers. comm.), and secondly on 0.28km^2 Herekopare Island with equivalent to 118 cats/km^2(Fitzgerald & Veitch, in prep.). Such high densities were only possible because large numbers of nesting seabirds provided an abundant year-round food supply. Other estimates of the density of feral cats on islands, reviewed by Macdonald & Apps (1978), are much lower, usually being 4–14 cats/km^2.

The ease of observing cat sign depends on the terrain, the type of ground cover and the type of food the cats are eating. The easiest sign to observe is dead birds (*Figure 2*). Cats prefer to carry their catch to an open area. They usually bite first into the back of the head and eat the brain or whole head, except one or both mandibles. Smaller birds may be eaten whole, although usually the wing tips and some body feathers are left. With larger birds, after eating part or all of the head, the cat turns the bird on its back and eats the breast meat. After creating an initial opening, the skin is usually pushed back from the area being eaten, rather than being torn off in chunks. The cat is then likely to eat the liver, heart, more flesh, intestines and finally bones. The tail, with some flesh attached, wing tips, bill and feet are usually left. In forests a scattering of plucked tail, wing and body feathers usually indicates that an owl or falcon, and not a cat, has made a kill. Cats do not deliberately pluck feathers before eating a carcase.

After eating birds, cats leave large distinctive droppings 10–15cm long and up to 3cm in diameter containing many feathers and masticated bones. Rodents are usually eaten whole, and the droppings contain fur and masticated bone; they may be 15–20cm long and 2cm or more in diameter (*Figure 2*). The scent of droppings containing rat remains is similar to those containing landbird remains, but B. J. Karl (pers. comm.) has observed that droppings containing seabird remains can smell strongly of the typical seabird scent. If a cat is feeding entirely on lizards or insects there may be no obvious prey remains, and the droppings may be round, smaller than 2.5cm in diameter, and difficult to find. Feral cat droppings do not contain noticeable quantities of the cat's own fur. Spherical or cylindrical pellets, frequently larger in size than cat droppings, containing feathers or fur and whole small bones, but no dirt or mucus, are regurgitations from a bird of prey. When fresh these have a distinct scent similar to wet woollen material. Cat footprints (*Figure 6*) left in soft or wet soil are distinctive, but cats will, if possible, avoid wet places.

THE GENERAL PRINCIPLE OF ERADICATION METHODS AND CHOICE OF ACTION

Eradication of cats is achieved by the combined and persistent use of several methods. To make the task as economical as possible a quick initial knock-down is required, followed by a large and persistent effort to remove the remaining animals.

This initial knock-down may be achieved by heavy doses of poison or the introduction of a biological control agent such as the viral disease feline enteritis, and must be followed by either poisoning, trapping, or hunting with dogs—or, preferably, all

---

Figure 2:   Cat sign. Upper—a cat-killed Black Petrel. Centre—a dropping as left by a cat. Lower—a typical dropping from a cat which has been feeding on rodents.

methods combined or varied as the situation demands. Trapping may be continuous, intermittent, seasonal, or with varied baits. Short-term immunity to feline enteritis and the low population density after the initial knock-down precludes the repeated use of this biological control agent.

As cat eradication programmes depend largely on using foods as baits or attractants to traps, it is important that the programmes be timed to take place when natural foods are at their lowest levels.

When it is known that cats on a particular island are detrimental to wildlife, careful consideration must be given to the course of action to be taken. Total eradication is the only long-term solution, but, before such action is started, there should be a good guarantee of success. If a high proportion of the cats are removed, and the programme then lapses, the resultant irruption of cats can be more detrimental to the island's wildlife than if no action had been initiated. Long-term control must receive similar careful consideration. Experience suggests that a considerable reduction in cat numbers is required before the affected species of birds begin to improve in numbers. It is therefore usually better to put more time and effort into the task to achieve total eradication. If eradication or effective long-term control is not possible then it is best to leave the cats alone and manage the wildlife concerned (e.g. Williams 1977).

METHODS OF EXTERMINATING FERAL CATS

Preparatory work

After deciding that the eradication of cats from an island is necessary, and before starting the work proper, some important preparations are required. A broad plan of attack prepared at this stage, bearing in mind possible public or other objections to some aspects of it, will assist greatly with all subsequent preparations. It is likely that the wildlife authority wishing to eradicate the cats will not own the island concerned. Therefore permission from the owner, and perhaps others who have rights to enter the land, will be required.

Throughout the project good publicity is necessary to reduce emotional and mis-informed criticism. It is probably desirable not to pursue publicity but, when asked, to ensure that the full story, emphasizing the damage done by wild cats and preferably not giving precise details of eradication methods, is received and published by the media. Every effort should be made to obtain binding agreements with the appropriate authorities to guarantee the continuing supply of finance and manpower. Particular emphasis should be given to the inclusion of people with the necessary expertise and authority to use the eradication methods proposed. If the proposed methods are not in accord with the law or the policies of interested organizations, then every effort should be made to amend the law, policy or work plan, while ensuring that the eradication project can still be successful.

The standard of accommodation on the island will depend on the size of the operation. Careful consideration should be given to providing several huts if it improves the ease and frequency of coverage of the island by the eradication team. Good tracks are important for the hunter and, usually, for the cats. Careful planning of the position of tracks in relation to the terrain, habitats for cats, and accommodation for hunters, is important. Cats show a preference for drier places, and in hilly terrain it is therefore better to put tracks on ridges. It is also important to have the vegetation on all tracks trimmed as close to the ground as possible, as this makes them better for both hunters and cats to walk on.

Baits

Baits are used beither to lure cats into traps or to carry poisons. Fresh fish has been the best readily-available bait for both traps and poison. If the supply of fresh fish for trap-baits fails temporarily then the old bait should be covered with cod-liver oil to refresh its scent. Cats have also been caught in new unbaited traps coated with 'fishoilene' (a cod-liver oil/petroleum product). This may be a suitable bait. Sawdust containing cat urine and/or faeces from a cattery has been an effective attractant, but has not been used during large-scale trapping. Analysis of the scents in cat urine, and the synthetic manufacture of those which attract cats, is being considered.

Tincture of valerian (*Valeriana officianalis*) has been effectively used in Scotland to attract cats to traps (R. Balharry, pers. comm.), but during tests on Frigate Island, Seychelles, it was ineffective. Catnip (*Nepeta cataria*) has not been tested for cat trapping, but it is known that not all cats respond to it (Todd 1962). The roots of Kiwifruit plants (*Actinidia chinensis*) are known to be attractive to cats but have not been tested during cat trapping. These plants are known to contain monoterpenoid alkaloids, some of which are proven to be attractive to cats (Eisner 1964).

Live birds and rodents have been used to attract cats to cage traps. The live bait is kept in a small cage placed so that the cat is trapped without harming the captive animal. Dead birds or rodents rarely attract cats, but if they are freshly killed and cut open they are more attractive. Fresh mutton was found by F. Woodrow (New Zealand Dept. Internal Affairs files) to be an effective bait, but not as good as fresh fish. Tinned pet foods have also been used—fish-flavoured was best, but none was as good as fresh fish.

Synthetic fermented egg (a Coyote (*Canis latrans*) attractant) and its flavour variants (Bullard *et al.* 1978), and the flesh of mammals not previously mentioned (e.g. Rabbit (*Oryctolagus cuniculus*) and deer (*Cervus spp.*) are possible attractants or poison carriers which have not been tested.

It is important that trap baits be changed frequently and that old baits not be left beyond their useful life-span at set or unset traps because stale scent may deter a cat from further investigating that bait, or future fresh ones. For the same reason all old baits should be disposed of where cats cannot possibly find them.

Cubed fish is the only medium which has been used effectively as a poison carrier. Dry pellets which can be stored and used as required would be preferable; these are being tested but so far no formula has proven to be more attractive than fresh fish.

Types of traps

Cage traps.   Two types are shown in *Figure 3*. These are baited with a food item on the trigger hook. Both types have been used in New Zealand but because of their bulk and relatively low capture rate are not recommended for use when large numbers of cats have to be killed or a large area of land covered. Type B is considered to be the better of the two because the door opening is higher (38cm), it does not have a hinged door (see section on trap setting) and, because it has a separate access door for rebaiting, it does not have to be moved during rebaiting. Type A is available from most New Zealand hardware stores. Type B was designed and constructed by Mr B. J. Karl (Ecology Division, D.S.I.R., Private Bag, Lower Hutt, New Zealand) and specifications are available from him.

Gin traps.   These are designed to catch the animal by the foot and, of the traps known to me, are clearly the most efficient method of trapping cats. This is mainly because of the way they can be set in a 'natural' manner (see section on trap setting), and the cat then has only to attempt to approach the bait rather than actually grasp it. There are probably many more varieties than those shown in *Figure 4*. The Lanes Ace trap, which was designed for rabbits in Australia, is widely used in New Zealand for catching

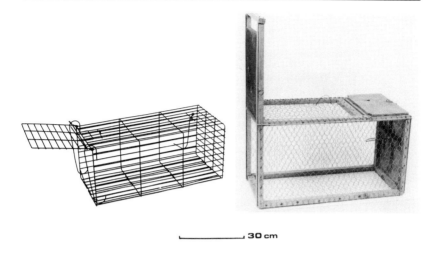

Figure 3: Cage traps. Left—type A, Right—type B.

Possums (*Trichosurus vulpecula*) and has been used extensively for feral cat eradication. It is made by Lanes Amalgamated Hardware Co. Ltd. (60 Bathurst Street, Sydney, NSW 2000, Australia) and is available from some hardware stores in New Zealand. While the Oneida Victor No. I has been used with some success for cat-catching, it is really too small and the lighter spring causes the jaws to close more slowly than the Lanes Ace. A cat reacts so rapidly that it can lift its foot clear of this trap before the jaws close. The Oneida Victor No. II has not been tested on cats, but appears to be a better size than the No. I, and is considerably lighter than the Lanes Ace. Oneida Victor traps are made in America by the Woodstream Corporation (Lititz, Pennsylvania 17543, USA) and are not commercially available in New Zealand.

Humane traps.   The traps shown in *Figure 4* have not been designed for killing cats, but both are capable of doing so in a humane manner. However, both have to be reset each time they are baited and this is an undesirable requirement (see section on trap setting). These traps are not recommended for an eradication programme, but are shown as examples and because they may have to be considered more seriously for humane reasons for future projects. There are also humane traps designed for species larger or smaller than feral cats (e.g. the Fenn trap designed for mustelids) which I do not recommend as they are likely to maim rather than kill cats.

Other traps.   There are a number of other traps which are commercially available or shown as drawings in publications. Some are probably capable of catching cats, but I know of none which is as efficient as those described above. Some are likely to maim and lose rather than catch cats, and others have jaws or loops of cord which do not close fast enough to catch a cat.

Setting traps

Cage traps.   As feral cats do not readily enter enclosed spaces, it is important that cage traps be carefully set to reduce additional suspicions. Human scent can be reduced by

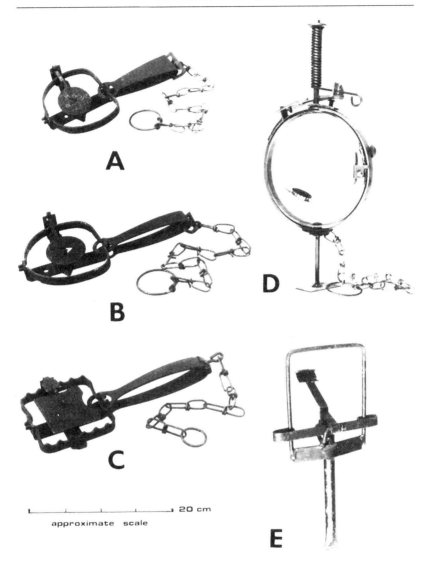

Figure 4:   A—Oneida Victor No. I gin trap. B—Oneida Victor No. II gin trap. C—Lanes Ace gin trap. D—Bigelow humane trap. E—Banya humane trap.

rubbing bait on the hands, or by wearing gloves covered in the scent of fresh bait. To reduce the 'closed-in' feeling the trap should be positioned so that the entrance is in, or facing the centre of, an area clear of long vegetation. The trap should be set squarely on the ground so that it will not wobble or slide when a cat enters it, and the floor of the trap should be covered with a light layer of soil or leaf litter. As it is possible for cats to reach a paw through the bars or mesh of some traps to touch the bait, and hence trip the trap, a few sticks should be leaned against the rear of the cage. Swinging doors hinged at the top should be at least horizontal when open or, preferably, bent upwards to reduce the 'closed-in' feeling. A weight can be placed on the door to speed its closing. Perpendicular, or 'drop', doors are better as the cat has a shorter distance to travel to the bait under a roof—again reducing the 'closed-in' feeling. Traps should always be set as finely as possible.

Gin traps.   For a 'baited set' (*Figure 5*) select a tree or other object onto which a bait can later be attached. It should also be broad at the base, have soil where the trap is to be placed, and be close to where cats usually walk (e.g. a track, opening in the forest, or dry stream bed). The end of the trap chain is secured to the tree so that the trap can be placed a handspan away from the eventual position of the bait. The smaller trigger plate should face towards the tree. The trap, finely set, is then placed firmly into the ground (it is important that there be no movement), preferably with its upper side level with the ground surface. Light fences made of sticks or stones are then extended from the tree to the outer edge of both sides of the trap jaws. These should not be too high or dense or the cat will feel 'closed-in', but must ensure that the only way a cat can sniff or eat the bait is by walking over the trap. These fences are also the best way to exclude non-target species (see section on non-target species). The set is completed by camouflaging the trap with a fine layer of soil and light leaves. It is important that this material does not jam the trigger plate, and that twigs and large leaves which might stop the trap from closing properly are not used. The bait is stapled to the tree about a handspan from the ground. A staple is used in preference to a nail so that the bait cannot be easily removed.

Figure 5: Setting a gin trap. Upper—the trap is placed in the ground a handspan from where the bait will be stapled. Centre—a fence of twigs is built. Lower—the trap is camouflaged.

The 'walk-through' set (*Figure 6*) can be used where non-target species are not at risk of being caught. It relies on the fact that cats avoid stepping on thin twigs, and the way they step through a gap between two obstacles (*Figure 6*). As with baited sets the trap must be finely set, placed firmly in the ground with the top level with the surface, and lightly camouflaged. If no natural sites are available fences of sticks may be built to guide the cat onto the trap. It is not usual when setting large numbers of gin traps to take special precautions to cover human scent. It is more convenient to work without precautions, and in any case the soil scents are strong and the operator's hands rapidly become dirty

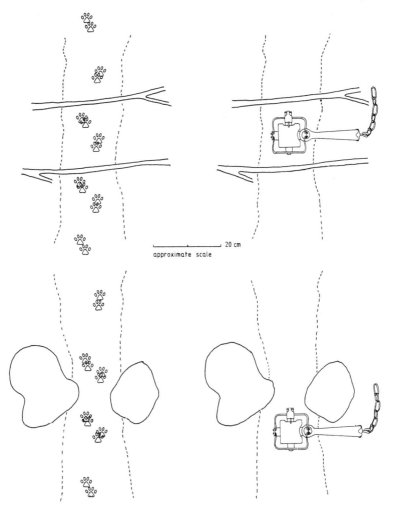

Figure 6: Methods of setting unbaited traps.

with soil. However, if possible, traps should be set some days before they are baited as this allows scents and signs of disturbance time to diminish. The scent of humans walking on tracks does not seem to affect the cat's use of those tracks. After setting, the traps may be left untouched for weeks providing the weather does not cause them to rust unduly, or wash soil under the plate and stop the trap working.

The spread of traps over an island must remain a matter of judgement for the operator, bearing in mind the likely range of the cats, their food supply, the terrain being covered and any other pertinent factors. For example, on Herekopare Island the traps were set at 30–60m intervals and on Little Barrier Island at 50–200m intervals (none were set in very steep places). Traps should be checked daily, as early as possible in the day, and any cats caught should be killed humanely. A swift blow with a hammer to the back of the head is recommended, although some operators prefer to shoot them with a small calibre rifle.

Use of feline enteritis

Feline enteritis (also known as feline pan leucopaenia) is a viral disease present in feral cat populations on all large land masses. It kills many cats in these areas, but if they do not die it leaves them with short-term immunity for up to four years. Therefore, on mainland areas waves of disease pass back and forth across the country. Islands are generally too small for such a pattern. First colonizers can be expected to be healthy, but are likely to have some residual immunity which soon dies out and leaves the population susceptible to later artificial introduction.

To introduce feline enteritis it is necessary to live-trap cats on the island concerned and keep them in captivity. There have been no precise studies of this subject, so, while the actual number of cats required must be a matter of judgement for the operator, I would recommend the capture of not less than 5 percent of the estimated total population. The live feline enteritis virus is best obtained from a laboratory which manufactures feline enteritis vaccines. When sufficient cats are held in captivity one is kept separate from the others as a test. This is given the recommended oral dose (usually 2ml) of live virus.

Feline enteritis produces an initial rise followed by a drop in body temperature, dehydration, loss of appetite, diarrhoea, vomiting and usually death. The time taken for this course may be from one day (West 1976) to 10 days (Veitch, pers. obs.). However, practical experience shows that in many cases there are no obvious signs until suddenly the cat is prostrate and close to death. Therefore, once the virus is proven to work on a test cat, all cats should be dosed and released immediately. Each cat should be released as far as possible from its capture site so that in endeavouring to return to its original home range it will have the greatest chance of contact with the maximum number of other cats.

Poisons

In New Zealand compound 1080 (sodium monofluoroacetate) is the only poison which has been used in cat eradication campaigns. In most countries the use of this and other poisons is strictly controlled by law, and any person using poisons should work within these laws.

Compound 1080 is supplied as an aqueous solution containing 20 percent active ingredient. The LD50 (i.e. dose to kill 50 percent of the sample) for cats is 0.3–0.5mg/kg body weight (Rammell & Fleming 1978). Fresh fish is the only bait that has been regularly used to convey this poison. Frozen fish does not work well because liquids readily leak out after it has thawed. A repeating veterinary syringe is used to inject the 1080, diluted to the dose-rate required, into bite-sized pieces of fish. The dilution rate will depend on the minimum volume which the syringe can dispense because it is important to inject as little liquid as possible. After establishing this volume the dilution should be calculated so that the heaviest cat expected will be killed by eating only one bait. This maximum weight is about 5.0kg (Orongorongo Valley, B. M. Fitzgerald, pers. comm.) in the New Zealand region, but island populations may differ. The weights of adult cats from Raoul, Little Barrier, and Herekopare Islands were: females, mean 2.17kg, range 1.25–3.8kg, n = 69; males, mean 2.67kg, range 1.1–4.1kg, n = 90.

The number of baits used and the manner in which they are spread is a matter of judgement for the operator, usually depending on the probable distribution of the cats; it may sometimes also be restricted by the availability of fresh fish. On Little Barrier Island we endeavoured to place baits at 20m intervals along tracks.

Other methods

Several other methods seem worthy of serious trial. A female cat in oestrus could be kept in a cage surrounded by suitable traps (gin traps are recommended, but an elaborate cage trap could probably be devised). On the only occasion this method has been used in New Zealand a male cat was attracted (D. V. Merton, pers. comm.). However it may attract cats of both sexes living in the vicinity. Oestrus can be artificially induced under the direction of a veterinarian.

Tape recorded calls have been used to attract other species, but have not been tried on cats.

Dogs were successfully used for cat hunting on Herekopare Island, but they did not find any on Little Barrier Island, despite adequate training on the mainland and at least 43 cats being present on the island.

Sterilization of male cats has been suggested as an eradication method. In the absence of proven chemical sterilants administered by baits, this approach requires the capture of all wild adult males from the population to be eradicated, their vasectomy by a veterinarian, and successful return to their normal home ranges. In view of the more efficient kill-trapping and poisoning methods available, sterilization of males is probably uneconomic.

DANGERS TO NON-TARGET SPECIES

Although there is probably no way of avoiding entirely the capture or poisoning of non-target species, it is clearly necessary to attempt to do so, both for the protection of non-target species and because every trap that captures something else is not available to catch a cat.

Proper setting of traps, as previously described, and, if need be, development of new trapping methods, will greatly reduce the number of such captures. In critical areas it may be necessary to cover or close traps during the day. Poison baits may have to be laid after dark and uneaten ones collected before dawn. However, in extreme situations it may be necessary to accept the mortality of some non-target animals as, in the long term, the eradication of the cats should more than compensate for that mortality.

ACKNOWLEDGEMENTS

I am particularly indebted to Dr P. J. Moors, N.Z. Wildlife Service, and to Dr B. M. Fitzgerald and Mr B. J. Karl, Ecology Division, D.S.I.R., for the information they have supplied and their extensive comments on the numerous drafts of this paper. I am also indebted to: Mr G. Aburn for his field assistance and comments; Mr R. A. Anderson, N.Z. Wildlife Service, for his field assistance, comments on earlier drafts of this paper and for the drawings he has provided; and to Dr I. A. E. Atkinson, Botany Division, D.S.I.R., Messrs R. Balharry, Nature Conservancy Council of Great Britain; B. D. Bell, N.Z. Wildlife Service; A. Cox, N.Z. Wildlife Service; A. G. Dobbins, Hauraki Gulf Maritime Park; D. V. Merton, N.Z. Wildlife Service, C. D. A. Smith, Department of Lands and Survey, and D. M. Todd for information which they have supplied. Thanks are also due to my typist, Mrs S. Hook, and to Mr S. J. H. Still and Mr R. Weber for technical assistance.

REFERENCES

Anon. (1981). *New Zealand official yearbook 1981*. Department of Statistics, Wellington.

Atkinson, I. A. E. 1973. Spread of the ship rat (*Rattus r. rattus*) in New Zealand. *J. Roy. Soc. New Zealand* **3**, 457–72.

Bullard, R. W., Spumake, S. A., Campbell, D. L. & Turkowski, F. J. 1978. Preparation and evaluation of a synthetic fermented egg coyote attractant and deer repellant. *J., Agric. Food Chem.* **26**, 160–3.

Eisner, T. 1964. Catnip: its raison d'être. *Science* **146**, 1318–20.

Leyhausen, P. 1979. *Cat behavior. The predatory and social behavior of domestic and wild cats*. New York, Garland STPM Press.

Macdonald, D. W. & Apps, P. J. 1978. The social behaviour of a group of semi-dependent farm cats, *Felis catus*: a progress report. *Carnivore Genetics Newsletter* **3**, 256–68.

Merton, D. V. 1970. The rehabilitation of Cuvier Island. *Wildlife—A Review* **2**, 5–8.

Panaman, R. 1981. Behaviour and ecology of free-ranging female farm cats (*Felis catus* L.). *Zeitschrift für Tierpsychologie* **56**, 59–73.

Pascal, M. 1980. Structure et dynamique de la population de chats harets de l'archipel des Kerguelen. *Mammalis* **44**, 161–82.

Prentiss, P. G., Wolf, A. V. & Eddy, H. A. 1959. Hydropenia in cat and dog. Ability of the cat to meet its water requirements solely from a diet of fish or meat. *American Journal of Physiology* **196**, 625–32.

Rammell, C. G. & Fleming, P. A. 1978. *Compound 1080: properties of sodium monofluoroacetate in New Zealand*. Technical Report to Ministry of Agriculture & Fisheries, Wellington, New Zealand.

Todd, N. B. 1962. Inheritance of the catnip response in domestic cats. *J. Heredity* **53**, 54–6.

West, G. P. (ed.) 1976. *Black's Veterinary Dictionary*. 12th ed. A & C Black, London.

Williams, G. R. 1977. Marooning—a technique for saving threatened species from extinction. *Int. Zoo Yearbook* **17**, 102–6.

Wodzicki, K. A. 1950. *Introduced mammals of New Zealand*. D.I.S.R. Bulletin No. 98. Government Printer, Wellington.

ICBP Technical Publication No. 3, 1985

ERADICATION CAMPAIGNS AGAINST *RATTUS NORVEGICUS* ON THE NOISES ISLANDS, NEW ZEALAND, USING BRODIFACOUM AND 1080

P. J. Moors

Wildlife Service, Department of Internal Affairs, Private Bag, Wellington, New Zealand

ABSTRACT

The Noises Islands lie in Hauraki Gulf about 24km northeast of Auckland. Most are bush-clad and none is permanently inhabited. Norway Rats (*Rattus norvegicus*) were first reported from the group in 1957. Eradication campaigns were carried out on Otata (21.8ha) and Motuhoropapa (9.5ha) Islands to test the practicability of such operations and as a conservation measure.

The first campaign on Otata was conducted in September 1979 using the acute poison 1080 (sodium monofluoroacetate) and the anticoagulant rodenticide 'Talon' (brodifacoum). Rat sign was absent until June 1980. A second campaign was begun in September 1980 using the same poisons in different baits. The baits were laid in places likely to be visited by rats, and were also maintained in 133 covered bait stations until December 1981. There has been no evidence of rats on Otata since April 1981.

Rats reappeared on Motuhoropapa in January 1981 after two years without definite signs of their presence. An eradication campaign was commenced in April 1981 using the same poisons, baits and procedures as in the second operation on Otata. Seventy-five bait stations were maintained until February 1983. The present status of the rats is uncertain, and efforts to ensure their removal are continuing.

The greatest practical difficulty encountered during the campaigns has been detecting the existence of rats when they are present in very low numbers.

INTRODUCTION

The three species of commensal rat (*Rattus rattus, R. norvegicus* and *R. exulans*) introduced to islands around the world have often had a severe impact on native birdlife (e.g. Atkinson 1977, this vol.; Moors & Atkinson 1984), as well as on other native animals such as reptiles and invertebrates (e.g. Ramsay 1978; Whitaker 1978).

Rats do their greatest damage to birds during the breeding season, when they prey on eggs, chicks and even adults. This predation has affected many island populations of birds, and sometimes has been responsible for the complete extinction of a species. For example, *R. rattus* colonized Big South Cape Island (930ha), New Zealand, about 1962. Within three years the rats had exterminated five species of native forest bird, including the last known population of the Bush Wren (*Xenicus longipes*) (Bell 1978).

The absence of introduced rats, especially the two European species *R. norvegicus* and *R. rattus*, is one of the main criteria used by the New Zealand Wildlife Service when choosing islands for the translocation of endangered fauna. However, there are few rat-free islands also suitable in other ways (geographical location, size, habitat, topography, climate) and more can be made available only by clearing rats from islands which are presently infested.

With this background in mind, the Wildlife Service mounted extermination campaigns against Norway Rats (*R. norvegicus*) inhabiting the Noises Islands in Hauraki Gulf. The aims of the project were firstly to test the feasibility of eradicating this species from forested, uninhabited islands of a reasonable size, and secondly to rehabilitate the islands for possible future releases of endangered fauna.

THE NOISES ISLANDS

The Noises Islands (36°42'S, 174°58'E; *Figure 1*) lie in Hauraki Gulf about 24km northeast of Auckland city. They have a temperate climate with regular rain and no frosts. Apart from Otata they are uninhabited and rarely visited. A small house on Otata was occupied until 1957, but since then has been used only for occasional holidays. However, the island is often visited during the day by summer boating parties.

Otata has an area of 21.8ha and a maximum altitude of 67m. Steep vegetated slopes skirt the shoreline, but elsewhere the topography is gentle. There is no permanent fresh water. The island is mostly covered with native forest regenerating after a fire sometime between 1925 and 1930. The canopy is generally closed and usually 4–8m high. It is composed mainly of *Myrsine australis*, *Pittosporum crassifolium*, *Melicytus ramiflorus* and *Pseudopanax lessonii*. Tall *Metrosideros excelsa* and *P. crassifolium* are common on the coastal slopes, and may form closed canopies up to 15m high. The understorey is generally open with the main ground cover being leaf-litter. Open grassy areas with dense clumps of Flax (*Phormium tenax*) persist on the western and northern slopes.

Motuhoropapa has an area of 9.5ha and a maximum altitude of 57m. An axial ridge runs northwest–southeast, with several side spurs falling steeply to the sea. The island is covered with mature forest having a closed canopy generally 6–10m high. The canopy is composed mostly of *Metrosideros excelsa*, *Pittosporum crassifolium*, *Melicope ternata*, *Melicytus ramiflorus* and two species of *Pseudopanax*. The understorey consists mainly of seedlings of the canopy species and *Dysoxylum spectabile*, with scattered dense stands of *Astelia banksii*. Leaf-litter is the main ground cover.

The remaining islands in the group are all 2ha or less in area, and are capped with a low scrub or forest of *P. crassifolium*, *Coprosma repens*, *Pseudopanax lessonii* and *Metrosideros excelsa*.

Six species of seabird and at least 13 species of landbird breed on Otata and Motuhoropapa, and a further 14 species of landbird have been recorded there. No reptiles occur on Motuhoropapa, but two species of skink and one of gecko inhabit Otata. The list of identified terrestrial invertebrates for the two islands exceeds 400 species.

COLONIZATION BY RATS

Rats were first recorded from the Noises Islands when one was seen on Otata towards the end of 1957. Unfortunately the other islands in the group were not checked at that time. Norway Rats were identified on Maria Island late in 1959, when they appeared responsible for the recent deaths of many hundreds of breeding White-faced Storm Petrels (*Pelagodroma marina*). Rat sign was found on David Rocks when they were

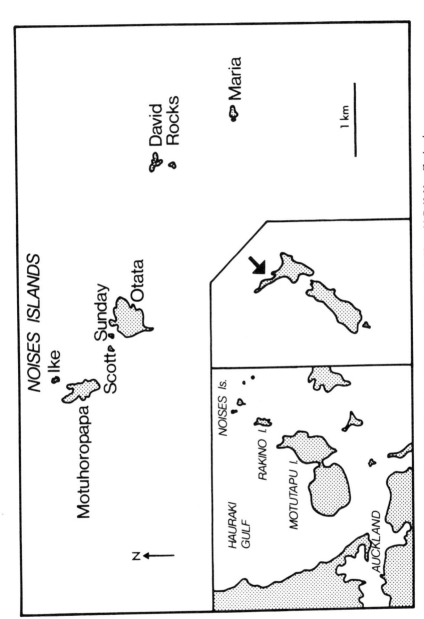

Figure 1: The Noises Islands and their location in Hauraki Gulf, New Zealand.

searched in November 1960. There is no contemporary information about the status of rats on Motuhoropapa.

There seem to be two routes by which Norway Rats are likely to have colonized the Noises Islands. From the late 1920s until 1972 garbage from ships used to be held on the Auckland waterfront and then dumped each day at sea several kilometres southwest of the Noises, and the floating remains were often washed onto the islands. Norway Rats commonly live in waterfront areas and sometimes infest ships. Any dumped with the garbage could have been carried ashore on rafts of refuse. Alternatively, the rats could have been transported by a strong ebb-tide current which passes the eastern shores of Motutapu and Rakino Islands (*Figure 1*), both of which are inhabited by Norway Rats. The Noises Islands lie directly across the northeasterly flow of this current. Norway Rats are strong swimmers and enter water readily. They are therefore well adapted to survive the water-borne journeys necessary for either colonization route.

There is no information about how the Norway Rats spread once they had reached the Noises Islands. Motuhoropapa and Otata are sufficiently close together for rats to have colonized one by swimming from the other using the islets in between (the widest water gap to be crossed is about 400m; *Figure 1*). However Maria Island and David Rocks are more isolated, the water gaps separating them from each other and from Otata exceeding 1.1km in width. It is possible therefore that these two islands were colonized independently, especially in the case of Maria, where rats could have gained access during the construction of a navigation light in 1953.

The rats disappeared from both David Rocks and Maria Island (each 2ha in area) during the mid-1960s, following sporadic laying of 'Warfarin' rodenticide between 1960 and 1964 by the Royal Forest and Bird Protection Society and the New Zealand Wildlife Service. The remaining islands in the group were not treated until the eradication campaigns described in this paper. Norway Rats were eliminated from Ike, Scott and Sunday Islands (all 0.6ha or less; *Figure 1*) during 1978 using warfarin and Epibloc (alpha-chlorohydrin) in permanent bait stations. Norway Rats were the only mammals on Otata and Motuhoropapa during the campaigns.

THE ERADICATION CAMPAIGNS

It is important to emphasize from the outset that *eradication* demands a different approach to *control* of rats: the objective of eradication is to kill every last individual, whereas control aims merely to reduce numbers to some acceptably low level. Eradication demands a long-term commitment, together with perseverance from the field operators. It is also essential that administrators and those supplying finance for the operation understand the distinction and do not stop the campaign when few rats are left and the cost becomes increasingly high for each rat killed. The last few rats are certainly the most expensive and exacting to destroy, but they are also obviously the most vital if the campaign is to succeed.

The campaigns on Otata and Motuhoropapa were designed bearing in mind the resources of equipment, manpower, money and time which could realistically be expected for future routine operations, perhaps on remote islands with difficult access. In these circumstances poisoning is the only practical and efficient method of extermination. I used two rodenticides added to different baits in order to reduce the effects of individual rats becoming shy of either poison or of particular baits. Such behaviour is well documented for Norway Rats, and can be passed from one generation to the next (e.g. see Barnett 1976). The first poison was sodium monofluoroacetate, more widely known as 'compound 1080', which was used to try and obtain a rapid initial reduction in rat numbers. It causes death after only a few hours, but produces poison-shyness in any rats which eat a sub-lethal dose. The second poison was brodifacoum, a new anti-coagulant rodenticide marketed in New Zealand under the proprietary brand name 'Talon WB'. Brodifacoum has a different mode of action from 1080, and death occurs 4–8 days after a lethal dose is consumed, so rats are less likely to develop an aversion to it. For this reason brodifacoum was used against those rats which had become shy of 1080, or had not been attracted to bait containing 1080. In contrast to earlier anti-coagulants, such as warfarin, brodifacoum is lethal to rats after only a single dose.

The LD_{50} (the dose likely to kill 50 percent of individuals) of 1080 for Norway Rats is 3.8mg/kg body weight (Barnett & Spencer 1949), and of brodifacoum is 0.26mg/kg body weight (Redfern *et al.* 1976). The concentrations of these poisons used in the campaigns were such that an adult rat would have consumed a lethal dose by eating one meal of only 3–4g of bait. This effectiveness after a single dose is especially important for eradication campaigns, where it is essential that rats need to feed from the bait only once to obtain a lethal dose.

The delayed death from brodifacoum is both an advantage and a potential dis-advantage. On the one hand rats eat a killing dose well before they begin to experience the toxic effects, whereas on the other they may continue feeding and consume far more bait than is needed to kill them. This wastes bait if rats are abundant, and the excess poison in carcases may present a hazard of secondary poisoning for predators or scavengers. A 'pulse baiting' method has been developed by Dubock (in press) in an effort to reduce these problems. However, these disadvantages were not considered serious for the Noises campaigns because rats were scarce and no species were at risk from secondary poisoning. In fact, rat numbers were sufficiently low to prevent us obtaining reliable information on bait consumption and the effectiveness of the two rodenticides. This in turn meant that it was extremely hard to determine the progress of the campaigns.

Otata Island

The eradication campaign on Otata was started in September 1979 at a time when the density of rats was naturally low (probably about 1 rat/ha). One hundred and seven covered bait stations were set out every 40m along 14 parallel transects and 26 additional stations were placed around the shoreline (*Figure 2*). The transects were themselves about 40m apart, so the bait stations formed a rough grid covering the island. The covered stations protected baits from ground-feeding birds and also the weather. They were constructed from sheets of plastic (45 × 35cm) bent into tunnels and held down with wire pegs. The 40m spacing was based on the movements of Norway Rats on Motuhoropapa, where the average distance between successive captures in live-traps was 113m for males and 49m for females (Moors 1979). Compound 1080 was used during the first stage of the campaign in a bait consisting of a 1:4 mixture by weight of rolled oats and fish-flavoured cat food. During trials elsewhere, wild Norway Rats had clearly preferred this bait above whole kernel corn, a 1:1 mixture of rolled oats and kibbled wheat, and feed pellets for rabbits. In order to encourage rats to feed at the stations about 100g of unpoisoned bait were provided for six nights at each one. The baits were checked daily and replenished when necessary. Many were attacked by insects, but only two showed evidence of being eaten by rats. All were then replaced with fresh baits containing 0.08 percent 1080, these being left out for a further two nights. Judging from the daily inspections of each station, rats ate little of these poison baits and I doubt that many were killed.

The second stage involved distributing brodifacoum bait blocks over the island. The blocks each weighed about 5g and contained whole kernels of corn, 0.005 percent brodifacoum, and paraffin wax as a weather-proofing agent. (The blocks were developed for the control of rats in Malaysian oil palm estates.) A team of five people spaced 10m

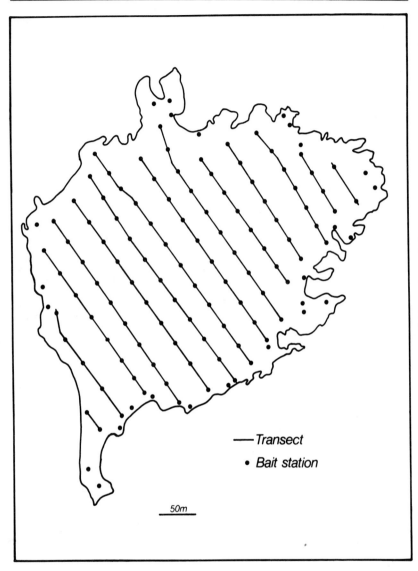

Figure 2:   The distribution of 14 transects and 133 bait stations on Otata Island during the two campaigns to eradicate Norway Rats.

Figure 3: A large white plastic container (30 × 14 × 15cm) used as a bait station during the second eradication campaign on Otata Island. The wooden base (26 × 8.5cm) and bait holder (with Talon WB bait blocks) fit through the mouth of the container and the lid is then screwed on.

apart walked line-abreast down each transect, placing a block every 5m or so. Blocks were left in sites likely to be visited by rats, such as hollow logs, under rocks and beneath overhanging vegetation. They were also distributed on the coastal slopes, along the shoreline and on offshore islets. About 7500 blocks were broadcast, giving an average density of 330 blocks/ha. One hundred marked blocks were examined at the end of October 1979: only six were intact, the remainder being in various stages of decay from insect attack and disintegration of the wax matrix.

The total manpower needed to cut the transects, install the bait stations, lay and inspect the baits, and broadcast the blocks amounted to 13.5 man-hours/ha, or about 37 man-days altogether.

Otata was visited on three occasions during the following nine months to check for fresh rat sign (e.g. droppings, food remains and tracks in mud and sand). Kill-traps were set for a total of 712 trap-nights, and 57 wooden gnawing sticks (25 × 2 × 2cm), previously soaked for 24 hours in hot vegetable oil, were continuously available. (Rats gnaw the edges of the sticks and leave distinctive incisor marks in the timber.) No fresh sign was found until June 1980, when droppings were discovered in the house on the island. A second island-wide poisoning campaign was mounted in September 1980. The bait stations used in the first operation were replaced with new ones made from large plastic containers (*Figure 3*). These gave better protection and were more durable than the sheets of plastic. About 40g of whole oats impregnated with 0.08 percent 1080 were placed in each bait station. Small amounts of 0.08 percent 1080 paste (containing petroleum jelly, soya oil, sugar and green dye) were left near the house, around the shoreline and in four small breeding colonies of Grey-faced Petrels (*Pterodroma macroptera*). This paste remains active for 6–9 months. Both it and the poisoned oats were manufactured by the New Zealand Agricultural Pests Destruction Council. In addition, 40 pullets' eggs were injected with 0.1 percent 1080 and distributed around the edges of the petrel colonies. Norway Rats are known to eat the eggs of these petrels (Imber 1976), which are slightly larger than pullets' eggs, and the poisoning campaign coincided with the petrels' breeding season. The poisoned eggs were removed after a month, none having been eaten by rats.

From October 1980 onwards, Otata was visited every 2–3 months to search for rat sign and to check the bait stations and gnawing sticks. The 1080 oats were replaced in December 1980 with Talon WB bait blocks developed in New Zealand by ICI Tasman Ltd. The blocks weigh about 20g each and contain grain, tallow, wax and 0.005 percent brodifacoum. These baits were removed in December 1981. The gnawing sticks were soaked in fresh vegetable oil on each visit, and were maintained until February 1984. From time to time additional applications of 1080 paste and also a similarly formulated 0.01 percent brodifacoum paste have been made, particularly around the coast. In April 1981 fresh droppings and the chewed remains of *Pittosporum crassifolium* fruits were found on two rocky outcrops connected to Otata by a boulder beach. Talon blocks and 1080 paste were laid in both places. Since then there has been no sign of rats anywhere on Otata, and it is likely that they have been eradicated. The island is still being checked periodically to confirm that rats are absent.

Motuhoropapa Island

My approach to the extermination of Norway Rats from Motuhoropapa was initially rather different from that on Otata. In 1977 I had undertaken a trapping study of the rats but by December 1978 the capture rate had declined to zero. From these results and other information it appeared that the rats had been inadvertently eliminated by trapping alone. In order to determine if this was so I postponed laying poison and instead regularly checked the island for evidence of rats.

Motuhoropapa was visited every 2–4 months from December 1978 onwards. Kill-traps of four different designs were set for 1375 trap-nights between February 1979 and October 1980, and 92 live-traps were set continuously from April 1979 until February 1980. No rats at all were caught during this intensive and prolonged trapping pro-gramme. The trapping was supplemented with searches for droppings, tracks and feeding sign, and the use of tracking tunnels (Moors 1978) and gnawing sticks. No indisputable evidence of the presence of rats was uncovered, although possible sign was found in February 1979 and February 1980. On both occasions the skulls of birds accidentally caught in kill-traps had been chewed in a similar way to known rat predations. However the damage could also have been caused by Moreporks (*Ninox novaeseelandiae*) or Kingfishers (*Halcyon sancta*).

The island was searched again for rat sign in January 1981. One gnawing stick was found with a single set of tooth marks, and the following day a female rat (weight 144g) was kill-trapped about 30m away. Next day a second female (weight 204g) was caught nearby. Both captures were at established trap-sites in an area which had been routinely examined without success on previous visits (*Figure 4*). Both rats were the progeny of the current breeding season, and were reproductively mature but had not bred. By April 1981 rat sign was encountered over the whole island: 12 of 36 gnawing sticks had been chewed (*Figure 4*), fresh droppings were found in coastal caves, gnawed fruits of *Pittosporum crassifolium* and *Planchonella costata* were present, and the rats had even

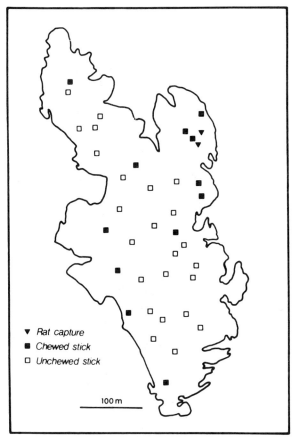

Figure 4:   Trap-sites at which Norway Rats were caught on Motuhoropapa Island in January 1981,
              and the positions of chewed gnawing sticks in April 1981.

recolonized Ike Island 150m offshore. Eighteen of 39 sticks had been gnawed by August
1981, including 10 which had not been chewed at the April inspection. I attribute this
unexpected reappearance of rats to a very small number surviving undetected throughout the preceding two years, and their numbers then increasing with breeding. Re-col-
onization of Motuhoropapa cannot be totally excluded as an explanation, but I think it
is most unlikely, especially in view of the two earlier occurrences of scavenging on
kill-trapped birds. In retrospect it seems certain that these were the work of rats rather
than birds. It may be significant that evidence for the presence of rats appeared at about
the same time in each of the three years and corresponded with the period when young
rats would have been entering the population. These individuals may not have
developed the behavioural aversion towards such things as traps and gnawing sticks
apparently displayed by adults.

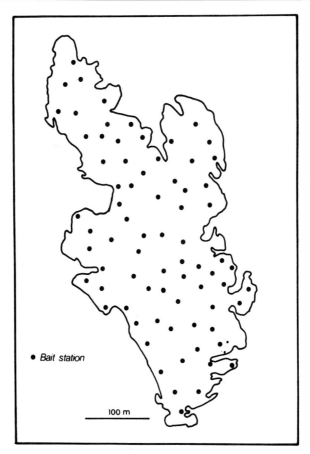

Figure 5:   The distribution of 75 bait stations on Motuhoropapa Island during the campaign to exterminate Norway Rats.

In April 1981 I reverted to the original plan to lay poison on Motuhoropapa. Forty-five bait stations of the design shown in *Figure 3* were placed every 50m along existing tracks, with another 30 around the coast (*Figure 5*). Oats impregnated with 0.08 percent 1080 were put in each station, and 0.08 percent 1080 paste was spread in likely rat haunts, particularly on coastal slopes, offshore stacks and in shoreline caves. Both types of bait were also distributed on Ike Island. The oats were replaced in August 1981 with 0.005 percent Talon bait blocks, which were maintained in the bait stations until their removal in February 1983. During five visits between February 1982 and April 1983 0.01 percent brodifacoum paste was also spread. During every visit the island was carefully searched for rat sign, concentrating particularly on areas where sign had been found during the irruption in 1981. Kill-traps were always set, the total trapping effort exceeding 1400 trap-nights, and 40–50 gnawing sticks were continuously available.

Fresh sign, mainly droppings and chewed gnawing sticks, was widespread in April and August 1981, and an adult female rat (weight 348g) was trapped in September. A rat was also trapped on Ike Island in August, and this, together with poisoning, eradicated the animals from there. Since 1981 the only evidence for the continuing presence of rats on Motuhoropapa has been an apparently rat-chewed carcase of an Indian Myna (*Acridotheres tristis*) found in February 1983. The bird had been caught in a kill-trap left set in August 1982 in the area where the irruption was first noticed in 1981.

Intensive searches and trapping produced no other sign of rats, nor was any found on the next visits in April and August 1983. The eradication campaign is continuing.

DISCUSSION

The eradication campaigns on the Noises Islands have been laborious and somewhat unpredictable. Four years—and several setbacks—after the first poison was laid, it now seems that Norway Rats have been eliminated from Otata, Scott, Sunday and Ike Islands, but possibly not yet from Motuhoropapa. The campaigns have required 20 field trips, the involvement at various times of 19 people (although most of the work was done by only three of these), and the expenditure of approximately 250 man-days of effort. The total cost of materials, transport and salaries is in the vicinity of $25,000 or about $760 per hectare of treated island. Success has been achieved through the distribution of two rodenticides in a variety of baits, and the availability of poisons for months at a time. The poison pastes have been especially useful, enabling poison to be laid in places where it was impractical to maintain bait stations. We have found no evidence that the poisoning has killed any animals other than rats.

The greatest practical difficulty encountered during the campaigns has been detecting rats when they are present in very low numbers. This problem may be more acute with Norway Rats than with *R. rattus* or *R. exulans*, both of which are generally less wary of man-made objects such as traps, bait-stations and gnawing sticks. It is also a problem not faced during control operations, which aim only to reduce the numbers of rats and which are counted a success if numbers become undetectably low. Nevertheless, efficient detection methods are essential if extermination campaigns are to be effective. Gnawing sticks soaked in cooking oil have been the most useful, but not infallible, means of detection on the Noises Islands. Additional and more reliable methods need to be developed. Techniques worth further investigation include the use of unpoisoned bait, devices for collecting hair (e.g. Suckling 1978), systems for obtaining rat tracks with ink or powder, detection of rat urine by fluorescence in ultra-violet light, and the use of specially trained dogs. These techniques should, however, always supplement careful searching for natural sign of rats.

Several deficiencies have become apparent during the course of the campaigns. The first operation on Otata probably failed because the pre-feeding period was not sufficiently long for the rats to become dependent on the unpoisoned bait, and also because the original brodifacoum blocks contained too much wax and so were unattractive to the rats. In addition, although earlier trials had shown the rolled oats-cat food bait for 1080 to be palatable, it had the disadvantage of being moist: this led to it rotting and becoming fly-blown after a few days of warm weather. The bait stations made from plastic containers (*Figure 3*) have been durable and convenient to use, but recent work elsewhere has shown that wild Norway Rats are reluctant to enter them (Moors, unpubl.). Covered bait stations are regularly used in poisoning operations against Norway Rats (e.g. Howard & Marsh 1976), and it is unclear why these plastic stations should be avoided. The same stations are, however, readily entered by *R. exulans* (I. McFadden, pers. comm.).

Rats have been eradicated from several other islands around the world. Intensive poisoning with the anticoagulant coumatetralyl in the winters of 1969–70 and 1970–71 removed Norway Rats from Flatey Island (50ha) in Iceland (Petersen 1979, in litt.). Bait stations were concentrated around the shoreline (where the rats obtained most of their food) and in places where rat tracks were common in the snow. Both winters were cold and hard, and Petersen (in litt.) considers that the resulting shortage of food forced the rats to feed on the baits. The poisoning apparently also eliminated House Mice (*Mus musculus*) from Flatey. The Castle Harbour Islands, Bermuda, are managed as a National Park, partly to protect the only breeding colonies of the rare Bermuda Petrel (*Pterodroma cahow*). Norway Rats and Ship Rats (*Rattus rattus*) are eradicated from these nine islands (total area 10ha) by intensive baiting with warfarin whenever the rats swim the few hundred metres from mainland Bermuda (Wingate, this vol.). Ship Rats were extirpated from Fisher Island (0.8ha), Bass Strait, by continuous trapping and poisoning between 1971 and 1974 (Serventy 1977). Rats (probably *R. rattus*) have also been removed from Heron Island (16ha) on the Great Barrier Reef (Kikkawa & Boles 1976). Finally, an attempt to kill off the Norway Rats on Furzey Island (20ha) in Poole Harbour, England, was unsuccessful, probably because of immigration from neighbouring islands (Lazarus & Rowe 1982).

The maximum size of island which can be successfully cleared of rats depends on a variety of factors. These include the location and accessibility of the island, its topography and vegetation cover, the ease of movement around it, the distribution of rats, and the amounts of money and manpower available. The species of rat being exterminated is also important, because the species differ in certain aspects of their behaviour (e.g. reaction to bait stations and traps, the extent of arboreal activity, and the size of movements and home ranges) which affect the design and conduct of the campaign. So far Flatey Island (50ha) is the largest island to be tackled successfully, and with current techniques it seems likely that 75–100ha is the practical limit at present. However, the development of chemosterilants, new rodenticides and effective attractants (e.g. synthetic rodent pheromones) may increase this size, as may the use of novel techniques like the introduction of single-sex populations of rat predators (see Fitzgerald 1978).

The campaigns on the Noises Islands have provided a valuable and largely successful test of the practicability of exterminating island populations of Norway Rats. Otata is now potentially available for the release of endangered fauna, and further effort will ensure that the same can soon be said for Motuhoropapa. I think intending rat exterminators can learn three main lessons from this work. Firstly, do not underestimate the size of the task, even if rat numbers seem small. Secondly, use as many methods of killing rats as you can, and never rely on one weapon alone. Thirdly, be aware that an absence of fresh sign does not necessarily guarantee that rats have been eliminated.

ACKNOWLEDGEMENTS

I appreciate the ready permission given by Mr B. P. Neureuter for the New Zealand Wildlife Service to have free access to the Noises Islands, to stay in the house on Otata, and to construct tracks and other facilities. He and his family have enthusiastically supported all stages of this work. A large number of people, not all of whom were staff of the Wildlife Service, helped with the eradication campaigns, and I am most grateful to them all. In particular, Duncan Cunningham and Ian McFadden provided indispensable technical and field assistance, and Dr Ian Atkinson was always ready to supply ideas, discussion and labour. ICI Tasman Ltd. donated some of the Talon baits, and together with Imperial Chemical Industries PLC made a grant towards my travel to the

18th World Conference of the International Council for Bird Preservation in Cambridge. Other travel funds were supplied by the New Zealand Wildlife Service and ICBP. I am grateful for comments on a draft of this paper by Dr J. M. Williams and Mr J. Innes.

REFERENCES

ATKINSON, I. A. E. 1977. A reassessment of factors, particularly *Rattus rattus* L., that influenced the decline of endemic forest birds in the Hawaiian Islands. *Pacific Science* **31**, 109–33.

ATKINSON, I. A. E. (this vol.). The spread of commensal species of *Rattus* to oceanic islands and their effects on island avifaunas.

BARNETT, S. A. 1976. The rat: a study in behaviour. Australian National University Press, Canberra.

BARNETT, S. A. & SPENCER, M. M. 1949. Sodium fluoroacetate (1080) as a rat poison. *J. Hygiene* **47**, 426–30.

BELL, B. D. 1978. The Big South Cape Islands rat irruption. *In:* Dingwall, P. R., Atkinson, I. A. E. & Hay, C. (eds) The ecology and control of rodents in New Zealand Nature Reserves. *New Zealand Dept. of Lands & Survey Information Series* **4**, 33–40.

DUBOCK, A. C. (in press). A practical technique for cost effective rodent control. *Acta Zool. Fenn.*

FITZGERALD, B. M. 1978. A proposal for biological control. *In:* Dingwall, P. R., Atkinson, I. A. E. & Hay, C. (eds) The ecology and control of rodents in New Zealand Nature Reserves. *New Zealand Dept. Lands & Survey Information Series* **4**, 223–7.

HOWARD, W. E. & MARSH, R. E. 1976. *The rat: its biology and control.* University of California Division of Agricultural Sciences Leaflet No. 2896.

IMBER, M. J. 1976. Breeding biology of the Grey-faced Petrel *Pterodroma macroptera gouldi. Ibis* **118**, 51–64.

KIKKAWA, J. & BOLES, W. 1976. Seabird islands No. 16. Heron Island, Queensland. *Aust. Bird Bander* **14**, 3–6.

LAZARUS, A. B. & ROWE, F. P. 1982. Reproduction in an island population of Norway rats, *Rattus norvegicus* (Berkenhout), treated with an oestrogenic steroid. *Agro-Ecosystems* **8**, 59–67.

MOORS, P. J. 1978. Methods for studying predators and their effects on forest birds. *In:* Dingwall, P. R., Atkinson, I. A. E. & Hay, C. (eds) The ecology and control of rodents in New Zealand Nature Reserves. *New Zealand Dept. of Lands & Survey Information Series* **4**, 47–56.

MOORS, P. J. 1979. Norway rats on islands in Hauraki Gulf. *Wildlife—A Review* **10**, 39–45.

MOORS, P. J. & ATKINSON, I. A. E. 1984. Predation on seabirds by introduced animals, and factors affecting its severity. *ICBP Tech. Pubn.* No. 2.

PETERSEN, A. 1979. The breeding birds of Flatey and some adjoining islets, in Breidafjordur, NW Iceland. *Natturufraedingurinn* **49**, 229–56. (In Icelandic; English summary pp. 252–6.)

RAMSAY, G. W. 1978. A review of the effect of rodents on the New Zealand invertebrate fauna. *In:* Dingwall, P. R., Atkinson, I. A. E. & Hay, C. (eds) The ecology and control of rodents in New Zealand Nature Reserves. *New Zealand Dept. Lands & Survey Information Series* **4**, 89–95.

REDFERN, R., GILL, J. E. & HADLER, M. R. 1976. Laboratory evaluation of WBA 8119 as a rodenticide for use against warfarin-resistant and non-resistant rats and mice. *J. Hygiene* **77**, 419–26.

SERVENTY, D. L. 1977. Seabird islands No. 49. Fisher Island, Tasmania. *Corella* **1**, 60–2.

SUCKLING, G. C. 1978. A hair sampling tube for the detection of small mammals in trees. *Aust. Wildl. Res.* **5**, 249–52.

WHITAKER, A. H. 1978. The effects of rodents on reptiles and amphibians. *In:* Dingwall, P. R., Atkinson, I. A. E. & Hay, C. (eds) The ecology and control of rodents in New Zealand Nature Reserves. *New Zealand Dept. Lands & Survey Information Series* **4**, 75–86.

WINGATE, D. B. (this vol.). The restoration of Nonsuch Island as a living museum of Bermuda's pre-colonial terrestrial biome.

ICBP Technical Publication No. 3, 1985

THE IMPACT AND ERADICATION OF FERAL GOATS ON THE GALAPAGOS ISLANDS

Luis Calvopina

Charles Darwin Research Station, Santa Cruz Is, Galapagos, Ecuador

Though the first reports of goat introductions to the Galapagos date back to the seventeenth century, sound evidence of early introductions date only from 1818 when four goats were accidentally introduced to James Island. Before the eradication campaigns were begun, ten islands supported populations of feral goats. From 1970 onwards a systematic extermination and control programme was developed, and research on the goats was begun later.

James is the most affected island, with a population of over 80,000 goats. Intensive studies of the vegetation inside and outside exclosures show that all canopy species and the majority of shrubs are failing to replace themselves successfully due to the consumption of seedlings by goats. Because of the goats' selective browsing, several palatable endemic species are near extinction and survive only in protected areas. On the other hand, a few annual herbs favoured by grazing have invaded and consequently changed the composition and dominance of communities at the expense of perennials. Of the 584.6km^2 of James Island, about 25 percent is lava without vegetation, and another 15 percent previously vegetated has been deforested by goats and is now either grassland or barren soil. However, exclosure studies on James, and permanent plots on other islands such as Barrington and Pinta, show that several species of tree and perennial herb are still able to regenerate into communities when protected from browsing.

Clearance of highland forest on James, and the subsequent immigration of weedy species normally restricted to the lowlands, has undoubtedly affected the distribution and diets of seed-eating birds (e.g. *Geospiza* and doves). Destruction of leaf litter and increased dryness of the soil due to decreased plant protection have largely affected those birds which feed mainly on seeds and litter invertebrates (e.g. *G. difficilis*). The endemic hawks feed on goat carcasses on James and other islands with feral goats. These non-territorial birds clearly benefited from the presence of goats after clearance of the thick vegetation in the highlands made food (prey) more available.

To combat the critical situation created by the goats, the Ecuadorian Galapagos National Park Service, advised by the Charles Darwin Research Station and with partial international funding, conducted an extensive campaign to eradicate these animals utilizing the only method available, heavy hunting pressure. This has been successful on five small and medium-sized islands. Up to ten well-trained park guards carried out the hunting during the past ten years. They also hunted other feral mammals on several islands, but spent about 16 percent of their time killing goats. Approximately 60,000 goats have been removed, using mainly .22 manual rifles. At first females were killed, both to decrease numbers and also to cause a decline in juvenile recruitment. A special campaign has been mounted to remove the last difficult goats. This has included an increase in the number of hunters, the use of dogs, and, when available, high-powered rifles.

BREEDING SUCCESS AND MORTALITY OF DARK-RUMPED PETRELS IN THE GALAPAGOS, AND CONTROL OF THEIR PREDATORS

R. J. TOMKINS

Department of Zoology, Monash University, Melbourne, Vic. 3168, Australia
Present address: 64 Tompson Road, Revesby, NSW 2212, Australia

ABSTRACT

A dramatic decrease of Dark-rumped Petrels (*Pterodroma phaeopygia*) in the Galapagos has been caused by predation by introduced mammals, mainly Black Rats, dogs and cats. Breeding success on Isla Santa Cruz was 1.9 percent during two years. Minimum adult mortality was approximately 15 percent per annum, and the average adult life expectancy was 6.2 years. Clearly this population is doomed to extinction. Breeding success was higher on other islands because predation was not as severe, but nevertheless most islands need management attention.

Inter- and intra-island variation in these petrels is mentioned briefly because it must be decided which is to be saved: the Galapagos subspecies (by preserving any one population in the Galapagos), *or* the distinct populations on each island. Priorities and costs of recommendations are made for management action to preserve these petrels. The recommendations have two objectives, firstly to reduce rat predation on eggs and small chicks, and secondly to protect adults from larger predators. They detail control of rats, dogs and cats by poisoning, the construction of rockpiles incorporating petrel nests, and the laying of large-mesh wire over burrows in soil banks.

Future conservation work should include monitoring breeding success to decide if predator control programmes are successful. The search should continue for predator-free colonies. Consideration should be given to establishing a colony by chick transplantation onto a relatively predator-free island (i.e. Pinta and Fernandina).

INTRODUCTION

The Dark-rumped Petrel (*Pterodroma phaeopygia*) breeds only on the Galapagos Archipelago and Hawaiian Islands. The subspecies on the Galapagos (*P. phaeopygia phaeopygia*) is the only seabird considered to be in danger of extinction there (King 1981). Reliable local inhabitants report a noticeable decline in the number of these petrels breeding on three islands (a fourth is uninhabited). These declines have been due to the relatively recent clearing of nesting habitat and to predation by introduced mammals (Harris 1970). Baker's (1980) census suggested Isla Santa Cruz had 9000 breeding pairs, and I estimated that the population of Isla Santiago was about 25 percent more than Santa Cruz, whilst Islas Floreana and San Cristobal were about 25 percent less (Tomkins 1980).

The objectives of this study were to determine if the low nesting success and high adult mortality previously documented at Media Luna, Santa Cruz, by Harris (1970) were typical for the rest of the archipelago, and if necessary to suggest methods of predator control.

By supplementing Harris (1970) with my unpublished data and observations we know that an adult is present for breeding on the Galapagos for eight to nine months in every twelve, after which it is thought to migrate to the region of the Panama Bight. On their return they reoccupy their nest of the previous season. Immature birds return three months later and stay for two months. Both partners of a pair are more often found together in their burrow before egg laying and soon after egg or chick failure than at any other time. When together they are very vocal. Only one egg is laid. Chicks are brooded and guarded for a total of two or three days before being left alone, and at this stage are very vulnerable to attack. The young fledge approximately 110 days after hatching.

I am preparing a discussion of the existence of distinct populations of these petrels within the Galapagos (based on inter- and intra-island variations in morphology, egg size, breeding timetable, vocalizations and possibly plumage) and this will be presented elsewhere. The variations have been allowed for in the suggestions for predator control made in this paper. Briefly, there appear to be two groups of birds on San Cristobal, one breeding in the austral summer and another significantly smaller one breeding in the winter. Those of the summer group are closer in size to Santiago birds than they are to the winter group. On Floreana birds on adjacent volcanoes (which differ in height and therefore climate) breed on average seven weeks apart, but there is no size difference. Birds on Santa Cruz breed last. Birds on Floreana are larger, and those on Santa Cruz are smaller than all other groups. However, the differences in size between the extremes are not noticeable in birds on the wing, and overlap exists.

METHODS

Groups of burrows on the four breeding islands (*Figure 1*) were numbered and monitored individually. Burrows at Media Luna were monitored in 1978 and 1979, and those at other colonies only in 1979. Several visits were made to each breeding island, and each time the marked burrows were examined as thoroughly as possible and a record of their contents kept. However, some burrows were long and twisted, and it was not always possible, even using a torch and mirror, to see the occupants. Adults and large chicks were banded with numbered metal bands from the British Museum. The ages of eggs (determined by comparing their weights with those of known-age eggs and by their cleanliness) and chicks were estimated. The stage of the breeding cycle for adults not found with eggs or chicks was estimated by examining the condition of their plumage and brood patch. Thus a breeding timetable was established for each nest and verified or adjusted in the light of subsequent visits. The reasons for breeding failures were determined by searching the immediate vicinity of the nest for evidence of desertion or predation. The method of killing and consuming petrels was diagnostic for each type of predator on the Galapagos, and carcasses found usually provided tell-tale signs of the identity of the predator. For example, Dogs (*Canis familiaris*) scattered limbs and feathers over a wide area and mutilated carcasses, owls neatly plucked the body and usually ate viscera and pectoral muscles only, whereas Cats (*Felis catus*) crunched the back of the skull and often left both wings attached to a slightly chewed carcass stripped of most flesh (often called a 'bridle carcass'). Black Rats (*Rattus rattus*) left pieces of eggshell unevenly chewed, moved eggs out of burrows, drank or ate the contents, and abandoned the almost empty shell. Rats dragged carcasses of chicks from the burrows to sheltered areas (called 'ratteries') where rat food debris, including petrel bones, accumulated. Occasionally the vegetation platform in the burrow was scattered,

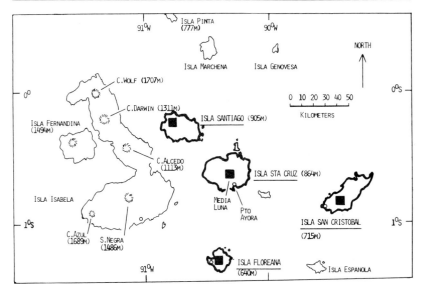

Figure 1:   Dark-rumped petrels are known to breed on four islands in the Galapagos Archipelago.
Colonies monitored in this study are represented by a solid square symbol.

and large quantities of fresh rat droppings were found in burrows from which chicks disappeared. If these signs were not present the predator was listed as unknown. It is unlikely that carcasses were carried far by predators, and very few injured birds would have died unnoticed in burrows because the smell of rapidly decomposing carcasses would have attracted my attention.

Thin short twigs were placed across the entrances to burrows, and depending on the pattern of disturbance it could be judged the next day in which direction a bird or rat had passed overnight. Burrows were usually inspected by day.

RESULTS

Search for colonies
Likely breeding sites on many volcanoes and islands were searched in 1978 and 1979 for petrels. They were seen or heard on Sierra Negra, Cerro Azul, C. Alcedo and Volcán Fernandina, but no nests were found. No trace of petrels was found on C. Wolf, C. Darwin, Isla Genovesa, Isla Pinta, nor on several other islands (Tomkins 1980). Several hundred were seen at sea off Isla Marchena in August 1978 (J. Grove & D. Kiehn, pers. comm.), but none were found on those parts of the island which were searched.

Breeding success
The results of 232 known breeding attempts in 444 burrows are shown in *Table 1*. Lack of funds caused cancellation of the final trip to Floreana and San Cristobal in 1979, and so the complete breeding cycle was not monitored. Harris (1970) reported a breeding success of 6.0 percent at Media Luna in 1966 and 1967 combined, and my study in the same area shows a success rate of 1.9 percent for both seasons combined. Breeding

Table 1: Success of breeding attempts in monitored burrows on the Galapagos in 1978 and 1979.

Island	No. of burrows	No. of eggs	Final status unknown	No. of fledglings or large chicks	Non-predatory losses[1]	Failures			% failure from predation	Overall breeding success %
						Predator	Unknown	Total		
Santa Cruz (1978)	87	64	0	0	2 non-pred. 1 human	61	0	64	95.3	0.0
Santa Cruz (1979)	95	39	0	2	4 non-pred. 2 human	31	0	37	79.5	5.1
Santiago (1979)	80	38	0	15	4 non-pred.	13	6	23	34.2	39.5
Floreana (1979)	72	47	0	23	4 non-pred.	15	5	24	31.9	48.9
San Cristobal (1979)	110	44	2	5	10 non-pred. 1 human	19	7	37	43.2	11.4
Total for 1979	357	168	2	45	25	78	18	121	46.4	26.8
Grand total	444	232	2	45	28	139	18	185	59.9	19.4

Note: 1. Addled eggs, intra-specific competition, etc.

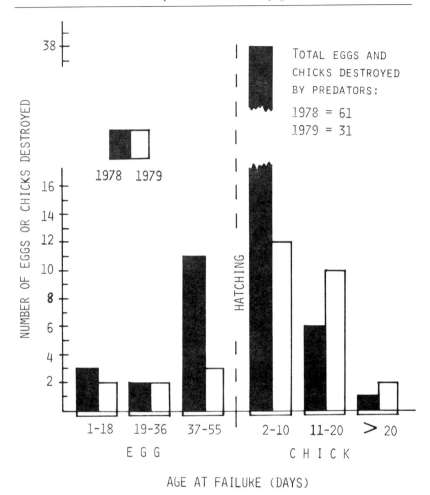

Figure 2: Age at which eggs and chicks failed because of rat predation at Media Luna, Isla Sta Cruz, in 1978 and 1979.

success was much higher on the other islands, the most successful being Floreana. Breeding success on most islands was lower than those of other Procellariiformes e.g. *Oceanodroma castro* 25 percent (Harris 1969a); *O. furcata* 39 percent (Boersma *et al.* 1980); *Puffinus lherminieri* 59 percent (Snow 1965); *P. puffinus* 75 percent (Harris 1969b); *P. tenuirostris* 60 percent (F. I. Norman *in* Harris 1969b); *Bulweria bulwerii* 57 percent (Cramp & Simmons 1977); *Phoebetria palpebrata* 31 percent and *P. fusca* 35 percent (Berruti 1979).

Predation

Figure 2 shows the estimated age at which 92 eggs and chicks were destroyed by Black

Table 2: Destruction of Dark-rumped Petrel eggs, chicks and adults on the Galapagos by predators and other causes. A dash indicates that the particular predator is absent from the island.

	Santiago	Floreana	San Cristobal	Sta. Cruz 1978	Sta. Cruz 1979	Total for each predator
DESTRUCTION OF EGGS AND CHICKS CAUSED BY						
Cat	—	0	2	0	0	2
Dog	—	0	1	0	0	1
Rat	5	15	16	61	31	128
Pig	2	0	0	0	0	2
Owl	(4)[1]	0	0	0	0	(4)[1]
Hawk	2	—	—	—	—	2
Minimum totals caused by predators only	13	15	19	61	31	139
Non-predatory losses	4	4	11[2]	3	6	28
Unknown	6	5	7	0	0	18
Total losses	23	24	37	64	37	185
DEATH OF ADULTS CAUSED BY						
Cat	—	3	5	0	0	8
Dog	—	3	8	19	9	39
Rat	0	0	0	0	0	0
Pig	5	0	0	0	0	5
Owl	0	0	1	3	0	4
Hawk	4	—	—	—	—	4
Minimum totals caused by predators only	9	6	14	22	9	60
Non-predatory losses	0	1	2	0	1	4
Unknown	2	1	13[3]	0	0	16
Total losses	11	8	29	22	10	80
GRAND TOTAL	34	32	66	86	47	265

Notes: 1. Deaths caused by either owls or hawks.

2. Intra-specific competition on San Cristobal was a major component in non-predatory losses.

3. Probably caused by cats and dogs.

Rats at Media Luna in 1978 and 1979. Most predation of eggs and chicks occurred in the 20-day period either side of hatching. Because nesting failures tended to be dated only approximately some failures indicated in *Figure 2* as having occurred immediately before hatching may have occurred immediately after hatching, and vice versa. As rats were a major predator on the other three islands I suggest this pattern was similar there too. *Table 2* summarizes the number of eggs, chicks and adults destroyed by each predator in the colonies monitored in this study. Some failures before hatching included in *Figure 2* may have been caused by rats eating eggs deserted for a few hours during the day (Harris 1970) or during the night. In 1978 and 1979, of 27 burrows studied, one bird indisputably left its egg temporarily unattended during the night and four others might have. Egg neglect has been reported in other species of *Pterodroma* and it is common among Procellariiformes (Boersma & Wheelwright 1979). However diurnal attendance but nocturnal egg neglect appears to be rare. Rats investigated all holes and cracks in a petrel colony, and if a sound egg was unattended or a chick was too small to defend itself

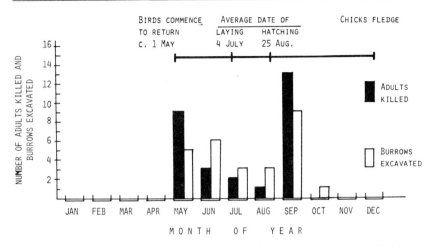

Figure 3:   Month of year and stage of breeding cycle at which 28 adult petrels were killed by dogs, and at which 27 petrel burrows were excavated by dogs at Media Luna in 1978 and 1979.

successfully they ate it. Rats in all colonies probably ate eggs and chicks on an opportunistic basis (D. & D. Clark, pers. comm.). Rats probably do not kill adult petrels (Harris 1970). From three or four days of age onwards chicks tended to wander up and down their burrows and often roamed outside the tunnel entrance. This activity was revealed by downy filaments along the length of the burrow and on pathways near entrances to burrows. Chicks also stand outside burrows at night and exercise their wings just prior to fledging, making themselves vulnerable to attack by larger predators such as cats, dogs and owls.

In 1978, in one sub-colony at Media Luna, dogs dug up 16 (70 percent) of the 23 burrows in which eggs were laid and also killed 12 adult petrels. In 1979 at the same site, eggs were laid in 12 burrows, five burrows (42 percent) were excavated by dogs and seven adult petrels were killed. The drop from 23 to 12 eggs represents a halving in the number of breeding pairs. This decrease can be largely, if not wholly, accounted for by the 12 dead adults found in 1978. Only three of the 16 burrows dug up in 1978 were used in 1979. Aerial activity over this sub-colony was noticeably less in 1979 compared with 1978. I suspect that dogs were relatively infrequent visitors to the colonies and were probably from nearby farms. The dogs dug mostly adult petrels out of soil burrows and killed them. Both dogs and cats also caught adults on the surface whilst walking to or from their burrows, or whilst engaged in courtship and pair-bonding activities on the ground, especially in clearings. *Figure 3* clearly shows that most adults at Media Luna were killed in May and September, which coincides with the period when both partners are most often together in their burrows. September is also the period when immature birds were most often in the colonies, and these would be more vulnerable than experienced adults. This pattern was similar on San Cristobal and Floreana, but because breeding was not as closely synchronized there these deaths were less concentrated. On San Cristobal and Floreana there were no signs of active cat dens, and I suspect that the cats were mainly from nearby farms. They visited the colonies infrequently and only on the former island were they a serious predator of petrels. Feral pigs (*sus scrofa*) killed chicks and adults on Santiago, but as most nests are safely under rocks their present influence on petrels is slight. If the current programme to reduce the pig population is continued by the Galapagos National Park Service no specific action need be taken in petrel colonies. Short-eared Owls (*Asio flammeus*) and probably occasionally Barn Owls (*Tyto alba*) and Hawks (*Buteo galapagoensis*) killed so few chicks and adults that their predation should be considered insignificant. It is possible that since rats formed part of the diet of both Short-eared Owls (Abs *et al.* 1965; Nelson 1968: 231) and Hawks (de Vries 1976) on the Galapagos, on Santiago they may have benefited petrels by controlling the number of rats and by inhibiting rat movement across goat-grazed areas between petrel colonies (see Management Recommendations).

Other causes of nest failures

Apart from predation there were several other causes of the failure of eggs and chicks, and these have been called 'Non-predatory losses' in *Tables 1* and *2*. The following are explanations of those 28 failures. The embryos of seven eggs did not commence development and their contents were usually rancid when examined: these have been called 'addled' here but other authors refer to them as 'infertile'. A nervous bird was seen sitting with the egg under its chest rather than beneath its brood patch, and this was regarded as 'inadequate incubation'. Ants and other small arthropods were not usually seen at most colonies, but on Santiago several burrows were infested with the latter from nearby pig and goat dust-baths. Two nests there had a large number of small ants, and since both of these failed it is possible that incubating adults were forced away by these arthropods. One nest on Floreana had many ants: this also failed. One eggshell on Santiago appeared to be much thinner than other eggshells. Relatively deep water was present in one nest, and at some stage after egg-laying water cascaded over two more nests. One cracked egg was not incubated on the usual vegetation platform of the nest. Eight eggs (six on San Cristobal) were ejected from nests by adult petrels, and I attributed this to intraspecific competition. 'Human failures' were caused when I accidentally broke one egg and inadvertently forced three adults to temporarily abandon their eggs which were then eaten by rats. One non-breeding bird flew into a cliff and broke its neck, and one egg cracked at the large end was not incubated; these two losses have been omitted from *Tables 1* and *2*.

The recorded incidence of addled eggs at Media Luna increased from two in 1978 (3.1 percent) to four in 1979 (10.3 percent). No data was available from other islands. Sound and addled eggs were tested for contamination with organochlorine residues by the Patuxent Wildlife Research Center. The results (*Table 3*) show very little contamination. This amount would not have contributed to the production of addled eggs, or to the formation of thin eggshells and subsequent crushing of eggs during incubation.

Adult mortality

The minimum annual mortality of banded adults caused by predators at Media Luna was estimated by averaging the data for the two seasons. Of the 46 banded there in 1978 five were found dead by the end of that season, and of the 22 banded in 1979 plus 20 banded survivors from 1978, five were found dead by the end of 1979. This yields an average minimum annual mortality of banded birds of 11.4 percent. Another estimate of predation mortality was made by counting how many banded and non-banded birds (31) were found dead by the end of the two seasons in an area where 103 eggs were laid (i.e. 206 breeding birds; *Table 1*). The answer of 15.0 percent is similar.

Index of annual population adjustment

To assist with deciding the priorities for predator control (see later) an Index of Annual

Table 3: Organochlorine contamination of Dark-rumped Petrel eggs from the Galapagos. All eggs had leaked before analyses so that wet weights of samples were less than wet weights of contents of whole eggs (c. 56g). No residue detected shown by a dash; and lower limit of reportable residues = 0.05ppm. Samples were also checked for presence of p,p'DDD, p,p'DDT, Dieldrin, Heptachlor epoxide, Oxychlordane, cis-Chlordane, trans-Nonachlor, cis-Nonachlor, Endrin, Est. Toxaphene, HCB, and Mirex, but none were detected.

Sample	Oven dried wt. (g)	Extractable lipid wt. (g)	DDE p,p' (ppm)	Ext. PCB (ppm)	Index of eggshell thickness[1]
81–486	NA	1.980	0.07	—	NA
487	3.124	0.781	—	—	1.4236
488	9.806	3.882	—	—	1.3111
489	12.221	4.490	0.06	—	1.3968
490	9.718	4.198	0.09	—	1.4007
491	9.833	3.941	0.11	—	1.4588[2]
492	5.522	1.878	0.07	—	1.3690[2]
493	13.082	5.493	0.12	—	1.4836
494	4.977	2.101	—	0.28	NA
Unnumbered	NA	NA	NA	NA	1.4057

Notes: 1. After Ratcliffe 1970.
2. Blowholes were bigger than for other eggs; therefore these indices are slightly lower than they should be.

Population Adjustment, expressed as a percentage of the population (IAPA%), was constructed using known and estimated values (Table 4). It is based on the assumption that the numerical stability of a population will depend on the balance between recruitment of new breeders (dependent on 'f' and 's' below) and losses of adults ('n' and 'u' below). Consideration is given to replacement of breeding individuals, not pairs. The formula is

$$IAPA\% = \frac{f \times s}{2} - n - u$$

where: f = overall % success per pair (Table 1)
s = estimated return of fledglings to colony, i.e. recruitment (an optimistic 75%: see Lack 1966; Harris 1977; Cramp & Simmons 1977)
n = % non-predatory deaths (unknown, but presumed to be equal on all islands, and given a value of 5% on the basis of data in Lack 1966; Ashmole 1971; Rowley 1975; Cramp & Simmons 1977)
u = % deaths due to known and unknown predators (Table 2) expressed as % of breeding birds in each colony (i.e. number of eggs × 2, Table 1).

The formula for IAPA% relies on recruitment into the breeding population to occur from natal islands, and would be biased if recruitment occurred from non-natal islands. There is no evidence for the recruitment of adults from one island to another. None of the 155 adults that I banded were subsequently found outside the banding colonies. However, in 1977 one bird nested in a colony six kilometers from the colony it used in 1975.

Many petrels are thought to live for more than 20 years and this is probably also true of Dark-rumped Petrels. Birds known from banding records to be at least seven years old (3 birds), 10 years old (1 bird) and at least 12 years old (3 birds) were recorded breeding in 1978 and 1979.

Table 4:   Index of Annual Population Adjustment (%) for Dark-rumped Petrels on four islands
in the Galapagos Archipelago.

Island	% breeding success[1] (f)	% non-predatory mortality[1] (n)	% mortality from predation[1] (u)	IAPA %
San Cristobal	11	5	31	−32
Santa Cruz 1978	0	5	17	−22
1979	5	5	12	−15
Santiago	40	5	14	−4
Floreana	49	5	7	+6

Note: See text for explanation of: f—taken from *Table 1*; n—estimated to be 5%; u—calculated from *Table 2*.

Discussion of predation

Isla Santa Cruz.   Assuming an annual mortality rate of 15 percent an adult of this
long-lived species will have on average only 6.2 years in which to replace itself in the
breeding population (calculated using $2 - m/2m$, where m = mortality rate as a decimal
(Lack 1954)). However, with an annual fledgling production of only 1.9 percent (i.e. two
fledglings from 103 eggs in 1978 and 1979), each breeder was successfully replacing itself
slightly more than once in a hundred years! Clearly, with this high level of adult mortality
and this disastrously high rate of predation on eggs and chicks, the population at Media
Luna will be wiped out in the near future. In fact, monitoring subsequent to this study
shows that compared with the 64 eggs laid in numbered burrows in 1978 and 39 in 1979,
32 eggs were laid in 1980 (Bass 1980) and only '20 burrows were occupied' in August 1981
(Harcourt, pers. comm.). Bass (1980) confirmed my suspicion that the very low
breeding success rate at Media Luna was typical of many breeding areas on Santa Cruz.
She also showed that the low success rate was not caused by disturbance from
investigators.

Index of annual population adjustment.   The petrels on Floreana are the least affected
by introduced predators and the population might optimistically be expected to increase
at 6 percent per annum according to these calculations (*Table 4*). However, recent
surveys by Coulter *et al.* (this vol.) suggest that at present this population is also
declining. The population on San Cristobal seems in an even worse condition, my
calculations suggesting that it might decrease annually by 32 percent. However, since
most petrels on San Cristobal are similar to those on Santiago (Tomkins, in prep.),
where the petrels are declining only slowly, and since the headquarters and facilities of
both the Galapagos National Park Service and the Charles Darwin Research Station are
on Santa Cruz, I suggest that the petrel population on Santa Cruz should have the first
priority for predator control.

MANAGEMENT RECOMMENDATIONS

Any management policy regarding predator control should attempt to maintain (i) a
population of the Galapagos subspecies, or (ii) possibly unique populations on each
island within the Galapagos. Unfortunately the choice of action will be dominated by its
cost, and therefore any action costing many thousands of dollars will not be feasible.

Table 5: Priority, additional production of fledglings and costs of predator control action in the Galapagos.

Priority	Action[1]	Estimated additional productivity[2]	Estimated cost in 1980 (US$)[3]
1	Rockpiles at Media Luna	—	4 × 250 each
2	Wire mesh over banks at Media Luna	—	2 × 150 each
3	Rat poisoning at Media Luna	+18	1700 p.a.
4	Dog poisoning at Media Luna	—	200 p.a.
5	Rat poisoning at selected groups of burrows throughout Sta. Cruz (if No. 3 is successful)	—	not estimated
6	Rockpiles on Floreana	—	4 × 500 each
7	Rockpiles on San Cristobal	—	4 × 500 each
8	Dog and cat poisoning on San Cristobal	—	250 & 200 p.a.
9	Wire mesh over banks on San Cristobal	—	2 × 250 each
10	Rat poisoning on San Cristobal	+12	950 p.a.
11	Rat poisoning on Floreana	+9	375 p.a.
12	Rockpiles on Santiago	—	4 × 500 each
13	Rat poisoning on Santiago	+3	250 p.a.

Notes: 1. Prohibitively expensive actions omitted (e.g. fencing and poisoning, and high intensity poisoning).
2. Figures shown represent estimated additional number of chicks which might fledge after rat poisoning, compared with number fledged in 1979.
3. Costs do not include inter-island transport or labour.

Thus it must be decided if relatively inexpensive but widespread annual action, which will produce few visible results immediately but which may allow a slow recovery, is preferable to no action or expense, resulting in the entire population of an island such as Santa Cruz being wiped out, possibly within 15 years.

Because the main diet of rats at Media Luna consists of berries, leaves and insects (Clark 1980), it is more likely that rats will wipe out all petrels from an area rather than, as predation continues, the reduced availability of petrels for food will cause a decrease in the numbers of rats. Thus it is obvious that rat control is essential if more chicks are to fledge. Control programmes for dogs and cats are also needed on most islands to protect adults (*Table 2*).

The most efficient method of protecting the petrels would be to construct a fence capable of excluding cattle, pigs, dogs and rats around an area containing many nests, and then poison the enclosed predators. But this would be prohibitively expensive (approximately US$ 750,000 based on 1980 costs of materials and transport to Media Luna, and labour). Many other methods were considered, and the most practical are listed in *Table 5*, with costs estimated in 1980.

Control of predators

Rats cannot be eliminated from a mountainous, heavily vegetated island honeycombed with lava tubes, tuff cones and fissures. Thus a major objective in the conservation programme should be to control the number of rats in the immediate vicinity of petrel nests for a specific part of the breeding season. Control of dogs and cats should be undertaken when they are most destructive. Control of these predators is needed each year. Birds breed at different times of the year on each island so the dates of commencement of protective action will vary between islands.

All methods of control should be tested *in situ* before more intensive and expensive programmes are commenced. The efficacy of poisons and baits in areas of very high relative humidity must be tested.

Table 6:   Dates of visits to petrel colonies to monitor breeding success and to poison predators.

Island	Date of visit	Purpose of visit[1]		
Santa Cruz (Media Luna)	(1) 15 May			D
	(2) 10 August	M	R	D
	(3) 1 October	M		
	(4) 10 November	M		
San Cristobal	(1) 1 January	M	R	
	(2) 1 March	M	R	D & C
	(3) 1 May	M	R	
	(4) 1 July	M	R	D & C
	(5) 1 September	M	R	
	(6) 1 November	M	R	
Santiago	(1) 5 June	M	R	
	(2) 1 August	M	R	
	(3) 1 October	M		
Floreana	(1) 5 May: C. Pajas	M	R	C
	(2) 15 June: C. Pajas, C. Alieri, C. Verde	M	R	C
	(3) 5 October all three	M		

Note: 1. Breeding success monitoring (M); rat (R), dog (D) or cat (C) poisoning.

Rats.   Three methods of rat destruction have been considered: kill-traps, live-traps, and poison. Several workers have discussed the merits and methods of each system (e.g. Moors, this vol.; Clark 1980; Fall 1977), and based on their comments I suggest that poisoning is the most suitable technique. I recommend that a 'second generation' anticoagulant rodenticide such as 'Brodifacoum' be used to control rats in the petrel colonies. These rodenticides have a high single-dose toxicity, a killing time of 1–4 days, and a reduced likelihood of secondary poisoning (Redfern *et al.* 1976; Dubock 1979).

Rat poisoning can be done on a 'high intensity' scale with bait stations being inspected every two or three days over several months, or it can be done on a 'low intensity' scale with bait laid only once or twice at a critical stage of the breeding timetable of the petrels. The former will be much more expensive and may allow only moderately higher production than the 'low intensity' scheme.

If a shortage of finances forces a compromise in the planned activities, then breeding monitoring and poisoning can be done on the same visit, and *Table 6* shows the approximate dates on which those visits should be made. Because poisoning should be centred on the average time of hatching at each colony (as this is when most rat predation occurs) separate poisoning trips could be made 20–25 days after the dates indicated if finances allow.

Dogs and cats.   Four methods of reducing the incidence of dogs and cats in colonies have been considered: shooting, trapping, M-44 cyanide-ejecting devices, and poisoning. Poisoning will produce the highest cost-benefit results, and I recommend that compound 1080 (sodium monofluoroacetate) be used (see Kruuk 1979). At Media Luna, dog poisoning should be most intensive in May and August. On San Cristobal, dog and cat poisoning should be done mainly in March and July.

Other management action
Two additional methods of providing safe nesting sites and protecting their contents from dogs and livestock are (i) to construct artificial rockpiles; and (ii) to lay wire mesh over soil and fern banks in which petrels breed or are likely to breed.

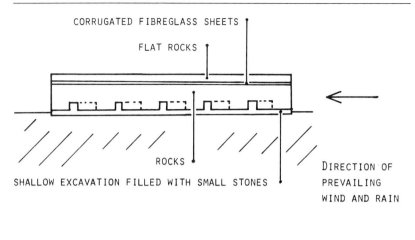

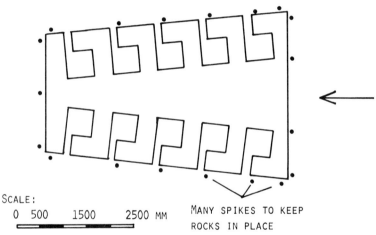

Figure 4: Side view (top) and plan view (bottom) of proposed rockpiles incorporating nest sites for petrels.

Rockpiles. There are several accounts of Procellariiformes breeding in artificial nest sites (e.g. Harper 1976; Kress 1981; Wingate 1977) but the last two are the most relevant to seabird conservation. Petrels investigated six experimental wooden and wire boxes which I installed in 1978 in soil banks at Media Luna, and eventually fledged a chick from one in 1980 (Bass 1980, pers. comm.). This success, and the obvious inaccessibility of petrels nesting among boulders on Santiago, encourage me to suggest that rockpiles be built in colonies. Designs for these rockpiles are shown in *Figure 4*, and construction and location details are provided in Tomkins (1980). They should be built in clearings with short grass, near active breeding colonies. Petrels investigate all cracks and holes at a colony, and will investigate rockpiles. Rats hesitate to enter a clearing unless the grass is long (but once they know an interesting feature is in a clearing they will enter it frequently—D. &. D. Clark, pers. comm.). The estimated cost of one rockpile at Media Luna in 1980 was US$ 250, but US$ 500 on other islands. Once installed they are very long-lasting and virtually maintenance-free. If rats trouble petrels breeding in the rockpiles, their control will be easier in a cleared area and at a concentration of say ten nests than if those ten nests were scattered across the hillside. To encourage occupation of the rockpiles, tape recordings of petrels' nocturnal calls should be played from within the rockpiles at night whilst petrels circle over the nearby colony. The peak of this aerial activity at Media Luna is August–September during attendance by non-breeding birds; but it should also be done in May–June when the breeders visit before laying. Petrel droppings and feathers from the nearby colony should be strewn at entrances of tunnels.

Wire mesh.   A simple and inexpensive way to prevent dogs digging petrels out of soil burrows is to lay wide strips of c. 120mm plastic-coated wire mesh over soil banks. This mesh will allow petrels access whilst preventing excavation. The estimated cost of installation in 1980 of one bank 15 metres by 2 metres at Media Luna was US$ 125, and US$ 250 on other islands. My trials at Media Luna in 1978 showed that plastic-coated wire was relatively impervious to moist soil, and once installed and pegged securely it would be maintenance-free for many years.

Priority for action
The suggested priority of predator control action shown in *Table 5* is a compromise between saving the subspecies and saving the island populations. Rockpiles and wire mesh are placed higher than poisoning because adults must be protected before young can be produced, and because these two actions will, after the initial outlay, continue to produce chicks without further expense, thus allowing resources to be directed at the more expensive yearly requirement for poisoning.

If it is decided to abandon island populations which are in serious trouble, and concentrate on 'healthier' populations (i.e. save the subspecies), rockpiles and predator poisoning should be undertaken on Floreana and then on Santiago. Coulter *et al.* (this vol.) have put forward a conservation programme for the petrels which concentrates on managing the large colony at Cerro Pajas, Floreana.

FUTURE WORK

Assessment of control action
The breeding success in treated colonies must be monitored to assess the effectiveness of predator control. I suggest that a scientist from the National Park Service or the Charles Darwin Research Station be made responsible for this monitoring and for subsequent analyses of its effectiveness. If alterations to the poisoning programmes beome necessary, these should be supervised by that officer.

Searches for other colonies
The search for additional breeding colonies should continue. There may be a substantial colony relatively free from predators which, with a small programme of predator control, may become a stronghold for this subspecies in the future. In particular the volcanoes Sierra Negra, Cerros Azul and Alcedo should be searched systematically.

Life cycle

Little is known about the life cycle of this species in the Galapagos because most studies have dealt with its death. The breeding success of pelagic seabirds fluctuates notoriously, and it is not known what constitutes 'normal' breeding success for this subspecies, or those factors in its life cycle which may naturally affect that success. Because of the relatively high breeding success and accessibility of colonies on Floreana, I suggest that a full-scale study be undertaken of the breeding biology of the Dark-rumped Petrels there.

Transplantation of chicks

The exciting success with transplants of Atlantic Puffin chicks (*Fratercula arctica*) and the recolonization of Leach's Storm Petrels (*Oceanodroma leucorhoa*) (Kress 1981) provides great encouragement to managers when drastic action is needed to save endangered seabirds. If rockpiles in Galapagos are successful, attempts to create a new colony in a relatively predator-free environment should be considered, for example on Islas Pinta or Fernandina. Chicks, preferably from Santiago or San Cristobal, could be extracted from their nests a few days before fledging and transported to Pinta or Fernandina. There they should be confined in rockpiles for a few days (and possibly fed squid and fish). Tape recordings of the nocturnal aerial calls of birds from the chicks' *natal* island should be played during internment. They should then be allowed to fledge from their foster island: they may return to it and breed, or they may not. Bearing in mind the work of Fisher (1971) on *Diomedea immutabilis*, J. Sincock on *Puffinus puffinus newelli* (Byrd *et al.*, 1984), and of others, this is an experimental question well worth investigating.

Because of the inter-island differences in these petrels any new colony created should maintain population identities if possible. If the Galapagos subspecies is to be maintained, rather than the island populations, transplanted chicks should be taken from Santa Cruz, which is the most 'unhealthy' population.

ACKNOWLEDGEMENTS

This is contribution Number 351 of the Charles Darwin Foundation.

The project was conceived by Dr R. W. Tindle and Craig MacFarland. Dr Tindle provided advice and encouragement throughout 1978 and part of 1979. I owe thanks to many people for their assistance in the field, usually in inclement weather. In particular I thank C. Brown, N. Stoyan, B. Lamoreaux, K. Belt, P. Curtis and especially W. Reed. I am deeply indebted to B. Best. Sras. Guldberg on San Cristobal, and Srs. Luisfilipe and Lenin Cruz and their family on Florenana gave freely of their knowledge of petrels and their hospitality. Srs. Gordillo on San Cristobal and Tupiza on Isabela were indispensable. Sr. O. Chappy, Dr T. de Vries, and K. Kunioki (Haleakala National Park, Hawaii) provided me with background information early in the study. Numerous residents of Puerto Ayora, Santa Cruz, notably J. and A. DeRoy, T. and A. Moore, C. and F. Angermayer, B. and S. Divine, Srs. M. Castro, A. Koelle, and Sra. V. Staply supplied me with past and present information about these petrels in the Galapagos. The cooperation of the then Intendente of the Galapagos National Park Service Sr. M. Cifuentes A. and his staff (in particular Srs. A. Villa, S. Olaya and P. Cartagena) was outstanding. I acknowledge and thank the former director of the Charles Darwin Research Station Dr H. Hoeck for his success in the difficult task of raising funds for this project. I also thank my numerous colleagues at the Station for their helpful discussions.

Discussions with officers of the U.S. Fish and Wildlife Service in Denver and Hawaii, as well as with Dr A. Dubock (ICI, UK) were most enlightening. Dr.D. Duffy and Prof. Mike Cullen kindly criticized manuscripts. The Smithsonian Institution, D. Gemmill, and the Department of Zoology at Monash University assisted greatly by allowing me to use their facilities whilst preparing this paper.

This study was financed by grants from the International Council for Bird Preservation; the Flora and Fauna Preservation Society of the United Kingdom; the Smithsonian Institution; the Stanford Alumni Association; the World Wildlife Fund (International); and by donations from Margery E. Plymire, Nancy N. Wachs, Kenneth W. Salter and Winifred E. Pettee. These grants and donations are gratefully acknowledged.

REFERENCES

ABS, M., CURIO, E., KRAMER, P. & NIETHAMMER, J. 1965. Zur Ernährungsweise der Eulen auf Galapagos. *J. für Ornith.* **106**, 49–57.

ASHMOLE, N. P. 1971. Sea bird ecology and the marine environment. *In:* Farner, D. S. & King, J. S. (eds) *Avian biology. Vol. 1.* Academic Press, New York.

BAKER, A. R. 1980. *Breeding distribution and population size of the Dark-rumped Petrel* (Pterodroma phaeopygia) *on Santa Cruz Island, Galapagos.* Charles Darwin Research Station. 1980 Annual Report: 72–4.

BASS, F. 1980. *Report of the Dark-rumped Petrel* (Pterodroma phaeopygia) *monitoring program on Santa Cruz Island, Galapagos.* 1980 Annual Report, 1–18, Charles Darwin Research Station.

BERRUTI, A. 1979. The breeding biologies of the Sooty albatrosses *Phoebetria fusca* and *P. palpebrata. Emu* **79**, 161–75.

BOERSMA, P. D. & WHEELWRIGHT, N. 1979. Egg neglect in the Procellariiformes: reproductive adaptations in the Forked-tailed Storm-petrel. *Condor* **81**, 157–65.

BOERSMA, P. D., WHEELWRIGHT, N., NERINI, M. & WHEELWRIGHT, E. 1980. The breeding biology of the Forked-tail Storm-petrel (*Oceanodroma furcata*). *Auk* **97**, 268–82.

BYRD, G. V., SINCOCK, J. L., TELFER, T. C., MORIATY, D. I. & BRADY, B. G. 1984. A cross-fostering experiment with Newell's race of Manx Shearwater. *J. Wildl. Mgnt.* **48**, 163–8

CLARK, D. A. 1980. Age- and sex-dependent foraging strategies of a small mammalian omnivore. *J. Anim. Ecol.* **49**, 549–64.

COULTER, M. C., CRUZ, F. & BEACH, T. (this volume). A programme to save the Dark-rumped Petrel, *Pterodroma phaeopygia*, on Floreana Island, Galapagos, Ecuador.

CRAMP, S. & SIMMONS, K. 1977. *Handbook of the birds of the Western Palaearctic.* Vol. 1. Oxford University Press, Oxford.

DUBOCK, A. 1979. *Alternative strategies for safety and efficacy of rodenticides.* Paper No. 14, Fifth British Pest Control Conference, UK.

FALL, M. 1977. *Rodents in tropical rice.* Technical Bulletin No. 36, Denver Wildlife Research Center, US Fish & Wildlife Service.

FISHER, H. 1971. Experiments on homing in Laysan Albatrosses, *Diomedea immutabilis. Condor* **73**, 389–400.

HARPER, P. 1976. Breeding biology of the Fairy Prion (*Pachyptila turtur*) at the Poor Knights Islands, New Zealand. *N.Z. J. Zool.* **3**, 351–71.

HARRIS, M. 1969a. The biology of storm petrels in the Galápagos Islands. *Proc. Calif. Acad. Sci.* 4th Series: **37**, 95–166.

HARRIS, M. 1969b. Food as a factor controlling the breeding of *Puffinus lherminieri. Ibis* **111**, 139–56.

HARRIS, M. 1970. The biology of an endangered species, the Dark-rumped Petrel (*Pterodroma phaeopygia*), in the Galapagos Islands. *Condor* **72**, 76–84.

HARRIS, M. 1977. Comparative ecology of seabirds in the Galapagos Archipelago. *In:* Stonehouse, B. & Perrins, C. (eds) *Evolutionary ecology.* Macmillan, London.

KING, W. B. 1981. *Endangered birds of the world. ICBP Bird Red Data Book.* Smithsonian Institution Press, Washington D.C.

KRESS, S. W. 1981. *Egg Rock update.* Newsletter of the Fratercula Fund of the National Audubon Society, 1981: 1–4.

KRUUK, H. 1979. *Report to the Charles Darwin Research Station on the ecology and control of feral dogs in Galapagos.* Unpublished report to Charles Darwin Research Station.

LACK, D. 1954. *The natural regulation of animal numbers.* Oxford University Press, Oxford.

LACK, D. 1966. *Population studies of birds.* Oxford University Press, Oxford.

MOORS, P. (this volume). Eradication campaigns against *Rattus norvegicus* on the Noises Islands, New Zealand, using brodifacoum and 1080.

NELSON, J. B. 1968. *Galapagos: island of birds.* Longmans, Green & Co., London.

RATCLIFFE, D. A. 1970. Changes attributed to pesticides in egg breakage frequency and eggshell thickness in some British birds. *J. Appl. Ecol.* **7**, 67–115.

REDFERN, R., GILL, J. & HADLER, M. 1976. Laboratory evaluation of WBA 8119 as a rodenticide for use against Warfarin-resistant and non-resistant rats and mice. *J. Hyg.* **77**, 419–26.

ROWLEY, I. 1975. *Bird life.* Collins, Sydney.

SNOW, D. 1965. The breeding of the Audubon's Shearwater (*Puffinus lherminieri*) in the Galapagos. *Auk* **82**, 591–7.

TOMKINS, R. J. 1980. *A study of the conservation of the Dark-rumped Petrel (*Pterodroma phaeopygia*): considered to be an endangered species in the Galapagos.* Unpublished report to Charles Darwin Research Station.

DE VRIES, T. 1976. Prey selection and hunting methods of the Galapagos Hawk, *Buteo galapagoensis. Gerfaut* **66**, 3–43.

WINGATE, D. 1977. Excluding competitors from Bermuda Petrel nesting burrows. *In:* Temple, S. (ed.) *Endangered Birds.* The University of Wisconsin Press, Madison.

A PROGRAMME TO SAVE THE DARK-RUMPED PETREL, *PTERODROMA PHAEOPYGIA*, ON FLOREANA ISLAND, GALAPAGOS, ECUADOR

MALCOLM C. COULTER, FELIPE CRUZ & JUSTINE CRUZ

Charles Darwin Research Station, Casilla 58-39, Guayaquil, Ecuador

INTRODUCTION

The Dark-rumped Petrel (*Pterodroma phaeopygia*) is a seabird that breeds only in the Hawaiian and Galapagos archipelagos. In both areas the populations are in danger of extinction. In Hawaii there are 400 to 600 pairs. In the Galapagos the situation is more favourable (Coulter, 1984). The birds breed on five islands: Santa Cruz, Floreana, Santiago, San Cristobal and Isabela. On Santa Cruz and Floreana, the only islands as yet surveyed, the populations consist of 9000 (Baker 1980) and 1000 pairs, respectively (Coulter *et al.* 1981). Yet we found in 1981 that on these two islands the populations were declining at 33 percent per year over the previous four years (Coulter *et al.* 1981, 1982). In 1982 the Floreana population declined by another 27 percent. If nothing is done, the Galapagos populations probably have only 10 to 15 years left. In 1982 we began establishing a programme to save the birds, with major initial efforts on Floreana Island.

CAUSES OF THE DECLINE

The decline in the petrel populations is largely a result of low reproductive success, about 5 percent on Santa Cruz (Harris 1970) and between 15 and 30 percent on Floreana, and to a lesser extent to adult mortality on the breeding grounds (see also Tomkins, this vol.). Both are attributable to predation by feral animals. Cats and dogs kill adults and young. Pigs excavate burrows and eat adults and young. Most importantly Black or Ship Rats (*Rattus rattus*) prey on both eggs and young. In addition, goats, donkeys and cattle cause severe habitat destruction and inadvertently destroy burrows. The problem of protecting the petrel, therefore, is one of controlling the feral animals.

The feral animal problems differ among the islands (*Table 1*). On Santa Cruz, and probably on San Cristobal and Isabela as well, dogs and rats are major problems. On Santiago goats, pigs and rats cause the most damage. Goats and pigs have trampled the ground so that now the soil in much of the area is too hard for burrowing by birds. The remaining nests are largely concentrated in rock outcrops where rats are an important predator. On Floreana, rats and feral cats (*Felis catus*) are the major predators. The inhabitants of Floreana eliminated wild dogs because the dogs killed cattle. Also, pigs are only a minor problem on Floreana because they remain in the lowlands during most of the petrels' breeding season.

177

Table 1: Facts on the Galapagos Islands where Dark-rumped Petrels breed. Fernandina and Pinta are listed in the ICBP Red Data Book as possible nesting sites. However, during various trips to these two islands no nests have been found.

Island	Size (km²)	Number of inhabitants	Major feral animal problems
Floreana	172.5	c. 50	Cats and rats (wild dogs no longer present; pigs only a minor problem)
Santa Cruz	985.6	1–2,000	Dogs and rats (pigs and cats may also be a problem)
Isabela	4,588.1	c. 1,000	Probably similar to Santa Cruz
San Cristobal	558.1	1–2,000	Probably similar to Santa Cruz
Santiago	584.6	none	Pigs and rats (this is the only petrel island without cats)

Note: Areas from Black (1973).

BREEDING CYCLE

In 1981 we conducted a preliminary study of the Dark-rumped Petrels on Floreana. The petrels nest in the highlands; on Floreana they nest at the tops of some of the volcanoes (called cerros) in the centre of the island. The birds return in January, and begin laying late in that month. A single egg is laid per pair, in a simple nest in an underground burrow that may extend to ten feet but is often shorter. Egg-laying lasts through March. Hatching occurs 50 days later, lasting from late March through May. Chicks remain in the burrows for the next 3½ months, and leave in August and September. If an egg is lost the parents visit the nest over the next few weeks but do not re-lay. The birds have only a single chance to breed each year.

The breeding season differs between the island populations. On Floreana eggs are laid in January through March, whereas birds on Santa Cruz lay in June and July. Less is known about the birds on the other islands. On Santiago they probably have a similar timing to those on Floreana, and Tomkins (this vol.) has reported that on San Cristobal birds in different colonies breed year-round. No nests have yet been found on Isabela, though petrels undoubtedly breed there. The timing of courting suggests that they lay sometime between February and June.

The time of breeding is an important consideration when establishing a programme to save the petrels. Working conditions in the highlands where the birds breed are difficult at any time of year. Vegetation is extremely dense and nests are hard to find. During the garua season (July through December) the highlands are shrouded in thick mist and there is no possibility of staying dry. During the rainy season (January through June) there are sparse downpours and conditions are hot and dry. Transporting water during this period generates great problems. Work is possible in the highlands only with proper logistical support.

CONSERVATION

We have chosen to concentrate our initial efforts on Floreana Island for four reasons. Firstly, the feral animal problems are less severe there than on the other islands. Secondly, four of the five islands on which petrels breed are inhabited, but Floreana has only 50 inhabitants. It is easy to develop support from such a small population. In fact, they already fully endorse the project and local people are involved in the work as well.

Thirdly, this involvement also means that we have local logistical support, such as water transport, which is extremely important during the rainy season when the birds breed. Fourthly, but not least importantly, we have located the largest petrel colony in the Galapagos on Cerro Pajas, Floreana Island, with about 1500 breeding birds.

At the suggestion of the International Council for Bird Preservation and the World Wildlife Fund, Dr J. Keith of the US Fish and Wildlife Service and Mr B. D. Bell of the New Zealand Wildlife Service were invited to the Galapagos to assist with the preparation of an effective conservation programme for the petrels. Both Bell and Keith have had extensive experience in the control of feral animals, and agreed with our choice of Floreana as the site of the first management efforts. The conservation plan for Cerro Pajas, which began in 1982, is as follows:

Rat control
We have tested a number of poisons and have chosen a trade formulation of coumate-tralyl known as 'Racumen'. It has proven to be effective in initial trials and also has good persistence. The poison will be placed in plastic tubes to increase its field life. We recognize the dangers for non-target animals of laying poison, but there are none in the area likely to suffer from secondary poisoning. Hawks are absent and the few owls also suffer from rat and cat predation. We will monitor the effectiveness of the rat control programme using snap-trapping and tracking tiles. Rat control will begin in late November, before the petrels return, and continue through the period of vulnerability until the end of May.

Cat control
Control of cats is a tough problem and we are still examining various methods, including hunting and trapping.

Control of pigs, goats and donkeys
We are presently controlling these animals with hunting. In addition we are planning to build a fence around the colony on Cerro Pajas to keep out donkeys and cattle, and to discourage goats and pigs. By keeping out these larger animals we should also discourage cats which prefer to travel along trails made by these other animals.

Monitoring the petrels
The aim of this conservation programme is to increase reproductive success and halt the decline of the population. We will evaluate the success of our efforts by monitoring the numbers and productivity of breeding petrels.

The campaign is still in its initial stages and is likely to be modified as we gain experience. As we understand progressively more about the specifics of controlling rats and cats we hope to reduce the costs and effort while still keeping the same effectiveness. Tomkins (this vol.) has also provided information and plans for a conservation programme for the petrels, including control of feral animals.

NOTE ADDED IN PROOF

The programme has been fully successful during the 1982–83 breeding season. To the end of June 1983, rat predation has been totally eliminated on Cerro Pajas and 51 percent of the monitored nests still had chicks, compared with 34 percent at the same time in 1982. In 1983/4 the breeding success was raised to over 70 percent.

ACKNOWLEDGEMENTS

We are grateful to Mr Brian Bell of the New Zealand Wildlife Service and Dr James Keith of the US Fish and Wildlife Service for their improvements to the programme. We have had the full support of the staff of the Charles Darwin Research Station and Servicio Parque Nacional Galapagos. The work was supported by a grant from the World Wildlife Fund.

REFERENCES

Baker, R. 1980. breeding distribution and population size of the Dark-rumped Petrel (*Pterodroma phaeopygia*) on Santa Cruz Island, Galapagos. *Charles Darwin Research Station 1980 Annual Report*, 72–4.

Black, J. 1973. *Galapagos Archipielago del Ecuador*. Charles Darwin Foundation, Santa Cruz, Galapagos.

Coulter, M. C. 1984. Conservation of seabirds in the Galapagos Islands, Ecuador. *ICBP Tech. Pub.* No. 2.

Coulter, M. C., Beach, T., Cruz, F., Eisele, W. & Martinez, P. 1981. The Dark-rumped Petrel, *Pterodroma phaeopygia*, on Isla Floreana, Galapagos. *Charles Darwin Research Station 1981 Annual Report*, 170–3.

Coulter, M. C., Duffy, D. C. & Harcourt, S. 1982. Status of the Dark-rumped Petrel on Isla Santa Cruz, 1981. *Noticias Galapagos* **35**, 24.

Harris, M. P. 1970. The biology of an endangered species, the Dark-rumped Petrel (*Pterodroma phaeopygia*), in the Galapagos Islands. *Condor* **72**, 76–84.

Tomkins, R. J. (this vol.). Breeding success and mortality of Dark-rumped Petrels in the Galapagos, and control of their predators.

ICBP Technical Publication No. 3, 1985

THE DIET OF THE OSPREY ON TIRAN ISLAND: MANAGEMENT IMPLICATIONS FOR POPULATIONS ON THE NORTHERN RED SEA ISLANDS

URIEL N. SAFRIEL, YEHUDA BEN-HUR & ADAM BEN-TUVIA

Department of Zoology, The Hebrew University of Jerusalem, Jerusalem, Israel 91904

ABSTRACT

The Osprey (*Pandion h. haliaetus* (L)) population on Tiran and adjacent islands in the northern Red Sea is dense (*c.* 50 pairs), stable and undisturbed by man and pesticides. In order to elucidate factors controlling the breeding density and dispersion of this population, a study of the population's food habits was carried out during three breeding seasons. The birds brought 52 fish taxa to nests, the mean and maximum lengths and weights of the fish being respectively 380 mm and 1060 mm, and 250g and 935g. Most birds were generalists (number of fish species, S = 17; Brilloin's diversity index, H = 2.02 nats), 50 percent of their diet consisting of herbivorous fishes; these birds nested along shores of shallow lagoons and wide intertidal platforms. About 20 percent of the birds were specialists (S = 5, H = 0.33), 92 percent of their diet being made up of predatory fishes, and these birds nested in front of a narrow fringing reef facing deep water. Ease of capture determined dietary composition and its variation with marine habitats near nests. The conservation implications of these findings are that management of Ospreys in areas of the Red Sea prone to future pollution and disturbance should be concentrated on shores with lagoons and wide platforms, rather than on shores with narrow fringing reefs facing deep water. A comparison of Osprey diet with the catch from Red Sea fisheries indicates very little potential clash between the protection and improvement of the Red Sea islands' Osprey populations and commercial fisheries.

INTRODUCTION

The Osprey (*Pandion haliaetus haliaetus* (L.)) breeds along the coasts of the Red Sea, especially on small near-shore islands. Recent information on distribution and population densities is lacking (Cramp & Simmons 1980), except for Sinai, where recent estimates have been made by Zu-Arets (1973) and Paz & Zu-Arets (1976). In 1973 there were 21 active nests on Tiran Island (27°57'N, 34°06'E; *Figure 1*), the only island off the Sinai coast. An adjacent, smaller island close to the Saudi Arabian coast had at least ten active nests. Ospreys do not breed along the Sinai coast of the Red Sea except around the southern tip of the peninsula, where there are three mangrove lagoons harbouring five active nests.

This Sinai population is part of a larger population mostly concentrated on several scores of islands (of which Tiran is the largest, with an area of 59km²) scattered along an 80km stretch of the east coast of the northern Red Sea. Similar islands, some of which are inhabited by Ospreys, are also common on the west coast near the entrance to the

Figure 1:   Tiran (white arrow) and its environs from an altitude of 200 miles.

Gulf of Suez (*Figure 1*). Most of these northern Red Sea islands are generally uninhabited by man and are devoid of mammalian predators. Desert trees suitable for nesting are rare near the Sinai shores, and Ospreys there are basically ground-nesters, the nests being highly vulnerable to ground predators. The high population densities on these small mammal-free islands may thus be regarded as an anti-predator adaptation.

The Red Sea Osprey populations are not only relatively dense, rather stable and undisturbed by man, but they are also free of pesticides since the northern Red Sea is surrounded by vast areas lacking modern agriculture and devoid of significant rainfall and run-off. Their positive intrinsic rate of increase may guarantee recolonization of areas where the species is now extinct once the agents of extinction have been removed. However, in recent years increased tourism has brought some disturbances and egg-stealing (at least on Tiran), and future regional economic developments may be associated with significant pollution. A thorough knowledge of the ecology of the Tiran Osprey population, apparently the largest in the region, is therefore essential. Here we report the diet of breeding birds on Tiran Island, and put forward recommendations based on these investigations for managing the Ospreys.

MATERIALS AND METHODS

Ospreys on Tiran nest in a variety of sites: on wide, rather flat seashores, on sandy beaches, on low bushes of *Suaeda fruteicosa*, and occasionally on tiny rocky islets just offshore. The nests are long-lasting, and often put to multiple use. Each pair 'owns' several nests which may be used in different seasons, or within the same season if the first breeding attempt fails. Incubation starts at the end of January or beginning of February and is performed by the female, which is then fed by the male.

Fish remains, mainly bones and dried parts (especially fins, heads and caudal sections), become scattered around the nests. This debris was collected from all nests on Tiran Island, and our basic data consists of 62 samples of food remains ('nest-collections'), each representing the food brought to a single nest during the breeding season in 1974, 1977 or 1978. The remains were identified from reference skeletons and preserved specimens in the fish collection of the Zoological Museum of the Department of Zoology at The Hebrew University of Jerusalem. Most remains which could be identified were heads or caudal sections, and these were also used to estimate the original length and weight of the fish. Lengths were calculated from regression equations of total length on head length and on tail length. The equations were derived from measurements of preserved museum specimens and fish in commercial catches. Weights were calculated from regression equations of weight on length, the equations being mainly derived from measurements of commercial catches and from Ben-Tuvia (1968). For some fish in the family Scaridae we used the equation $W = H^2L/C$, where H is the largest circumference, L is the length of the fish and C is a constant related to the general shape of the body (Smith 1953).

THE DIET OF THE POPULATION AS A WHOLE

We identified 984 items in the 62 nest-collections. These items were divided between 52 taxa, of which 32 taxa could be identified to species and 13 only to genus. Thirty-two items could not be identified, but were allocated to one of seven unnamed taxa. The fish belonged to 21 families (*Figure 2*), and the frequency distribution for families and species (*Figure 3*) each produced a skewed ranked-abundance curve—a few families and species were very common, but most were rare. Fistulariidae was the commonest family, its only species *Fistularia commersonii* Rüppell also being the commonest prey, comprising 28 percent of the diet.

Only 107 prey-items were represented by remains which were insufficient for estimating their lengths. The calculated lengths of other items ranged from 76–1066mm, with a mean length of 383mm. The frequency distribution is bimodal (*Figure 4a*). The left-hand peak corresponds to *Acanthurus nigrofuscus* (Forsskal) and *Siganus argenteus* (Quoy & Gaimard) (second and third commonest species, respectively), while the right-hand peak corresponds to *F. commersonii* and *Tylosurus sp.* (first and fourth commonest species, respectively).

Weights were unobtainable for 122 items. The mean for all other prey-items was 247g (heaviest item 936g). The frequency distribution of weights (*Figure 4b*) does not correspond to that of lengths, but is skewed to the left. This is because the long fishes were narrow, whereas many of the short fishes were broad, relative to their respective lengths.

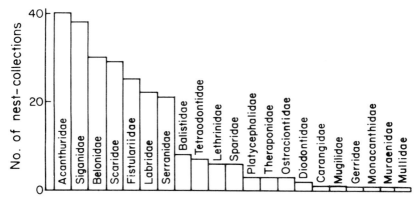

Figure 2:   Frequency distribution of fish families in the nest-collections.

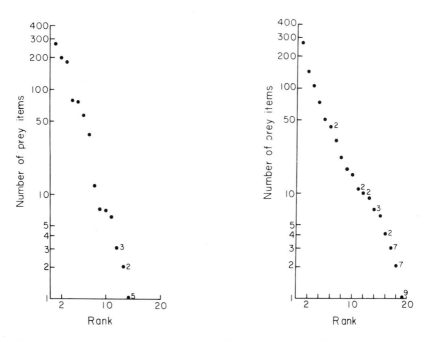

Figure 3:   Ranked-abundance curves for families (left) and species (right) for all nest-collections combined. Numbers indicate families or species with the same rank.

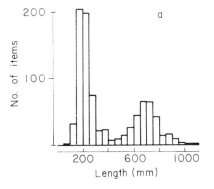
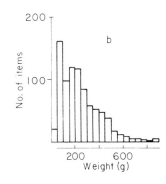

Figure 4:   Frequency distribution of lengths (a) and weights (b) for all nest-collections combined.

THE DIETS FROM INDIVIDUAL NESTS

The numbers of fish in individual samples varied depending on the number of chicks in each nest, and on how long the chicks survived. The species richness and species diversity of samples increased with the number of items found in a nest-collection, but both curves reached asymptotes at about 35 items (*Figure 5*). Thus, it is safe to assume that for the seven nests with more than 35 prey-items the collections represent an unbiassed estimate of the diet of the birds involved. Four of these nest-collections lie near the asymptotes for richness and diversity, hence they can be defined as generalists, feeding on a varied diet; but three are deviates with low species richness and diversity because they specialized on *F. commersonii* which comprised about 90 percent of these diets. The differences in diet between the generalists and extreme specialists are statistically significant (*Table 1*).

Do differences in diet between specialists and generalists depend on the marine habitats available in the vicinity of the nest? Tiran, like most other seashores and islands in the region, is surrounded by fringing coral reefs. In the southern and southwestern parts of the island, where high mountains plunge to the sea, the reef is extremely narrow

Table 1:   The dietary characteristics of generalist versus specialist Ospreys on Tiran Island[1].

| | Species richness[3] | Species diversity[4] | Percentages[2] | | | |
			Fistularia commersonii	*Acanthurus nigrofuscus*	*Siganus argenteus*	*Tylosurus* sp.
Generalists	16.7	2.02	15	22	19	9
Specialists	5.0	0.33	89	4	2	1

Notes: [1]Mean values: in all columns, differences between generalists and specialists are significant, $P < 0.001$ (t-tests).
[2]Percentages only for the four commonest species in the diet.
[3]Number of species.
[4]Expressed by Brilloin's H, in nats (Pielou 1966).

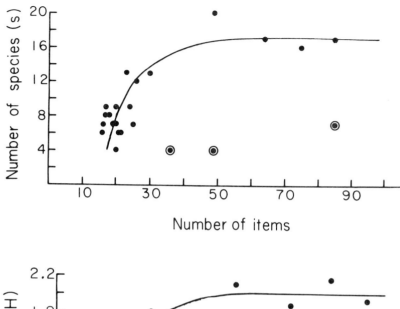

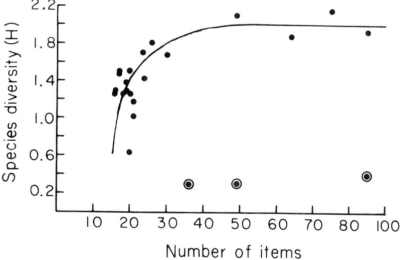

Figure 5:   Species richness (number of species) (top) and species diversity (expressed by Brilloin's H, after Pielou 1966) (lower) as functions of the number of items in nest-collections. Points surrounded by circles indicate samples from specialist feeders (see text). Collections with less than 16 prey items excluded.

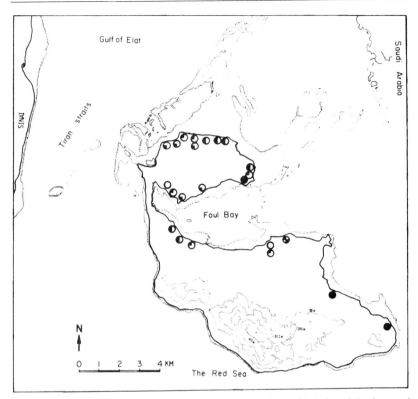

Figure 6: Tiran Island, its fringing coral reef, the location of nests (circles), and the degree of dietary specialization (black part of circles) or generalization (white part of circles). Criteria for generalized diet (white sections):
    High species diversity (top right section)
    High species richness (top left section)
    Low proportion of *Fistularia* (bottom right section)
    Relatively high proportion of the reef fish *Scarus* (bottom left section)
Criteria for specialized diet (black sections):
    Low species diversity (top right section)
    Low species richness (top left section)
    High proportion of *Fistularia* (bottom right section)
    Low proportion of the reef fish *Scarus* (bottom left section)
For further explanations see text.

and Ospreys do not nest there (*Figure 6*). The nests on Tiran are mostly concentrated in front of wide reefs and around the shallow lagoon at Foul Bay. In other places where a few nests occur the narrow reefs drop abruptly to great depths close to the shore.

As indicated by *Figure 5*, the degree of generalization or specialization in the diet seems to be a discrete rather than continuous variable. In order to rank nests according to their degree of generalization or specialization we selected from a list of parameters that characterize a diet (species richness, diversity and evenness; weight and length diversity and evenness; proportion of representation of each species) four variables with distributions exhibiting an extremely high variance and strongly deviating from normality (as expressed by their kurtosis values). These variables were used for ranking the degree of dietary specialization (or generalization) of each nest. The nests and their classifications are shown in *Figure 6*. It is evident that a generalized diet is strongly associated with nests in front of wide shallow reefs, whereas a specialized diet is associated with nests near narrow fringing reefs with very deep water in their lee.

DETERMINANTS OF THE COMPOSITION OF DIETS

Are there other factors apart from nest location that contribute to the variation between nests in dietary composition? We ranked the 'catchability' of each fish species that appeared in the diet using attributes that affect the ease of detecting it, such as the fish's size and its tendency to swim in groups, and attributes that affect the chances of its capture, such as the timing of its activity (with respect to the amount of light), and the fish's preferred habitat. Large fish swimming in schools during daylight in surface waters were regarded as highly 'catchable' (ranked 5), whereas small, mainly nocturnal fish swimming alone in deep water were regarded as the least catchable (ranked 1). We also ranked with a score of 1–5 the relative abundance of each species. Information for these rankings was gathered from Smith (1953), Porter (1973), Carcasson (1977), Fishelson (1977), M. Goren (pers. comm.) and our own observations at several locations along the Gulf of Elat and in the vicinity of Tiran.

The proportion of each fish species in the diet was not correlated with its relative abundance at the reef or with its weight, but was significantly correlated with the species' 'catchability index' (*Table 2*). Hence, Ospreys on Tiran do not seem to select their food with respect to the relative abundance of the fish, or with regard to the prospective reward (e.g. weight alone); rather, ease of capture plays a significant role in the determination of the composition of the Osprey's diet.

Thus the predominance of *Fistularia commersonii* in the specialists' diet is not related just to its size, but primarily to the fact that it is easy to capture. This fish (*Figure 7*) is a predator that habitually lies in ambush close to the bottom at the seaward side of the reef, from which it darts to the surface in pursuit of prey (Fishelson 1981). The predominance of another large and common fish *Tylosurus sp.* is also related to ease of capture. This fish is a predator that often 'perches' close to the surface of the water, nearly motionless, with body (and eyes) pointing slightly downwards. From this vantage point it darts into the depths to capture its prey. *Fistularia* and *Tylosurus* are therefore common where the seaward face of the reef plunges abruptly to the depths because in these places they can scan great expanses of the vertical face of the reef. Such reefs are usually narrow, like those in front of the specialists' nests. On the other hand, most

Table 2: Coefficients of correlation between proportions of the different species in the diet, and some attributes of these fishes[1].

Proportion in the diet	'Catchability' index	Index for the relative abundance on the reef
Spearman's rank-correlation[2]	0.395*	0.246
Kendall's partial rank-correlation[3]	0.131	−0.135

Notes: [1]The value with an asterisk is the only significant one, $P < 0.01$.
[2]Correlation with the variables denoted at the head of each column.
[3]The proportion of each fish species in the diet is partially correlated with the fish's weight; the controlled variable is denoted at the head of each column (Siegel 1979, p.462).

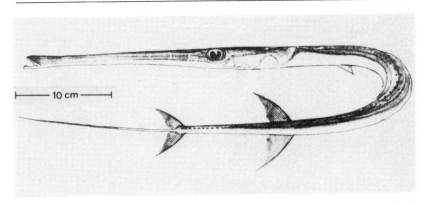

Figure 7:   Fistularia commersonii, the commonest fish in the diet of Ospreys on Tiran Island and almost the exclusive prey of specialist feeders.

species of reef fish occur in shallow waters where the fringing reefs are wide. This makes a varied selection of species available to the Ospreys, whose food habits are correspondingly diversified.

THE OSPREY'S TROPHIC POSITION ON TIRAN ISLAND

We used the sources cited above to determine the trophic positions of the fish found in the Osprey's diet (*Table 3*). Altogether at least 30 percent of the biomass brought to nests belonged to herbivorous fish and thus this biomass had been transferred through just one link of the food chain. About 50 percent of the biomass belonged to fish from other trophic levels, and hence had passed through more than one link. At least 10 percent of the biomass had passed through three links before being removed from the marine ecosystem and into the top-carnivore level of the Ospreys. Thus, if the Red Sea becomes polluted with pesticides the potential for Tiran Ospreys to concentrate pesticides in their bodies is quite high. This is because pesticides tend to concentrate in the upper levels of food chains, and the Osprey is positioned at the top of a relatively long chain.

However, not all the Ospreys are equally at risk. Only those nesting in front of narrow reefs (22 percent of nests) are highly vulnerable (*Table 4*), since they rely on prey near the top of the food chain, and in which pesticides can become highly concentrated. Since the percentage of predatory fishes in the diets of all other nests is significantly lower (*Table 4*), these nests are definitely safer.

THE OVERLAP BETWEEN THE OSPREY'S CATCH AND COMMERCIAL FISHERIES

Of the 45 taxa identified in the Osprey's diet, only 14 species have a commercial value. Listed in decreasing order of commercial importance, these are *Siganus rivulatus* (Forsskal), *S. luridus* (Rüppell), *S. argenteus* (Quoy & Gaimard), *Epinephelus fasciatus* (Forsskal), *Cephalopholis miniata* (Forsskal), *Plectropomus maculatus* (Bloch), *Crenimugil crenilabis* (Forsskal), *Rhabdosargus haffara* (Forsskal), *Gerres oyena*

Table 3:   The trophic position of fish in the diet of the Tiran Osprey.

A. Fish with single trophic position

	Herbivores %	Primary predators %	Secondary predators %
Species	22	7	31
Individuals	41	2	7
Weights	29	2	10

B. Fish with mixed diets (omnivores)

	Mixed herbivory & primary predation %	Mixed herbivory, primary & secondary predation %	Mixed primary & secondary predation %
Species	16	9	15
Individuals	8	4	38
Weights	16	3	40

Notes: Values are percentages of totals obtained from all nest-collections combined; for example—22% of species, 41% of individuals and 29% of total diet biomass belonged to the herbivorous trophic level.

(Forsskal), *Lethrinus mahsenoides* C.V., sparids, *Pseudupeneus forsskali* (Fourmanoir & Guézé), *Acanthurus sohal* (Forsskal), *Therapon jarbua* (Forsskal), *Tylosurus* sp., *Epinephelus summana* (Forsskal), *Siganus stellatus* (Forsskal), *Platycephalus indicus* (L.) (Smith 1953; Ben-Tuvia 1968; Porter 1973; Carcasson 1977; Randall, pers. comm.). Together these species comprised 30 percent of the total number of items collected from nests.

Only four of the eight most important commercial fish in the Gulf of Elat appear in the Osprey's diet—*R. haffara* and *C. crenilabis* (frequency in diet less than 1 percent), and *S. rivulatus* and *S. luridus* (each only 4 percent of the diet). The two species of *Siganus* may reach 35 percent of the commercial catch taken by trammel nets. Of the five most important fishes in the Osprey's diet only *S. argenteus* (*c.* 10 percent in the diet) is commercially important, though it is less so than the other two *Siganus* species. Ospreys and fishermen take similar sizes of *S. luridus*, but Ospreys tend to take smaller sizes of the other two species (*Figure 8*). If the age of fish does not contribute much to the variance in size within the range taken by Ospreys and fishermen, then for all practical purposes Ospreys on Tiran hardly compete with commercial fisheries.

Table 4:   Percentage biomass of fish brought to Osprey nests in relation to the type of reef adjacent to the nest and the trophic status of the fish.

	Width of reef in front of nest[2]		
	Narrow	Intermediate	Wide
Number of nests[1]	2	3	18
Proportion of trophic levels in diet			
Predator	95	83	35
Herbivore	5	6	50
Omnivore	0	11	15

Notes: [1]Twenty-three nests contained sufficient remains to have raised at least one nestling (Ben-Hur 1982).
[2]The differences between the types of nest sites are significant, P < 0.001 (Variance test for homogeneity of the binomial distribution, Snedecor & Cochran 1967, p. 240).

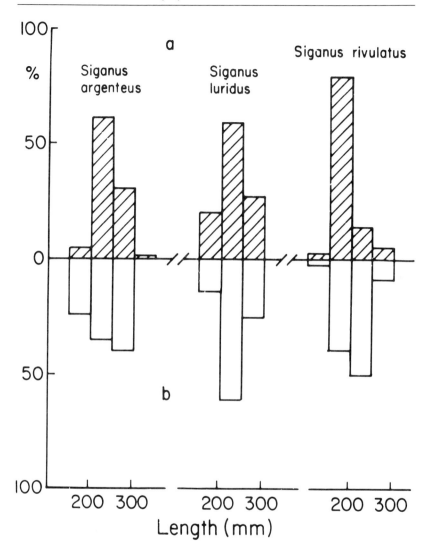

Figure 8:   Size distribution of *Siganus* species in Osprey diet (a), and in the commercial catch from the Gulf of Elat (b).

MANAGEMENT IMPLICATIONS AND RECOMMENDATIONS

The plight of the European Osprey has already been described in detail (for references see Odszo & Sondell 1976). The northern Red Sea islands, especially Tiran, maintain an unusually healthy and dense breeding population of the European subspecies. These Ospreys do not seem to compete, nor to have the potential to compete, with commercial fisheries. On the other hand this population could provide stocks for the recolonization of areas in which Ospreys have become extinct, or for introductions into previously uninhabited regions. Future developments in the northern Red Sea may endanger this population, and it should therefore be carefully protected.

The results of our investigation which have management implications, together with our recommendations, are as follows:

- The association between composition of the diet and nest location on Tiran suggests that the Ospreys forage at sea immediately in front of their nests. They select their prey with respect to the ease of its capture, and hence prefer to nest in front of wide shallow reefs and lagoons where their prey and diet are highly diversified. Furthermore, the proportions of predatory fish in their diet is low.
- The few Ospreys nesting in front of deep waters prey almost exclusively on predatory fish, most of which are fish predators themselves. The birds seem to select these species because their foraging habits make them detectable and relatively easy to catch.
- Wide reefs are common along many of the Sinai shores, yet Ospreys rarely nest in front of them. Their preference for islands, and their extremely high density there, is probably related to the islands' inaccessibility to mammalian predators (see Introduction).
- The breeding density of Ospreys can be increased on the mainland and on other areas accessible to mammalian predators by providing them with raised nesting platforms. This has been tried successfully by the Israeli Nature Reserves Authority in Sinai. It is advisable to site such poles in front of wide reefs and shallow lagoons, firstly because Ospreys prefer these habitats (hunting success there is greater than elsewhere), and secondly because of reduced risk of Ospreys being poisoned with pesticides should pesticide pollution become prevalent in the Red Sea (because fish eaten near such sites come from the lower levels of the reef's trophic web).
- For similar reasons, protection efforts on islands should be concentrated on Ospreys nesting in the vicinity of wide reefs and shallow waters, rather than on those nesting in front of narrow reefs and deep waters.

ACKNOWLEDGEMENTS

We wish to thank S. Zu-Arets for invaluable information on the distribution and biology of Ospreys on Tiran Island; A. Baranes for help with the Hebrew University fish collection; K. Porter for information on commercial fisheries, M. Goren for information on the biology of Red Sea fish, R. W. Bruce for information on weights of fish, I. Noy-Meir, P. J. Moors and an anonymous reviewer for comments and criticism, the Israeli Nature Reserves Authority, and the Israel Defence Forces for arrangements to stay, collect and observe on Tiran Island.

REFERENCES

BEN-HUR, Y. 1982. *The diet of a top-predator of a coral reef—the diet of the Osprey* (Pandion haliaetus) *population on the Island of Tiran.* (in Hebrew) MSc Thesis, The Hebrew University of Jerusalem, Jerusalem.

BEN-TUVIA, A. 1968. Report on the fisheries investigations of the Israel South Red Sea Expedition, 1962. *Sea Fish. Res. Stn. Haifa Bull.* **52**, 21–55.

CARCASSON, R. 1977. *A field guide to the coral reef fishes of the Indian and West Pacific Ocean.* Collins, London.

CRAMP, S. & SIMMONS, K. E. L. (eds) 1980. *The birds of the Western Palearctic. Vol. II.* Oxford University Press, Oxford.

FISHELSON, L. 1977. Sociobiology of feeding behaviour of coral fish along the coral reef of the Gulf of Eilat. *Isr. J. Zool.* **26**, 114–36.

FISHELSON, L. 1981. *Eilat coral reef fishes.* (in Hebrew) Hakibbutz Hameuchad, Tel-Aviv.

ODSZO, T. & SONDELL, J. 1976. Reproductive success in Ospreys *Pandion haliaetus* in southern and central Sweden, 1971–1977. *Ornis. Scand.* **7**, 71–84.

PAZ, U. & ZU-ARETS, S. 1976. *Annual Report for 1973 on bird observations in Israel.* (in Hebrew) Nature Reserves Authority, Tel-Aviv.

PIELOU, E. C. 1966. Shannon's formula as a measure of specific diversity: its use and misuse. *Amer. Natur.* **100**, 463–465.

PORTER, K. 1973. *Ecology and distribution of commercial fishes of the Gulf of Elat (=Gulf of Aqaba) and the Gulf of Suez.* (in Hebrew) MSc Thesis, The Hebrew University of Jerusalem, Jerusalem.

SIEGEL, P. 1979. *Non-parametric statistics for the behavioural sciences.* McGraw Hill, New York.

SMITH, G. L. B. 1953. *The seafishes of Southern Africa.* Central News Agency Ltd, Capetown.

SNEDECOR, G. W. & COCHRAN, G. 1967. *Statistical methods applied to experiments in agriculture and biology.* Iowa State College Press, Ames.

ZU-ARETS, S. 1973. *Survey of breeding birds on Tiran (Southern Sinai) in the breeding season of 1973.* (in Hebrew) Nature Reserves Authority, Tel-Aviv.

ICBP Technical Publication No. 3, 1985

STATUS, HABITS AND CONSERVATION OF *CYANORAMPHUS* PARAKEETS IN THE NEW ZEALAND REGION

ROWLAND H. TAYLOR

Ecology Division, DSIR, Private Bag, Nelson, New Zealand

ABSTRACT

The genus *Cyanoramphus* comprises four extant species and eight extant subspecies; in addition two species and two subspecies have become extinct in the last 210 years. Extant forms occur on widely scattered islands in the New Zealand region. Information is given for each form on distribution, abundance, habitat preferences, feeding, breeding, population trends, threats to survival and conservation.

INTRODUCTION

Parakeets of the genus *Cyanoramphus* (subfamily: Psittacinae) occur in the South Pacific from the tropics to the subantarctic (*Figure 1*). From an apparent centre of origin in New Zealand the genus has successfully dispersed across ocean barriers to many islands in the region (Fleming 1976). Because of the high degree of subspeciation that has occurred on isolated islands, some forms have a very limited distribution and are thus vulnerable to extinction. There are six currently recognized species, of which two from the Society Islands—the Black-fronted Parakeet (*C. zelandicus*) and the Society Parakeet (*C. ulietanus*)—have become extinct since 1773. The range and need for conservation of the four remaining species vary widely.

The purpose of this paper is to compare and summarize information on the surviving species and subspecies. Data have been gleaned from the literature and unpublished reports and notes. My own field interest in New Zealand parakeets dates from 1950. Since that time I have made observations on Red-crowned Parakeets (*C. novaezelandiae*) in several North Island forests, on the Chicken Islands in 1969, on Kapiti Island in 1961, on Stewart Island and nearby smaller islands in 1950, 1973, 1975 and 1978, and on the Auckland Islands in 1954, 1966, 1973 and 1978. Expeditions to Raoul and the Meyer Islands in 1978 and Macaulay Island in 1980 enabled me to obtain data on the Kermadec Parakeet (*C. n. cyanurus*). The Chatham Island Red-crowned Parakeet (*C. n. chathamensis*) and Forbes' Parakeet (*C. auriceps forbesi*) were studied during three trips to Chatham, Pitt, South-East and the Mangere Islands in 1970, 1973 and 1976; while expeditions to the Antipodes Islands in 1969 and 1978 provided the opportunity to

195

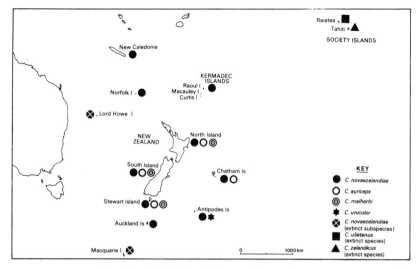

Figure 1:   Distribution of *Cyanoramphus* parakeets.

study Reischek's (*C. n. hochstetteri*) and Antipodes Island Parakeets (*C. unicolor*). I have made regular observations on Yellow-crowned Parakeets (*C. a. auriceps*) in beech (*Nothofagus*) forests of the northern South Island since 1962, and also studied this species on the Chetwode Islands in 1974, Titi Island since 1980, and on several trips to Fiordland, Stewart Island and the Auckland Islands. Personal observations on Orange-fronted Parakeets (*C. malherbi*) in the wild have been confined to the Hope River area, North Canterbury, during two visits in 1981. Localities mentioned in the text are shown in *Figures 2, 3* and *4*.

SPECIES ACCOUNTS

Antipodes Island Parakeet (*Cyanoramphus unicolor*)

Distribution and abundance.   Restricted to the Antipodes Islands where it is common on Antipodes Island (2000ha) and Bollons Island (54ha); and occurs in small numbers on Leeward (11ha), Inner Windward (8ha) and Archway (6ha) islets. Following a survey in 1978 I estimated the total population to number 2000–3000 birds.

Habitat.   There are no trees on the islands and the vegetation is mainly grassland composed of *Poa litorosa* tussocks interspersed with patches of sedge, various herbaceous plants, the fern *Polystichum vestitum* and scattered low *Coprosma antipoda* shrubs. There are numerous Rockhopper Penguin (*Eudyptes crestatus*) and Erect-crested Penguin (*E. sclateri*) colonies near the coast.

Antipodes Island Parakeets occur all over the islands, but are most common in tall dense tussocks or sedges, especially on steeper slopes and along watercourses.

Habits.   Over 400 observations of *C. unicolor* feeding during February 1969 and November 1978 indicated that leaves of tall tussocks (*Poa*) and sedges (*Carex*) were the

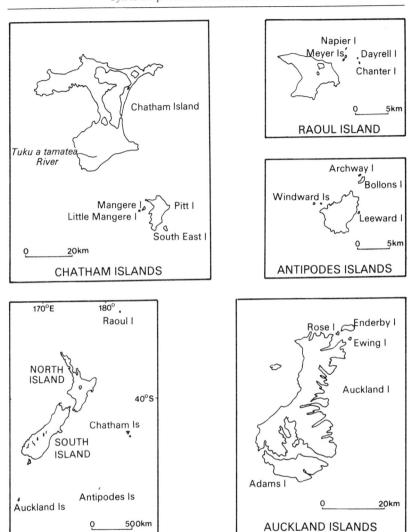

Figure 2:   New Zealand and outlying islands.

main foods (70 percent of all observations), supplemented with seeds (13 percent), berries, flowers, other vegetation (10 percent), and the remains of dead penguins and petrels (6 percent). When eating tussock leaves the parakeets cut lengths up to 20cm long with the bill and, while holding them in one foot, chew them progressively towards the tip. When feeding intensively a bird can chew more than 15 lengths in a minute and may remain in the one place for long periods. Piles of crushed and twisted chewings, each still attached to an unchewed leaf tip, are a distinctive sign of feeding.

The Antipodes Island Parakeet is capable of strong flight, but when feeding moves mainly by walking and climbing. If approached quietly they will remain feeding less than 2m away. They sometimes appear inquisitive and are attracted by human activity, and like a Kea (*Nestor notabilis*) may peck at tent seams and ropes. When alarmed they become furtive, keep silent or give only a short call and disappear into thick vegetation. The birds feed most intensively from early to mid morning and before dusk. Throughout the middle of the day they spend much time basking and preening in sheltered sites on or near the ground. They bathe regularly in freshwater pools and roost in burrows or tunnels under thick vegetation. Flocking has not been observed. Very few territorial disputes are seen. During the breeding season males are well spaced and mainly sedentary, and females have overlapping home ranges.

The nesting season is from October to January. Nests are built in well drained burrows often more than 1m deep in the fibrous peat beneath vegetation or in the thick matted bases of tall tussocks. Clutch size in the wild is unknown. At Antipodes Island broods of one to three newly-fledged young were seen being fed by adults during the first two weeks of February 1969. Fledged young are fed by both parents for at least one week, by which time they can fly strongly.

Conservation status.   Common within its endemic range. Population stable.

The species is under no immediate threat. The Antipodes Islands are strict Nature Reserves and permits are required to land. The islands are uninhabited by man. The habitat remains unmodified except for abundant House Mice (*Mus musculus*) on the main Antipodes Island. Although mice compete with the parakeets for seeds, superficially they appear to have little effect on the birds. However, they may seriously compromise the long-term survival of the Antipodes Island Parakeet by making the island a far more favourable habitat for Cats (*Felis catus*) or other small carnivores should they ever arrive (Taylor 1979).

Twelve birds were transferred to Kapiti Island off the west coast of the North Island of New Zealand in 1907 (Chilton 1909) and several survived there until at least 1923. None have since been released on other islands, but the species has adapted readily to captivity and has bred successfully at the Mt Bruce Native Bird Reserve since 1969. It is also held in several private aviaries in New Zealand. Matings with Reischck's Parakeets in aviaries have resulted in hybrid young, though hybrids are unknown in the wild (Taylor 1975).

Red-crowned Parakeet (*Cyanoramphus novaezelandiae novaezelandiae*)

Distribution and abundance.   New Zealand and Auckland Islands. Previously widely distributed on the North, South, Stewart and Auckland Islands and on many of their adjacent islands and islets (Oliver 1955). The species is now very scarce on the two main islands of New Zealand, where the only recent records are from large forest remnants in Northland and the Waitakere, Coromandel, Hauhungaroa, Urewera, Tararua, Rimutaka, Nelson and Fiordland Ranges (Bull *et al.* 1978). The species is rare on Great Barrier Island (Ogle 1981). It is still widespread and in good numbers on Stewart Island and nearby smaller islands, and many small offshore islands including Three Kings, Poor Knights, Hen and Chickens, Sail Rock, Little Barrier, Arid, Mokohinau, Mercury, Aldermen and Kapiti (Falla *et al.* 1979); and on Enderby, Rose, Ewing and Adams Islands in the Auckland group. Surprisingly it is absent from the many islands in the Marlborough Sounds, South Island (pers. obs.).

Habitat.   Forests, scrublands and open areas. This parakeet is usually found more at forest edges and at lower altitudes than is the Yellow-crowned Parakeet.

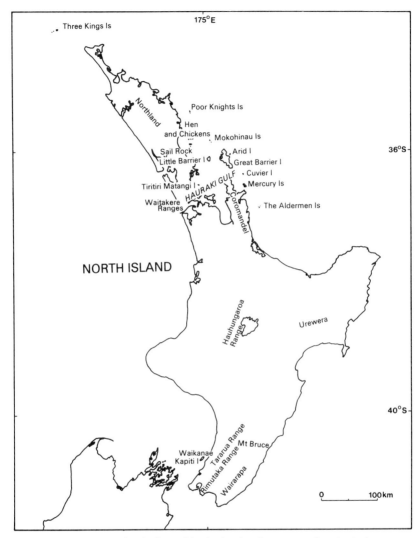

Figure 3:   North Island and adjacent islands, showing place names referred to in the text.

Habits.   Many kinds of seeds, berries, fruits, buds, flowers and shoots are eaten. On Tiritiri Matangi and Little Barrier Island, Dawe (1979) found that Red-crowned Parakeets ate about 90 plant species. Considerable variation occurred seasonally. The diet on Tiritiri Matangi was: spring—buds and flowers (37 percent) with some fruit and seed capsules; summer—fruit (36 percent) and some buds, flowers, seed capsules and seeds; autumn—seeds (32 percent) with fruit and fallen seeds; winter—fallen seeds (24 percent) and fruit (23 percent), seed capsules, leaves and shoots. The diet was different on Little Barrier Island with more buds and flowers and less fruit eaten in spring and summer, and no seed eaten in autumn. This parakeet also feeds on invertebrates, nectar and honeydew, and regularly drinks water. Commonly recorded foods on offshore islands include the seeds of *Phormium, Leptospermum, Acaena*, and of several rushes, sedges and grasses, and also the flowers and succulent shoots of *Disphyma* and *Muehlenbeckia*.

Pairs remain together throughout the year but territorial behaviour is restricted to the vicinity of the nest. Birds flock to an abundant food source at any season. On islands with limited fresh water, they congregate at springs and seepages to drink and bathe.

Ecological and behavioural barriers keep this species apart from the Yellow-crowned Parakeet in the wild. Inter-breeding by the two species in unmodified habitats has been recorded only rarely (Veitch 1979). Occasionally hybrids may become locally abundant where the habitat has been drastically modified, as on the Auckland Islands (Taylor 1975).

A hollow branch or tree trunk is a favourite site for nesting, but holes in cliffs or among rocks, and burrows in the ground or in densely matted vegetation are also used. Nests in decaying trees are commonly lined only with powdered wood, but feathers, moss, grass stems, tree-fern scales and small amounts of other dry plant material may be used. Often the same nest site is used year after year. In the wild most eggs are laid in October, November and December. Clutch size is variable, 2–10 being reported (Dawe 1979). All young leave the nest at about the same time, five to six weeks after hatching, when the smaller ones in a large brood may be noticeably less developed. Both parents continue to feed the young for a week or so after fledging.

Conservation status.   Locally common to rare. Population now essentially stable.

Red-crowned Parakeets were considered serious pests of crops, orchards and gardens during the 1870s and 1880s. However, introduced cats, Stoats (*Mustela erminea*) and other predators have drastically reduced parakeet populations on the main islands, and wild birds now have little contact with man. The species is under no immediate threat and is abundant on a number of small islands that are Nature Reserves free of introduced predators.

Red-crowned Parakeets have been kept and bred very successfully in captivity both in New Zealand and overseas. They are often crossed with Yellow-crowned Parakeets and many birds in private aviaries show hybrid characters (pers. obs.). In recent years aviary-bred Red-crowned Parakeets from Mt Bruce Native Bird Reserve and the Nga Manu Trust have been released in the Wairarapa, at Waikanae, in the Waitakere Ranges, and on Tiritiri Matangi and Cuvier Islands in the Hauraki Gulf (C. Roderick, pers. comm.; P. McKenzie, pers. comm.; Dawe 1979). The long-term success of the mainland liberations is uncertain, but the two island releases have resulted in new self-sustaining populations (Dawe 1979).

Kermadec Parakeet (*Cyanoramphus novaezelandiae cyanurus*)

Distribution and abundance.   Confined to the Kermadec Islands. Abundant on forested Raoul Island in 1836, but exterminated from there by wild cats probably before 1854. A population of about 100 parakeets still occurs on the Meyer Islands 1km northeast of Raoul, and others inhabit the smaller nearby islets of Napier, Dayrell and the Chanters (Merton 1970). The species is now very abundant on Macauley Island and straggles to Curtis Island approximately 80 and 120km, respectively, to the south-west of Raoul. I estimated the population on Macauley Island to number over 10,000 birds in November 1980.

Habitat. The two Meyer Islands cover about 16ha and rise to over 100m a.s.l. The steep slopes above the sea cliffs support coastal scrub and stunted forest up to 8m high. The ground beneath is mostly bare because of the activity of petrels. Around the shore and on steeper rocky slopes there are often areas vegetated by low shrubs, herbs, sedges and other salt-tolerant species.

Macauley Island (325ha) was denuded of trees and shrubs by Goats (*Capra hircus*) many years ago, and the vegetation became predominantly short grassland. Parakeets were the most common landbird then (J. O'Brien, unpub.). The goats were exterminated during expeditions in 1966 and 1970, and the vegetation is changing rapidly. In 1980 the rank grassland was being invaded by stands of tall sedges (*Cyperus* and *Scirpus*) and fern (*Hypolepis* and *Pteris*), and Ngaio trees (*Myoporum obscurum*) were starting to spread from seed sources on the cliffs.

Habits. Over 690 observations of Kermadec Parakeets feeding at Macauley Island in November 1980 indicated that seeds of sedges (*Cyperus* and *Scirpus*) and of various grasses and herbs were the main foods (69 percent of all observations), supplemented with *Solanum nodiflorum* berries (12 percent), various leaves, flowers and other vegetation (12 percent), seaweeds (4 percent) and small intertidal limpets (*Scutellastra kermadecensis*) (3 percent).

In 1966 J. O'Brien (unpubl.) observed Kermadec Parakeets feeding on the carcasses of goats shot by his party on Macauley Island. On Meyer Island Merton (1970) recorded birds feeding on the terminal shoots of trees and shrubs and particularly on the seeds of sedges and other plants.

Birds flock at any season, and flocks of 50–100 were commonly seen on Macauley Island in November 1980. On North Meyer Island in January 1966 Merton (1970) saw two loose flocks of about 20 and 30 birds on the summit ridge at dusk. They were apparently congregating to roost and none could be found at lower levels on the island immediately afterwards. On Macauley Island many birds roost close together in thick stands of tall sedges and ferns, in scattered sites under rock ledges, and in burrows in open ground. There is no permanent freshwater on Macauley and the birds commonly bathe in shallow intertidal pools.

Territorial behaviour has not been recorded although males defend the immediate vicinity (*c*. 5m) of the nest (pers. obs.). Three nests found on the Meyer Islands in 1966 were all near ground level, one in a bank and the others in hollow tree trunks or stumps (Merton 1970). Most eggs are laid in October and November and the clutch size varies from 2–5 (pers. obs.; Merton 1970). On the Meyer Islands in 1966–67, a nest with five chicks fledged on 24 December; another contained two chicks which flew before 8 January; and numerous family parties of 3–5 young were seen in late December (Merton 1970). On Macauley Island, where trees are few, nests are in holes in the cliffs or in burrows in the ground. In November 1980 nests were found with eggs and young chicks.

Conservation status. Locally common to rare. There has been a recent major population increase on Macauley Island since the removal of goats by the New Zealand Wildlife Service. There were over 1000 birds there in 1966 (J. O'Brien unpubl.), 2000 in 1970 (B. D. Bell unpubl.), and over 10,000 in 1980 (pers. obs.).

The Kermadec Islands are all strict Nature Reserves and permits are required to land. The habitat of the Meyer Islands remains unmodified, but Raoul Island has feral cats and Norway and Polynesian Rats (*Rattus norvegicus* and *R. exulans*). Birds from the Meyer Islands are known to disperse to Raoul where occasional parakeets have been seen and parakeet feathers disgorged by cats have been found (Merton 1970), but the species is unable to re-establish itself there. Polynesian Rats are abundant on Macauley Island but appear to have little effect on the birds.

The subspecies is not held in captivity.

Chatham Island Red-crowned Parakeet (*Cyanoramphus novaezelandiae chathamensis*)

Distribution and abundance. This species is restricted to the Chatham Islands where it formerly occurred on all forested islands. It is now uncommon on the two main islands of Chatham (72,000ha) and Pitt (6415ha), but abundant on South East Island (237ha), where earlier massive populations (Fleming 1939) are at more moderate levels due to the recent regeneration of forest and scrub that followed the removal of sheep in 1961 (Taylor 1975). Presently controlled by man to low numbers on Mangere (120ha) and Little Mangere Islands (16ha) to prevent inter-breeding with the rare Forbes' Parakeet (see Forbes' Parakeet).

Habitat. Forest margins, bush patches, scrublands and open areas are favoured. On South East Island in November 1976 these birds were most numerous around the coast and about clearings and forest edges, and were much less numerous inside the thickly regenerating forest. The recent shrinking of the forest cap on Little Mangere Island has allowed the Red-crowned species to become established there within the last decade.

Habits. Over 580 feeding observations of this species on South East and Mangere Islands between 1970 and 1976 (Taylor 1975; and unpubl.) indicate that in October–November the main foods are leaves and shoots (60 percent), flowers (19 percent), seeds (10 percent) and small amounts of nectar, invertebrates and fruits. In March–May more seeds are eaten but leaves and shoots are still the main foods. Small grits of volcanic glass have been found in the crops of birds collected on Mangere Island (Nixon 1982). Territorial behaviour has not been recorded. Birds are often encountered in groups and flock to an abundant food source at any season. This species is far less sedentary than the Chatham Island Yellow-crowned Parakeet and flies in the open much more often. On Mangere and SouthEast Islands they visit springs and freshwater pools to drink and bathe.

Nests are built in hollow limbs and trunks of trees. The breeding season is extended. Most eggs are laid in October to December. Clutch sizes recorded range from 5–7 eggs. On South East Island, eggs and recently-fledged young have been recorded in early November. Fleming (1939) found numerous nests in late December, the contents ranging from eggs to well feathered young.

Conservation status. Locally common to rare. Population now essentially stable.

South East and Mangere Islands are strict Nature Reserves requiring landing permits. Fortunately there are now no introduced mammals on these islands—sheep (*Ovis aries*) having been removed from the two islands in 1961 and 1968 respectively (Ritchie 1970). The vegetation of both islands is now changing rapidly and should return to an almost complete forest cover. Recently the New Zealand Wildlife Service has been reducing the numbers of Chatham Island Red-crowned Parakeets on Mangere and Little Mangere islands to decrease the possibility of their hybridization with Chatham Island Yellow-crowned Parakeets (Taylor 1975; Nixon 1982).

A few birds of this subspecies are held in New Zealand aviaries.

Reischek's Parakeet (*Cyanoramphus novaezelandiae hochstetteri*)

Distribution and abundance. Restricted to the Antipodes Islands where it is common on Antipodes Island and Bollons Island and occurs in small numbers on Leeward, Archway and Windward islets. In 1978 I estimated the total population of the islands to number 4000–5000 birds.

Habitat. The topography and vegetation of the Antipodes Islands are described under *C. unicolor.* Reischek's Parakeets occur on all parts of these islands, but are most common on the more open areas of the central plateau and in coastal places with low vegetation and penguin colonies.

Habits. Over 450 feeding observations at the Antipodes Islands in February 1969 and November 1978 showed that seeds—mainly tussock and sedge—were the major food (55 percent of all observations). Other important foods were flowers (20 percent), berries (9 percent), succulent leaves and buds (8 percent) and invertebrates (5 percent).

The birds are capable of strong flight and flock to abundant food sources at any season. They can be approached closely, and when alarmed take to the wing, calling as they fly. They feed most intensively during mid-morning and late afternoon. On fine days when not feeding they spend much time basking and preening in the lee of sheltering vegetation. They bathe regularly in shallow freshwater pools. At night they roost among thick tussocks or ferns. Nests are built in tunnels about 40cm deep in the crowns of tall *Poa litorosa* tussocks or clumps of *Polystichum* fern. The nest cavity is lined with small cut pieces of vegetation. This species nests from November to March about four weeks later than *C. unicolor,* the difference in timing being associated with the availability of preferred foods. The clutch size in the wild is unknown. At Antipodes Island three nests found in early February each contained only a single nestling, two in down and one almost fledged. Both parents continue to feed the fledged young for about a week.

Conservation status. Common within its endemic range. Population stable.

Reischek's Parakeet is under no immediate threat (see comments under *C. unicolor*). A wide ecological separation exists between this species and *C. unicolor.* These sympatric species have different food habits, breed at different times and nest in different sites. Direct interspecific competition is not seen at the island and wild hybrids are unknown (Taylor 1975). The species has adapted readily to captivity and has bred successfully at Mt Bruce Native Bird Reserve since 1969. It is now held in several aviaries in New Zealand and has hybridized with *C. unicolor* in captivity.

Norfolk Island Parakeet (*Cyanoramphus novaezelandiae cookii*)

Distribution and abundance. Restricted to Norfolk Island (3455ha). Only 17–30 birds were found during special parakeet surveys in 1977 and 1978 (Forshaw 1980), and the total population was estimated at about 20 in 1983 (D. Crouchley, pers. comm.).

Habitat. The birds prefer the tall dense forest of Norfolk Island Pine (*Araucaria heterophylla*) and other native vegetation around Mt Pitt (Forshaw 1980). They also occur in *Eucalyptus* plantations near native forest and occasionally range wider afield to feed (Smithers & Disney 1969).

Habits. The food of this species is mainly seeds, berries and buds. The birds feed in the tops of Norfolk Island Pines and on the seeds of the introduced Wild Olive (*Olea africana*) (Forshaw 1980). They also feed in forest litter scratching for seeds (and invertebrates?). They visit nearby gardens to feed on ripening fruit, particularly peaches (Smithers & Disney 1969).

Norfolk Island Parakeets are usually seen in pairs and small groups, but very large flocks were reported in earlier times. They are not shy and can be approached quite closely.

The nesting season is variable and well spread out, but most eggs are laid from October to December. The nest is built above the ground in a hollow limb or hole in a tree. About five eggs are laid (Forshaw 1969).

Conservation status. Endangered. Population presently fairly stable.

The subspecies has declined drastically in the past and is subject to many pressures, notably loss of habitat, avian disease, competition from introduced species and predation by rats (*Rattus rattus* and *R. exulans*) and feral cats (Forshaw 1980, Phipps 1981). The Mt Pitt Forest Reserve (474ha) is the last substantial remnant of native vegetation on the island (Forshaw 1980). It seems that competition from the introduced Crimson Rosella (*Platycercus elegans*) has been, and still is, a major threat to the parakeets on Norfolk Island. Forshaw (1980) and Phipps (1981) have recommended the transfer of some Norfolk Island Parakeets to another island, possibly Lord Howe, where there is no competing species. Unfortunately there seems to be little chance of any easing of the pressures on these parakeets at Norfolk Island, short of drastic reduction in the numbers of Crimson Rosellas and stronger measures to protect areas of native vegetation (King 1981). In 1983 five Norfolk Island Parakeets were taken into captivity in an attempt to establish a captive breeding population on the island (D. Crouchley, pers. comm.).

New Caledonian Red-crowned Parakeet (*Cyanoramphus novaezelandiae saisseti*)

Distribution and abundance. This parakeet is restricted to the main island of New Caledonia. The extent of its range is uncertain, but there are recent reports of small numbers from widely scattered parts of the island (Forshaw 1973; Hannecart & Letocart 1980; Orenstein 1972; Vuilleumier & Gochfeld 1976).

Habitat. Occurs in indigenous mountain forests.

Habits. The New Caledonian Red-crowned Parakeet feeds both on the ground (Mayr 1945) and in the lower and middle storeys of the forest (Forshaw 1973) on seeds, including those of *Casuarina*, and fruits (Hannecart & Letocart 1980). Although not shy, the species is apparently hard to observe. It is reported to make little noise, fly swiftly and often perch or rest high in the canopy. Mayr (1945) considered it 'a quiet and rather rare bird; usually seen singly or in pairs'.

The nesting period is from November to January. Nests have been found in hollow trees, the eggs (2–4) being laid on a bed of leaves (Hannecart & Letocart 1980).

Conservation status. Orenstein (1972) considered this parakeet to be 'still reasonably common in undisturbed areas'. The population is presumably stable and is not known to be at risk (King 1981).

Yellow-crowned Parakeet (*Cyanoramphus auriceps auriceps*)

Distribution and abundance. Yellow-crowned Parakeets were formerly common throughout New Zealand, the Auckland Islands and many of their offshore islands (Oliver 1955). Now they occur only in the larger forest tracts of the North and South Islands (Bull *et al.* 1978) and on Three Kings, Hen and Chickens, Little Barrier (Falla *et al.* 1979), Great Barrier (Ogle 1981), Kapiti, Inner and Outer Chetwodes, Titi (pers. obs.), Ruapuke (K. Morrison, pers. comm.), Big and Little Solander, Codfish, Stewart Island and surrounding smaller islands, and Auckland and Adams Islands in the Auckland group (Falla *et al.* 1979, pers. obs.). Numbers vary locally from rare to fairly common on the North and South Islands; they are rare on Great Barrier and Kapiti Islands, but common on the other islands listed.

Habitat. Native forest, particularly mixed beech/podocarp forest, is preferred on the North and South Islands. On offshore islands where both Yellow-crowned and Red-crowned Parakeets occur, the former favours taller unbroken forest and scrub, whereas the latter prefers more open areas with low vegetation.

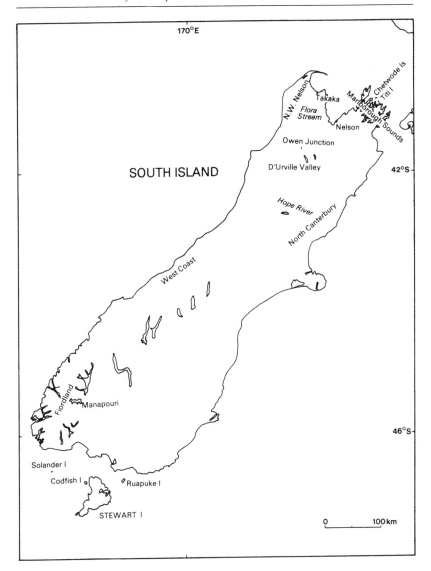

Figure 4: South Island and adjacent islands, showing place names referred to in the text.

Habits. The birds' food consists of a wide range of shoots, buds, flowers and seeds (including those of beech (*Nothofagus* spp.) and various podocarps) and invertebrates. Although this list is similar to that of the Red-crowned Parakeet, observations on feeding Yellow-crowned Parakeets and their habits and habitat preferences suggest that invertebrates are much more important in the diet of the latter. In South Island beech forests, scale insects (*Ultracoelostoma assimile*) and caterpillars (*Heliostibes vibratrix*) are eagerly sought from beneath beech bark on twigs and branches (pers. obs.). Early observers recorded that Yellow-crowned Parakeets often followed flocks of Whiteheads (*Mohoua albicilla*) in the North Island and Yellowheads (*M. ochrocephala*) in the South Island (Oliver 1955).

On the Chetwode Islands in early October 1974 most Yellow-crowned Parakeets were taking seeds and invertebrates from loose soil and leaf litter on the ground (77 percent of all observations). Other foods at this time were seeds of *Pseudopanax*, *Leptospermum* and thistles, and flowers of herbaceous *Senecio*, *Hymenanthera obovata*, *Phormium* and *Coprosma*.

Buller (1888) recorded that this species was 'less gregarious' than the Red-crowned Parakeet and was 'seen generally in pairs'. Nowadays on the main islands of New Zealand, pairs or small groups are usually seen feeding in the forest canopy or on the outer foliage of shrubs, and are only seen very infrequently on or near the ground. However, on offshore islands without introduced predators they commonly feed on the forest floor.

On Outer Chetwode Island in early October 1974 at least 68 percent of 232 Yellow-crowned Parakeets observed were in pairs and many males were seen aggressively chasing other pairs. This species hybridizes very occasionally with Red-crowned birds in the wild (see Red-crowned Parakeet).

Nesting sites are similar to those of the Red-crowned species, the most common being in natural holes in living or dead trees. In some areas breeding may extend over the greater part of the year, the timing probably being adjusted to the availability of food. Young birds have been seen from July through the summer until April, but most eggs are laid in October, November and December. Clutch size varies from 5–9 (Oliver 1955).

Conservation status. Locally common to rare. Population now essentially stable.

After declining markedly on the mainland during the first part of this century, the Yellow-crowned Parakeet increased again and since 1950 has been regularly observed in the larger tracts of forest in both the North and South Islands (Oliver 1955; Falla *et al.* 1979). However it is still largely absent from the mainland north of Auckland where Buller (1888) found it so numerous about 100 years ago. Recent accelerated felling of lowland native forests in both the North and South Islands, and their conversion to exotic pines (*Pinus* spp.), now threatens to further reduce mainland populations. Fortunately the species is abundant on several small island Nature Reserves free of introduced predators. It is noteworthy that following the disappearance of Norway Rats from Titi Island about 1975, Yellow-crowned Parakeets quickly recolonized the island. They now occur there in good numbers and are breeding.

This species is successfully bred in captivity both in New Zealand and overseas, but unfortunately is often cross-mated with Red-crowned Parakeets.

Forbes' or Chatham Island Yellow-crowned Parakeet (*Cyanoramphus auriceps forbesi*)

Distribution and abundance. Restricted to the Chatham Islands where it formerly occurred on Pitt Island (Fleming 1939). Breeding is now confined to Mangere Island (120ha) with about 40 birds, and Little Mangere Island (16ha) with about 16 birds.

Habitat. These birds disappeared on Pitt and Mangere Islands after early destruction of the forest, and all available evidence suggests that this subspecies prefers dense unbroken forest and scrub (Taylor 1975). This conclusion is supported by a recent population decline on Little Mangere Island, where the 4ha forest on the summit is rapidly deteriorating, and by their slow recolonization of Mangere Island since its bush patch has regenerated.

Habits. Over 100 observations of birds feeding on Little Mangere Island between 1973 and 1976 indicated that in October–November the main foods were invertebrates (40 percent), flowers (35 percent) and seeds (18 percent). In March–May more leaves and berries were eaten, but invertebrates were still important. On Mangere Island birds feed more on leaves and seeds and less on invertebrates (Nixon 1982), perhaps reflecting the different availability of these foods on the two islands.

Forbes' Parakeet is most commonly seen singly or in pairs. Flocks other than small (probably family) groups have not been reported in recent years. Observations on both Little Mangere and Mangere Islands suggest that pairs are sedentary and attached to their nesting areas throughout the year. During the breeding season on Little Mangere the birds are strongly territorial and aggressively defend boundaries, calling loudly. The females are less aggressive but fly with their mates in aerial chases of intruding birds. The birds' territorial system cannot be maintained in open areas. The destruction of forest leads to this species being displaced by, or hybridizing with, Red-crowned Parakeets (Taylor 1975; Flack 1976).

Nests are built in holes in living or dead trees. One freshly prepared nest found inside a dead trunk on Little Mangere Island in November 1976 was lined with powdered wood. The breeding season is extended, eggs being laid at any time between October and March. On Little Mangere Island Fleming (1939) saw numbers of immature birds with their parents in December 1938, and in recent years newly fledged juveniles have been seen until late May.

Conservation status. Vulnerable. Population now increasing slowly.

The population on Little Mangere Island has declined since Fleming (1939) reported more than 100 birds in 1938. A New Zealand Wildlife Service survey in 1968 revealed 20–30 birds. Taylor (1975, and unpubl.) counted ten breeding pairs in November 1973 and eight pairs and several unmated males holding territories in November 1976. More recent reports suggest that numbers on Little Mangere are still declining slowly (Nixon 1982), almost certainly because of rapid deterioration of the forest, mainly from natural causes—including a succession of dry seasons and extremely numerous burrowing petrels which inhibit regeneration.

Forbes' Parakeet is threatened by genetic swamping through large-scale hybridization with the Chatham Island Red-crowned Parakeet on Mangere and Little Mangere Islands (Taylor 1975; Flack 1976; Nixon 1982). The critical situation is due to the past drastic reduction of forest on Mangere. Continued active management of the birds may be necessary until the former forest cover is re-established.

Fortunately regeneration and large-scale planting by the New Zealand Wildlife Service is now well under way on Mangere. The Service is also attempting to eliminate hybrid parakeets and limit the numbers of Red-crowned Parakeets on both Mangere and Little Mangere. These operations have been most successful. In a total of about 100 parakeets on Mangere in 1973, six were Forbes', 47 were Red-crowned and 47 were hybrids (Taylor 1975). By comparison in 1982 there were 40 Forbes', 12 Red-crowned and very few hybrids (D. Crouchley, pers. comm.).

A Yellow-crowned Parakeet was seen on 29 December 1982 near the Tuku a tamatea River in the south of the main Chatham Island (D. Melville, pers. comm.) where only

Chatham Island Red-crowned Parakeets have previously been recorded. Whether this bird was a stray from the Mangere Islands or part of a small resident population is unknown.

A few Forbes' Parakeets are held in captivity at Mt Bruce Native Bird Reserve, where they have bred successfully.

Orange-fronted Parakeet (*Cyanoramphus malherbi*)

Distribution and abundance. This parakeet is extremely rare and has been recorded at only seven localities during this century—Stewart Island (1904), Takaka (1913), Owen Junction (1928), Manapouri (1949), Flora Stream in north-west Nelson (1955), D'Urville Valley (1965), and Hope River in North Canterbury (1963, 1980, 1981, 1982).

Habitat. Recorded from subalpine scrub to near sea level, but recent records are mostly from edges of beech forest below 800m altitude (Harrison 1970). In the Hope River area nesting birds have only been found in tall Red Beech (*Nothofagus fusca*) dominant forest between 600m and 900m altitude, and they seem to prefer areas bordering on Mountain Beech (*N. solandri*) forest (D. Crouchley, unpubl.).

Habits. Very little has been recorded of their feeding habits. Reischek (1886) mentions berries and seeds. The label on a specimen taken on the West Coast of the South Island states 'stomach small grubs' (Harrison 1970). Different food preferences may be the major factor separating this species ecologically from the Red-crowned and Yellow-crowned species (Harrison 1970; Taylor 1975). Recent observations in the Hope River area in November 1980, March 1981, September/October 1981 and October 1982 have indicated that scale insects, flower and leaf buds, flowers, young leaves and seeds are commonly eaten (pers. obs., A. Cox, unpubl.; D. Crouchley, unpubl.).

Most Orange-fronted Parakeets observed have been associated with parties or flocks of Yellow-crowned Parakeets. Haast was well acquainted with the two species in the field and collected several Orange-fronted birds for Buller; he stated that the two species always occur together, but that Orange-fronted Parakeets were 'not so bold' as the Yellow-crowned species (Buller 1870). Orange-fronted Parakeets seen near the Hope River in 1980 and 1981 were often in small flocks which included Yellow-crowned birds. In October 1981 a mixed pair (Yellow-crowned male and Orange-fronted female) attempted to nest there in a hole high in a dead beech tree, but unfortunately deserted the one egg laid after the nest became waterlogged in a storm. In October 1982 two pairs of Orange-fronted birds were located near the same area. One pair nesting in a cavity behind a knot-hole about 10m up a live Red Beech produced a clutch of three eggs.

Conservation status. Rare. Population essentially stable as far as known.

In European times the Orange-fronted Parakeet has never been as common as either of the other two mainland parakeets. However, Haast considered it the predominant parakeet in some South Island localities (Buller 1870), and it appears from Buller (1888) and available museum specimens that it was not uncommon in the hills around Nelson in the 1880s. There are also numerous reports of the species from various parts of the South Island during the nineteenth century. Five specimens were collected from the one flock of parakeets at Owen River in 1928 (Fleming 1980). Reischek reported that he obtained specimens of Orange-fronted Parakeets from Hen and Little Barrier Islands, Hauraki Gulf, in the 1880s but the validity of these records has been questioned on the grounds that 'the species has not been recorded there before or since' (Harrison 1970). However these grounds are weak considering that very few parakeet specimens have been taken from these islands since Reischek's time, and the poor success recent ornithologists have had anywhere in identifying the species from field sightings alone.

After examining at the Vienna Museum Reischek's two labelled Orange-fronted Parakeet skins from Hen Island, I am prepared to accept their validity and the previous occurrence of the species in the North Island.

After reviewing the status of the Orange-fronted Parakeet, Harrison (1970) suggested that it might be more common than generally thought, but some other authors have considered it to be close to extinction (Mills & Williams 1978). In September 1980 a small number of Orange-fronted Parakeets were discovered by the New Zealand Wildlife Service near the Hope River in North Canterbury, where this species comprises about 8 percent of a parakeet population of predominantly Yellow-crowned birds (A. Cox, unpubl.; D. Crouchley, unpubl.).

Holyoak (1974) suggested that the Orange-fronted Parakeet is a colour morph of the Yellow-crowned Parakeet, and is not a distinct species. He found that the often-quoted differences between the two forms in body size and bill structure are based on too few specimens and these are mostly of unknown sex. He also found that consistent structural differences appear to be lacking, and that colour differences can be explained in terms of small changes in carotenoid pigmentation, which is probably under simple genetic control. Nixon (1981) agreed with Holyoak after studying further museum specimens. However, the apparent lack of real structural differences between the two forms is not proof that they belong to the same species, and there is some contrary ecological evidence (Buller 1870; Fleming 1980). Although Holyoak's hypothesis is persuasive, the Orange-fronted Parakeet is retained here as a valid species until further evidence becomes available.

Five male and two female Orange-fronted Parakeets are now held for breeding in captivity. Four of these birds were caught with mist nets and the others were reared from eggs removed from a nest near the Hope River in 1982. Limited experimental cross-breeding using male Orange-fronted Parakeets and female Yellow-crowned Parakeets is also under way in an attempt to clarify the taxonomic status of the Orange-fronted birds.

CONCLUSION

The *Cyanoramphus* parakeets are a characteristic component of the landbird fauna of islands in the New Zealand region. The six species and ten subspecies have adapted to a remarkably wide range of habitats from subantarctic tussock grassland to tropical rainforests.

The Antipodes Island Parakeet is endemic to the isolated subantarctic Antipodes Islands where it is common. The Red-crowned Parakeet includes eight island subspecies. Of these the Lord Howe Island Parakeet (*C. novaezelandiae subflavescens*), last seen about 1870, and the Macquarie Island Parakeet (*C. n. erythrotis*), last seen in 1890, are already extinct. Extant island forms in New Caledonia, Norfolk Island, the Kermadec Islands, New Zealand (including adjacent islands) and the Chatham Islands are now either rare and endangered, or have reduced ranges owing to habitat loss and the introduction of alien predators. An exception which has not declined in numbers or range is Reischek's Parakeet from the unmodified Antipodes Islands. The Yellow-crowned Parakeet has two subspecies. One survives with reduced range and numbers on the main islands of New Zealand and in substantial numbers on several offshore islands free of introduced carnivores. The second is endemic to the Chatham Islands where it is rare and endangered by habitat changes and consequent hybridization with *C. novaezelandiae*. The status of the rarely seen Orange-fronted Parakeet of the New Zealand mainland is being investigated, and it may prove to be a colour morph of *C. auriceps*.

Most species have shown a striking resilience to the large-scale habitat modification which followed European settlement. However, on small islands some parakeets have not been able to adapt rapidly enough to cope with a wide range of environmental changes, including the introduction of predators such as cats. These factors have forced two species and two subspecies to extinction. Most of the surviving forms are not seriously threatened. The Norfolk Island Parakeet and Forbes' Parakeet in the Chatham Islands are exceptions. The present precarious status of the former (Forshaw 1980) demands urgent action, but Forbes' Parakeets are already responding to active management involving habitat improvements and elimination of wild hybrids.

In view of the broad range of proven conservation techniques which are now available, there is no reason for further extinctions of *Cyanoramphus* parakeets in the foreseeable future. All species do well in captivity, and aviary-bred Red-crowned Parakeets have been re-established in the wild on offshore islands and mainland New Zealand.

ACKNOWLEDGEMENTS

I gratefully acknowledge the co-operation of the New Zealand Wildlife Service and the Department of Lands and Survey during many expeditions. Numerous people have helped with valuable records, discussion and field assistance. It is impossible to name them all but special thanks are due to Brian Bell, Don Merton, John Warham, Rodney Russ, Doug Flack, Andy Cox, David Crouchley, Bruce Thomas and Peter McKenzie. Jocelyn Tilley prepared the figures and several colleagues in Ecology Division commented on the manuscript.

ADDENDUM

Since the manuscript of this paper was submitted for publication, experimental cross-breeding has proven that the Orange-fronted Parakeet is a colour morph of the Yellow-crowned Parakeet, and is not a distinct species (Taylor, in prep.).

REFERENCES

BULL, P. C., GAZE, P. D. & ROBERTSON, C. J. R. 1978. *Bird distribution in New Zealand.* Ornithological Society of N.Z., Wellington.
BULLER, W. L. 1870. Notes on the ornithology of New Zealand. *Trans. N.Z. Inst.* 2, 385–92.
BULLER, W. L. 1888. *A history of the birds of New Zealand.* Second Edition. Published by the Author, London.
CHILTON, C. 1909. *The subantarctic islands of New Zealand.* Vol. 1. Philosophical Institute of Canterbury, Wellington.
DAWE, M. R. 1979. *Behaviour and ecology of the Red-crowned Parakeet* (Cyanoramphus novaezelandiae) *in relation to management.* M.Sc. thesis, University of Auckland.
FALLA, R. A., SIBSON, R. B. & TURBOTT, E. G. 1979. *The new guide to the birds of New Zealand.* Collins, Auckland.
FLACK, J. A. D. 1976. Hybrid parakeets on the Mangere Islands, Chatham Group. *Notornis* 23, 253–5.
FLEMING, C. A. 1939. Birds of the Chatham Islands. Part II. *Emu* 38, 492–509.
FLEMING, C. A. 1976. New Zealand as a minor source of terrestrial plants and animals in the Pacific. *Tuatara* 22, 30–7.
FLEMING, C. A. 1980. Orange-fronted Parakeet: Record of flocking. *Notornis* 27, 388–90.
FORSHAW, J. M. 1969. *Australian Parrots.* Lansdowne Press, Melbourne.

Forshaw, J. M. 1973. *Parrots of the World*. Lansdowne Press, Melbourne.

Forshaw, J. M. 1980. The Norfolk Island Parakeet (*Cyanoramphus novaezelandiae cookii*). A threatened population: status and management options. *In:* Pasquier, R. D. (ed.) Conservation of New World Parrots: 461–9. *ICBP Tech. Pub.* **1**.

Hannecart, F. & Letocart, Y. 1980. *Oiseaux de Nlle Caledonie et des Loyautes: New Caledonian birds*. Vol. 1. Hannecart & Letocart, Noumea.

Harrison, M. 1970. The Orange-fronted Parakeet (*Cyanoramphus malherbi*). *Notornis* **17**, 115–25.

Holyoak, D. T. 1974. *Cyanoramphus malherbi*, is it a colour morph of *C. auriceps?* *British Ornithological Club Bulletin* **94**, 4–9.

King, W. B. (Editor) 1981. *Endangered birds of the World. The ICBP Bird Red Data Book.* Smithsonian Institution Press. Washington, D.C.

Mayr, E. 1945. *Birds of the Southwest Pacific.* Macmillan, New York.

Merton, D. V. 1970. Kermadec Islands Expedition Reports: A general account of birdlife. *Notornis* **17**, 147–99.

Mills, J. A. & Williams, G. R. 1978. The status of endangered New Zealand birds. *In:* M. J. Tyler (ed.) *The status of endangered Australasian wildlife*. Roy. Zool. Soc. South Australia, Adelaide.

Nixon, A. J. 1981. External morphology and taxonomic status of the Orange-fronted Parakeet. *Notornis* **28**, 292–300.

Nixon, A. J. 1982. *Aspects of the ecology and morphology of* Cyanoramphus *parakeets and hybrids from Mangere Island, Chatham Islands*. M.Sc. thesis, Victoria University of Wellington.

Ogle, C. C. 1981. Great Barrier Island wildlife survey. *Tane* **27**, 177–200.

Oliver, W. R. B. 1955. *New Zealand Birds*. 2nd Edition. A. H. & A. W. Reed, Wellington.

Orenstein, R. 1972. The endangered birds of New Caledonia. *Animals* **14**, 364–7, 373.

Phipps, G. 1981. The Kakarikis. *Australian Aviculture*—June 1981: 126–39.

Reischek, A. 1886. Observations on the habits of New Zealand birds, their usefulness and destructiveness to the country. *Trans. N.Z. Inst.* **18**, 96–104.

Ritchie, I. M. 1970. A preliminary report on a recent botanical survey of the Chatham Islands. *Proc. N.Z. Ecol. Soc.* **17**, 52–6.

Smithers, C. N. & Disney, H. J. de S. 1969. The distribution of terrestrial and freshwater birds on Norfolk Island. *Australian Zoologist* **15**, 127–40.

Taylor, R. H. 1975. Some ideas on speciation in New Zealand parakeets. *Notornis* **22**, 110–21.

Taylor, R. H. 1979. How the Macquarie Island Parakeet became extinct. *N.Z. Journal of Ecology* **2**, 42–5.

Veitch, C. R. 1979. Parakeet hybridisation. *Notornis* **26**, 395.

Vuilleumier, F. & Gochfeld, M. 1976. Notes sur l'avifaune de Nouvelle-Caledonie. *Alauda* **44**, 237–73.

ICBP Technical Publication No. 3, 1985

THE PUERTO RICAN PARROT AND COMPETITION FOR ITS NEST SITES

JAMES W. WILEY

Puerto Rico Field Station, Patuxent Wildlife Research Center, U.S. Fish and Wildlife Service, P.O. Box 21, Palmer, Puerto Rico 00721

ABSTRACT

The Puerto Rican Parrot (*Amazona vittata*) once occurred throughout Puerto Rico and its satellites but suffered tremendous population losses beginning in the mid-seventeenth century. Today the entire population, consisting of less than 30 individuals, is restricted to the Luquillo Mountains of eastern Puerto Rico. Early population declines were clearly related to habitat destruction and human harassment. The remnant population has been under continuous protection in what is now the Caribbean National Forest, where substantial areas of virgin or slightly degraded forest remain. Yet, despite protection of habitat seemingly suitable for parrots, the Luquillo population continued to decline. Through systematic surveys for cavities in parrot nesting areas it has been determined that optimal nesting cavities are scarce, and that this scarcity may have been one cause of the poor reproductive performance of the parrots in recent decades. Competition for the limited sites has been intense and the high incidence of observed parrot injuries may be related to the excessive nest site competition among parrot pairs. Introduced Honeybees (*Apis mellifera*) occupy cavities within the volume range used by parrots and have taken over some parrot nests after the young have fledged. However, in recent years the most threatening competitor for nest cavities has been the Pearly-eyed Thrasher (*Margarops fuscatus*). When searching for nest sites, these birds prey on unguarded parrot eggs and young chicks. Thrashers and parrots are now provided with adjacent artificial or improved natural nest sites with optimal dimensions for each species. While defending their own nest, resident thrasher pairs effectively defend the parrot nest from other pairs of thrashers prospecting for nests. Since this strategy was incorporated into the parrot management programme in 1976 there have been no thrasher-related losses of parrot eggs or chicks.

INTRODUCTION

At the time of their discovery, the West Indies had no fewer than 26 species of macaws, parrots and parakeets. Five hundred years later 14 of these species are extinct, primarily as a result of the detrimental effects of man. Each of the 12 surviving species has undergone massive declines in populations, though with less than 30 birds in the wild none is closer to extinction than the Puerto Rican Parrot (*Amazona vittata*).

When Columbus arrived in the West Indies in 1492 Puerto Rico was completely forested (Hill 1899; Murphy 1916; Wadsworth 1949), and Puerto Rican Parrots were widespread and abundant. The parrot occurred throughout the wet and dry forests of the island, and on at least three of Puerto Rico's four offshore islands (Culebra, Vieques and Mona). Although no population estimates were made for the species before its decline, there were probably several hundred thousand birds, possibly more than a

213

million, before Europeans began extensive forest clearance in the eighteenth century.

The history of the parrot's decline is closely linked with man's population growth and its effect on parrot habitat. People shot parrots for food and to protect their crops, and took young birds for pets. However, the most important factor contributing to the decline has been the almost total destruction of Puerto Rico's forests. The small-scale slash-and-burn agriculture of the aboriginal Taino Indians resulted in little modification of the forests, but with the arrival of Europeans the human population escalated and forests disappeared rapidly. Within 400 years the island's population had increased from a few scattered bands of Tainos to 1 million residents (114 people/km^2) in 1900. By that time three-quarters of the island was under agriculture and less than 1 percent of the virgin forest remained (Murphy 1916; Wadsworth 1949).

Remnant populations of the parrot survived in several refuges of partially degraded forests in rugged mountain and karst regions. However, after about the mid-1930's, because of attrition through harvesting and continued habitat reduction, these populations died out. Parrots remained only in the Luquillo Mountains where about 7000ha (Wadsworth, pers. comm.) of old forest had been preserved, first as crown lands when the forest was under Spanish rule and later as a United States National Forest. Still, despite the preservation of this habitat, the population declined until in 1975 only 13 birds were left in the wild.

The decline of the Luquillo Forest population during the past 50 years was due to extremely high mortality within the population and consistently poor reproductive success. This had five main causes:

- Nest robbing by man for pets.
- Nest-site scarcity and inadequacies.
- Nest predation by the Pearly-eyed Thrasher *Margarops fuscatus*.
- Raptor predation on adult and young parrots.
- Parasitism of nestlings by Warble Flies (*Philornis [Neomusca] pici*) (Wiley 1980).

In this paper I shall concentrate on the factors responsible for the scarcity of nest sites, the competition problems that resulted and the conservation measures being used to alleviate these problems.

FACTORS RESPONSIBLE FOR NEST SITE SCARCITY

Availability of natural cavities

Because of its requirement for cavity nests, the Puerto Rican Parrot needs mature forests for its survival. Although the remaining population is protected within the Caribbean National Forest, where sizeable tracts of virgin or slightly-culled forest have been preserved, nevertheless successional changes, degradation and destruction of the forest have led to a scarcity of nest sites. This scarcity has been responsible for lowered breeding effort and success in the parrot because some potential pairs are known to have foregone nesting and others have been forced to use inadequate cavities (e.g. wet, shallow sites). Lack of sites has also intensified competition for nest cavities among parrots, and also among parrots and other cavity-nesting species.

Snyder (1977) systematically examined trees and cavities in 27.5ha of the palo colorado (*Cyrilla racemiflora*) and tabonuco (*Dacryodes excelsa*) forest types encompassing the four areas where parrots nest and roost. I conducted subsequent surveys in parts of the forest (colorado and tabonuco types) where parrots were not currently nesting. From these studies it was learned that the traditional nesting areas were exceptionally well endowed with natural cavities (*Table 1*). However, based on the characteristics of

Table 1: Frequency of trees and cavities in surveys conducted in parrot nesting and non-nesting areas (total 43.5ha) within the Luquillo Forest, Puerto Rico.

Tree species[1]	No. of trees	No. of cavity-bearing trees (%)	No. of cavities
Parrot nesting areas			
Palo colorado	720	201 (27.9)	252
Laurel sabino	194	24 (12.4)	31
Caimitillo	119	16 (13.4)	17
Tabonuco	71	4 (5.6)	4
Cupeillo	44	0	0
Miscellaneous	68	5 (7.4)	6
Total	1,216	250 (20.6)	310
Non-nesting areas			
Tabonuco	223	18 (8.1)	19
Palo colorado	159	29 (18.2)	35
Laurel sabino	35	6 (17.1)	7
Caimitillo	74	9 (12.2)	11
Cupeillo	25	2 (8.0)	2
Palo de pollo	65	9 (13.8)	10
Miscellaneous	51	3 (5.9)	5
Total	632	76 (12.0)	89

Note: Scientific names of trees: Palo colorado, *Cyrilla racemiflora*; laurel sabino, *Magnolia splendens*; caimitillo, *Micropholis garciniaefolia* and *M. chrysophylloides*; tabonuco, *Dacryodes excelsa*; cupeillo, *Clusia krugiana*; palo de pollo, *Pterocarpus officinalis*.

successful parrot nests (i.e. internal dimensions, height from ground and dryness), only about 0.4 optimal cavities per hectare were present even in the favoured parts of the forest.

Successional changes in stands of palo colorado may be an important cause of the present scarcity of optimal nest sites. During the past 35 years, 24 of the 25 nests in the Luquillo Forest have been in palo colorados. This high use of palo colorados is probably related to the frequent development of cavities in these trees. Systematic surveys in the Luquillo Forest revealed that in nesting areas more than 80 percent of all cavities occur in palo colorados, even though these trees account for only about 50 percent of those inspected (*Table 1*). Many of the parrot nesting areas now appear top-heavy with old palo colorados, and I predict a decline in the availability of cavities as larger colorados die without being replaced.

In the two western nesting areas the numerous large palo colorados that in recent decades have died and fallen may have been the result of the severe hurricanes that devastated the Luquillo Forest in 1928 and 1932. These storm-related die-offs of colorados have probably contributed to the low availability of nest sites in some areas.

Human activities
Several of man's activities within the forest have undoubtedly affected the abundance of cavities:

- Timber harvesting and charcoal-making.
- Destruction of nest cavities by people harvesting chicks.
- Destruction of potentially good nest cavities by honey gatherers.

Timber was cut within the National Forest from 1931 to 1953. Within the 3400ha of colorado forest type, 2800ha were considered 'timber areas' and about 430ha (13 percent) of the type was cut-over (Wadsworth, pers. comm.). Although palo colorado has little commercial value as timber and was not included in Forest Service timber estimates, it was selectively removed for charcoal from at least 400ha of prime colorado forest between 1945 and 1950. Also, from 1935 to about 1960 a programme of timber-stand improvement by girdling 'weed trees' (including the palo colorado) was implemented. Except for an experimental 0.4ha plot, the improvement operations did not intentionally penetrate the colorado type, but still may have thinned out palo colorados along the upper edge of the tabonuco type where parrots are known to nest. These removal programmes must have resulted in some loss of suitable nest cavities, although the magnitude of effects on the parrot is difficult to assess.

Honeybees (*Apis mellifera*) have figured prominently in the reduction of nest sites for parrots. Introduced to Puerto Rico by Europeans, they presumably became established in the wild early in the colonial period and are now common in the upper Luquillo Mountains. With overlapping preferences for cavity sizes, honeybees and parrots compete for tree hollows. Because parrot chicks normally fledge by the first week of June and honeybees mostly swarm between 1 June and 1 September, there is only a short period when swarms might directly threaten the safety of active nests. Nevertheless, honeybees appropriate nests after the parrot breeding season and also occupy unused but potentially good nest sites, thus rendering many cavities unavailable to parrots until the hives expire. In one valley in 1981 seven of the nine (78 percent) optimal sites for parrot nests were taken over by honeybees.

Up to the late 1960s honey harvesting was a common activity in the Luquillo Forest. Climbing the rotting, hollow trees that held hives was dangerous, and harvesting typically was done by felling the tree. This selective destruction of cavities certainly reduced the availability of suitable cavities to both parrots and honeybees.

From the 1930s until the 1960s parrot nests were harvested in at least four of the five parrot nesting regions. Judging by the number of people involved in this enterprise (determined by interviewing former parrot harvesters), nestlings were probably taken from nearly every nest in the Luquillo Mountains by the 1950s and 1960s. As with honey gathering, the nest tree was sometimes chopped down rather than risk a hazardous climb to remove the chicks. Even if the tree could be climbed the nest cavity might be too deep to reach the chicks, in which case a hole was hacked into the cavity from the outside. This practice selectively rendered the best (i.e. deep and successful) cavities unusable for future nesting.

COMPETITION FOR NEST SITES

The destruction of nesting habitat has exacerbated competition for nest sites among the several cavity-nesting species in the forest. Many of the injuries observed in territorial parrots may be the outcome of intense battling over the limited nest sites. Of eight nesting pairs studied since 1973, five have had one or both members sustain a permanent injury such as a broken limb or damaged eye. The selective advantage in successfully defending a good site must be considerable because there are significant risks in these territorial battles. For example, wounded birds are more susceptible to predation, and fighting birds may fall victim to predators because of inattentiveness to their surroundings. Intensive defence of nest sites may waste energy which would otherwise be available for general breeding activities. It may also require substantial time away from the nest, thereby allowing predators to take eggs or young chicks.

Aside from the honeybee there are two other species that are potential competitors for parrot nest sites: the Puerto Rican Screech Owl (*Otus nudipes*) and the Pearly-eyed Thrasher. The screech owl is the most common raptor in the Luquillo Forest. Although both it and the parrot utilize cavity nests, we have observed no competition between the two for nest sites because the owl begins egg-laying about six weeks later than the parrot. Also, the owl is nocturnal and the parrot diurnal, so there is little chance of a prospecting owl finding a parrot nest unguarded. This might occur only if a nest has been deserted through the loss of the adult female or some other catastrophe. There have been no failures of parrot nests attributable to owls.

The Pearly-eyed Thrasher, the only other common secondary hole-nesting bird (i.e. it does not excavate its own cavity) in the Luquillo Mountains, has recently become the most important cause of parrot nest failure. In fact, competition for nest sites and predation of parrot nests by thrashers are together probably an adequate explanation for the decline of the Puerto Rican Parrot during the last 30 years.

Pearly-eyed Thrashers were uncommon in Puerto Rico in the early 1900s, but were clearly increasing by the 1930s (Wetmore 1927; Danforth 1931). Thrashers expanded into the Luquillo Forest in appreciable numbers around 1950, and are now among the most abundant birds in the forest's palo colorado zone. The breeding seasons of the thrasher and parrot overlap, and thrashers are commonly exploring potential nest cavities while parrots are laying. As long as the adult parrot is on the nest, prospecting thrashers present no problems and are easily supplanted by the larger parrot. But parrots do not attend their nests constantly, which allows thrashers the opportunity to steal eggs and chicks. Between 1968 and 1975 all 19 parrot nests studied were threatened, at least to some degree, by thrashers. Five nests are known to have failed because of thrasher predation, and at least two and up to six successful nests would have been lost if we had not intervened. Parrots seem behaviourally ill-equipped to deal with thrashers, and this inability may be a reflection of the recent colonization of the Luquillo Forest by the thrasher.

A minimum of seven species of exotic parrots and parakeets are now breeding in Puerto Rico (Raffaele & Kepler, ms; pers. obs.). Although none occur yet within the Luquillo Forest, there are sizeable populations in the lowlands which surround the habitat of the Puerto Rican Parrot. Areas being considered as future re-introduction sites for the native parrot also have populations of these exotics. In the future introduced psittacines could become serious competitors with the Puerto Rican Parrot for food and nest sites.

RECENT EFFORTS TO REDUCE COMPETITION FOR NEST SITES

Since the present research programme began in 1968 a series of techniques has been developed for improving the reproductive success of Puerto Rican Parrots by reducing interspecific and intraspecific competition. These techniques include:

- close guarding of parrot nests from hides;
- improvement and maintenance of active nest sites;
- providing additional artificial nest sites for parrots;
- providing alternative sites for Pearly-eyed Thrashers; and
- protection of parrot nests from occupation by honeybees.

Each of these procedures is described below.

Initially, nests were guarded daily from dawn until dark by members of the research team. Most of the parrot eggs were taken to a field station for artificial incubation, with plaster dummy eggs left in the nest in their place. Some control of thrashers was attempted through removal of the birds, but this only caused additional exploration of the parrot nests by thrashers replacing the eliminated birds.

Today all active parrot nests are still watched as often as possible from dawn until dark from hides, especially during the most critical periods for the parrots, which are the exploration and selection of nest sites, egg-laying, hatching and fledging. This technique has proven invaluable in detecting problems (particularly with the thrashers) in time to make corrections, and has prevented the loss of many parrot nests.

Experiments by Snyder & Taapken (1977) revealed that the Pearly-eyed Thrasher prefers a shallower nest cavity than do parrots. Parrots have used some very deep holes, and even in the deepest they consistently seek the darkest, most sheltered corner of the floor. These experiments and observations led to the development of an artificial cavity with a depth acceptable to parrots but not favoured by thrashers. All nesting pairs of parrots are currently using artificial or 'improved' natural sites that incorporate a number of weather-proofing and anti-predator features (*Figure 1*). For example, natural cavities have been structurally reinforced and sealed against wet weather with fibreglass and polyester resin; furnished with dry, draining floors; deepened to at least 1.5m; fitted with baffles and angles so that eggs or chicks cannot be seen by predators looking in from the entrance, and have had their entrances constricted to prevent the entry of large predators such as Red-tailed Hawks (*Buteo jamaicensis*).

Natural cavities have a relatively short life expectancy (average 10–15 years), and when a site can no longer be repaired it is replaced with a long-lasting artificial nest fixed to the remains of the nest tree. These artificial boxes are fabricated from 25.4cm diameter polyvinyl chloride ('PVC') tubing, and have the improvements and predator-proofing described for the upgraded natural sites (*Figure 2*). Several box designs have been constructed. Typically the nest boxes are 210cm deep (180cm from nest entrance lip to floor) with a 60° bend 150cm below the lip. A roof with a 7.5cm overhang is bonded to the top of the nest tube. The entrance, measuring 13.5cm wide by 17.8cm high, is large enough to allow easy entry by the parrots but keeps larger predators out. A block of pine wood is fastened to the outside lower lip for parrots to chew, which is an important displacement behaviour during nest exploration and acceptance. A wire-mesh ladder leads from the entrance to the bottom of the nest. Inspection and manipulation of nest contents is facilitated by a 15cm wide by 18.5cm tall door near the bottom of the tube. The nest floor has several 8mm holes for drainage and fresh colorado tree bark is used as litter in the bottom. The boxes are given a final coat of brown-pigmented polyester resin, then sprinkled with colorado tree bark for a more natural appearance. Also, this roughened surface furnishes epiphytes with a better purchase on the box. Nest boxes are attached to live trees with aluminium straps and steel lag bolts and then adorned with bromeliads and orchids. To provide parrots with easy access to the boxes large vines are run from nearby trees to the nest entrances. Both the modified natural sites and the artificial cavities have been accepted by the wild pairs.

Because of the limited number of suitable natural cavities, since 1977 we have installed 25 polyvinyl chloride nest structures in the three remaining nesting areas to provide sites for new parrot pairs as they reach maturity. Pairs have been observed inspecting at least three sites but eggs have not yet been found in these boxes. Although there have continued to be cases of territorial pairs failing to breed, it does not appear to be attributable now to a scarcity of suitable nest sites.

Snyder & Taapken (1977) observed that after Pearly-eyed Thrashers settled on a nest site they rarely visited parrot nests and did a reasonably efficient job of excluding other prospecting thrashers, thereby giving significant protection to the parrots. To take

Figure 1: Adult male Puerto Rican Parrot on vine leading to entrance of improved nest cavity. The nest hollow has been sealed against rain with coats of polyester resin and fibreglass cloth, provided with baffles so that predators cannot see the bottom of the nest from the entrance, and deepened with a polyvinyl chloride tube extension. A foster chick reared in captivity is looking out of the entrance.

Figure 2: Polyvinyl chloride tube nest for Puerto Rican Parrots. Nest box is attached to palo colorado with aluminium straps. Nest entrance (arrow) is covered with piece of polyvinyl chloride to prevent the entry of honeybees during the non-breeding season of the parrots.

Figure 3: Artificial nest box for Pearly-eyed Thrashers. The box is secured to a tree within sight of an active Puerto Rican Parrot nest. In defending their own nests territorial thrashers exclude non-resident thrashers from the vicinity of the parrot nest.

Table 2: Summary of Pearly-eyed Thrasher visits to nests of Puerto Rican Parrots where alternative nest sites had or had not been provided for the thrasher. Nests of parrots were modified by deepening and providing baffles to block the view of eggs and chicks from the entrance. Data are from six parrot nests watched between 1973 and 1981.

Stage	Alternative thrasher box	Parrot nest modified	No. of days of observ.	No. of thrasher visits per day		Number of thrashers shot or frightened away per day
				Nest lip	Inside	
Pre-incubation	None	No	11	2.3	0.5	1.6
	Present	No	42	2.8	0.7	0.0
	Present	Yes	91	0.3	0.1	0.1
Incubation	None	No	31	0.8	0.2	0.4
	Present	No	26	0.9	0.2	0.6
	Present	Yes	145	0.2	0.0	0.1

advantage of this territorial behavior, each parrot nest has been provided with nearby artificial wooden nest boxes with dimensions preferred by thrashers (i.e. 23cm × 23cm × 65cm deep; *Figure 3*). These boxes are usually installed within 6m of the parrot nest, and are oriented so that the residents can spot intruding thrashers in the vicinity of the parrot nest.

Prospecting visits to parrot nests drop dramatically when parrot nests have been modified and thrashers are provided with alternative nest boxes (*Table 2*). For example, at the 'North Fork' nest in 1973, 26 thrashers were shot during the breeding season to ensure the safety of the parrot eggs. Thrasher visits to that nest were infrequent, but were the result of the continual turn-over of prospecting birds, rather than repeated visits by resident birds. In 1974 a nest box for thrashers was installed near the parrot nest and, although thrashers were not shot, the rate of thrasher visits initially remained at the 1973 level. These early visits took place while the resident thrashers were exploring their territory before they had finally settled on the nearby nest box. Once they had chosen the box visits to the parrot nest dropped almost to zero. With the incorporation of this strategy into the parrot conservation programme, a low frequency of visits by thrashers to all parrot nests is now the norm (mean = 0.2 visits/day), and nesting parrots have had no further problems from competition with thrashers.

Between 1973 and 1981 honeybees invaded parrot nests seven times during the non-breeding season, necessitating the removal of the hives before the next parrot breeding season. To prevent take-overs by swarming honeybees, all nest entrances are now sealed after the chicks fledge and re-opened before the start of the next breeding season.

Overall, parrot breeding success since 1973 has been averaging about 75 percent of the nests that reach the egg stage, compared with a historical rate of 11–26 percent. This improvement can be attributed largely to the prevention of thrasher depredations and to the maintenance of parrot nest sites in sound, dry condition. Additionally, since improving the parrots' natural sites and providing artificial ones, intraspecific fighting over nest sites has dropped substantially in frequency and intensity, and we have observed no parrots with injuries resulting from combat. The wild population is increasing and in 1982 there was a minimum of 29 birds.

FOOTNOTE

This research was conducted in collaboration with the Institute of Tropical Forestry, Southern Forest Experiment Station, US Forest Service, and the Commonwealth of Puerto Rico Department of Natural Resources

REFERENCES

DANFORTH, S. 1931. Puerto Rican ornithological records. *J. Dept. Agric. Puerto Rico* **15**, 33–106.

HILL, R. T. 1899. Notes on the forest conditions of Puerto Rico. *US Dept. Agric. Forestry Bull.* **25**, 1–48.

MURPHY, L. S. 1916. Forests of Porto Rico, past, present, and future, and their physical and economic environment. *US Dept. Agric. Bull.* **354**.

RAFFAELE, H. A. & KEPLER, C. B. (manuscript). The feral exotic avifauna of Puerto Rico.

SNYDER, N. F. R. 1977. Puerto Rican parrots and nest-site scarcity. *In:* Temple, S. A. (ed.) *Endangered birds—management techniques for preserving threatened species:* 47–53. Univ. Wisconsin, Madison.

SNYDER, N. F. R. & TAAPKEN, J. D. 1977. Puerto Rican parrots and nest predation by pearly-eyed thrashers. *In:* Temple, S. A. (ed.) *Endangered birds—management techniques for preserving threatened species:* 113–20. Univ. Wisconsin, Madison.

WADSWORTH, F. H. 1949. *The development of forest land resources of the Luquillo Mountains, Puerto Rico.* Ph.D. dissertation, Univ. Michigan, Ann Arbor.

WETMORE, A. 1927. The birds of Puerto Rico and the Virgin Islands. *N.Y. Acad. Sci. Scientific Survey Puerto Rico and the Virgin Islands* **9** (parts 3 & 4): 245–598.

WILEY, J. W. 1980. The Puerto Rican parrot (*Amazona vittata*): its decline and the program for its conservation. *In:* Pasquier, R. F. (ed.) Conservation of New World parrots: 133–159. *ICBP Tech. Publ. No.* 1.

ICBP Technical Publication No. 3, 1985

THE RESTORATION OF NONSUCH ISLAND AS A LIVING MUSEUM OF BERMUDA'S PRE-COLONIAL TERRESTRIAL BIOME

DAVID B. WINGATE

Department of Agriculture & Fisheries, P.O. Box 145, Flatts 3, Bermuda

ABSTRACT

Bermuda is the world's most densely populated oceanic island and its indigenous terrestrial ecosystem has been drastically modified. Nevertheless some of the endemic flora and fauna have survived, and the rediscovery of the endemic Bermuda Petrel or Cahow in 1951 resulted in the establishment of the 10ha Castle Harbour Island National Park. The largest island, Nonsuch (6ha), was selected in 1962 for restoration as a living museum of the terrestrial biome because of its isolation and because its diverse topography is representative of most Bermuda habitats. Nonsuch was a desert island when the project began, because it had been ravaged by feral goats, dogs and rats, and its forest of Bermuda Cedar had been killed by a scale insect epidemic between 1947 and 1951. Restoration has involved the elimination and/or exclusion of exotic species, the re-introduction of native fauna, reforestation with indigenous flora and the artificial creation of additional habitats and niches to accommodate endangered species. The island's small size and isolation have made it possible to eliminate or exclude most exotic species including rats, and the restored native flora, including the Bermuda Cedar, has thrived in the absence of exotic competitors. Species successfully re-introduced include the endemic race of the White-eyed Vireo from Bermuda's main island and the Yellow-crowned Night Heron from Florida. Other experimental re-introductions from abroad include the Green Turtle and the West Indian Top Shell. Habitat manipulation has included the construction of two ponds to allow the establishment of native wetland species. The development of a 'baffler' to eliminate nest-site competition with the White-tailed Tropicbird, and artificial burrows to increase the availability of nesting sites, have enabled the Cahow to increase, with the potential for a large population. The advantages and limitations of satellite islands for endangered species conservation are discussed in the light of the Nonsuch Island experience.

INTRODUCTION

Oceanic islands have been recognized as crucibles of rapid speciation in the grand process of evolution ever since the publication of Charles Darwin's *Origin of Species*. More recently, they have also been identified as having the highest species extinction rates following the era of rapid colonial expansion and subjugation of remote corners of the planet by European nation states since the fifteenth century (see IUCN Red Data Book Series including King 1981). Not so generally recognized is the fact that many of the unique and endangered species which still survive on islands are dependent for their survival not so much on the main islands of the group, where they evolved, but on small adjacent satellite islets which have fortuitously escaped the main thrust of man's exploitation and exotic introductions. This is especially true of seabirds and other marine-living species which are dependent on islands only for breeding. Cousin Island in the Seychelles and Boatswain Bird Island off Ascension Island are two examples which come immediately to mind, but there are numerous others.

This paper examines the potentials and limitations of small satellite islands for conserving endangered species or aiding their restoration by detailing the Cahow conservation project and the Nonsuch Island 'living museum' project which have been under way on the Castle Harbour Islands of Bermuda since 1951 and 1962, respectively.

These projects are possibly unique in that they have involved the successful long-term rehabilitation of an indigenous oceanic island ecosystem on a group of satellite islets where that ecosystem had been almost obliterated.

HISTORICAL BACKGROUND

The isolated oceanic island of Bermuda is located at 32°17'N and 64°45'W in the Atlantic. It is the most northerly coral atoll in the world, a circumstance made possible by the warming effects of the Gulf Stream. The emergent land area, totalling 53km², consists of one large and numerous closely-adjacent small islands on the southeastern rim of the shallowly-submerged Bermuda volcanic platform (775km²). The topography is hilly and is formed from beach-derived calcareous sediments deposited as dunes by the wind and cemented to form aeolionite (Bretz 1960; Land & Mackenzie 1970). Brackish, peat-filled marshes occupy some of the deeper interdune valleys, and small areas of mangrove occupy the sheltered coves.

At the time of its discovery by European explorers in the early sixteenth century, Bermuda had no indigenous human inhabitants or other mammals. The fauna was dominated by large nesting colonies of seabirds, notably the endemic Bermuda Petrel or Cahow (*Pterodroma cahow*), the Audubon Shearwater (*Puffinus lherminieri*), the White-tailed Tropicbird (*Phaethon lepturus catesbyi*), various terns (*Sterna* spp.), Noddies (*Anous stolidus*) and boobies (*Sula* spp.) (Lefroy 1877; Verrill 1902a,b). There were also a few extremely tame endemic landbirds and marshbirds, now known only from the early historic accounts and the largely undescribed subfossil remains preserved in limestone caves (Shufeldt 1916, 1922; Wetmore 1960, 1962; Wingate, unpubl.). The only non-flying, non-marine vertebrate was the Rock Lizard (*Eumeces longirostris*), an endemic skink (Wingate 1965). The relatively impoverished flora, with 8 percent endemism, was dominated by Bermuda Cedar (*Juniperus bermudiana*), Bermuda Palmetto (*Sabal bermudana*) and a few species of woody shrubs, which together formed a dense evergreen forest over most of the island (Britton 1918).

Permanent human settlement did not begin until 1612 when a British colony was established. By that date pigs (*Sus scrofa*), which had been released by Spanish voyagers about 1560, had already decimated the seabirds on the main island. *Rattus rattus* (and probably *Mus musculus*) arrived accidentally in 1613, and domestic cats and dogs were introduced at about the same time. The impact of these new predators, combined with extensive burning and deforestation for tobacco cultivation during the first two decades of settlement, reduced the seabird population to a pitiful remnant and caused the rapid extinction of most landbirds. Thereafter, changes in the native fauna and flora appear to have occurred at a more gradual pace. However, the period from 1680 to 1840 is poorly documented. The small size of Bermuda enabled the settlers to exterminate the feral pigs before 1630, and rabbits, goats and other ungulates were never permitted to become feral except on a few small harbour islands. The Brown Rat (*Rattus norvegicus*) probably became established in the eighteenth century, but was not specifically recorded before 1840 (Jones 1859).

Prior to the nineteenth century, the human population never grew beyond 10,000 and was supported primarily by shipbuilding and sea trading. Following the American War of Independence, however, Bermuda became of great strategic importance to Great Britain, and vast sums were spent in fortifying and garrisoning the island as a 'Gibraltar of the West'. This not only stimulated a rapid population growth which has continued up to the present, but laid the cultural foundation for a more sophisticated economy based initially on agriculture and tourism and more recently on tourism and international 'off-shore' company business (Hayward *et al*. 1981). The island presently enjoys one of the highest standards of living in the world, and threats to the remaining natural resources come mainly from the excesses of luxury developments, for there is no poor population dependent directly on Bermuda's resources for subsistence, as is the case with most developing nations.

The natural history has been well documented since 1840, at first by governors and officers in the British military and colonial service and later by local naturalists and scientists from American and European universities. Increased communication with the outside world resulted in a new wave of faunal and floral introductions during the Victorian era, but most of these were relatively benign and their impact on surviving native species was cumulative rather than catastrophic. The most notable exception was the House Sparrow (*Passer domesticus*), introduced in 1870–4, which caused a drastic decline in the native cavity-nesting Eastern Bluebird (*Sialia sialis*) through competition for nest-sites (Bradlee *et al*. 1931).

It was not until 1940 that the deterioration of Bermuda's remaining native heritage accelerated sufficiently to arouse public concern for conservation action. From 1941–43, as part of a wartime land-lease agreement between the United States and Great Britain, portions of the island were leased for the construction of an airport and naval base. The dredging for this destroyed many small islands, including Cooper's Island (31ha) in Castle Harbour, and increased Bermuda's land area by more than 6 percent. The opening of the new airport to commercial air traffic after the war stimulated an unprecedented growth in tourism and a boom in hotel and house construction, all of which was facilitated by modern construction equipment such as bulldozers. By 1982 new housing units were being built at a rate of over 300 per year, and Bermuda had become the most densely crowded oceanic island in the world, with a housing density of more than 5 per ha and a human population density of 12 per ha. The endemic *Juniperus bermudiana* forest remained dominant, forming a virtual monoculture until 1946, but two accidentally-introduced scale insect pests destroyed 96 percent of the forest before 1951 (Challinor & Wingate 1971). This disaster stimulated a major reforestation effort by the government, but the use of 'exotic' species was emphasized so heavily in this programme that naturalized introductions and garden ornamentals now comprise more than 90 percent of the flora biomass (Wingate, unpubl.).

The landbird fauna suffered equally dramatic changes after 1950 (Wingate 1973). The rapid urbanization and floral changes favoured natural colonization by Mourning Doves (*Zenaida macroura*) and Starlings (*Sturnus vulgaris*) from the American continent, and in 1957 the Kiskadee Flycatcher (*Pitangus sulphuratus*) was deliberately introduced from Trinidad as part of a government-sponsored biological control programme. All three species increased rapidly during the 1960s, while the native birds suffered a further decline. By 1980 urban habitat was sufficiently prevalent to allow a population explosion of the domestic pigeon (*Columba livia*), which now competes with tropicbirds for nest-sites in the coastal cliffs.

The loss of Bermuda's cedar forest and the unexpected rediscovery of the Cahow (Murphy & Mowbray 1951) became the chief catalyst for government involvement in conservation on Bermuda. Although non-government organizations such as the Bermuda National Trust and the Bermuda Audubon Society still play a primary role in the

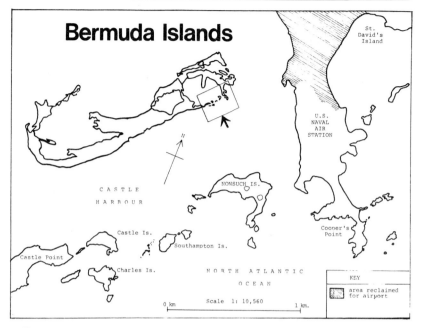

Figure 1: Location of Nonsuch Island and the other Castle Harbour Islands in Bermuda.

establishment of nature reserves, the government parks system now covers more than 242ha including the Castle Harbour group of islands (Jones 1979). In 1966 the government also established a Conservation Division within the Department of Agriculture and Fisheries with a mandate to protect and restore habitats of indigenous flora and fauna.

THE LIVING MUSEUM PROJECT ON NONSUCH ISLAND

Origins and Methods

The Castle Harbour Islands National Park consists of nine small islands totalling 10 ha within an area of approximately 2km² at the eastern end of Bermuda (*Figure 1*). Nonsuch Island (6ha) is the largest, and once served as a quarantine hospital for yellow fever. In 1962 I moved to that island as warden in charge of the conservation programme for the Cahow. The idea of managing Nonsuch as a living museum of Bermuda's pre-colonial terrestrial biome was conceived at that time, and after 1966 it received full government recognition and support as a project of the Conservation Division.

Nonsuch was ideally suited for such a project because its size and diverse topography made it potentially capable of representing most of the habitat types found on the main island of Bermuda. Also it was sufficiently isolated from the main island to permit the exclusion by quarantine measures of most of the exotic species which had become naturalized on the main island. Indeed, at that time many of the exotic introductions had not reached the Castle Harbour Islands, making them the only sanctuary for the Cahow and the last area on Bermuda where the endemic skink remained abundant.

Figure 2:   Bermuda Cedar forest above North Cove Beach on Nonsuch Island in 1945 before the scale insect epidemic.

Nevertheless when the project began Nonsuch itself was essentially a desert island. Its dense evergreen forest of *Juniperus bermudiana*, which had formed a monoculture until 1947 (*Figure 2*), had been totally destroyed by the scale insect epidemic before 1953. By 1962 free-roaming goats had further reduced the flora to a herbaceous cover virtually devoid of landbirds (*Figure 3*).

The living museum project is best described, therefore, as a long-term experiment in restoration. This restoration has been based on a review of all previous literature on the natural history of Bermuda, together with first-hand study of the few intact remnants of the indigenous floral communities on Bermuda's main island.

The work has proceeded in three ways:
- Introduced and naturalized 'exotics' have been eliminated by selective culling, insofar as possible, or prevented from colonizing by the imposition of quarantine measures.
- Missing elements of the indigenous floral and faunal communities have been re-introduced from Bermuda's main island or from other parts of their native range abroad, as necessary, and habitat restoration has been accelerated by mass reforestation with nursery-propagated native trees and shrubs, all planted in their appropriate niches at the appropriate spacing.
- Additional habitats and ecological niches have been created artificially by modifying the topography and making use of man-made structures and manipulative techniques.

Figure 3:   Dead cedar trees in the Central Vale of Nonsuch Island in 1963.

ELIMINATION AND EXCLUSION OF EXOTIC SPECIES

Flora
In 1962 Nonsuch had not yet been colonized by the majority of exotic trees, shrubs and forbs which now dominate Bermuda's main island. Indeed, only five naturalized species were sufficiently aggressive on Nonsuch to pose a threat to the native flora, and all were eliminated or reduced to insignificance by selective culling before 1966. Three of these continue to reach the island via bird droppings from a night roost of starlings, but are prevented from establishing by a continuing culling programme. A small number of cosmopolitan forbs and grasses which disperse by burrs or wind cannot be readily eliminated from the island, but these only compete with native species along the mown trailways.

Fauna
Of the 15 introduced terrestrial vertebrate species which are currently naturalized on Bermuda, only five species of birds, the two *Rattus* species and the Jamaican Anole (*Anolis grahami*) had succeeded in establishing on Nonsuch before the project began. Goats were removed from the island in 1962 and domestic dogs and cats are now excluded under the management regulations. Quarantine measures have effectively excluded the toad (*Bufo marinus*), two whistling frogs (*Eleutherodactylus johnstonei* and *E. gossei*), two species of lizard (*Anolis leachii* and *A. roquet*), and the House

Mouse (*Mus musculus*). Of these, only the toad regularly makes the water crossing by swimming from Cooper's Point at an average rate of three per year, but the immigrants have so far been detected by night searches and removed before they could reproduce.

Rats of both species have been totally eliminated by the use of bait stations containing anticoagulant rodenticides, either Warfarin in cornmeal or diphacinone in wax-impregnated blocks of grain. The stations are spaced at 40m intervals throughout the island. Because rats are strong swimmers and Nonsuch is only 170m from the nearest source of re-infestation on Cooper's Point, the island is recolonized at rare intervals. No attempt has been made to eliminate House Sparrows, Starlings or European Goldfinches (*Carduelis carduelis*) because they are too abundant and mobile. Starlings use the island mainly for cliff-nesting and more recently for night-roosting in the restored forest, but they feed mainly on the main island. House Sparrows are relatively uncommon in the restored native habitats and the Goldfinches, though abundant, occupy a seed-eating niche which became vacant with the extinction of native finches in the 17th century. The only introduced bird which poses a significant threat to the living museum project (by virtue of its potentially heavy predation on the endemic skink and a native cicada (*Tibicen sp.*)) is the Kiskadee. While Kiskadees are abundant on the main island they are relatively sedentary, and their rate of immigration to Nonsuch is sufficiently low (less than 50 per year) that it has been feasible to prevent them from establishing by shooting. Partly as a result of this control programme, Nonsuch is now the only place on Bermuda where the native cicada survives and the only place where the skink remains common.

An attempt to eliminate the lizard *Anolis grahami* by intensive culling was unsuccessful. Culling began in 1963 when the population was still small and localized, but was discontinued in 1972 when the forest cover became too dense and it became apparent that the population was increasing and spreading anyway. By 1980 the population density was comparable to that on the main island.

DELIBERATE RE-INTRODUCTIONS AND HABITAT RESTORATION

Flora

The most urgent task of the living museum project was a general reforestation programme to replace the windbreak and wildlife habitat lost when the cedar forest was destroyed. The dead cedars were left standing because of their historic and aesthetic interest, and for the windbreak and rigid support for other vegetation that their highly durable timber still provided. Most of these trees were still standing in 1982.

In 1966–67 two rapid-growing and evergreen exotic species, the Tamarisk (*Tamarix gallica*) and the Casuarina (*Casuarina equisetifolia*), were planted around the periphery of the island to provide a temporary windbreak while the slower-growing native species became established. These exotics were selected because they do not self-seed in Bermuda's soils and thus could easily be eliminated by girdling when they had served their purpose. The initial native planting of approximately 6000 trees and shrubs between 1963 and 1968 involved all species which are known to have formed the canopy of Bermuda's pre-colonial forest, except the Bermuda Cedar. The main species planted were Bermuda Palmetto, Bermuda Olivewood (*Cassine laneanum*), Sea Grape (*Coccoloba uvifera*), Buttonwood (*Conocarpus erecta*), Forestiera (*Forestiera segregata*), White Stopper (*Eugenia axillaris*), Jamaica Dogwood (*Dodonaea jamaicensis*) and Yellow-Wood (*Zanthoxylum flavum*). Cedars were not used in the initial planting because seedlings available at that time were not able to withstand scale insect attack. By 1970, however, a scale-tolerant strain, aided also by the deliberate introduction of specific biological control insects, was becoming prevalent again on the main island. Six

Figure 4: Advanced stage of reforestation on Nonsuch Island in 1983, with Bermuda Cedar
sapling in foreground and dense growth of Bermuda Palmetto, Bermuda Olivewood and White
Stopper.

hundred cedar seedlings were propagated from seed in that year and planted on
Nonsuch in 1972. Although less than half of these have survived, the healthiest
specimens have rapidly overtaken the other native trees in height and now form a
significant part of the canopy over 20 percent of the island.

It took ten years for the native plantings to form a thicket and another ten years before
a proper canopy was established (*Figure 4*), which then allowed the introduction of
more fragile and shade-loving native understorey species.

One measure of success of the reforestation effort since 1980 has been the vigorous
regeneration from seed of all species which is taking place naturally in the absence of
exotic plant competitors.

Fauna
With the exception of the Eastern Bluebird, the accelerated restoration of the native
forest by reforestation enabled surviving species of indigenous fauna to recover on, or
to recolonize Nonsuch Island naturally. Only the endemic race of the White-eyed Vireo
(*Vireo griseus bermudianus*) required deliberate re-introduction from Bermuda's mainland in order to achieve recolonization within a reasonable time. This sedentary
forest-dependent species died out on Nonsuch in 1963 due to the loss of the cedar forest
and the effects of a hurricane. Three pairs were netted on Bermuda's mainland and
released on Nonsuch in 1972. In the absence of mammal predators and Kiskadees the
vireo quickly attained a population density almost twice as high as in the equivalent

habitat on the main island. This population is also beginning to exhibit tamer behaviour and a greater tendency to feed on or near the ground.

Re-introductions are now being attempted with species which were extirpated entirely from Bermuda in the early colonial period. Herons of various species were recorded as resident by the early settlers. One of them has recently been identified from sub-fossils as an undescribed race of the Yellow-crowned Night Heron (*Nycticorax violacea*) which was adapted for feeding on land crabs. Between 1976 and 1978 44 nestlings of the nominate race were transported to Bermuda from Tampa Bay, Florida, and weaned into the wild at Nonsuch on a diet of native land crabs (*Gecarcinus lateralis*). A majority survived and remained resident, feeding almost exclusively on land crabs, which are abundant on the Castle Harbour Islands. Successful breeding was subsequently confirmed on a larger nature reserve on the main island in 1980, and at least 16 pairs were breeding there by 1982 (Wingate 1982).

Early historical accounts also confirm that Bermuda supported a major nesting rookery for Green Turtles (*Chelonia mydas*). Bermudan waters still support a large population of immigrant juveniles from elsewhere, but the population which used to breed on Bermuda was reduced to insignificant numbers as early as 1620 and was totally exterminated before the mid 1950s. An experimental attempt to re-establish a breeding rookery has been under way since 1967 by transplanting clutches of eggs from Tortuguero, Costa Rica, and allowing the hatchlings to swim to sea from South Beach on Nonsuch. Approximately 16,000 hatchlings were released to sea between 1967 and 1978, but it may take several more years before the outcome of the experiment is determined because Green Turtles may take up to 25 years to reach maturity. The Top Shell (*Cittarium pica*), a large marine gastropod, is another species which was apparently extirpated on Bermuda by over-harvesting before the nineteenth century. In 1982 82 specimens were re-introduced to the inter-tidal zone of Nonsuch from the northern Bahama Island (Bickley & Rand 1982). The survival rate during the first year was 79 percent, and all of the survivors grew rapidly. If the re-introduction proves successful, this species will once more provide shells for the native Land Hermit Crab (*Coenobita diogenes*), which has become increasingly rare on Bermuda since the original population of Top Shells was extirpated.

HABITAT RESTORATION WITH THE AID OF MAN-MADE STRUCTURES AND MANIPULATIVE PROCEDURES

Cahow Conservation Programme

The history of the Cahow has been thoroughly documented by Verrill (1902b), Murphy & Mowbray (1951), and Zimmerman (1975). Suffice it to say here that a combination of factors so decimated the Cahow population after human settlement of Bermuda that the birds were ultimately restricted to four of the smallest Castle Harbour Islands totalling less than 1ha. But even these islets were marginal breeding habitat because they were accessible to rats and were so eroded that they lacked sufficient soil to enable the birds to excavate nesting burrows. As a consequence the Cahows were forced to nest in the few deep natural holes and crevices in the cliffs, but these also happened to be the optimum breeding habitat of the White-tailed tropicbird. The resulting nest-site competition invariably favoured the later-nesting and larger Tropicbirds, and was causing the deaths of more than 60 percent of Cahow chicks when the population was first rediscovered.

In addition to the rat elimination procedure described above, two manipulative procedures have been developed since 1954 to overcome this problem and to increase the number of safe nesting sites (Wingate 1978). In 1954 Richard Thorsell and Louis Mowbray devised an artificial entrance for the Cahow nesting crevices which they called a 'baffler'. This excludes the larger Tropicbird by taking advantage of the size difference, in the same way that a 4cm entrance hole on a Bluebird nest-box excludes the larger Starling. Since 1961 the baffler has completely prevented mortality from tropicbirds, effectively trebling the Cahows' reproductive success.

The second manipulative technique has been the construction of artificial nesting burrows on the level tops of the Cahow nesting islets. This has been done in an effort to re-establish the original separation in breeding niches between the soil-burrowing Cahow and the cliff-nesting tropicbird. The burrows are made by excavating trenches into the soft rock with a mattock and roofing them over with concrete. Their major advantage is that they can be added as required, built anywhere and duplicated indefinitely until they completely saturate the smaller islands. Now that nest-sites are no longer a limiting factor and full protection is afforded from predators and competitors, the Cahow population has responded with a gradual but accelerating increase from 18 pairs in 1962 to 35 pairs in 1983. Ultimately, this increasing population is expected to spill over onto the larger neighbouring soil-covered islands such as Nonsuch, where soil-burrowing will once again become possible. Nonsuch Island could easily accommodate a naturally burrowing population in excess of 1000 pairs, but the use of artificial burrows could increase the potential to many thousands.

Creation of Marsh Habitats
One of the major factors limiting the scope of the living museum project when it began on Nonsuch was the lack of any natural marshland or ponds on the island. Fortuitously, the topography of Nonsuch made it possible to create two small ponds, one providing saltmarsh/mangrove habitat and the other freshwater marsh habitat, by comparatively minor enhancement of two natural swales or valleys. In 1975 the availability of funds and equipment made it possible to develop both ponds simultaneously. The slightly tidal saltmarsh pond was created by excavating an area of 3000m² behind the South Beach dune to a depth of 50cm below the water table. The freshwater pond (*Figure 5*) was created by deepening a natural swale between two hills, installing a 25×55m impermeable PVC liner, and covering it with a 40cm layer of soil. The resulting impermeable basin filled naturally with rainwater because the annual rainfall exceeds the evaporation rate on Bermuda (Macky 1957).

Completion of these ponds made it possible to introduce the native flora and fauna associated with such habitats on Bermuda's mainland, and was regarded as a necessary prerequisite to the re-introduction of the Yellow-crowned Night Heron. With the exception of the slow-growing mangroves, mature communities essentially indistinguishable from their counterparts on the main island were established in these ponds within three years (*Figure 5*). One species successfully introduced to the brackish pond in 1976 was an endemic killifish (*Fundulus bermudae*), known only from two other inland ponds on Bermuda (Beebe & TeeVan 1933).

At least two other rare and localized native species are expected to benefit significantly from the creation of these ponds. The Giant Land Crab (*Cardisoma quanhami*), limited to two small colonies in mainland mangrove swamps, was successfully introduced to the saltmarsh pond in 1980. The Moorhen (*Gallinula chloropus cachinnans*), which presently numbers less than 15 breeding pairs on the main island, is expected to breed on the freshwater pond if it can be deliberately introduced, and it may even colonize Nonsuch naturally. In the absence of mammalian predators its high reproductive potential could result in good breeding success, and provide a boost to the main population by dispersal from Nonsuch.

Figure 5: The freshwater pond on Nonsuch Island in 1983. Dense stands of *Typha* grow on the edge of the pond, with restored native forest behind (Bermuda Palmetto, Bermuda Olivewood and Bermuda Cedar). Dead trees are girdled Casuarinas.

DISCUSSION

There are two important features of the living museum nature reserve procedure described in this paper. Firstly, it is concerned with restoring a whole ecosystem rather than any particular component species. This is advantageous because of commensal relationships which might not be anticipated beforehand. Secondly, it exploits the isolation and manageable size of small islands in order to maintain, re-adjust or enhance species and habitats in a way that is either self-sustaining, or at least is sustainable in the long term with a minimum of energy input.

The achievements of the Cahow and living museum projects on the Castle Harbour Islands demonstrate that satellite islands can play a unique and vital role in the conservation of endangered species, provided that they are sufficiently isolated from the parent island and are representative of at least some of its habitats.

In the case of seabirds and other marine animals which need land only for breeding and which are colonial nesters, satellite islands are theoretically capable of supporting the entire world population. The Castle Harbour Islands, for example, are the only remaining breeding station for the Cahow, but clearly have the potential to support a large and viable population with the aid of bafflers and artificial burrows. These islands also support a stable population of more than 500 nesting pairs of White-tailed Tropicbird, which represents approximately 15 percent of Bermuda's total breeding population. This is significant, too, in view of the fact that the bulk of the population, which nests on cliffs on the main island, is declining.

Satellite islands can likewise perform a vital role as predator-free or competitor-free sanctuaries for species which are entirely terrestrial in habit. However, in this case the size of the island can be a serious limiting factor for two reasons:

Firstly, small size may limit the number or diversity of habitats, so precluding the establishment of certain species altogether. An extreme example of this problem would be a mountainous oceanic islet with a low satellite islet which could not be used as a refuge for endangered cloud forest species. Even Nonsuch, which is fairly representative of Bermuda, has problems of this type. Its small size places it entirely within the coastal distribution of the soil-burrowing Land Crab and greatly increases exposure to wind and salt spray during gales. Although these factors did not prevent the artificial creation of self-sustaining marshlands, it has precluded the creation of a typical inland valley habitat because some of the component species cannot survive the combined stress of salt spray and burrowing by Land Crabs. Such species could only be maintained on Nonsuch by continuous and intensive horticultural care, thus blurring the important distinction between a living museum nature reserve and a botanical garden or zoo.

Secondly, small size may preclude large species or species with large foraging territories from maintaining viable populations on the island. Although the endemic Rock Lizard has a sufficiently large population on Nonsuch to survive in isolation indefinitely, it is extremely doubtful whether the White-eyed Vireo could do the same if it became extinct elsewhere on Bermuda, because Nonsuch is capable of supporting only ten breeding pairs.

Notwithstanding this, small satellite islands free of predators or competitors can still provide a crucial *temporary* role in a crisis, even for species with large territories in relation to the size of the island. The case history of the re-introduction of Yellow-crowned Night Herons is pertinent here because it revealed that Nonsuch Island by itself was not sufficient to meet the herons' breeding requirements. The success of the project was ultimately dependent on their access to a much larger reserve on the main island.

If there is a moral in these examples, it is that satellite islands may assist in the preservation of unique island ecosystems, but they are no substitute for, and should not become an excuse to neglect, the greater challenge of establishing or rehabilitating large reserves on the parent islands themselves. Rather, the operative principles of the satellite island approach should be employed wherever possible in the design of those large reserves on the parent island.

In order to illustrate how this might be done I offer the following proposal involving Cooper's Headland on the eastern boundary of the Castle Harbour Islands National Park. Prior to its connection to St. David's Island with dredged fill during the construction of the airport in 1943 (*Figure 1*), Cooper's Point was an island of 31ha separated from St. David's Island by a water gap of 700m. This island was part of the land leased to the United States for a military base in 1941 for a period of 99 years. Much of it has since been bulldozed, quarried or otherwise modified for a variety of installations, including storage bunkers, a 4ha concrete water catchment and a NASA tracking station. Nevertheless, the headland has not been used for residential development, and even today the greater part of its varied coastline (which includes 7 percent of Bermuda's total beach area), together with about 2ha of sheltered inland habitat, remains unspoiled and dominated by native species.

Assuming that the formidable political and planning problems of handing Cooper's Island back to Bermuda and relocating its vital installations elsewhere could be overcome, it would be a comparatively easy engineering task thereafter to isolate the island again by dredging a wide channel through the reclaimed area. It could then be restored as an extension of the living museum project within an expanded Castle Harbour Islands National Park. Considering what has been achieved on Nonsuch with only one fifth of the land area, the potential of Cooper's Island as a living museum would be almost unlimited.

ACKNOWLEDGEMENTS

Since 1951 the Cahow conservation programme and some of the research on Nonsuch have been partly funded by grants from the New York Zoological Society. I have been employed as Conservation Officer in the Bermuda Government Department of Agriculture and Fisheries since 1966, and most of the work on Nonsuch Island has been supported by the Bermuda Government since then. The Caribbean Conservation Corporation provided funding and the family of Dr H. Clay Frick has played a leading role in the Green Turtle rookery restoration experiment since 1967. Numerous other friends and colleagues from the Department of Agriculture, the Bermuda Biological Station and research institutions abroad have provided encouragement, scientific advice and voluntary assistance over the years.

REFERENCES

BEEBE, W. & TEEVAN, J. 1933. *Field book of the shore fishes of Bermuda*. G. P. Putnam's Sons, New York & London.

BICKLEY, E. & RAND, T. G. 1982. Reintroduction of West Indian Top Shells on Bermuda. *Dept. Agric. & Fish. Bull.* **53**, 64–6.

BRADLEE, T. S., MOWBRAY, L. L. & EATON, W. F. 1931. A list of birds recorded from the Bermudas. *Proc. Boston Soc. Nat. Hist.* **39**, 279–382.

BRETZ, J. H. 1960. Bermuda: a partially drowned, late mature, pleistocene karst. *Bull. Geol. Soc. Amer.* **71**, 1729–54.

BRITTON, N. L. 1918. *Flora of Bermuda*. Hafner Publ. Co., New York & London.

CHALLINOR, D. & WINGATE, D. B. 1971. The struggle for survival of the Bermuda Cedar. *Biol. Conserv.* **3**, 220–2.

HAYWARD, S. J., GOMEZ, V. H. & STERRER, J. W. (eds.) 1981. *Bermuda's delicate balance*. Bermuda Biol. Station for Research Inc., Spec. Publ. No. 20.

JONES, J. M. 1859. *The naturalist in Bermuda*. Reeves & Turner, London.

JONES, J. H. 1979. *The guide to Bermuda's public parks and beaches*. Dept. Agric. & Fish. Publ., Island Press Ltd, Hamilton.

KING, W. B. 1981. *Endangered birds of the world: ICBP Bird Red Data Book*. Smithsonian Inst. Press, Washington DC.

LAND, L. S. & MACKENZIE, F. T. 1970. *Field guide to Bermuda's geology*. Bermuda Biol. Station for Research Inc., Spec. Publ. No. 4.

LEFROY, J. H. 1877. *Memorials of the discovery and early settlement of the Bermudas or Somers Islands 1511–1687: Compiled from the Colonial Records and other original sources*. Vols 1 & 2. Longmans, Green & Co., London.

MACKY, W. A. 1957. *The rainfall of Bermuda*. Bermuda Meteorological Office Technical Note No. 8.

MURPHY, R. C. & MOWBRAY, L. S. 1951. New light on the Cahow (*Pterodroma cahow*). *Auk* **68**, 266–80.

SHUFELDT, R. W. 1916. The bird caves of the Bermudas and their former inhabitants. *Ibis* **10**, 623–35.

SHUFELDT, R. W. 1922. A comparative study of some subfossil remains of birds from Bermuda, including the 'Cahow'. *Ann. Carnegie Mus.* **13**, 333–418.

VERRILL, A. E. 1902a. *The Bermuda Islands*. Reprinted from the Transactions of the Connecticut Acad. Sci., Vol. 11, with some changes. New Haven, Connecticut.

VERRILL, A. E. 1902b. The 'Cahow' of the Bermudas, an extinct bird. *Ann. Mag. Nat. Hist.* **7**, 26–31.

WETMORE, A. 1960. Pleistocene birds in Bermuda. *Smithsonian Misc. Collections* **140**, 1–11.

WETMORE, A. 1962. Notes on fossil and subfossil birds. *Smithsonian Misc. Collections* **145**, 1–17.

WINGATE, D. B. 1965. Terrestrial herpetofauna of Bermuda. *Herpetologica* **21**, 202–18.

WINGATE, D. B. 1973. *A checklist and guide to the birds of Bermuda*. Bermuda Press Ltd., Hamilton.

WINGATE, D. B. 1978. Excluding competitors from Bermuda Petrel nesting burrows. *In* Temple, S. A. (ed.) *Endangered Birds: management techniques for preserving threatened species*. Univ. Wisconsin Press, Madison.

WINGATE, D. B. 1982. Successful re-introduction of the Yellow-crowned Night Heron as a nesting resident on Bermuda. *Colonial Waterbirds* **5**, 104–15.

ZIMMERMAN, D. R. 1975. *To save a bird in peril*. Coward, McCann & Geoghegan Inc., New York.

MULTIPLE USE OF COUSIN ISLAND NATURE RESERVE, SEYCHELLES

A. W. Diamond

Edward Grey Institute of Field Ornithology, Zoology Department, South Parks Road, Oxford, England
(Present address: *Canadian Wildlife Service, Environment Canada, Ottawa K1A OE7, Canada*)

ABSTRACT

Cousin is the only internationally-owned nature reserve in the world. It was bought by ICBP in 1968, and gazetted a Special Reserve by the Seychelles Government in 1975. It is only 27ha in area, and 2km from its nearest neighbour, but maintains over a quarter of a million breeding seabirds of seven species, one endemic species of landbird and another found on only two other islands, and is the most important breeding ground of Hawksbill Turtles in the region.

The development of research, conservation and tourism on Cousin since 1968 is described, with particular attention to the interactions between these three uses and the constraints they place on each other. Likely future trends in all three are predicted, taking into account the most recent changes—the transfer of responsibility from the British Section of ICBP to the ICBP Secretariat, and the appointment of a Seychellois Chief Warden.

Cousin's three main uses—conservation, education (including tourism) and research—are clearly inter-dependent. Most time and money are devoted to tourism, whose profits subsidize conservation and research. The security of Cousin's future will depend on imaginative use of its potential for conservation and research as well as tourism, in ways that will generate income as well as knowledge and goodwill.

INTRODUCTION

In January 1968 the British Section of the International Council for Bird Preservation (ICBP) bought the tiny island of Cousin in the Seychelles and began to run it as a nature reserve. In 1970 the first resident ICBP representative—titled the 'Resident Scientific Administrator'—arrived with his family, beginning a dual scientific and conservation presence that has continued uninterrupted to the present day. The salary of that first scientist was provided by Lindblad Travel Inc. in a first link with tourism which has also continued uninterrupted ever since. Conservation, scientific research and tourism have thus played major roles on Cousin from the first. An examination of their respective influences on the management of the reserve may be useful not only in guiding future policy on Cousin, but also perhaps in the wider context of the management of small islands for conservation.

THE ISLAND

Cousin is described in detail in the Management Plan (Diamond 1975). It is a very small, low island, 27ha in area and 69m high. Physically it is dominated by a core of granite running directly into the sea on the rocky south and west coasts, but bordered to the north and east by a broad flat plain of phosphatic sandstone fringed by beaches of sand over beach-rock. The hill carries dense stands of low trees (*Euphorbia pyrifolia*), tall stands of native *Ficus* spp. and introduced *Eucalyptus camaldulensis* trees, patches of sedge, grass, herbs and creepers, and much bare rock. The flat land—known locally as 'plateau'—was planted early this century with coconuts (*Cocos nucifera*) and little natural vegetation remains, except a tiny patch of mangroves (mainly *Avicenna marina*) on the south coast. Tall clumps of *Casuarina equisetifolia* and patches of halophytic shrubs (*Scaevola taccada* and *Suriana maritima*) dominate the beach-crests. Fortunately the planting was not complete and a number of large native trees did remain in several parts of the island. Since ICBP acquired Cousin the plantation has become overgrown with regenerating trees of native species, notably *Pisonia grandis*, *Morinda citrifolia* and *Phyllanthus casticum*. Over half the 130 or so species known from the island are considered to have been introduced (Fosberg 1970).

The climate is humid and tropical; annual rainfall averages about 160cm, and monthly temperatures average between 24°C and 26°C (Prys-Jones & Diamond, in press). Southeast winds blow steadily and strongly from April to October or November, and northwest winds more erratically between December and February; most rain falls between October and February. An important effect of the seasonal change in wind direction through 180° is that the beach sand moves constantly between the east and north coasts; the resulting changes in beach topography have major consequences for nesting turtles (Diamond 1976) and for boat-landings, and prevent the construction of jetties.

Cousin is one of the smallest of the inhabited islands of the Seychelles; its population since 1968 has remained at four Seychellois estate workers and boatmen, plus the expatriate Scientific Administrator and his wife. In 1968 several of the Seychellois lived permanently on Cousin with their families, but the last family left in 1973 and the workers now keep their families on a larger island (where school and hospital are available) and see them chiefly at weekends. A feature of Cousin's Seychellois staff is its remarkable constancy; there have been no staff changes since 1974, a record unique on such an island. Cousin is about 2km from Praslin—the nearest large island—with which contact is maintained by boat (from both islands) and by radio. The nearest airstrip is on Praslin and connects with the main island of the group—Mahé—where there is an international airport.

The biota of Cousin is of course the justification for its unique status as the world's only internationally-owned nature reserve. One species of bird—the Seychelles Brush Warbler (*Acrocephalus sechellensis*)—(formerly *Bebrornis*, see Diamond 1980b)—is endemic to the island (though formerly slightly more widespread). Of the other landbirds endemic to Seychelles, the Seychelles Fody (*Foudia sechellarum*) occurs on only two other islands; the sunbird (*Nectarinia dussumieri*) is widespread in the archipelago; and the native race *rostrata* of the Madagascar Turtle Dove (*Streptopelia picturata*)—probably now extinct through hybridization with the introduced nominate race—was confined to Cousin and the neighbouring island of Cousine. The Madagascar race of the turtle dove, the Madagascar Fody (*F. madagascariensis*), the Barred Ground Dove (*Geopelia striata*), the Indian Myna (*Acridotheres tristis*), and the Barn Owl (*Tyto alba*) have become established following introduction to the Seychelles at various times. The landbird fauna thus contains one species endemic to the island, one found on only two other islands, a widespread Seychelles endemic, and five introduced species.

The seabird fauna is of less conservation interest, but is much more spectacular to the ordinary visitor. Seven species breed (four terns, two shearwaters and a tropicbird) and numbers exceed a third of a million birds a year, Black Noddies (*Anous tenuirostris*) alone contributing over 100,000 pairs (Diamond & Houston 1974). White or Fairy Terns (*Gygis alba*) breed commonly, and Cousin is now perhaps the only island in Seychelles where they abound as they did elsewhere in the islands before the introduction of Barn Owls (*Tyto alba*) to control rats in the early 1950s, an introduction which apparently led to the decimation or extinction of other Seychelles populations of Fairy Terns (Penny 1974).

Other notable components of the fauna include several species of skink, gecko and shore- and land-crabs, a blind-snake and giant millipedes. Between 20 and 30 Hawksbill Turtles (*Eretmochelys imbricata*) lay on the beaches each year, and Cousin is recognized as one of the most important breeding sites in the western Indian Ocean of this endangered species (Frazier 1974, 1975; Diamond 1976; Garnett 1978; Brooke & Garnett 1983). A small herd of Giant Tortoises (*Geochelone gigantea*), initially captive but now free-ranging, are a considerable tourist attraction but their conservation interest depends on their taxonomic status which is clouded in doubt (Diamond 1980a). The only mammals are fruit-bats (*Pteropus seychellensis*) which commute from Praslin to feed on ripe fruits, and the Black-naped Hare (*Lepus nigricollis*) introduced from India. Neither rats nor cats, which have wiped out so many native bird populations elsewhere in the islands (Diamond & Feare 1980), are established on Cousin.

CONSERVATION

Cousin's conservation interest was of course the prime reason for its acquisition by ICBP, and conservation remains the first priority. But conservation of what? The endemic warbler has always been cited as the most important conservation priority, but the fody, turtle dove, the seabirds and the vegetation have always been recognized as of great interest in their own right. It was not long after the reserve was established that its importance as a breeding ground for Hawksbill Turtles was recognized, and this must now be recognized as an additional major focus of conservation (Diamond 1980a).

One of the initial goals of management was to re-create the original vegetation. By 'original' was meant, most probably, the vegetation in existence before Europeans colonized the island; it is not known clearly what this was, other than that it was a dense woodland of some sort, but Fosberg (1970) suggested that it was mainly a mature forest of *Pisonia grandis*. The primary goal of management, however, was the conservation, and if possible the increase, of the tiny population of Brush Warblers. These were thought to be limited chiefly by lack of habitat; it was assumed that the 'original' habitat would hold more warblers, and so the way to increase their numbers was to allow the original habitat to regenerate. This was done by stopping the regular clearing of bush regenerating under the coconut trees, and continuing to collect fallen coconuts chiefly as a conservation measure—to prevent regeneration of coconut trees—and only incidentally as a source of income. The urgent goal of increasing warbler numbers therefore coincided with a less well-defined, and clearly less urgent, objective of recreating the original vegetation of the island. No conflict between the various goals of conservation occurred so long as the assumption on which they were all based—essentially that the native vegetation would hold maximum numbers of all the native birds—remained true. Indeed so comfortably did the various objectives seem to coincide that it proved difficult for ICBP's two management bodies (an Advisory Panel in London, and a Local Committee in Seychelles) to decide on an order of priorities when it became necessary to clarify these in order to produce a Management Plan (Diamond 1975). The order of priorities agreed then was:

- To maintain the maximum possible populations of three endemic landbirds—Brush Warbler, Fody and Turtle Dove.
- Within this framework to restore the original habitats of the island. Where this seems to conflict with the primary objective, the primary objective takes precedence.
- To make full use of the island's educational and research potential.

In 1980 two further primary objectives were added (Diamond 1980a), to be placed in priority between items 2 and 3 above:

- To maintain the maximum possible population of Hawksbill Turtles on and around the island.
- To maintain the maximum possible populations of seabirds breeding on the island.

The order of priority of conservation objectives thus became in summary: native landbirds (excluding sunbirds); habitat regeneration; turtles; seabirds.

It became necessary to define clearly an order of priorities because the early work on the Brush Warbler suggested that it might achieve its highest densities not in climax *Pisonia* forest, as had been assumed, but in secondary, regenerating *Morinda-Pisonia* woodland or scrub (Diamond, unpub.). Later research on the warblers' habitat preferences has confirmed this suggestion (Bathe & Bathe 1982; Anon. 1982) and justified the clear ordering of priorities embodied in the Management Plan. Research is being continued to clarify the species' habitat requirements more precisely before any management action is taken.

Whatever the possible shortcomings of the conceptual basis for vegetation regeneration as a tool for conserving Brush Warblers, it has so far been spectacularly successful. Warbler numbers increased from 30 in 1959 to about 300 in 1981 (Anon. 1982, Bathe & Bathe 1982); the increase was linear, rather than sigmoidal, suggesting that it was due to a steady increase in available habitat (Diamond 1980b). Bathe & Bathe concluded that the population levelled off between 1978 and 1981, but their data are open to alternative interpretations; certainly, as they showed very clearly, between 1975 and 1981 there had been a marked re-distribution of warbler territories among the available habitats. The 'laissez-faire' policy of allowing vegetation to regenerate has been abundantly vindicated by the increase not only in warblers but also in Seychelles Fodies, though the evidence for this increase is subjective and is likely to remain so until a census technique for this very difficult species can be devised.

Conservation of landbirds by habitat management has thus been successful in raising numbers of two of the threatened endemic species. It has also brought the vegetation closer to its presumed primeval state. It has not succeeded in preventing the probable extinction of the endemic race of the turtle dove, though it was not expected to because this bird was doomed not through habitat loss, but by hybridization with its introduced relative, which no technique possible in the circumstances could have prevented. Reservations about this management policy are expressed for the future rather than the past, and concern not only the possibility that the climax vegetation—if it exists or is ever achieved—may hold less landbirds than an arrested succession would, but also that it might carry fewer seabirds, particularly Brown Noddies (*Anous stolidus*) which nest chiefly in the crowns of coconut trees (Diamond & Houston 1974; Bathe 1982a).

The other major conservation programme has protected the nests and breeding

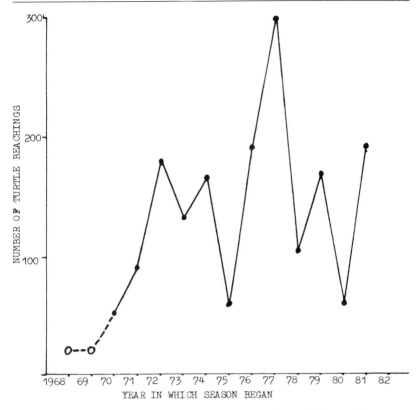

Figure 1: Number of turtle beachings recorded in each season since establishment of the reserve. Hollow circles and dashed lines refer to hearsay evidence from local staff; later figures (solid circles, continuous line) are results of supervised beach patrols. Data from records of Cousin Island Research Station.

females of Hawksbill Turtles from poaching (Diamond 1976; Garnett 1978; Brooke & Garnett 1983). The number of turtle beachings increased dramatically in the first few years of regular beach-patrols. Since then it has shown no trend but instead has fluctuated widely around an apparently fairly constant level (*Figure 1*). Although set up primarily to conserve birds, Cousin has from the beginning been run as a nature reserve rather than simply as a bird reserve, and has certainly made an important contribution to turtle conservation in the region. Turtle conservation consumes a high proportion of the time and efforts of the reserve staff throughout the turtle breeding season (September to March) and is likely to continue to do so as long as the programme is successful.

ICBP has always given complete protection to the whole Cousin environment, including those parts of the surrounding reef over which effective protection can be exercised. Collecting on the reef, and even picking up dead shells washed ashore, has been totally forbidden; the result is easily seen subjectively in a profusion of shells of many species on the beach and one of the richest reef biotas in Seychelles (Robertson 1972; Frazier & Polunin 1973), but no attempt has been made to monitor this aspect of the conservation programme.

TOURISM

There was no tourist industry as such when ICBP bought Cousin, the few visitors to Seychelles being businessmen or independent travellers rather than tourists. But the islands even then were on the brink of developing a tourist industry, of which a significant proportion was to be directed towards the wildlife attractions. The cruise ship *Lindblad Explorer* was the first large-scale tourist enterprise to exploit this market, and needed to be able to visit Cousin. ICBP would not allow this unless they could install their own full-time warden to control the visitors, and agreed with Linblad Travel Inc. to allow visits by the cruise ship if Lindblad would provide funds for a warden. This they did, and ICBP took the opportunity to appoint a scientist who could carry out research as well as guide and control tourists. These visits took place in 1970 and in 1971, when an international airport was opened on Mahé and it was no longer profitable for the cruise ship to visit Seychelles. Visitors then began to reach Cousin by small boat from Mahé or from Praslin, normally as part of a package tour or holiday.

The pattern of visiting and type of visitor changed drastically when the cruise ship gave way to the package tour. Most of the cruise passengers were interested in wildlife, knew that they were coming to a nature reserve, and were guided on board and ashore by knowledgeable naturalists who themselves were often committed conservationists. They came ashore in very large parties, often up to 80 at a time, and toured the island in groups of up to 20. Such parties came to Cousin at widely spaced intervals, and in between there were only sporadic visits by very small numbers of local visitors from within Seychelles. Package tours, on the other hand, bring parties of up to 20 at a time, often several times a day on the three days a week when the island is open to visitors. Many of the visitors do not even know that they are coming to a nature reserve, and most start their tour with no particular interest in wildlife. The couriers who accompany them often have less knowledge of, or interest in, Cousin and its wildlife than even their clients do. To increase the value of the tour, as well as to minimize the disturbance they cause, all parties are shown around the island by a member of the staff.

The rare but large and demanding parties which first visited Cousin probably had more effect on the wildlife than the later, smaller but more regular and less interested groups. The only bird on which an effect could be clearly seen is the Fairy or White Tern (*Gygis alba*), which breeds low down near paths, and often allows a very close approach. Its single egg is precariously balanced on a flimsy perch, and if not knocked to the ground when its startled parent flies off, it then becomes vulnerable to predation by skinks (*Mabuya* spp.) and Seychelles Fodies. The large parties of visitors frightened many Fairy Terns off their eggs, and because they came so rarely the birds did not have the opportunity to become habituated to them. An early study by Mary Penny (the wife of the first Scientific Administrator) suggested that Fairy Terns nesting along paths used by visitors had lower breeding success than those on paths closed to the public (C. M. Penny, unpub.). This led to the imposition of a strict limit of 20 people allowed ashore at any one time. This limit has remained in force long after the pattern of visiting had changed. Not until 1975–76 was a serious attempt made to see whether the new pattern affected Fairy Tern breeding success. It was concluded that there was no demonstrable effect along the paths open to the public (Wilson 1982). In 1980–81 a further study found that proximity to a tourist path did not influence the selection of breeding sites by the terns (Bathe 1982b).

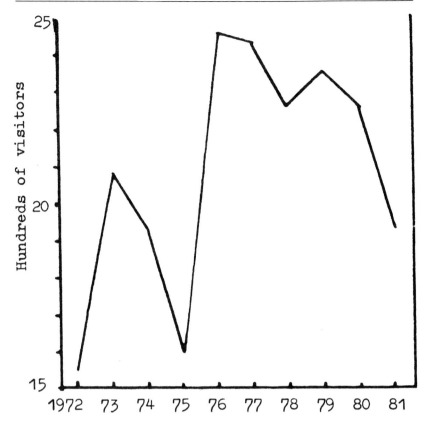

Figure 2: Annual number of visitors to Cousin Island Nature Reserve since the opening of the international airport on Mahé.

Thus the only demonstrably harmful effect of tourism on conservation—reduced breeding success of Fairy Terns—no longer seems to occur. Less tangible conflicts concern mainly the time and resources taken up in administering the island's tourist trade, and in shepherding the visitors ashore, around the island and back to their boat. (An important part of the conservation policy in relation to tourism is that all visitors shall be landed in a Cousin boat; this is to prevent the introduction of rats and other noxious aliens). The work that might be done by island staff if they were not looking after tourists includes research, administration, maintenance, beach patrols, estate work and other conservation work.

Numbers visiting the island have fluctuated unpredictably in the past (*Figure 2*), and will no doubt continue to do so in the future. This will continue to make financial planning very difficult so long as income from visitors remains a major proportion of total income. No serious effort has been made to promote tourism on Cousin, either within Seychelles or abroad.

RESEARCH

ICBP's early decision to maintain a scientific as well as a conservation presence on Cousin reflected the need for a solid knowledge of the island's biota on which to build sound conservation policies. A research committee set up to guide the Pennys' research soon fell into disuse, and research by successive Scientific Administrators was controlled only very loosely and so reflected their personal interests.

Most of the research carried out on Cousin has been done by the Scientific Administrators or their wives. A few projects have been carried out by visiting scientists, staying from a few weeks to as long as six months, occasionally involving short-term university expeditions. Most of these have received prior approval from ICBP, but very few have been at ICBP's invitation or been projects of direct and immediate conservation interest (Fosberg's (1970) vegetation report; Frazier & Polunin's (1973) reef survey; and Kirk's (1981) study of the hare, have been notable exceptions). Some of the research has been published in scientific journals (see Appendix 1), but most results, especially from Scientific Administrators of Cousin, now appear in an internal ICBP series of 'Technical Reports' from the Cousin Island Research Station (see Appendix 2).

The physical conditions for carrying out research were much improved in 1973 when a new house and laboratory (the latter donated by Prof. Rudolf Geigy) were opened. The laboratory has ample working space and living accommodation for visiting scientists. But the main problems hindering research are not on Cousin at all; they lie thousands of miles away in the committees which allocate research grants to biologists in Europe and North America. It is extremely difficult to raise money for research so far away, and especially so for work oriented more towards practical conservation than to prestige science. Clearly there are enough dedicated people prepared to work on a shoestring budget to have kept a trickle of scientists passing through Cousin, but the unquestioned potential for long-term work in this uniquely tractable island ecosystem has not yet been realized.

Many of the research priorities identified in ICBP's Management Plan and its revision (Diamond 1975, 1980a) have not been achieved, even by ICBP's own staff. Yet a commendable amount of research has been done; the published papers and Technical Reports (see Appendices 1 and 2, respectively) attest to that, and as much material lies unworked in many salt-stained notebooks. All of this, whether or not identified beforehand as an ICBP priority project, has contributed to our knowledge of the Cousin ecosystem and its biota, and provides a useful basis for future work. There are acute problems in trying to co-ordinate, much less direct, research by gifted and ambitious scientists so far away who are dazzled by research opportunities often much more attractive than those suggested by the remote advisers in ICBP. Staff recruited primarily from the ranks of researchers can only be expected to follow their own interests to a large extent. In future, those projects seen by ICBP as essential will have to be done mostly on a project basis with funding and recruitment from outside.

EDUCATION

Most of the education carried out on Cousin has been of tourists as they go around the island with a guide; the bulk of the education programme has thus been incorporated into the tourist section of the island's work, and has taken no extra resources. However, most Scientific Administrators have recognized the importance of educating the Seychellois public not only about Cousin, but also about conservation in the islands in general. The first Scientific Administrator, M. J. Penny, was particularly active in this respect, addressing schools, broadcasting on Radio Seychelles, writing a book (Penny

1974) and newspaper articles, and even composing and recording a popular song ('Follow the wind to Cousin') which spent some time in the islands' hit parade. His successors have frequently talked to schools, to the Teachers' Training College and to the Police Training School, and have encouraged free visits by parties of local school-children.

COUSIN'S ROLE IN SEYCHELLES

Cousin's first Scientific Administrator was the only trained biologist in the islands apart from Agriculture Department staff. He was therefore useful to the government for advice on conservation matters affecting other islands, and for many years the biologist on Cousin was often called upon to help with conservation and research problems elsewhere in Seychelles. ICBP has always valued its contribution to the islands in this respect, and the tradition of using its Cousin staff in this way has continued through several changes of government and in spite of the establishment on Mahé of a Conservation Department with qualified Seychellois staff. Visiting researchers have often kept close contact with those on Cousin, and the island has undoubtedly played a useful role as a base and as a source of scientific contact for many of the researchers who have been active in the islands during the last decade.

THE FUTURE

The future uses to which Cousin will be put will continue to be constrained by financial problems. The capital raised to buy the island was never enough to provide sufficient annual income in perpetuity. Thus capital has been run down over the years, sup-plemented from time to time by grants (notably from the World Wildlife Fund and the Fauna and Flora Preservation Society), income from coconuts and landing fees from visitors. The capital is now almost exhausted, and the regular World Wildlife Fund grant withdrawn, so unless a major endowment can be secured Cousin will have to be run within a much tighter budget, and with more emphasis on raising income. The tourist side of the operation will therefore become more important, consuming more of the time and resources of the staff and leaving less for research. This, in turn, will require a major effort to attract researchers on a project basis, funded from outside ICBP's budget for running Cousin. Conservation will remain the main priority in an overall policy sense, but much more of the island's resources will have to be devoted to tourism (and other activities that produce an income) than has been the case in the past. This will certainly strain conservation resources at some times of year; for example, turtle patrols will have to be reduced, which will make the turtles more vulnerable to poaching and will curtail the long-term research programme quite seriously.

The recent transfer of responsibility for Cousin from ICBP (British Section) to ICBP International coincides with a re-assessment of the respective roles of research, conser-vation and tourism in the management of the reserve. In late 1982 the staff structure was also changed. The post of Scientific Administrator was replaced by the posts of Warden and Research Officer, these being filled by a Seychellois and a British biologist, respectively. Likely future trends for each of the island's main uses can be summarised as follows:

Conservation
Protection of the island from invasion by exotic predators and competitors is the most essential part of conservation management. Indian Mynas (*Acridotheres tristis*) will need to be monitored closely for possible effects on the native biota, and if these are

found they may have to be controlled. Control of Barn Owls—as always, on a modest scale—will need to be continued. Further research on habitat management may indicate a need for selective felling to maintain sufficient successional vegetation for Brush Warblers. For this a critical re-evaluation of the objectives will probably be required: to encourage a maximum warbler population and accept rotational felling of woodland *or* to accept a large but not maximum warbler population and minimal interference with the current succession.

Turtle conservation on Cousin is expensive in time and facilities such as boats, engines and radios. To date, almost all this cost has been borne by ICBP (with grants from the Fauna and Flora Preservation Society), but since this programme so clearly benefits a natural resource of great value to the Seychelles as a whole, it is reasonable to expect some contribution in the future from the Seychelles Government and from other international conservation bodies more directly concerned with turtles than ICBP. Secondment of a Parks Ranger to Cousin throughout the turtle season would be one way of ensuring adequate protection for the nesting animals and, if the ranger were a trainee, could very usefully be repaid by the training given to the ranger by Cousin staff. Closer links between Cousin's conservation work and that of the other bodies involved in conservation in Seychelles (Government, Seychelles Islands Foundation, Royal Society for Nature Conservation, International Union for the Conservation of Nature and Natural Resources, World Wildlife Fund, etc.) would clearly be beneficial to all.

Tourism

Tourism will continue to loom large in Cousin's future, both as a source of income and as a target for education. Tourists were accepted initially with some reluctance, but since they are now a welcome necessity they should not only be accepted but encouraged and used to a much greater extent than formerly for furthering conservation goals. The tourist market will exercise considerable influence in Seychelles for some time to come, and if that influence can continue to be shaped, as it has in the past, to improve the climate for conservation, such opportunities should be exploited to the full. A serious and professional effort to promote tourism on Cousin is essential to the island's future.

Research

Research will continue to be carried out partly by ICBP staff resident on the island and partly by visiting scientists. But the balance between the two is likely to shift. If the predicted trends in conservation and tourist activities materialize, more staff time will be devoted to those and less will be available for research. It is also likely that the Research Officer will be concerned more with practical conservation work and directed monitoring work, than with furthering a research career. In view of the poor correspondence in the past between research priorities identified by ICBP and the research actually carried out, ICBP will have to move beyond merely identifying priorities to ensuring that they are met. Routine monitoring work can be included in the resident staff's terms of reference; more demanding or time-consuming work will have to be commissioned, and the funds raised and personnel recruited, by ICBP. Such projects will of course have to compete with others within ICBP's programme.

There is some scope for funding essential research work from outside on a project basis. The turtle research, for example, would be more appropriately supported by other bodies; to date, apart from occasional relatively small grants by the Fauna and Flora Preservation Society, ICBP (British Section) has supported this work almost unaided. Detailed research projects suitable for Ph.D theses abound, several of them of direct conservation interest (e.g. Brush Warbler and Seychelles Fody life-histories, social behaviour and habitat preferences). Successful pursuit of this kind of research goal requires the interest of an established university department, which unfortunately remains to be kindled to a fiercer heat than that of short-term undergraduate expeditions.

APPENDIX 1

List (to July 1983) of all scientific publications based on work done wholly or partly on Cousin. Full bibliographic details of publications marked with an asterisk are given in the References.

ANON. 1982.*

BOURNE, W. R. P., BOGAN, J. A., BULLOCK, D., DIAMOND, A. W. & FEARE, C. J. 1977a. Tern diseases and deformities in the Seychelles. *Auk* **94**, 405.

BOURNE, W. R. P., BOGAN, J. A., BULLOCK, D., DIAMOND, A. W. & FEARE, C. J. 1977b. Abnormal terns, sick shorebirds, chlorinated hydrocarbons and arboviruses in the Indian Ocean. *Mar. Poll. Bull.* **8**, 154–158.

BROOKE, M. de L. 1981a. Size as a factor influencing the ownership of copulation burrows of the ghost crab (*Ocypode ceratophthalmus*). *Zeit. Tierpsych.* **55**, 63–78.

BROOKE, M. de L. 1981b. The nesting biology of the Seychelles potter wasp *Eumenes alluaudi* Perez. *Ecol. Entom.* **6**, 365–377.

BROOKE, M. de L. & GARNETT, M. C. 1983.*

BROOKE, M. de L. & HOUSTON, D. 1983. The biology and biomass of the skinks *Mabuya sechellensis* and *M. wrightii* on Cousin Island, Seychelles. *J. Zool. Lond.* **200**, 179–95.

CROOK, J. H. 1961. The Fodies (Ploceinae) of the Seychelles Islands. *Ibis* **103a**, 517–548.

DIAMOND, A. W. 1975.*

DIAMOND, A. W. 1976a. Subannual breeding and moult cycles in the Bridled Tern *Sterna anaethetus* in the Seychelles. *Ibis* **118**, 414–419.

DIAMOND, A. W. 1976b.*

DIAMOND, A. W. 1978. Feeding strategies and population size in tropical seabirds. *Amer. Natur.* **112**, 215–223.

DIAMOND, A. W. 1980a.*

DIAMOND, A. W. 1980b.*

FEARE, C. J. 1976. Desertion and abnormal development in a colony of Sooty Terns *Sterna fuscata* infested by virus-infected ticks. *Ibis* **113**, 112–115.

FRAZIER, J. 1974.*

FRAZIER, J. 1975.*

FRAZIER, J. G. 1979. Marine turtle management in Seychelles: a case-study. *Envir. Cons.* **6**, 225–230.

FRAZIER, J. G. 1980. Exploitation of marine turtles in the Indian Ocean. *Human Ecol.* **8**, 329–370.

HELLAWELL, C. E. 1979. *The Seychelles Magpie Robin on Aride*. ICBP (British Section) Research Report.

HOUSTON, D. C. 1979. Why do Fairy Terns *Gygis alba* not build nests? *Ibis* **121**, 102–104.

PENNY, M. J. 1974.*

PERCY, LORD R. 1970. Cousin Island Nature Reserve in the Seychelles. *Biol. Cons.* **2**, 225–227.

PRYS-JONES, R. P. & DIAMOND, A. W. (in press). Ecology of land birds on granite and coral islands. *In* Stoddart, D. E. (ed.) Biogeography and ecology of the Seychelle islands. Junk, the Hague.

ROBERTSON, I. 1972.*

WATSON, J. 1978. *The Seychelles Magpie Robin (Copsychus sechellarum)*. WWF Project 1590: Final Report 1(a).

APPENDIX 2

List (to 1 February 1983) of Cousin Island Research Station Technical Reports. Full bibliographic details of publications marked with an asterisk are given in the References.

FOSBERG, F. R. 1970.*

LLOYD, D. E. B. 1971. Survey of the giant tenebrionid beetle *Pulposipes herculeanus* on Frigate Island, November 1971.

FRAZIER, J. G. & POLUNIN, N. C. 1973.*

DIAMOND, A. W. 1971. Report on a visit to Fregate Island, L'Ilot and St. Marie, 17–20 November 1973.

LLOYD, D. E. B. 1973. Habitat utilisation by land birds of Cousin Island and the Seychelles. (Incomplete).

DIAMOND, A. W. & HOUSTON, D. 1974.*

WILSON, J. & WILSON, R. 1976. A survey of the Seychelles Magpie Robin on Frigate Island, May 1976.

DIAMOND, A. W. 1976. Monitoring vegetation changes on Cousin Island.

COWX, D. 1978. Observations on the Giant Tortoise population on Cousin, August 1978.

GARNETT, M. C. 1978.*

HARTLEY, N. J. W. 1979. Monitoring vegetation changes on Cousin Island—a comparative summary of surveys to establish changes.

WILSON, J. R. 1980. Observations of shearwaters on Cousin Island Jan. 1975–June 1976.

WILSON, J. R. 1980. Ornithological observations on Cousin Island, Jan. 1975–June 1976. 2. Tropic birds, boobies, and frigates.

WILSON, J. R. 1980. Ibid. 3. Skuas, gulls and terns (except Fairy Terns Gygis alba).

KIRK, D. A. 1981.*

BATHE, G. M. & H. V. 1982. A record of the distribution of vascular plants on Cousin Island, 1980/81.

BATHE, G. M. & H. V. 1982. The distribution and feeding ecology of the Giant Tortoise (Geochelone gigantea) on Cousin Island, Seychelles.

BATHE, G. M. & H. V. 1982.*

BATHE, H. V. 1982.*

WILSON, J. R. 1982.*

SORENSEN, A. E. 1982. The spatial distribution and foraging behaviour of the Seychelles Brush Warbler (Acrocephalus (Bebrornis) sechellensis).

BATHE, H. V. 1982.*

BATHE, G. M. 1982. The terrestrial fauna of Cousin Island, Seychelles. Insecta: Odonata.

GARNETT, M. C. 1977. The effect of Giant Tortoises (Geochelone gigantea) on the vegetation and the density of nesting seabirds, on Cousin Island, Seychelles.

BATHE, G. M. 1982. The terrestrial fauna of Cousin Island, Seychelles. Insecta: Formicidae (ants).

BATHE, H. & G. 1982. Feeding studies of three endemic landbirds, Acrocephalus sechellensis, Foudia sechellarum, and Nectarinia dussumieri, on Cousin Island, Seychelles.

HOTTINGER, L. 1980. Apatitic cementation of coral sands produced by bird excrements.

PHILLIPS, J. 1982. Report on the gale of 3–4 July 1982.

BATHE, G. M. 1982. The terrestrial fauna of Cousin Island, Seychelles. Apoidea (bees).

WILSON, J. R. 1982. The breeding biology of Fairy Terns (Gygis alba) on Cousin Island, Seychelles. Part I.

WILSON, J. R. 1982. The breeding biology of Fairy Terns (Gygis alba) on Cousin Island, Seychelles. Part II.

REFERENCES

(*Signifies an unpublished report in the Cousin Island Technical Report series; see Appendix 2).

ANON. 1982. The brush warbler and the island sanctuary. New Scientist 95, 486.

BATHE, G. M. & BATHE, H. V. 1982. Territory size and habitat requirement of the Seychelles Brush Warbler Acrocephalus (Bebrornis) sechellensis.*

BATHE, H. V. 1982a. A minor study of some seabirds nesting and roosting on Cousin Island, Seychelles.*

BATHE, H. V. 1982b. Some aspects of the breeding biology of the Fairy Tern (Gygis alba) on Cousin Island, with particular emphasis on any factors influencing nest site selection.*

BROOKE, M. de L. & GARNETT, M. C. 1983. Survival and reproductive performance of Hawksbill Turtles Eretmochelys imbricata L. on Cousin Island, Seychelles. Biol. Cons. 25, 161–170.

DIAMOND, A. W. 1975. Cousin Island Nature Reserve Management Plan 1975–79. ICBP (British Section), London.

DIAMOND, A. W. 1976. Breeding biology and conservation of Hawksbill Turtles, Eretmochelys imbricata L., on Cousin Island, Seychelles. Biol. Cons. 9, 199–215.

DIAMOND, A. W. 1980a. *Cousin Island Nature Reserve Management Plan revision 1980–1984.* ICBP (British Section) London.

DIAMOND, A. W. 1980b. Seasonality, population structure and breeding ecology of the Seychelles Brush Warbler *Acrocephalus sechellensis. Proc. 4th Pan-Afr. Orn. Congr.*, 253–266.

DIAMOND, A. W. & FEARE, C. J. 1980. Past and present biogeography of central Seychelles birds. *Proc. 4th Pan-Afr. Orn. Congr.*, 89–98.

DIAMOND, A. W. & HOUSTON, D. 1974. Census of tree-nesting terns, Cousin Island, Seychelles: September 1974.*

FOSBERG, F. R. 1970. Cousin Island report.*

FRAZIER, J. 1974. Sea turtles in Seychelles. *Biol. Cons.* **6**, 71–73.

FRAZIER, J. 1975. Marine turtles of the western Indian Ocean. *Oryx* **13**, 164–175.

FRAZIER, J. G. & POLUNIN, N. C. 1973. Report on the coral reefs of Cousin Island, Seychelles (November 1973).*

GARNETT, M. C. 1978. The breeding biology of Hawksbill Turtles (*Eretmochelys imbricata*) on Cousin Island, Seychelles.*

KIRK, D. A. 1981. The ecology of the Cousin Hare *Lepus n. nigricollis,* in the Seychelles. (B.Sc Honours Zoology thesis, University of Aberdeen).*

PENNY, M. J. 1974. *The birds of Seychelles and the outlying islands.* Collins, London.

PRYS-JONES, R. P. & DIAMOND, A. W. 1984. Ecology of the land birds on the granitic and coralline islands of the Seychelles, with particular reference to Cousin Island and Aldabra Atoll. *In* Stoddart, D. R. (ed.) Biogeography and ecology of the Seychelle islands. Junk, the Hague. 529–58

ROBERTSON, I. 1972. *Marine National Parks, Seychelles.* IUCN/WWF Project No. 726(39-3).

WILSON, J. R. 1982. An investigation into the effect of tourists on the breeding of Fairy Terns along paths on Cousin Island, Seychelles.*

PART IV
A PROGRAMME FOR THE PROTECTION OF ISLAND ECOSYSTEMS

ICBP Technical Publication No. 3, 1985

CONSERVATION OF ISLAND ECOSYSTEMS

CAMERON B. KEPLER[1] & J. MICHAEL SCOTT[2]

1   *Patuxent Wildlife Research Center, Maui Field Station, 248 Kaweo Place, Kula, Hawaii 96790*
2   *Patuxent Wildlife Research Center, Mauna Loa Field Station, P.O. Box 44, Hawaii National Park, Hawaii 96718*

ABSTRACT

To protect birds within secure island ecosystems requires a global perspective and intensive local effort. To begin we must divide the world's oceans into regions organized along biogeographical or political lines. Regional working groups should be formed to determine conservation needs and oversee management programmes. The groups would firstly identify key resource people and sources of information, and then compile a list of all major islands or island groups in each region. Simultaneously, a set of international criteria must be developed to enable conservation needs to be placed in an order of priority. Using these criteria, the regional groups would pinpoint islands that have important resources needing protection and, if possible, delineate any sites that require further investigation. On-site surveys would be conducted to determine if the priorities are accurate and how essential habitats can best be protected. Regional priorities would be reassessed in the light of these survey results.

The programme would then begin to acquire the necessary rights to manage important natural areas, with existing conservation and government agencies playing a crucial supporting role. Because stresses on islands are rarely reduced just by securing an area, management plans must be developed and implemented as soon as possible. We see a compelling need to develop a Red Data Book outlining proven techniques by which introduced ungulates, predators and exotic plants can be eliminated from island reserves.

This plan for island conservation has been developed in the light of experiences in Hawaii, and the final section of the paper discusses past and current conservation programmes within the Hawaiian archipelago.

INTRODUCTION

We live on a water planet: 70.8 percent of the earth's surface is covered by salt water, a formidable barrier to the dispersal of terrestrial life forms. Scattered over slightly more than $361,000,000km^2$ of ocean are tens of thousands of islands harbouring some of the world's most remarkable ecosystems. Varying degrees of isolation, combined with sets of physical, environmental, and biological conditions peculiar to each island have produced unique assemblages of species, small altered samples from sources near and far (Carlquist 1965). The isolation that has led to the evolution of so many endemic taxa has also produced vulnerability and high extinction rates: 93 percent of all avian extinctions since 1600 have been island species, and the majority of endangered taxa are island endemics (King 1981). There is growing evidence that high rates of avian

255

extinction on islands followed their settlement by humans long before the period of European exploration (Olson & James 1982; Diamond 1982). Because islands are so widespread, numerous and vulnerable, our efforts to conserve them must be well planned with a clear image of the global task required. Otherwise island conservation efforts could become lost in a scramble to save scattered components of island ecosystems or to achieve public relations or political objectives.

The subject of our concern in this symposium is the conservation of birds. We must realize, however, that the long-term protection of birds requires that we protect their habitats. Some eurytopic species (i.e. those tolerant of a range of environmental conditions) may easily adapt to disturbed vegetation but be stressed for other reasons— the Seychelles Magpie Robin (*Copsychus sechellarum*), threatened by introduced cats in the suburban environment on Frigate Island, is an example (King 1981), as are many seabirds that need land free from predators more than particular habitat types. The majority of species, however, are stressed primarily as a result of habitat degradation. With the list of endangered species of all taxa growing daily, we will be increasingly unable to protect all species with problems, and therefore our efforts must focus on saving functioning native ecosystems. Programmes such as Wingate's (this vol.) and those of the New Zealand Wildlife Service (Mills & Williams 1978) inspire us as much by their efforts to recreate lost habitats as they do by their efforts to secure the future for particular species. However, if we act now to protect ecosystems we will reduce the number of heroic efforts needed to save birds from extinction in the future. Thus our primary goal is to protect critical ecosystems. This can be done by identifying, legally securing, and managing island areas.

Under natural conditions avian diversity on islands is a function of area and habitat diversity (MacArthur & Wilson 1967), factors of prime importance in planning for the conservation of island birds. A comparison of birds on land-bridge islands with those on nearby continents (Diamond 1981; Lack 1969; Terborgh & Winter 1980) clearly shows a dramatic loss of species, as has been reviewed in this symposium (J. M. Diamond, this vol.; King, this vol.). Identical processes have been documented for Barro Colorado Island in Panama (Willis 1974; Terborgh 1974; Karr 1982), and on habitat fragments on continents (Terborgh 1974).

As islands are developed their natural habitats become fragmented into smaller units, and some habitats essential to many species, particularly those most specialized, may be lost. On high islands the native vegetation at lower elevation is normally the first to be destroyed, often with disastrous consequences. Olson & James (1982) show that at least 40 species of birds disappeared as a result of habitat destruction in Hawaii before Europeans arrived. Mesic and xeric forests at low elevations are often species-rich relative to montane wet forests (Kepler & Kepler 1970) and can harbour rich endemic faunas not represented at higher altitudes. In addition, lowland dry habitats are rich in potential inter-island (or inter-refuge) migrants (Lack 1976); losing these habitats could reduce rates of gene flow between or within populations, and inhibit or prevent normal patterns of movements between islands. Range contraction up the slopes permanently restricts species to typically cooler and wetter habitats that are likely to be suboptimal, and may deny them essential resources (Diamond 1982). These insularization effects (Wilcox 1980) may be most severe when habitats are lost in concentric rings around mountains, the typical island pattern following human colonization.

Vulnerability of birds to extinction has been related to increased body size (Willis 1974), to particular taxa (Terborgh & Winter 1980), to certain guilds requiring specific microhabitats (Karr 1982), and to species that disperse poorly (Diamond 1981). For birds on oceanic islands other factors such as flightlessness, naiveté in the face of introduced predators, or susceptibility to disease, can lead to quick extinction when their habitats are broached by man and his commensal animals. J. M. Diamond (this vol.) argues that the probability of extinction is inversely correlated with population size. Obviously population size will decrease when a species' range contracts through fragmentation of its habitat. What might be less well appreciated is that density declines even in the remaining prime habitat fragments (Scott & Kepler, in prep.), which is what we would predict if populations surviving within the fragment depended in part on some resources beyond its borders. The increasing vulnerability of these small populations results from many interacting forces, some environmental and others genetic (Shaffer 1981; Franklin 1980). Species facing severe novel stresses (such as introduced avian diseases) may need large populations if resistance is to be developed, as has been the case for several Hawaiian species (van Riper *et al.* 1982). The near loss of the Puerto Rican Parrot (*Amazona vittata*) and the extinction of the Heath Hen (*Tympanuchus cupido cupido*) are classic examples of the number of unrelated stresses that can together threaten small populations (Shaffer 1981; Wiley, this vol.; Snyder *et al.*, in press).

These considerations and many others all argue strongly for large reserves (Diamond 1976, 1982; Terborgh 1976; Whitcomb *et al.* 1976). An opposite view, which proposes that several small reserves with a combined area equal to a single large one may be a better strategy (Simberloff & Abele 1976a, 1976b, 1982; Simberloff 1982) does not seem appropriate for many birds (see Diamond 1976, and especially Whitcomb *et al.* 1976). Small reserves may be useful, however, for unique ecosystems such as wetlands, or for offshore islands as 'marooning sites' for endangered birds (Wingate, this vol.; Williams 1977). Simberloff (1982) argues that many small reserves protecting diverse habitats will increase the number of protected species. However, in many instances the vulnerable birds, such as predators, frugivores and larger members of other guilds, need large areas, not small fragments with much edge. The species that add to greater species richness may not, in fact, need protection: many can survive well outside the reserves.

A problem with many discussions of reserve area is that 'large' and 'small' are rarely defined. Proponents of large reserves generally mean the largest possible, believing that even huge fragments will lose some species (Terborgh & Winter 1980). We believe that size must be determined by defining what is to be protected. A reserve for elephants must be larger than one protecting bog orchids. Waterfowl or seabirds, adapted to small patchily distributed habitats, might thrive in a series of small reserves; systems of comparable size would be inadequate for montane forest birds. Frugivorous nomads such as parrots, toucans or hornbills require larger areas than warblers or flycatchers. Not only must reserves contain essential microhabitats, they must also maintain viable populations. It has been suggested that a viable population must contain at least 500 individuals simply in order to maintain the genetic integrity of the population (Franklin 1980; Soulé 1980), and this number might be an order of magnitude too small to protect some species against environmental perturbations.

If we are to protect the birds of the world's islands we need two categories of essential information. Firstly, we must have an international priority listing of goals to help focus on those species or constellations of species most in need of protection. Secondly, we must obtain reliable information about these species and their ecosystems and then plan what is needed to protect them. Essential data include range, densities within that range, and critical ecological needs such as nest-site preferences, food, migration patterns, etc. Only then can realistic reserve boundaries be drawn on a map. Without this information reserves may not be able to fulfill their intended goals. As an example, on the island of Hawaii there are eight reserves totalling an enviable 106,673ha (9.8 percent of the island), yet none of the island's endangered forest birds are adequately protected (*Figure 1*). Such a system makes it difficult to convince sceptics of the need to protect additional areas.

Our global task is to protect major self-sustaining island ecosystems. By doing so we

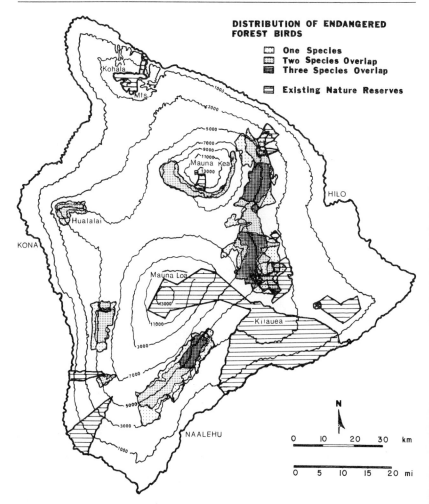

Figure 1:   Distribution of endangered forest birds in relation to existing nature reserves on the island of Hawaii in 1982.

will protect the greatest number of birds for future generations. We will be building arks for our planet's island biota. Each will be a unique assemblage of plants and animals. Although we may select one dramatic species as the flagbearer for the ecosystem, our efforts must protect life-forms in all taxa, many of them as yet undescribed. Reserves must be located according to the biological and political idiosyncrasies of each island group upon which we work. We must order the priorities for our tasks both worldwide and within regional subdivisions. This requires that we maximize our effectiveness, understand our resources and strive to protect outstanding natural areas. This demands detailed knowledge of each island, and requires that local experts in each region become involved. We must 'think globally but act locally', to quote a motto of the US Nature Conservancy. We propose the following plan as a means of achieving these objectives.

PLAN FOR ISLAND CONSERVATION

We introduce here a ten-step plan for the protection of island ecosystems. Although the plan specifically addresses birds and island ecosystems, we feel that it serves equally well as a blueprint focusing conservation efforts on a wide variety of other taxa and areas. We will present the overall plan first and then follow this with a discussion of our own Hawaiian programme as a specific example of how it might work on other islands. The plan is organized into a series of steps, although action in many regions will be on a number of steps simultaneously. The final step is ubiquitous and will be a logical part of most of the others. Global regions (see Appendix 1) differ enormously in the number of steps they have completed; the urgent task is to complete the first eight steps as rapidly as possible and begin active management of many additional key reserves around the world.

Identify Conservation Regions
The first task is to subdivide the world's islands into manageable units in order to simplify our understanding of the myriad conservation problems worldwide. We suggest that regions be delineated biogeographically (i.e. the Caribbean, Tropical Indian Ocean, Madagascar and Mascareres, etc.). We realize that political realities may require modifications to this approach. Thus biogeographic regions such as the Subantarctic Islands or the Southwest Pacific may necessarily be subdivided into smaller units. The specific delineation of areas such as the Philippine Islands south through Indonesia present special challenges. Current conservation efforts by specific people or organizations will also modify what might otherwise be straightforward biological or political decisions. We feel that the reasoned input of an international group of concerned biologists is essential in determining regions that will become, in essence, global management units (see Appendix 1).

Locate Key Resource People and Information
After identifying geographic regions, the next step is to identify key resource people in each region who are willing to serve on a working group whose main function will be to determine which resources need protection. These groups would gather all the information, published and unpublished, relevant to their areas.

The first requirement will be the production of a complete list of the area's islands. This has already been done in some places: examples include Nicholson (1969) for the Pacific, Elliott (1972) for the Indian Ocean and Watson (1975) for the Antarctic and Subantarctic. The list should contain the names, area, height, primary climate and vegetation, land use and a bibliography for each island or island group. Data on native and introduced species, their populations, status and major threats are also essential, although much of this information can be added after the list is prepared.

Develop International Ranking Criteria
With a completed list each working group can determine which islands have high priority for conservation. To do this and also allow global comparisons to be made, each group must have the same internationally accepted set of criteria for ranking the ecosystems. Ogle (1981) compared four schemes for their abilities to rank New Zealand forest habitat, finding no significant differences between them. He concluded that 'all habitat ranking systems employing sound ecological criteria would produce rankings which

differ only slightly.' His final system (see Appendix 2 in Ogle 1981), however, is a particularly appropriate framework for developing a global ranking scheme for island bird habitats. He gives a numerical score graded according to the condition or status for each of eight ranking criteria: representativeness (locally, regionally, nationally), habitat diversity, habitat modifications, degree of isolation, size (larger areas yield higher scores), number of indigenous forest bird species, rarity of indigenous birds, and rarity of other fauna. The scheme addresses the major concerns of reserve size and habitat diversity, and considers known avian parameters. Although other 'elements' such as additional taxa and habitat types could be added (see Hoose 1981), they would increase the time needed to rate potential reserves.

Place Conservation Needs in Order of Priority
The working groups, using the international ranking scheme, should synthesize all available information for their areas. The US Nature Conservancy's Heritage Program provides an excellent example of how to proceed (Bill Burley, pers. comm.; Hoose 1981). The ICBP Red Data Book for birds (King 1981) will be useful in pinpointing areas of particular concern. The end product will be a preliminary list ranking the conservation needs of all major avian habitats. All priority lists should be described in sufficient detail to allow other working groups to assess them. Gaps in our knowledge should be pointed out.

Develop Regional Action Plans
Once this preliminary list has been developed the working group should develop regional action plans. Regional boundaries may be modified or adjacent regions merged if this seems appropriate for the action that needs to be taken. Major stresses should be identified and mapped, and areas of similar stress be combined to allow a unified approach to the general problem.

Study High Priority Areas
At this point the groups have worked only with known information. This will often be inadequate to determine exactly what needs to be done and not sufficiently detailed to allow the actual drawing of reserve boundaries. As we demonstrate below, the information available can be misleading. It will be necessary to begin surveys in those areas that *appear to be* of highest priority, using guidelines already established for the entire project. Before reserves are acquired and managed we must be satisfied that we have a sound data base. Management decisions made without adequate data are likely to waste time and money protecting areas that really do not need protection, and may preclude protection of critically important areas. In the long run the time taken to procure or summarize the available information will amply repay the efforts required to obtain it.

Birds are easily censused indicators of stress, and excellent methods for surveying them have been developed (Caughley 1977; Eberhardt 1978; Burnham et al. 1981; Ralph & Scott 1981) and used on islands (Scott et al. 1981). While not always necessary, we feel that there is frequently a special need to determine the numbers of birds over their entire range. If we are unable to protect the entire range of a species, we will want to set reserve boundaries which embrace the largest number of individuals. Studies to gather this type of information have been conducted in Hawaii, and the methods used there are suitable for other islands (see Scott et al. 1981). Daily, seasonal or irregular movements to peripheral areas should be determined in addition to density estimates. For example, Amazon parrots now restricted to montane forests in the Lesser Antilles move to the lowlands following severe hurricanes (Snyder et al., in press). If reserves for them include only high mountain forests the parrots will be forced to fly to the agricultural lowlands after hurricanes.

Surveys will reveal the true status of the avifauna and, using a botanical team in conjunction with the bird survey, will help determine the habitat preferences of the birds (Scott *et al.* 1981). Habitat can be described in terms of canopy height, cover and species composition, and understorey type. We feel that habitat stresses (introduced ungulates and plants) should also be described. The survey can be designed to identify the key 'elements' if they are needed to complete the ranking process on each island. Elements listed for all natural areas provide an index to natural diversity that may be applied to the final ranking process.

Design Reserves

After surveys of areas with potentially high priorities, the regional working group will need to meet the survey team to finalize conservation priorities, design reserves and make management recommendations. The primary guidelines will be to maximize the size and habitat diversity of the reserves so that they embrace those areas which are essential to the survival of the species, and those where the birds are most abundant. The general rules described by Diamond (1975) provide excellent guidelines for such a design. Once this is accomplished the conservation programme moves into its third phase, the commencement of conservation action.

Acquire Property

Acquiring and managing reserves are perhaps the most difficult steps. They rely on individuals and agencies that may not have been directly involved with the working groups: the landowners, local and national governments, and conservation organizations that have the power, money, or expertise to negotiate land deals. The working groups should introduce their findings and goals to the landowners and conservation agencies, and they will certainly want to evaluate progress, but at this point much of what happens will be undertaken by others. A vital requirement will be the cooperation of landowners, who in many regions will be local villagers (reserves may straddle village boundaries, and negotiations will have to be made with chiefs who value their control of the land above all else). Land arrangements will need to be worked out which fully recognize the needs of residents. The attitudes of the landowners towards conservation programmes can be evaluated before the surveys begin, and the behaviour of survey teams will have a strong influence on the success of subsequent negotiations for land. The importance of these personal relationships cannot be overemphasized.

Acquisition of reserves must be imaginative, and recognize that there are many types of protection other than outright ownership. For example, conservation easements, leases and rental or management agreements are all common and proven alternatives to purchasing the land (Hoose 1981). The local people will often have to be persuaded that their land is important for conservation, and their fears will have to be allayed at the outset. Local people should be employed whenever possible so that they can gain a clear understanding of the conservation objectives and pass them on to their friends. It then remains to negotiate an agreement with the local landowners.

Managemement

Management of the land requires just as close coordination with local peoples as does control of the land. Most reserves will need management, and at the very least they must be regularly inspected. We have an excellent example from the Hawaiian island of Maui of what benign neglect can do to a protected ecosystem. Kipahulu Valley was relatively pristine when first surveyed in 1967, and it gained international recognition as an outstanding natural area (Warner 1968). Due to the purchase of half the valley by the US Nature Conservancy and to the gift of the other half by the State of Hawaii, the entire valley (3600ha) was incorporated into Haleakala National Park. Although in good condition, Kipahulu harboured feral pigs (*Sus scrofa*) which were damaging the vegetation, although some investigators thought that they were not a serious threat (see Banko & Wilson 1968). The survey team urged that the pigs be eradicated and that human activity in the area be strictly controlled.

When management began in 1969 Kipahulu was closed to the public and access by scientists was restricted. Lacking adequate resources, however, staff at Haleakala National Park did not attempt to control the pigs. Formerly the pigs had been avidly hunted by residents from nearby communities, but we suspect that hunting pressure decreased after the implementation of the strict National Park policies. As a result the valley ecosystem began to fall apart. Recently Diong (1982) has suggested that the pig population increased substantially in the late 1960s and early 1970s. Exotic plants increased in abundance and diversity, the native forest understorey was severely reduced, and large areas of bare, uprooted soil developed. Even worse, the exotic strawberry guava (*Psidium cattleianum*) began to take over the forest below 1200m altitude. Management needs have now reached crisis proportions as the entire lower forest is threatened.

Whether or not these problems are directly attributable to the policies initiated in 1969, the decline in natural values of Kipahula Valley demonstrates several important points. Firstly, many of the threats facing island ecosystems, such as introduced plants and animals, are pervasive and stem indirectly from man's activities. Secondly, these problems are not solved merely by securing an area—their solution needs active management. Thirdly, if management cannot be initiated immediately, at the very least the reserve must be monitored so that adverse changes can be detected and remedied before they become severe. Finally, we must make certain that our management will be better than that provided freely by nearby inhabitants.

Management plans should be written by those most interested in and knowledgeable about each area. They should clearly describe and rank all the major stresses, and develop a plan setting out the steps that must be taken to alleviate them. The plan becomes a working document: it stimulates a planned and educated course of action and helps evaluate progress. A flexible plan will need regular revision as particular projects are completed.

Once a management plan is developed, the real work—active management—begins. Major stresses must be tackled aggressively. We point out that if the threats come from large mammals such as goats or pigs the primary goal should be eradication: it is not important how many are killed, as impressive as these figures can be, but how many are left behind to breed (Baker & Reeser 1972). The effort required to remove the last 10 animals may equal that required to kill the first thousand; getting the last is absolutely essential. We should not look so much at cost per animal, the job being best viewed as a sustained effort until the last animal is eliminated. The high expense of eliminating the last individuals must be realized from the beginning. Managers need to be aware that achieving this goal will be frustrating and difficult.

When the major stresses have been eliminated management of the reserve will move either to a maintenance phase, or to active rehabilitation. It is important during this period that managers be able to quickly identify new threats and the re-appearance of old ones. This will take additional time and dedication. The restoration of 6ha Nonsuch Island over a period of 20 years provides a graphic illustration of the magnitude of the task (Wingate, this vol.). We are dealing with decades, not years. However, the rewards of seeing unique ecosystems return fully justify the costs.

Island ecosystems seem to be stressed far more than continents by the indirect consequences of man's activities. A host of browsing and predatory mammals, exotic insects and plants, and avian diseases have been introduced to islands (Atkinson, this vol.), and they continue to degrade protected and unprotected habitats alike. Most of the most damaging predators and browsers introduced to islands—pigs, goats, rats, cats, dogs, mongooses and mustelids—occur worldwide, and there are many biologists and land managers who have dealt effectively with them (Veitch, this vol.; Baker & Reeser 1972; Calvopina, this vol.; Merton 1978; Moors, this vol.). We see a compelling need for a single volume, perhaps in the style of the ICBP Red Data Book (King 1981), which describes practical methods for reducing or eliminating these mammals. Many imaginative management techniques lie scattered through journals or reports (e.g. Temple 1978), and we have come across managers, particularly those on isolated islands, scrambling to locate, or even re-invent at great cost in time and effort, methods already proven elsewhere.

Staff from the New Zealand Wildlife Service have recently travelled to the Seychelles and the Galapagos Islands to advise local managers on the control of cats, goats and other pests (C. R. Veitch, pers. comm.). We perceive the need for a team of professional wildlife field staff available when necessary for work throughout the world. They would help solve critical conservation problems on the spot and train local managers to continue the initial efforts. We strongly urge that such a team be formed.

Community Support and Education

The development of community support for conservation efforts is essential. The benefits of the reserve—economic, aesthetic, and practical (e.g. better watershed)—should be emphasized to the local people. Local residents should be employed whenever possible, thus providing income for their economy and making the conservation programme a community effort. Tourism such as that developed in the Galapagos Archipelago and Cousin Island (A. W. Diamond, this vol.) should be encouraged if it is compatible with the aims of the reserve. Tourism helps the local economy and can provide some of the money needed for management of the reserve, although it rarely covers all expenses. The reserves should thus serve not only to protect species, they should also act as educational tools to train local inhabitants to protect even more land. Wherever they are sited, most reserves will partly depend on land outside their boundaries for the survival of species within. This requires the support of people living in adjacent areas.

In addition to their role within local communities, reserves are also immensely valuable educational resources for visitors. Millions of people each year visit national parks, wildlife refuges and privately-owned sanctuaries, thus gaining first-hand impressions of naturally functioning ecosystems. These experiences, augmented by such interpretive features as leaflets, books, self-guiding nature walks, interpretive signs and resource personnel have given thousands of people the background and incentive to appreciate and understand the need to protect natural areas. Many of these people become members of conservation organizations, or at least are more sympathetic towards new conservation programmes elsewhere.

CONSERVATION IN THE HAWAIIAN ARCHIPELAGO

The Hawaiian Archipelago is the world's most isolated land, the high islands being located more than 4000km from the nearest continent and over 3000km from the Marquesas, the nearest high islands. Its diverse, highly endemic fauna and flora are an inspiration to biogeographers and a cause for despair among conservationists. Much that is uniquely Hawaiian has been lost since the first Polynesians stepped ashore around

500 A.D. There were still about 70 species of native land and freshwater birds present when Captain Cook first landed on the Hawaiian Islands in 1778. Today 24 are extinct and an additional 29 are endangered (Berger 1972). As imposing as these numbers are, they are only a fraction of the losses induced by man. Olson & James (1982) have identified at least 40 additional species from fossil and sub-fossil remains, and they believe that most were contemporaneous with the early Polynesian Hawaiians. Thus more than 60 species have become extinct within 1500 years—over 60 percent of the original avifauna.

Hawaii's vascular plants, 98 percent of which are endemic, have also suffered: approximately 1172 of 1765 known species (66 percent) are either extinct (273), endangered (800) or rare (99), and although this compilation is tentative, it clearly reveals the magnitude of the losses (Fosberg & Herbst 1975). Similar losses have occurred in other taxa, most notably the insects (Zimmerman 1970) and land snails (Hart 1975).

We do not wish to dwell on these losses, for they are well known (see Gagne 1975). What we want to emphasize is that many of them have occurred in spite of important conservation programmes begun early this century.

In 1903 the Hawaiian Territorial Government passed legislation for the creation of a system of forest reserves. The first reserve was proclaimed in 1904 and by 1910 most of Hawaii's State Reserve System, now containing 485,000ha, was completed. Watershed protection was the primary concern, and reserve management consisted primarily of fencing to exclude cattle, irregular hunting of ungulates, and the planting of exotic trees, primarily in denuded areas. The status of these lands can be changed so they are not inviolate reserves (e.g. in 1918 the reserve on Kahoolawe Island was withdrawn to allow cattle ranching), and many are inadequately fenced and thus grazed by cattle from adjoining ranches. In spite of this the reserves hold about 30 percent of the state under forest cover and they are essential for the survival of most of Hawaii's endemic birds.

The US Government has been active in the islands since early this century. In 1909 Theodore Roosevelt established the Hawaiian Islands National Wildlife Refuge to protect the immense seabird colonies in Hawaii's Leeward Islands. Although the group of seven islands within the refuge contain under 730ha, they hold some 10 million seabirds of 18 species (Harrison *et al.*, 1984) and are the only habitat for four endemic landbirds.

Conservation received a boost on the main islands in 1916 when the US National Park Service dedicated lands on Maui and Hawaii that were the genesis of Haleakala National Park and Hawaii Volcanoes National Park. Together these two areas now encompass about 96,500ha. Their management programmes show increasing effectiveness and their research programmes are helping to control many of Hawaii's most severe threats to the flora and fauna (Baker & Reeser 1972).

In spite of the impressive list of protected areas set aside early this century, very little systematic management accompanied their initial establishment. The important point is that with over 35 percent of the archipelago under some form of legal protection, species in all taxa continued to decline in number and many became extinct. For example the following seven endemic birds disappeared during this century (King 1981): Laysan Rail (*Porzana palmeri*), Lanai Thrush (*Phaeornis obscurus lanaiensis*), Laysan Millerbird (*Acrocephalus f. familiaris*), Hawaii O'O (*Moho nobilis*), Black Mamo (*Drepanis funerea*), Laysan Honeyeater (*Himatione sanguinea freethi*) and Lanai Creeper (*Paroreomyza maculata montana*).

To this list we can probably add the Kauai Akialoa (*Hemignathus procerus*) and, in the last five years, the Lanai population of the Common Amakihi (*Hemignathus virens*). Several other species barely survive with small populations. For these and other extinct species the management efforts have clearly not been sufficient to save them.

Table 1: The Hawaii Forest Bird Survey team at maximum staffing level (from Scott *et al.* 1981).
Reproduced with the permission of the Wildlife Society, which holds the copyright.

Position	No.	% of year employed	Primary responsibilities
Senior Scientist	1	100	Experimental design, data analysis, write-ups, daily schedule, training, overall responsibility for programme.
Statistician	1	30	Experimental design, data analysis.
Administrative Officer	1	30	Handles hiring, payroll, etc.
Field Supervisor	1	100	Ensuring that equipment is ready for use, vehicles running properly, teams in woods, first response in case of accident.
Field Assistants	2	50	Radio checks, pickups and drop-offs, equipment repair.
Ornithologists	8	30	Documentation of bird distribution and abundance.
Botanists	2	50	Documentation of rare plant distribution,
	3	30	characterization of vegetation structure, species composition and phenology of selected species of plants: 4 in field, 1 in office working with vegetation mapping.
Trail crew	6	50	Responsible for flagging trails, detailed notes on safety hazards, presence of water, and camp sites.

In recent years a new wave of conservation activities has begun. The State of Hawaii has initiated a Natural Area Reserve System, dedicating the first reserve in 1973. The system to date totals 11,705ha in eight reserves, and an additional six areas totalling 21,945ha have been approved but not formally dedicated (B. Lee, pers. comm.). In 1978 the State of Hawaii extended protection to 36 islands as the Hawaii State Seabird Sanctuary. In 1972 the US Fish and Wildlife Service began a wetland programme that now includes five important reserves totaling 568ha for endangered waterbirds (R. Shallenberger, pers. comm.). These areas are being actively managed. In 1965 the US Fish and Wildlife Service sent the first of three biologists to determine what could be done to protect the endangered remnants of the formerly large endemic avifauna, and from 1976–1982 the US Forest Service fielded an independent avian research team.

In 1975 Fish and Wildlife Service biologists decided that a thorough survey of all extant forests was essential to determine the distribution, density, population size, habitat correlates, and ultimately the management needs of the native forest birds. The field work began in 1976 and required six years of seasonal effort on five islands, 1300km of survey transects, and 10,000 sampling stations (*Table 1*). Data analysis is still under way. The survey methods have been described in detail by Scott *et al.* (1981; see also references therein) and are well adapted to rugged terrain. We feel that if surveys can be completed in the highly eroded and very wet Hawaiian ecosystems, they can be conducted almost anywhere.

Our gain in knowledge from the surveys has been impressive, allowing us to rank conservation needs and pinpoint stresses in a way not previously possible. At its most basic, the project has substantially altered our understanding of the distribution of Hawaii's forest birds. For example, the Akiapolaau (*Hemignathus munroi*), until recently thought to occur in only two localized areas (Berger 1972; King 1981), actually ranges around the eastern, southern and western slopes of Mauna Kea and Mauna Loa (*Figure 2*). It is dependent on upper-elevation Koa (*Acacia koa*) and Ohia (*Metrosideros collina*) forest for its survival, and this habitat is severely threatened by logging and

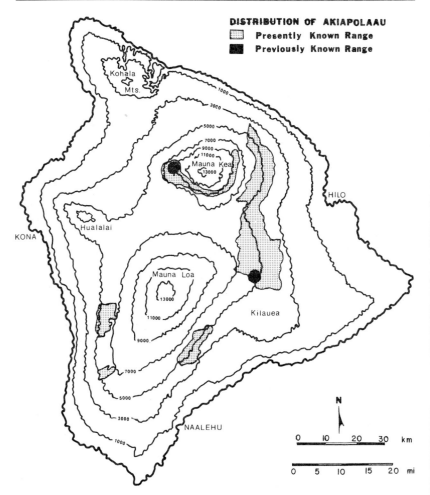

Figure 2: Present (1982) and previously (1972) known distribution of the Akiapolaau (*Hemignathus munroi*).

grazing. Its distribution on the western slopes of Mauna Loa is clearly relictual, and the severe fragmentation of habitat there has undoubtedly resulted in local extinctions. We can expect a similar fate in other populations if land clearing progresses much further.

Detailed knowledge of the range and densities of populations enables us to establish realistic boundaries for areas needing protection. When the survey was completed we were surprised to realize how inadequately protected Hawaii's forest birds were (*Figure 1*), a point we stressed earlier. If areas now reserved were all that could be protected, many species would undoubtedly disappear, as they have on much of the west side of the island.

The forest bird surveys have demonstrated that 'locked-up' forests provide ineffective protection for Hawaii's ecosystems. The best habitat is typically found in those areas most accessible to hunters, and the most devastated areas are generally more than 1km from the nearest access point. Remoteness is detrimental because hunters rarely penetrate such areas, and populations of feral pigs, goats, deer, cattle, sheep and other introduced ungulates range unchecked with severe effects on the ecosystem. This does not suggest that unstructured hunting is an efficient management tool for large reserves; clearly in Hawaii it has done little more than alleviate damage to the habitat at forest edges. Given the high fecundity of most feral mammals (Baker & Reeser 1972; Kramer 1971), the only permanent solution lies in an integrated programme utilizing fencing to restrict movement and organized hunting, trapping or chemical controls to eliminate feral animal populations.

The results from the Hawaiian Forest Bird Survey have identified real needs for conservation and management. The broad scope of the surveys allows conservation to proceed from an objective data-base that takes into account all potential forest areas and the stresses to which they are exposed. These data, and a series of recovery plans derived in part from them, have attracted the US Nature Conservancy (an efficient, privately-funded land protection agency) to the islands. Working closely with state and federal biologists and land managers, they have drawn up a 5-year plan to acquire management rights for critical areas of bird habitat on each island. In less than four years the Conservancy has purchased options on nearly 5000ha of land on Maui, Molokai, Hawaii and Kauai, and is actively pursuing other important areas (H. Little, pers. comm.). The negotiations to acquire easements have taken time and effort nearly equivalent to that required for the surveys themselves. Management plans are being developed for each reserve and tentative steps taken to develop strong and lasting relationships between the government, the Conservancy, landowners and residents. Of added significance, the Conservancy and the Hawaii Department of Land and Natural Resources (which has jurisdiction over the forest reserves) are discussing ways to manage jointly their respective holdings. If Hawaii's remaining prime forests can be included in such integrated, active management programmes, real progress can be made to protect what remains.

The programmes described above illustrate many important points:
- legal protection, even on a large scale, may be insufficient in itself to help insular ecosystems;
- published information, even on well-known islands, can be unreliable;
- without a good data-base, it is difficult to identify key areas or core populations which need protecting;
- good information can be obtained from the most topographically difficult areas;
- the conservation of island ecosystems on inhabited islands involves a large number of people and agencies with overlapping responsibilities. Their interactions can be most positive when they perceive a set of shared goals and work together to achieve them;
- the most serious stresses on islands in many cases come from introduced plants and animals, rather than from the direct activities of man;
- active management programmes that directly address these stresses are essential to the ultimate protection of many island ecosystems.

ACKNOWLEDGEMENTS

We gratefully acknowledge the insightful comments on early drafts of this paper by J. D. Jacobi, A. K. Kepler, P. H. McEldowney, and F. R. Warshauer, and thank

R. L. Walker for his drafting of the figures. We also thank the many people in the Hawaii Department of Land and Natural Resources, the US National Park Service, the US Forest Service, the University of Hawaii, the US Nature Conservancy and our own agency for their help over the years.

NOTE ADDED IN PROOF

J. Michael Scott's present address is Condor Research Center, 2291A Portola Road, Suite 300, Ventura, California 93003, USA.

APPENDIX 1: REGIONAL GROUPING OF ISLANDS

The following list of major island regions was compiled by A. K. Kepler, C. B. Kepler and P. J. Moors following the recommendations and discussion of members of the ICBP Island Management Workshop, held on 13 August 1982 in Cambridge, England.

Atlantic Ocean
Northwest Atlantic (islands off Canada and Greenland)
Northeast Atlantic (islands off Iceland and Norway south to Gibraltar)
North American Continental Shelf (Maine to Florida)
Caribbean (Gulf of Mexico, Bahamas to 'bump' of Brazil)
Central Atlantic Oceanic Islands (Azores through Cape Verde)
African Continental Shelf (Tangiers to Algoa Bay, South Africa)
South American Continental Shelf ('bump' of Brazil to southern tip of Argentina)
South Atlantic Oceanic Islands (Ascension, St. Helena)
Mediterranean and Black Seas

Indian Ocean
Arabian Sea (includes Red Sea and Persian Gulf)
Madagascar and Mascarenes (includes Comoro)
Tropical Oceanic (Laccadives through Chagos, Seychelles, Cosmoledo)
East African Continental Shelf
Indian Continental Shelf (included Andamans and Nicobars)

Southeast Asia
Indo-Malayan islands (Indonesia, Malaya, mainland north to China)
Philippines
Chinese Islands (Mainland China, Taiwan and Korean islands)
Japan and its dependencies

Pacific Ocean
Russian Pacific
Alaskan Islands
North American West Coast (British Columbia south to Baja California)
Central American West Coast (Mexico through Colombia)
Galapagos
South American West Coast (Ecuador south to Concepcion, and Chilean Pacific—Easter, Juan Fernandez, etc.)
South American Southwest Coast (Concepcion through southernmost Chilean islands)
Australia and dependencies
Papua New Guinea, Solomons, Bismarcks
New Caledonia and New Hebrides
New Zealand and dependencies
Southwest Pacific (Fiji, Tonga, Samoa, Wallis and Fortuna, Niue, Cooks, Tokelau)

South Pacific (French Polynesia, Pitcairn, Henderson)
Central Pacific (Kiribati, Tuvalu, Nauru)
American Pacific (Marianas, Marshalls, Palau, Carolines, Hawaii, other dependencies)

Southern Ocean
Subantarctic Islands
a.   South American, Falklands, South Georgia, etc.
b.   'African' sector (Tristan, Gough, Bouvet, Marion, Prince Edward, Crozet, Kerguelen, Heard, etc.)
c.   Australasian Sector (Macquarie, New Zealand dependencies)
Antarctic Islands

Other
Russian Arctic Islands

REFERENCES

ATKINSON, I. A. E. (this vol.). The spread of commensal species of *Rattus* to oceanic islands and their effects on island avifaunas.

BAKER, J. K. & REESER, D. W. 1972. Goat management problems in Hawaii Volcanoes National Park. *U.S. Nat. Park Service Nat. Res. Report* **2**, 1–22.

BANKO, W. E. & WILSON, N. 1968. Notes on mammals of Kipahulu Valley, Maui. *In:* Warner, R. (ed.) *Scientific Report of the Kipahulu Valley Expedition*, 125–7. Unpublished report, The Nature Conservancy.

BERGER, A. J. 1972. *Hawaiian birdlife*. Univ. of Hawaii Press, Honolulu.

BURNHAM, K. P., ANDERSON, D. R. & LAAKE, J. L. 1981. Line transect estimation of bird population density using a Fourier series. *In:* Ralph, C. J. & Scott J. M. (eds) Estimating the number of terrestrial birds. *Stud. Avian Biol.* **6**, 466–82.

CALVOPINA, L. (this vol.). The impact and eradication of feral goats on the Galapagos Islands.

CARLQUIST, S. 1965. *Island Life*. The Natural History Press, Garden City, New York.

CAUGHLEY, G. 1977. *Analysis of vertebrate populations*. Wiley, New York.

DIAMOND, A. W. (this vol.). Multiple use of Cousin Island Nature Reserve, Seychelles.

DIAMOND, J. M. 1975. The island dilemma: lessons of modern biogeographic studies for the design of natural preserves. *Biol. Conserv.* **7**, 129–46.

DIAMOND, J. M. 1976. Island biogeography and conservation: strategy and limitations. *Science* **193**, 1027–9.

DIAMOND, J. M. 1981. Flightlessness and fear of flying in island species. *Nature* **293**, 507–8.

DIAMOND, J. M. 1982. Man the exterminator. *Nature* **298**, 787–9.

DIAMOND, J. M. (this vol.). Population processes on island birds: immigration, extinction and fluctuations.

DIONG, C. M. 1982. *Population ecology and management of the feral pig* (Sus scrofa) *in Kipahulu Valley, Haleakela National Park, Island of Maui, Hawaii*. Ph.D. Dissertation, Dept. of Zoology, Univ. of Hawaii, Honolulu.

EBERHARDT, L. L. 1978. Transect methods for population studies. *J. Wildlife Manage.* **33**, 28–39.

ELLIOTT, H. F. I. 1972. Island ecosystems and conservation with particular reference to the biological significance of islands of the Indian Ocean and consequential research and conservation needs. *J. Mar. Biol. Assoc. India* **14**, 578–608.

FOSBERG, F. R. & HERBST, D. 1975. Rare and endangered species of Hawaiian vascular plants. *Allertonia* **1**, 1–72.

FRANKLIN, I. R. 1980. Evolutionary change in small populations. *In:* Soule, M. E. & Wilcox, B. (eds) *Conservation Biology: an evolutionary-ecological perspective*, 135–50. Sinauer Assoc., Sunderland, Mass.

GAGNE, W. C. 1975. Hawaii's tragic dismemberment. *Defenders* **50**, 461–70.

HARRISON, C. S., NAUGHTON, M. B. & FEFER, S. I. 1984. The status and conservation of seabirds in the Hawaiian islands and associated island groups. *ICBP Tech. Pubn.* No. 2.

HART, A. D. 1975. Living jewels imperiled. *Defenders* **50**, 482–6.

Hoose, P. M. 1981. *Building an ark*. Island Press, Covelo, California.

Karr, J. R. 1982. Avian extinction on Barro Colorado Island: a reassessment. *Amer. Nat.* **119**, 220–339.

Kepler, C. B. & Kepler, A. K. 1970. Preliminary comparison of bird species diversity and density in Luquillo and Gaunica forests. *In:* Odum, H. (ed.) *A tropical rain forest*, E 183–6. US Atomic Energy Comm., Wash., DC.

King, W. B. 1981. *Endangered birds of the world*. Smithsonian Inst. Press, Wash., DC..

King, W. B. (this vol.). Island birds: will the future repeat the past?

Kramer, R. J. 1971. *Hawaiian land mammals*. Charles E. Tuttle Co., Rutland, Vermont.

Lack, D. 1969. The number of bird species on islands. *Bird Study* **16**, 193–209.

Lack, D. 1976. *Island biology, illustrated by the land birds of Jamaica*. Blackwell Sci. Pub., Oxford.

MacArthur, R. H. & Wilson, E. O. 1967. *The theory of island biogeography*. Princeton Univ. Press, Princeton, NJ.

Merton, D. V. 1978. Controlling introduced predators and competitors on islands. *In:* Temple, S. A. (ed.) *Endangered birds: management techniques for preserving threatened species*, 121–8. Univ. of Wisconsin Press, Madison, Wisc.

Mills, J. A. & Williams, G. R. 1978. The status of endangered New Zealand birds. *In:* Tyler, M. J. (ed.) *The status of endangered Australasian wildlife*, 148–68. Royal Zool. Soc. of South Australia.

Moors, P. J. (this vol.). Eradication campaigns against *Rattus norvegicus* on the Noises Islands, New Zealand, using brodifacoum and 1080.

Nicholson, E. M. 1969. Draft check list of Pacific oceanic islands. *Micronesica* **5**, 327–463.

Ogle, C. C. 1981. The ranking of wildlife habitats. *New Zealand J. Ecol.* **4**, 115–23.

Olson, S. L. & James, H. F. 1982. Fossil birds from the Hawaiian islands: evidence for wholesale extinction by man before western contact. *Science* **217**, 633–5.

Ralph, C. J. & Scott, J. M. (eds). 1981. Estimating numbers of terrestrial birds. *Stud. in Avian Biol.* **6**, 1–630.

Scott, J. M., Jacobi, J. D. & Ramsey, F. L. 1981. Avian surveys of large geographical areas: a systematic approach. *Wildlife Soc. Bull.* **9**, 190–200.

Shaffer, M. L. 1981. Minimum population sizes for species conservation. *Bioscience* **31**, 131–4.

Simberloff, D. S. 1982. Big advantages of small refuges. *Nat. Hist.* **91**, 6–14.

Simberloff, D. S. & Abele, L. G. 1976a. Island biogeography theory and conservation practice. *Science* **191**, 285–6.

Simberloff, D. S. & Abele, L. G. 1976b. Comments. *Science* **193**, 1032.

Simberloff, D. S.& Abele, L. G. 1982. Refuge design and island biogeographic theory: effects of fragmentation. *Amer. Nat.* **120**, 41–50.

Snyder, N. F. R., Wiley, J. W. & Kepler, C. B. In press. *The parrots of Luquillo: The natural history and conservation of the endangered Puerto Rican Parrot*. Western Foundation. Los Angeles.

Soulé, M. E. 1980. Thresholds for survival: maintaining fitness and evolutionary potential. *In:* Soulé, M. E. & Wilcox, B. A. (eds) *Conservation biology: an evolutionary–ecological perspective*, 151–70. Sinauer Assoc., Sunderland, Mass.

Temple, S. A. 1978. *Endangered birds: management techniques for preserving threatened species*. Univ. Wisconsin Press, Madison, Wisc.

Terborgh, J. W. 1974. Preservation of natural diversity: the problem of extinction prone species. *Bioscience* **24**, 715–722.

Terborgh, J. W. 1976. Comments. *Science* **193**, 1029–30.

Terborgh, J. W. & Winter, B. 1980. Some causes of extinction. *In:* Soulé, M. E. & Wilcox, B. (eds) *Conservation biology: an evolutionary–ecological perspective*, 119–34. Sinauer Assoc., Sunderland, Mass.

van Riper III, C., van Riper III, S. G., Lee Goff, M. & Laird, M. 1982. *The impact of malaria on birds in Hawaii Volcanoes National Park*. Technical Report 47. Cooperative National Park Resources Studies Unit, University of Hawaii at Manoa.

Veitch, C. R. (this vol.). Methods of eradicating feral cats from offshore islands in New Zealand.

Warner, R. E. 1968. *Scientific report of the Kipahulu Valley expedition*. Unpublished report, The Nature Conservancy.

Watson, G. E. 1975. *Birds of the Antarctic and Subantarctic*. Amer. Geophysical Union, Wash. DC.

WHITCOMB, R. F., LYNCH, J. F., OPLER, P. A. & ROBBINS, C. S. 1976. Comments. *Science* **193**, 1030–2.

WILCOX, B. A. 1980. Insular ecology and conservation. *In:* Soulé, M. A. & Wilcox, B. A. (eds) *Conservation biology: an evolutionary–ecological perspective*, 95–118. Sinauer Assoc., Sunderland, Mass.

WILEY, J. W. (this vol.). The Puerto Rican Parrot and competition for its nest sites.

WILLIAMS, G. R. 1977. Marooning—a technique for saving threatened species from extinction. *Intern. Zoo Yearbook* **17**, 102–6.

WILLIS, E. O. 1974. Populations and local extinction of birds on Barro Colorado Island, Panama. *Ecol. Mon.* **44**, 153–69.

WINGATE, B. D. (this vol.). The restoration of Nonsuch Island as a living museum of Bermuda's pre-colonial terrestrial biome.

ZIMMERMAN, E. C. 1970. Adaptive radiation in Hawaii with special reference to insects. *Biotropica* **12**, 32–8.

NOTES

NOTES

NOTES

NOTES

NOTES